# "THEY" Cripple Society

## Who are "THEY" and how do they do it?

## Volume 1

*An Exposé in True to Life Narrative Exploring Stories of Discrimination*

by Cleon E. Spencer

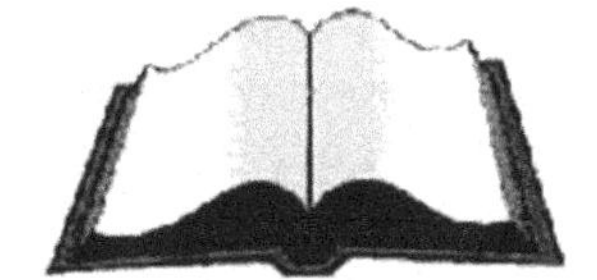

CCB Publishing
British Columbia, Canada

"THEY" Cripple Society
Who are "THEY" and how do they do it? Volume 1: An Exposé in True to Life Narrative Exploring Stories of Discrimination


ISBN-13 978-0-9809995-6-3
Second Edition, Revised

Library and Archives Canada Cataloguing in Publication

Spencer, Cleon E.
Fine, But Hardly Dandy: An exposé in true to life narrative / written by Cleon E. Spencer.
Vol. 1, 2nd ed. ; Vol. 2, 3rd. ed.
ISBN-13 978-0-9809995-6-3 (v. 1 : bound)
ISBN-13 978-0-9809995-7-0 (v. 2 : bound)
1. Envy. 2. Envy--Religious aspects--Christianity. 3. Interpersonal relations.
I. Title.
BF575.E65S64 2008 152.4'8 C2008-903328-0

This revised edition previously published as Fine, But Hardly Dandy Volume 1.

Extreme care has been taken to ensure that all information presented in this book is accurate and up to date at the time of publishing. Neither the author nor the publisher can be held responsible for any errors or omissions. Additionally, neither is any liability assumed for damages resulting from the use of the information contained herein.



Publisher: CCB Publishing
British Columbia, Canada
www.ccbpublishing.com

## Dedication

This book is humbly written with respect and dedication to all the good, well motivated people in North American Society, and that means most of them. The others are much written of in a different light in both Volume One and Volume Two of "THEY" Cripple Society.

# Introduction

This book, an exposé, focuses mainly on illustrating that the element of envy can be a far greater problem in adult life than any lingering sore spots from childhood. The writing reflects somewhat on improperly disciplined sibling rivalry and other childhood problems. Yet it shows that even with the damages of these overcome in adulthood, the evil of envy, more widespread and injurious than is recognized, can be a far more damaging problem particularly for some types of people.

Fine, dignified, often highly intelligent, well-charactered and cultured people who have to live in the unsheltered ebb and flow of everyday life bear the brunt of that envy far more than most people. Since they are a minority, their plight is not widely known. This book seeks to serve the purpose of bringing into common knowledge the cruel mental abuse some types of good people have to endure; having their lives and careers and characters stymied, blocked, and disrupted quite significantly. It is also a story of victorious, though difficult living on the part of the victims, despite the cruelty inflicted upon them.

Some of the tactics, maneuvers and mind-games used by envy's perpetrators, either openly or subtly, according as circumstances permit without them revealing themselves for what they are, are illustrated with true to life stories of the victims, as told in a fictitious support group on a university campus. The idea for this setting was conceived in the writer's mind many years earlier as he studied evening courses at a university and at that time attended a support group with a different agenda. This first book was written twenty years ago and recently revised so as to take care of some of the technicalities of society which have changed with time. But the essence of the content is still as valid as ever. In fact, due to the continual worsening of the problems herein portrayed, the need for such an exposé is ever greater.

The author is not a psychologist per sé, although he is widely read in the subject. In fact, he has many disagreements with formal psychology and psychiatry. These are backed by his uniquely wide experiences in many occupations and industries, rubbing shoulders with people in all walks of life.

However, not from personal experience only has the writer gained his insights, but from observations of others and listening to the stories of numerous people, as their work mate, or, as their minister in the church, each over a period of decades.

This book is followed with another by the same author and on the same topic, but with more relevance to adult life in the present time when the problem is grossly worsening and spreading in North America. The second writing shows more vividly the sheer cruelty and often brazen mental abuse with deceptive cover-up that is that is inflicted on fine, well charactered, cultured and intelligent people, not only by individuals as in the first book, but by groups of people — birds of a feather acting together.

Also the types of people who practice this malady are described and characterized, with stories to illustrate their behavior, including breaking the law by, often intentionally, inflicting emotional distress on adults; which law, to date, has been generally applied to spousal and child abuse.

Places and people have been disguised for the usual reasons. Simple Latin names have been used for locations. Names of characters have been chosen for their meaning, and coincide with their general character make-up. This was, more or less, a matter of convenience in finding suitable names, though it adds authenticity to the characters and the story.

The writer makes no claim to academic excellence, much less to what he sees as the over-sophistication of psychological theory. On the contrary, considering his background as a constantly assailed fine person he regards himself to be very fortunate indeed to have attained even one university level degree. He has only the intention, in both books, to have the problem exposed so that it may be more adequately dealt with both on a personal level and legally through litigation.

The books are written within the Christian perspective of the author, although there is much in them for people of other faiths, and more expressly for people in all of life's occupations.

Cleon E. Spencer

# CHAPTER ONE

Collin Seldon walked, at his usual brisk pace, up the sidewalk towards the glass doors of the Arts building of Quilibet University. The impressive glass front of the several storied structure caused him to glance upward as he approached. His face brightened and his lips showed the trace of a smile at the inviting warmth of the building. He swung open the street level door and entered. But then as if by intrusion of some other feelings the smile disappeared. He wondered now, *would the inside be as inviting as the outside appeared to be*. As he took the few steps across the entrance way, he gave a little shrug, as if to say to himself, *oh well, take it as it comes*.

Thoughts ran through Collin's mind as on this September Tuesday evening he proceeded up the half set of stairs that led to the first floor. On the previous Thursday he had taken the downward section of the divided stairway to the below ground hall where he had registered in an evening course in Psychology. Classes would begin this evening.

From the stair top he proceeded down the sizeable foyer of Floor One, to the elevators. There he became somewhat absorbed in ambivalent thought as he pushed the up button, waited a moment or two, stepped with other students onto the elevator, disembarked on floor three, all the while thinking how pleasant it could be to be back in the student world. Collin had a liking for a reasonable amount of this part of life. But his thoughts were juxtaposed with unpleasantness as well. His past academic life hadn't been all roses. Many people find university life pleasant, but not a person such as Collin Seldon. *Have I been a fool to come back for more*? he wondered.

Why, just now as he had crossed the busy foyer, he received a variety of unpleasant reactions from people who had only his appearance to go by as their motivation for their negative attitudes towards him. Of course there were some pleasant reactions towards him too, by those good people who took the trouble to even glance at him. But he much more caught the attention of people who didn't like him.

As he rode up the elevator, he wondered again if he had been a fool to come. Being now past middle-age he perhaps should be gearing down with regard to things like this, and spend more time with his fine and lovely wife, and their children and grandchildren.

And what is it about Collin Seldon that brought negative reactions exemplified by such gestures as pushing up a lip in contempt; raising one's head high momentarily in an 'I'm better than you' gesture; by a shaking of the head when passing by to intimidate and lessen his self-esteem; or by simply turning the head away as if to imply, I don't even see you, or, you're not worth looking at.

Although approaching retirement age, Collin had still retained a goodly measure of his youthful appearance and his vim and vigor. There were some signs of aging: his light brown hair graying at the sides; his wholesome, healthy looking facial complexion just beginning to show wrinkles in its past middle-age fullness; his once athletic body showing to be somewhat overweight; his average height being lessened, to a glancing eye, by shoulders that have begun to round. Collin was really just beginning to show his years, but he looked, and was still a fine, dignified looking person, as he had been all his life. His fine appearance was augmented by his modest, yet tasteful clothes and mannerism.

Good, well cultured people like and respect Collin Seldon for what he is — a fine smart looking, well charactered person of discerning mind. Although little or no attention is paid to it in society, the fact is, numerous others in all walks of life hate him and people similar to him, for the same reason, and often cause them much trouble. It is this latter reality which kept crossing his mind as he now returned to a campus as an evening student.

Collin had, over the years, learned to take these facts of his life in his stride as an unavoidable part and parcel of the life of a person such as he, yet he could not help but be aware of and affected by it.

At any rate he was coming back to the classroom again, if only on a limited scale. Collin Seldon was a clergyman by profession — a good one to whom many nice people easily confided their troubles and joys, their fears and hopes; to whom people turned, sometimes for advice, and often for approval or disapproval of a deed or desire or plan of action.

Collin, although not academically specialized in the area of counseling, was quite adept with this aspect of his ministry, coming by it naturally. He had a fairly broad basic training in the field, which he augmented occasionally by reading the latest books on the subject. In fact, the reason he was on his way to the classroom now was to take this course in "Current Trends in Psychology, Psychiatry and Relevant Social Problems." The name had caught his eye one day as he looked through the university catalog while helping a young member of his congregation plan a study program. Mostly it was the last three words of the course's title that had caught Collin's attention, namely, *Relevant Social Problems*.

*Maybe*, he thought to himself at the time, *maybe there is some new breakthrough here. Please God, could there be? Heaven knows there is a need — and I know from personal experience. Could there be*? He was looking for something to be at last formally recognized in psychology about the problems of fine, well cultured people like himself, often in some ways exceptional individuals; also the numerous hitherto unrecognized ways this matter so drastically affects society.

Collin was hopeful, well, sort of, so he had registered for the course. But he was doubtful too. That's the kind of person Collin Seldon was — always with a mind open at both ends, so to speak; as in this instance, hopeful, but with a mind tuned and ready for whatever reality might evolve from the situation. That way, he believed, the shocks of life are not so great, and although when using this method one may not ride through life as high as the proverbial eternal optimist, nevertheless the shocks are much better absorbed. Not all people live that way, but for such a person as Collin, experience had taught him that it was the only viable way.

Room 307 was brightly lit, and as Collin entered the open door at the front of the room his mind cleared itself entirely after a passing thought that perhaps there is no need here for fear or anxiety. At any rate he would think positively and give the situation the benefit of the doubt. He was a little early and the professor's chair was still vacant.

Collin glanced down across the room. Groups of students stood around chatting vigorously as though catching up with each others news after a summer apart. Most likely they had studied here the previous year, and some perhaps at summer semester too. Obviously the majority of them knew each other well. But here and there were students who were strangers to the scene, as one could guess; one walking around, hands in pockets, looking at the pictures on the wall; another just standing and looking here, there and everywhere, as though looking for some place or time to get in and mix with the crowd. Some others had already chosen chairs, were seated and ready, but temporarily passed the time by doodling with a pen or leafing through a book.

Collin, a newcomer himself, not only to this classroom but to this university, after inconspicuously surveying the geographics of the situation, chose a seat about three-quarters of the way down from the front and just to the right side of the center of the singly placed seats. After placing his briefcase on the writing arm of the chair he looked around. A pleasant and friendly looking young man was sitting two rows to the left. They caught each others glance.

The chap smiled, held up his hand and said, "Hi."

Collin did likewise, adding as a gesture of friendship, "How are you this evening?"

"Good," answered the stranger as he rose from the chair and proceeded towards Collin to make acquaintance. "Owen Winslow is my name," he said, as he put forward his hand to shake.

"Collin Seldon," said Collin, as he arose and shook hands.

*So far, so good*, thought Collin. For here introducing himself was a pleasant type indeed.

Owen Winslow, in his mid thirties stood a good deal taller than Collin Seldon. His somewhat heavy-set, yet trim, well-built body, obviously kept in good condition physically as well as with regard to neatness and appearance, as made evident by, among other things, good taste in clothes, would cause him to stand out as a fine person in any crowd. He looked down at Collin as the two now stood talking.

"I'm teaching here at this university, temporarily", said Owen.

"Oh then," said Collin with a smile as though well pleased, "you are to be our professor for this class."

"No," replied Owen, "I teach History of Religion, but I intend to take this course in Psychology 3004 to acquire a little more general knowledge of the subject. I find that basic training in psychology helps me to understand my students and colleagues a little better, which adds to the quality of my regular work. It also contributes to my personal growth."

"Sounds interesting, Owen, and somewhat of a coincidence. I am a clergyman. I too come to this course for much the same reasons as you, and I do use it in my work to some extent, but...."

Collin's words were interrupted by a call from the front of the room. "May I have your attention please. Could I ask you to take your seats. It is time to begin. Thank you."

The professor had entered the room and taken a standing position behind his desk. In response to his call, the students cutting off their conversations, spread themselves around the room filling almost all of the chairs.

"Nice to have met you", said Owen Winslow as he gestured toward his chair.

"Likewise," said Collin Seldon. "No doubt we'll have more opportunity to talk."

"Right," Owen responded as he proceeded to his seat.

Collin sat down. There would be no need to take notes at the beginning, perhaps not at all the first evening. He leaned a little to the right, placed his right elbow on the writing arm of the chair, extending his forearm upward so as to allow his extended thumb to connect with his chin. Simultaneously his loosely extended fingers covered a portion of the side of his face, the lower right side of his nose, and also a portion of his upper and lower lip and chin. *It has been very profitable on many previous occasions to sit in such a manner as this, at least to start*, he mused. Time would prove him out on that before the class was over. Collin outwardly looked relaxed in his chair, but there were tensions on the inside.

Professor Yates, a man in his middle fifties, briefly introduced himself to the class. He was an assistant professor in the psychology department he said. After extending a welcome to the students, he proceeded to outline the course, its purpose and scope. "The name of the course, 'Current Trends in Psychology, Psychiatry and Relevant Social Problems' indicates its broad scope. This in turn is indicative that with such all inclusive terms of reference we cannot possibly go into it with a detailed and prolonged study. You won't be a specialist when you have finished with this class," he quipped clumsily, belittling himself, rather than making his point in a humorous manner, as he had intended.

Then the professor quickly, and quite noticeably to Collin, set out positively to retrieve the stature he felt he had lost. He did so by expounding the merits of his "very comprehensive update" on this "all important subject" as he emphatically called it. "This is the essence of humanity," he said, "the insight into behavior, that enables people to cope with and react to society in a healthy manner."

Now gaining control of his composure before the class, he continued, "This is a survey course that I am sure you will find to be a valuable aid in helping you to chart your future course in the field of psychology; or, you may find it to be an excellent prerequisite that will open other doors to you; or, you may simply value it as good general knowledge."

The professor was now showing signs that he was already in control of things, standing tall, and as he continued speaking, moved about behind his desk with assurance and an air of ascending towards cloud nine.

Collin retained the same position in his chair as he had begun with. Being an ardent observer of people, he glanced around the room at the students that he was able to observe without turning his head, and being careful to do so only when Professor Yates' attention was directed away from the area where Collin sat. Without detracting the professor he was able to observe that the students were well absorbed in what they heard. Owen Winslow was deeply engrossed and obviously interested, so much so that he seemed unaware that Professor Yates avoided looking in his direction. The professor did look in Collin's direction without problem, as Collin's hand continued to cover a significant portion of his face. Collin too thought it would be a good course, but he wondered how things would turn out for himself. His inner tensions were somewhat quieted by his absorption with the lecture, but they were still there, and for good reason.

"In this course", continued Professor Yates, "we will survey the latest in mind exploration; such things as memory, thought processes, mind body interaction, and so on".

*I've recently read some interesting articles on this*, thought Collin as his own mind went into gear. *This will be an opportunity to get first hand professional views on the subject, just for the sake of curiosity, and general knowledge to help with my ministry, of course, as I am not now or not likely to get involved in such work to any great extent.*

After a little more detail on this aspect of the course, the professor swung into psychological testing methods. "Here", he said, "we will look at some new techniques, comparing and evaluating them alongside the methods that have been in use for considerable time." He spoke briefly on the indispensible value of testing, stating that this matter would be gone into more fully in due time.

*That's a little outside my sphere*, Collin reminded himself silently. *But the knowledge will never go astray, especially when speaking with any professional person to whom I may have to refer a parishioner for specialized help. At least I will be able to understand the language if a psychologist should need to speak to me about such things.*

Professor Yates next zeroed in on psychotherapy. "First we will survey the traditional uses of psychoanalysis and psychotherapy, looking at some of the merits and criticisms of each, with some case histories for illustration purposes. We will give attention to the wide use and misuse of transference, counter-transference and projection. Over and against these we will place some of the types of therapies that have evolved in recent years, with case histories which show the positive values they can have, as well as their weaknesses. We will touch on Bioenergenetics, Reality Therapy and Gestalt Therapy, to name only some." As Professor Yates mentioned the names of these newer methods, they struck a note in Collin's mind. He had read books on them, but he would be pleased to hear about them in the lecture room. There was always so much more to learn that way.

After a few minutes outlining just how the therapy comparisons would be done, the professor went into the final aspect of the course.

"We are finding more and more as time goes by," he said, "that the social aftermath of all that is done in the treatment of mental disorders is a key issue. It is an extremely important factor in deciding whether the patient will make the grade in society or whether he returns again, and perhaps again and again for further therapy of one kind or another."

Collin became so intensely interested at the sound of what he had just heard, that he forgot himself completely. His hand came unknowingly down from his face and lodged on the arm of his chair. His self awareness was now almost nil. Perhaps what was coming was what he had been searching and hoping for for many years.

"The social problems related to the treatment of the mentally ill are numerous and difficult," said Professor Yates. He continued to talk confidently, surveying his domain as he spoke, looking here and there at the students sitting before him. Then it happened. Professor Yates, in his surveillance of the class as he lectured, caught a glimpse, for the first time, of Collin Seldon with his hand down from his face. As their glimpses connected, the professor paused for a split second during which time there was a slight break in the flow of his speech as well as momentary stoppage in his head and body swinging. But then he turned very quickly away from Collin, looking out over the students to his right as he continued to lecture.

Collin, so absorbed in the content of the lecture, was only partly aware of what was happening as the professor turned back to venture another glimpse of him. Then with paling face he suddenly turned away from him again as if with fright.

This brought Collin's self awareness back to full capacity. He kept his cool and casually placed his hand to the side of his face as before, meanwhile observing that the professor's proud and elated swinging mood had now subsided. Whether his confidence had too, he could not detect, but the tone of the lecture was now definitely on the down beat.

Collin braced himself, expecting Professor Yates might venture another look. Within a short period he did, this time nodding slightly towards Collin, then turning away, only to look once more, bristle, then turn away to ignore Collin's presence throughout the remainder of the class period.

*I won't have much of a rapport with this one,* thought Collin. *I know from previous experiences that this professor perceives me, just by my presence, to be too much for him. By his bristle he has indicated he is going to handle it by being unfriendly, perhaps hostile towards me, maybe even try to drive me away. Time will tell.*

"The problems of social acceptance generally, the home environment wherein lies the root of the patients' problems, the acquisition of social and employment skills; these we will consider in the final phase of our course," continued Professor Yates. He was now somewhat subdued, but self-consciously endeavoring to regain his former stance.

*Not much new there*, thought Collin; *well, there maybe some new approaches to these familiar problems. That will be interesting and helpful, but really not what I was hoping for.*

Professor Yates continued the session towards its ending with an outline of how he would present these social problems with some experiments and case histories added. After presenting a list of text books and readings the period had passed and he dismissed the class, stating that he would be happy to talk to students individually in the fifteen or so minutes at his disposal immediately following dismissal.

Collin stayed in his chair as the students dispersed. At first he sat for a while looking over the list of text books he had written down. Slowly then he stood, purposely lingering some more, and allowing other students to talk to Professor Yates first. Collin would then approach him and, so he thought, try to befriend him.

Owen Winslow had lingered too, also for a purpose. Now that the other students had cleared away from the vicinity of Collin, Owen proceeded toward him somewhat hurriedly, meanwhile making an effort to control the smile that was breaking out over his face.

"You must be one of us," said Owen enthusiastically.

"One of us?" questioned Collin, expressing complete surprise. Thoughts went through his mind. *Was this some sort of shady approach*? Then, *no, it can't be. Unless my guess is wrong, this man is a good type. I'll trust him further*. "Just what do you mean by 'one of us'?" he asked curiously.

He was reassured by an apologetic reply from Owen, "I'm sorry I said that *one of us* so crudely, but my observance is you are a fine, well cultured, clean-cut looking person who stands out in public. Because of that, it brings on problems peculiar to people like you and I and the other members of a support group we have going here at the university. It was this group of fine people I had in mind when I said you must be one of *us*."

As Collin paused and pondered this unusual experience, Owen enthusiastically continued the conversation, "I couldn't help but notice Mr. Yates' reaction to you, and how you partially covered your face again. I recalled then that you had your hand up to your face from the beginning, but I didn't realize the significance of it until the moment Professor Yates turned so quickly away from you. A neat maneuver you have there — think I'll try that one!"

Collin began to see what Owen meant by *us*. "Might be a good idea for you too," he said as he smiled. "Then the professor will look in your direction also." They both laughed together in subdued tones.

Collin, looked toward the professor's desk. "I wish to make acquaintance with Professor Yates. We'll talk again later, okay?"

"That's a good maneuver too, Collin," said Owen, more seriously. "I think you can help us."

Surprise and curiosity came over Collin's face again.

"I mean — well — would you, that is, if you had it explained to you, I'm sure you would be interested," Owen said fluctuating between stammering and excitement.

"I think I know what *us* means now," replied Collin, "and if I can help anyone, I'd be glad to. There are lounging benches placed around the foyer. I'll meet you out there in a few minutes, if that's all right with you."

"Good" said Owen, obviously pleased. "I'll wait for you."

Collin, now left alone, approached the area where Professor Yates stood talking to a student. There was one other student still waiting. Mr Yates had been putting them through about one every two minutes. He glanced at Collin approaching the area. The student with whom he had been talking was breaking away with the usual courtesies. The next student stepped up. Professor Yates engrossed himself in a lengthy conversation with him. Two minutes passed, three, four, five. Collin had experienced this before. He looked at his watch and thought of leaving.

On second thought though, he decided to stay and ride it out. At least he would stay long enough to be sure whether this delay was a coincidence or a standoff. His wondering about which it would be was soon answered. The conversation between the professor and the other student continued for about two minutes longer. Meanwhile Collin stood his ground, giving the impression he intended to stay in there. Looking at his watch, the professor sent the student on his way and Collin stepped up to him immediately.

"What do *you* want?" Professor Yates asked disdainfully and curtly of Collin, with emphasis on the *you*.

Collin braced himself, as he had done on many similar occasions. In fact he was able to handle such a situation so well now, that no notice of shock to his system was visible. "Just thought I would discuss some aspects of the course with you," replied Collin in a calm and friendly tone that also seemed to say by its inference, *Well for what other reason would I be here*?

The Professor glared at Collin intensely and silently.

*I could ride out that glare too*," Collin thought to himself, *but then I know what it would lead to eventually; a complaint to the department head about me, a wayward student*. Instead, he looked at his wrist watch, and then at Professor Yates, "Of course, if there is no time left, we can skip it. I'm sure the questions I have to ask will be answered as the lectures go by."

"Yes", said the professor, emphatically, lifting his shoulders a little, as if by the face saving opportunity Collin had just given him he was now in control again. "I'm sure they will, and time is running out." He turned and began to pick up the papers from his desk and place them in his briefcase.

Collin bade him good night in a courteous manner and turned to leave the room. There was no reply. It had been a standoff indeed, from the beginning. Collin left the room, casually and unhurriedly, and went out to look for Owen Winslow.

As he entered the foyer, he didn't have to look far to find Owen who now bounded towards him half smiling, half excited. The two met a safe distance from the lecture room door.

"You'll have to excuse me for being so forward," remarked Owen in a subdued voice, "for I did snoop on your meeting with Professor Yates, from a distance that is. I couldn't hear the conversation, but the reaction was obvious, even from such a distance."

"Come" replied Collin, "let's go across the foyer a piece and have a seat, and we'll see what it is you have in mind about 'us'. In my whole life, you're the first one I've met who has been so open about this matter."

The two proceeded to an empty bench. Other students were

scattered throughout, going and coming, talking, standing and sitting.

"I'm very sorry to be bothering you so this evening," remarked Owen, "but I do think you can help us; you see we have a support group of fine cultured people, as we call them, formed here under the auspices of the Student Health and Counseling Services of this University."

"Uh-ah" Collin answered disinterestedly, "that's years behind me."

"That's what I expected, Collin, and that's just the point," Owen continued to press, "but you've make the grade. Our support group is made up of people like you, only much younger, who haven't yet made the grade. You can help them I'm sure."

Collin chuckled as he answered, "yea, I've made the grade. You saw what happened in the lecture room this evening."

"But," said Owen eagerly, "you did become a clergyman. I cannot help but surmise, judging from what happened this evening, that the going for you has been difficult at times, but you did make it, didn't you?"

"Well, yes, after a fashion I suppose I did make it," replied Collin. "Are you the overseer of the group?"

"I'm the facilitator, I got it together, but a psychiatrist from the Student Health and Counseling Services oversees all our meetings."

"Ugh," responded Collin. "Much to my regret, in my younger years I had an ugly experience with a couple of psychiatrists, and after that, brief encounters with two or three others, till, with God's help, I took my life back into my own hands. I have no desire to be involved with them again, not for my particular life experiences."

Owen's exuberance faltered as he said in a disappointed tone, "Aw, I'm sorry I bothered you with this."

Collin was moved by Owen's disappointment. "Okay," he said, more cheerfully, "we'll say I made the grade. What can I do to help? Would you explain your support group further?"

Owen became obviously happy. "We meet once a week," he said, "room 405, of this building— just one floor up. We meet under the guidance of Dr. Eldren, a retired psychiatrist who offers his services to the Student Health and Counseling Services, no connection to the Psychology Department. You won't have to worry about Professor Yates. Dr. Eldren is a very mature, understanding and friendly man — no problem for you there, I'm sure. Would you, I wonder, come along to the meeting tomorrow evening at seven? Dr. Eldren will explain the purpose of the group much better than I. Will you come?"

"Psychiatrists are years behind me," responded Collin, "but you've aroused my curiosity so much that I'm all ears. Will it be all right with Dr. Eldren if I come along to the meeting?"

"I feel sure it will," said Owen with renewed enthusiasm, "but I will contact him tomorrow and let him know about you."

Collin asked of Owen further, "How does your wife fit into this, or are you married?"

"I'm not married *yet,*" said Owen, with a twinkle, "but I have my eye on a fine woman at present. She is a member of our support group. She seems to like me too."

"I see," responded Collin. "My wife won't want to be attending the meetings, but she may accompany me on the drive here occasionally, and wait for me at the library. She has done things like that with me before. Anyway, please phone me by five o'clock tomorrow evening, and confirm that it will be in order for me to be present," said Collin as he reached into his pocket for a business card containing his phone number and gave it to Owen.

The two shook hands, exchanged parting courtesies, and separated, Owen heading for the stairs to floor four, Collin taking the elevator to floor one and the door out into the street.

*I may not find what I was hoping for in Psychology 3001*, he thought to himself, *but I may find it in room 405 — maybe! Hope to heaven I do.*

# CHAPTER TWO

The support group met as scheduled on Wednesday evening at seven in room 405 of the Arts Building. This fourth floor was taken up mainly with faculty offices. It was a quiet area, with occasionally a professor or secretarial personnel moving about, as well as a student now and then going to or coming from an interview. Amid this rather private atmosphere, room 405 was set aside as a meeting room for use of staff or other approved groups.

Collin Seldon, in accordance with his usual practice arrived a little early, but the open door of room 405 revealed that three others were already present. He entered the room, and as he did, he entered upon a new experience in life — well, not entirely new, it was to be old and familiar content, but with a new approach and emphasis. Collin sensed that already, even with all it may take out of him, he was glad he had come.

"So pleased you came" said Owen Winslow, one of the three early comers, as he went to Collin and shook hands. "Come, meet Dr. Eldren," he continued as he gripped Collin's shoulder and led him toward the senior person present.

Dr Eldren gave a hearty hand shake. "Most welcome to the group" he said, obviously well pleased at Collin's attendance. "Owen has told me a great deal about you already, even though he has known you for so short a time. He has great expectations for the contribution he feels you can make to our group — now I would like you to meet the youngest member of the club, Albin Anders."

Albin was standing beside the doctor. He blushed slightly at the mention of his own name. Obviously shy, he shook hands with Collin, rather hesitantly.

"How do you do," he said quietly and without the hearty exuberance that had been shown by the older men present. It was evident Albin Anders was very shy indeed.

Quickly Owen moved to his vacant side, the side opposite to

where Dr. Eldren was standing, placed his arm around Albin's shoulder, "Albin has become unofficially our prime charge in this venture," said Owen as he affectionately ruffled Albin's young shoulders with his powerful arm. "He is young, eager, and to date not too badly scathed in life. We hope to see him through to better days."

Collin could not help but look at Albin and size him up. Young, twenty one years of age or so, he would guess; fair complexioned, blonde hair, average height, with a youthful body and appearance; striking to look at. Collin's mind went into a swirl of thought and reflection. Past, present and future all sprang to his mind. Tears of emotion came to his eyes. Nobody would notice, he hoped. He fought it back, and kept it hidden as best he could. *Yes, Albin Anders would need help and support from the strong arm of Owen Winslow — and many others*, went Collin's flashing thoughts. *Life is not a bed of roses for Albin Anders, I'm glad I came*, was his thought on the matter as three other persons entered the door.

Owen Winslow did the introductions again as two ladies and a man now joined those already present in room 405. "This is Gilda Emerson, and this is Donna Coyne," he said as he turned to Collin. "Collin Seldon, ladies, a new member of our group." There was an exchange of handshakes. They were ladies indeed. Collin's thoughts shot into action again concerning what flak such fine people as they must have to put up with in society. It was interrupted this time, as Owen went on to say with a grin "and this is Leo Aidan, a man who brings such life and vigor to our group as you have never seen before."

"Oh, just listen to the reputation this guy is giving me," he shot back mischievously. "You just wait and decide for yourself Collin, and you'll find me to be one of the most peaceful people you ever met." Everyone laughed and the ice was well broken.

Dr. Eldren looked at his watch. "Is Brett planning to continue his attendance in this group?" he asked of Owen.

"Yes," replied Owen with a smile, "but you know he'll be late!"

"Well, we can arrange the chairs and sit down at any rate," suggested the doctor.

Chairs were placed in a circle, and as they were about to sit, the remaining member, Brett Culver rushed into the room.

"Sorry I'm late again folks," he apologized, and greeted the other members of the group with handshakes and a warm comment of how nice it was to be here and see them all again. He included Collin in his greeting without introduction, as a part of his effort not to delay the meeting. "I'm making a real effort these days to be on time for appointments, and its working — almost! I almost made it on time this evening, but will have to do better in the future," he said in self-criticism of a light nature. There was laughter and everyone was at ease as they sat down.

Dr. Eldren took the initiative. He spoke in the mellowing tones of a sympathetic man of seventy years of age. "As you already know, I am Dr. Eldren, a psychiatrist retired from private practice, and doing part time work in counseling here at Quilibet University. For the benefit of our new-comer, Collin Seldon, whom we are pleased to have join us, and also to refresh the memories of the remainder of us who met three times last spring, we will survey our purpose and accomplishments to date. Then hopefully we will be able to chart a course for the semester we are just beginning. Do you all agree with that approach?" he asked.

The doctor apparently wanted a shared planning and responsibility for this group — a mutual effort for the highest benefit. Collin was pleased immeasurably with that. He had already taken a cautious liking to this psychiatrist whom he learned had had a great deal of experience in a notable private practice which had involved him in the broader realms of the field. A man so experienced and mature would no doubt have a mind open enough to take in and deal with the ordinary, the extra-ordinary, the unexpected, even the unbelievable. Collin was becoming more impressed by the minute as Dr. Eldren spoke. His understanding tones befitted his humane appearance. His gray hair, almost white, yet thinned very little, rose up somewhat at the front, then swept back over his head in a medium length as though a crew cut had grown too long. Yet it was well trimmed at the sides, making it obvious that it was not really overgrown, but intentionally groomed that way. Dr. Eldren had put on very little extra weight in his older years. He was not exactly thin, but less than medium build, and a little on the tall side. His face showed slightly bulging jowls, common to a man of his years. He appeared to be holding his age well, except for one thing — his face appeared to be pale. He had a pleasant face, but it was very pale, Colin noticed. *There could be a thousand and one reasons, either temporary or permanent for a person to have a pale face,* he thought.

"This group was formed last spring, mainly on the initiative of Owen Winslow," continued the likable doctor. "Albin Anders," he said, as he looked at Albin with an affectionate smile, "was in Owen's class. Perhaps you would like to tell us Owen, how you and Albin came to be here."

"Yes," replied Owen, "I teach a history of religion course and Albin was in my class. I half noticed, half guessed that he was probably having similar difficulties as I had when I was younger and struggling through college, so after I got to know him better through routine class work, I approached him on the matter. Sure enough it was with him as I had thought. I came and spoke to Dr. Eldren about him. Dr Eldren just about that time had Leo Aidan referred to him by a department head for counseling because of the difficulty he was having with a professor in the department. During the same semester in another of my classes I was getting to know Gilda Emerson. In this case I had no reason to believe she had any problem — she appeared to be doing well — until one day in an after-class discussion she revealed to me that she had been having problems in the past, but was now doing fairly well. Because of this information and further observation, I thought she could both help with and benefit from this group. I invited her and here she is. So with the project unintentionally growing into a support group, I began to scout around intentionally for more members, feeling sure by then that I was coming up with a gathering of people who had problems in common. Leo told me about a friend of his, Donna Coyne, whom he thought could 'qualify,' he said with a smile and making the gesture of quotation marks with his forefingers, 'qualify for this group,' he re-emphasized as he smiled at Donna nearby.

Owen continued, "Last but not least, till now anyway, is Brett Culver. Brett was the last to join us last spring. Although he has been registered in evening courses here at the university for the past two years, it was really from patronizing one of his business establishments that I came to know him well. Then to my surprise one evening, I met him in the registrars office here at the university. Once again from observation and conversation, I realized he was another one for the group."

"Another one of *us*" jested Collin.

"Yes" said Owen, "another one of us. I seem to have developed a nose for such people now," he quirked, "guess you could call it 'attraction to one's own kind,' or something like that."

The members chuckled collectively as Owen continued, "Then it happens that just last evening I met Collin Seldon in, of all places, a psychology class. He is not only the latest addition to our numbers, but the one I've been able fastest to recruit — just took one class and a very brief but intensely productive meeting with him."

"You're getting to be very good at this Owen, you'll straighten us all out yet," interjected Leo. Everyone laughed — except Collin. He knew the remark was intended only as a jest, but for him it contained a grave misstatement which had cost him dearly in the past, which he could never accept, and which would always keep him wary. *Attempting to straighten us out will never work for us*, he thought to himself.

"Thank you, Leo," responded Owen, and, as he looked at the unsmiling Collin, "I only hope he decides to stay with us for a while."

"Don't worry, Owen, I'll be here for a while," Collin reassured him.

"All right, that's how we all came to be together," intervened Dr. Eldren. "Referring again to our progress to date, last spring each of the members present did an I.Q. and other relevant testing, mainly to verify what we already thought, that here we have a group with this in common, that you are all highly intelligent, and there is little or no indication of serious personality problems. There was an interruption from Leo as he rolled his eyes, stretched the upper part of his body upward as he rocked it from side to side in a mocking gesture of mimicking a conceited one. "Yea, we do rate after all—maybe not as we should in society, maybe not always in the classroom, but at least in the results of psychological testing, we do rate," he blurted out in a rollicking manner that brought smiles and laughter.

Collin smiled only, but a mixed feeling of amusement and satisfaction went deep, O so deep inside him, for here he was at last in the company of people with whom he had much in common. As humorous as Leo's antics went over though, Collin couldn't laugh aloud, for again Leo had unknowingly struck a meaningful and painful note. Collin glanced across at Albin, who also had smiled only. But he knew that young Albin's laughter was being stifled by the weight of his burdens rather than by any mature and meaningful thoughts on the matter. *I will stay on here just as long as it takes to help that young chap*, thought Collin with a feeling of sympathy towards him. *There are limitations to what I can do for him, but I'll help him somehow.*

Dr. Eldren took control again after laughing with the others. "I'm glad you can accept it in such a good frame of mind Leo." He then turned to Collin, "Leo in his fun making has just stated the purpose of this group." Then looking around at them all, "as previously indicated, all members of the group have an above average I.Q., you are all well behaved, well cultured, well groomed— smart and smart looking people. For all intents and purposes you should be doing extremely well in life, including academic life which is our most obvious concern since we are involved with the university in our respective ways. But I do not think we should try to isolate concerns pertaining to academic experiences only. I would suggest that in our discussions in this group we include any and all relevant life experiences. By exploring various aspects of your lives we will hopefully come up with some answers for you which will be helpful to you in the academic sphere as well."

Dr. Eldren continued to the group of very attentive listeners who had much at stake in this venture, "I gather from experiences described during the group discussions held last spring that you all have something else in common besides being smart and smart looking; you all have a feeling of being discriminated against one way and another by certain people." He turned to Collin, "Of course Collin, this being your first meeting with us, you haven't had any input into the group, but may I ask, does the brief, and no doubt incomplete description I have just given of the problem register with you? Have you had similar experiences?"

"Yes sir" responded Collin most emphatically, "but you've put the problem very mildly. Discrimination is hardly the word." Collin Seldon had never talked so freely to a psychiatrist for many years. He felt more free already with Dr. Eldren and this group, and besides, he wasn't here for any purpose other than to help out, so if at any time he was told he was paranoid, he could simply walk out.

But there was no mention or inference of paranoia by Dr. Eldren, who continued on in a probing fashion, "In our previous discussions, incidents in the lives of each participant were told to the group; it was enough to illustrate that each of you did have common experiences. Now we need to go into the matter in more depth. If you have problems in common, there may be a common cause or causes. Over the next several weeks or months, whatever it takes, I would suggest that each of you take a turn in reviewing significant parts of your life history, but paying particular attention to experiences of discrimination or times when you were up against other people. Then maybe if as Collin suggests, the word 'discrimination' is not a suitable description, we may be able to find a more accurate way of describing the phenomenon. Maybe also, and this is most important of all, perhaps, we can come up with some of the causes, something perhaps that you have in common that you are going about in a wrong or ineffective or inefficient manner, that brings this attitude of others upon you."

Collin Seldon froze in his chair at the sound of what he had just heard. *Good heavens*, he thought to himself, *when will some people tune in to the world of reality*. His thoughts raced on, *What am I doing here anyway. Getting myself into trouble again, needlessly*. He glanced around at the other members. They were listening intently. Obviously they hadn't become perturbed by what they had just heard. At least there was no visible sign of disturbance. But then Collin himself was showing no outward reaction to Dr. Eldren's statement. He had become quite adept over the years at not showing his feelings when necessary or expedient. It was one of his better means of protection. *Is this how it is with the other group members*, he wondered as he now surveyed them. *Maybe with some of them. But the younger ones would probably not yet know the difference*. He looked at Albin who appeared undisturbed about the issue. Collin felt compassion for him again. *I will stay on*, thought Collin again, *to help Albin Anders — otherwise he's done for — he will end up in an irreparable mess. I'll stay on, at least until I am compelled to drop out by the circumstance I already see on the horizon*. He then thought on the other side of the coin, so to speak, *Dr. Eldren is a good man. He may understand, he may see things in a different light — maybe — but then again he has his professional training to stand by*.

Collin was abruptly disturbed from his thoughts when Dr. Eldren addressed him by name, "Collin, as I indicated earlier, all members of the group have had psychological testing. Since you are our guest and have come to us because of our invitation rather than out of your own need, you can be exempt from any testing; or, if you think testing will be of any benefit in this instance, then we can arrange to have it done."

Collin declined. "I'd rather not Dr. Eldren. I've had many tests, and from them have learned that I have a very high I.Q., and not much else wrong with me except that."

There was laughter again. Even Albin laughed loud enough to be heard as he was attracted to Collin as a mentor. He spoke also, and, with a smile, "Mr. Seldon," he said, still too shy and lacking in self esteem to be on a first name basis with an older person such as Collin, "Do you regard having a high I.Q. as being a liability rather than an asset?"

"Collin is my first name" replied Collin, warmly, "A high I.Q. in itself is not a liability, but in certain other combinations it certainly can be, although I wouldn't exchange it, Albin, for a lesser I.Q."

"Thank you sir" responded Albin nervously, with his shyness settling in on him again.

"That's interesting" added Dr. Eldren, "I think we should explore that avenue more fully as you relate your experiences to one another. One would, off-hand, think of a higher I.Q. as being an asset at anytime — if a person has the initiative and is willing to put it to good use."

*Not always, Dr. Eldren, not always*, Collin thought again, but dared not yet say aloud. *There's a whole big world out there that just hates high I.Q's when they are in certain combinations with other traits. You're a good type, doctor, maybe you'll understand that when we talk about it later. But I have to know you better first. I wouldn't discuss it at this stage of the game — not yet.*

There was a pause. A silence came over the whole group. Dr. Eldren was waiting for more discussion on the I.Q. matter. He looked at Collin expectantly. Collin did a fast maneuver to avoid the subject. It would be ill-timed indeed to discuss it now. Discussions of life experiences should come first for needed illustrations.

"Your group discussions last spring, apparently will be continued now," shot Collin quickly changing the trend of thought. "So could I have at least a briefing on what was said, and the general attitude in the group towards it."

"Yes, yes," responded Dr. Eldren with a slight jump in his speech, in reaction to the change in the subject. Then he simmered down quickly. "Well, on second thought I would suggest we start from the beginning again as though no experiences were related at all last spring. As we know, we only barely got started, and it was very sketchily done at that time. Let us have a new beginning, with each of you telling relevant portions of your life's story with more detail and depth, which in turn will allow a more thorough analysis.

Everyone agreed to start anew and to go into more detail and depth.

The unconventional support group proceeded immediately and in earnest with Leo Aidan telling his story. He had had a clash with an English Professor whom he claims was discriminating against him. English was important to Leo. He wanted to major in it, feeling this would be a stepping stone into journalism.

To look at Leo, one wouldn't take him to be a person to initiate trouble. His pleasant manner befitted his clean-cut appearance. His little better than average height balanced well with his broad well developed shoulders and the medium build of the remainder of his body. His casual-business clothing was tasteful — navy blue pants with a contrasting light blue blazer with small, subdued checks and an appropriate conservative bluish tie. His black shoes were polished and in good condition. Leo Aidan undoubtedly had a cultured taste for quality. His attire went well with his black wavy hair, cut to medium length and parted at the left side, which had the effect of minimizing any possible bushiness that sometimes accompanies wavy hair. The roots of his hair came low on his forehead to meet the permanently planted lines that ran horizontally across his brow. At the sides his hair was neatly trimmed. At its roots it crowded in toward the sides of his forehead and upper face.

*Yes, Leo has a good head of hair*, observed Collin to himself, *it blends wonderfully well with the slightly darkened tincture of his complexion and his full and rounded face. In addition, his pleasant general facial expression, augmented at times by a broad seemingly uncontrollable smile produces the effect of a smart looking chap indeed, — and more. Yes, Leo Aidan would stand out in any crowd. Not that he would want to though. Yes, he would stand out in any crowd no matter what clothes he wore. Very interesting indeed*, mused Collin in his private thoughts.

Collin Seldon was the new-comer to the group. But now, with his curiosity and enthusiasm aroused as they had never been before, he could not help but take the initiative in leading the group the way he would like to see it go in order to attain the highest degree of accomplishment possible. He was still able to conceal his feelings. That, out of necessity, he had developed well over the years so that it was now a part of him. But he was stirred on the inside.

"Leo" he asked, "I wonder if before you review any of your family and earlier life's experiences with us, would you first relate in detail your skirmish with the English professor. Having done that, you could then turn to experiences in your earlier life and bring us up to the present time. In that manner we would be able to compare past and present and observe whether or not there are similarities in circumstances, causes, etc."

"Wonderful idea," interjected Dr. Eldren.

Leo agreed, "I think so too, O.K., here goes," he said as his face grimaced a little. "Well it's simple really. I was taking two evening courses in English last year. It is important to me that I do well in English especially. In one course I was doing well, very well—getting A's in my papers and tests. In the other course I was getting B's, and many B minuses at that. Now I fully recognized that it is not an uncommon occurrence for a student to do well in one course and not so well in the other, even possibly two courses in the same subject, but this was different."

Everyone present listened intently to Leo as he continued, obviously feeling the pain of the matter. "To go back to the beginning of the year: I was registered in English 2002 and English 2007. It was in English 2007 I had my first paper to hand in. I was pleased when I was given a B grade for it, but also I wanted to improve. I went to the professor with my paper, asked him how I could improve my future grades in that subject. His response was pleasant and co-operative. In fact he was delighted I was taking such an interest. He spent considerable time with me, as he did with other students who approached him. My work improved to A grade in a short time and remained so throughout the year — in English 2007 that is."

"In English 2002 it was an altogether different story," said Leo as he leaned forward in his wooden arm chair, and with his forearms placed on the chair arms, then bringing his hands upward and shaking them in a gesture of frustration. "I just couldn't get anywhere with that — that, how can anyone be like that anyway," he said with a mixture of anger and frustration.

"I know already that it is a disturbing experience for Leo," interjected Dr. Eldren, "perhaps even somewhat traumatic. However may I suggest that we refrain from expressing our feelings and opinions about people involved in the experiences we relate, at least until we have the whole factual story in sufficient detail so as to allow us to view the problems involved objectively. Then after our objective assessment has been made, we will be able to discern whether adverse feelings are justified or not."

"I'm sorry sir" replied Leo, "I'll try to keep better control of my feelings."

"No harm done Leo," said Dr. Eldren, sympathetically. "To express ones feelings is often therapeutic, but in this case we need an objective account as much as is possible. So if you can, just keep calm and tell us in as objective a manner as possible, your experiences with the professor of English 2002."

"Right sir," replied Leo as he tossed his head slightly in a gesture of disgust with himself, "I'll have to keep my cool, won't I."

The doctor smiled and nodded his head in approval.

Leo proceeded with his story. "In English 2002 my first paper brought a B minus. I felt I had done a little better than that because I had already picked up a few pointers from the professor of English 2007. However, it didn't bother me too much. I just decided I would talk to this professor as well, and ask him how I could improve my grade in his subject, fully realizing in the meantime that the two professors may well have different approaches to certain aspects of their presentations. I was ready to make allowances for that, but as time went by I was to find that it would not be so simple.

"I approached the second professor as I had the first, without complaint, and with an earnest enquiry as to how I might improve my grade in that subject. I approached him in the classroom after the lecture one evening. His reception of me was cold and seemingly lacking interest. He looked at his watch and told me he didn't have time to talk now, but if I would make an appointment to see him in his office next week, perhaps he would have time to spare then."

Collin smiled. He was familiar with the watch trick, the not having time — the put-off. *For sure*, he thought, *there will be more avoidance to come*.

Leo continued, "The professor spoke in such a condescending tone and manner that I felt strangely alienated from him at once. As I have already said, however, getting good grades in English is very important to me, so I continued to press him courteously but firmly, 'You set the date and time for next week sir, and I'll be there."

"We-l-l," he said vaguely, "I hardly know at this distance when it can be. You may speak to me about the matter again after class next Tuesday." I suspected then that he might be putting me off. Nevertheless, on the next Tuesday I approached him again, this time before class. He fumbled a little for words, perhaps for a way out, I can't be sure. Then, as if cornered he condescended again, "You may come to my office for a few minutes this evening, about fifteen minutes following this class. I'll see what I can do to help you."

"I wondered why he couldn't speak to me in the lecture room," Leo went on with his story. "But just as he suggested, I went to his office at the time stated. As I was about to knock on the half opened door, he beckoned me to come in. He sat behind his cleared desk looking very official, motioned to me with his hand and in a cold tone suggested I take the chair beside the wall, move it up to his desk and sit down a minute — a minute mind you," emphasized Leo.

"Now,' said the professor, leaning forward and with a low growl as I sat before him, 'you think you should be getting a higher grade in your work?'

'Not exactly, sir,' I replied, 'I would like to know how I can improve my work so that I can earn a higher grade.'

'The professor came back as sharply as he dared without being openly hostile, 'And what makes you think you have the ability to get a higher grade in this subject?'

"'Well," I said, as I shrugged my shoulders, 'I won't know till I try will I professor?"

'The professor's face dropped noticeably, and for a second or two he was stuck for words. Then finding his way out, he responded, "If I remember correctly, your composition is not too bad"——then he paused as if waiting for reaction from me. There was none. I was waiting for him to play his hand more fully. The pause came to an end. "This is a very complex and often difficult course. Some of the authors we are studying have a great deal of ambiguity about them, and it will require a well developed skill to really see through to their deeper meaning and interpret it in a sound and acceptable manner. Throughout the year, Mr. Aidan, you may develop this skill, but only time will tell to what extent."

There was a dead silence in the support group at the sound of what Leo had just related. Collin, half smiling, half moved to anger, shook his head, not in disbelief, for this type of behavior was all too familiar to him, but in disgust. He thought it through to himself: *the professor was sending Leo on a fool's errand to search for the answers himself throughout the year. Of course he would never find them to the satisfaction of the professor, who would continually indicate to him that he wasn't doing well with it. The end results—Leo's confidence and self-esteem would be lowered. Also, he may be worn out from trying. The professor is envious of Leo because he stands out in public in a dignified way, which is how he would like to be. But he doesn't have what it takes to do so. Therefore he turned on Leo. It is a mind-game. One of the foremost used by wayward educators. We will have to go into this one more thoroughly, later when it will more readily believed.*

Dr. Eldren, his attention attracted by Collin's head shaking, gazed at Collin in a mixture of wonderment and respect. His lips showed just a faint trace of a smile. The doctor was catching on but said nothing. It was too soon for comment.

Collin could have finished that story for Leo, but he remained silent, and Leo continued, "'well professor', I said, no doubt you can tell me what critics I can read on the works we are covering in this course. Especially since I am just a first year student, I would say it would be in order for me to allow myself to be guided by them, would it not?"

"'Yes of course" the professor responded quickly, and defensively; then leaning forward again and in a slower, colder tone he added, 'but the critics too can be very ambiguous. No! 'he said sharply, 'it will depend mostly on your own ability to discern. As for the critics you should read, the names of these will be given in class at the appropriate times to cover each author we study.'"

"'Yes of course sir,' I replied. I could not help but feel at the time that there was prejudice involved, but I wasn't sure. I would give him the benefit of the doubt. 'I will try my best sir to develop the skills necessary to get a better grade in this course. Thank you for your time. Good night,' I said as I rose to leave.

"'Good night', he said, with a churlish smile as I turned and walked out of his office."

The group remained silent, waiting for Leo to continue. The pause was broken by Albin with a premature and ill-constructed question. "Why was he prejudiced against you Leo," asked Albin. "Was it the quality of your work, or was it you yourself?"

Leo was embarrassed. Collin jumped to Leo's rescue, "Albin, I would say it is too early in Leo's story for us to discuss whether there was prejudice involved, although at present it certainly seems such is the case. Why not wait until he has related his whole story. Then we will in all probability be better able to determine and understand more surely whether prejudice was definitely involved and why. If we do eventually determine that it was prejudice, I would suggest that the 'why' of it — the motivation for it, be explored at that time."

"What do you think, Dr. Eldren," asked Owen courteously.

"I think Collin has a good point there," responded the doctor. "After all, you people seem to have a basic problem in common. So then there is a good possibility you all have something in common when it comes to the 'why' of it — in fact I suspect already that you truly have.

However, I agree with Collin, leave the whys and wherefores, so to speak, or the analysis, until we have heard more experiences to give us better understanding. Is that what you had in mind Collin?"

"Yes, Dr. Eldren, plus the fact that by waiting until more stories are told, the whys and wherefores of the matter will be clearly illustrated, I feel sure," replied Collin confidently.

Dr. Eldren nodded approval.

"Sounds super to me," remarked Owen. The others expressed agreement also.

Dr. Eldren was pleased. "It seems we are off to a good start folks, and we are getting our format in order as we proceed. The experience Leo has just related to us took place nearly a year ago. I talked to him about it at that time. Now I think it will be interesting and helpful to our purpose to hear the remainder of the experience as it progressed through the university year. Would you mind continuing the story Leo?"

"Not at all sir," replied Leo. "I continued in the course and worked very diligently at it. I could not help but feel that the professor was cold toward me in classes."

"Was that a feeling only?" asked Gilda Emerson, "or were there some actions or tangible attitudes to cause you to feel that way. It's difficult to describe attitudes, I know, but not impossible."

"It turned out to be more than a feeling," responded Leo, "there were actions and attitudes throughout the year to substantiate my feelings."

"Can you describe these actions and attitudes?" pressed Gilda.

"A-h-h-h, he was just a screwball," Leo replied in disgust.

"Maybe so," came back Gilda, "but you are falling into the very common booby-trap that allows such screwballs to go on their miserable way, trampling on whomever they choose, according to their own whim and fancy. Then good people like yourself simply walk away from them and stay away from them, shrugging them off as funny or ill-natured characters with whom you want nothing further to do. Such an attitude as that by you and many others like you in similar circumstances, just serves to allow them to set up and rule their own little domain. In it they can include and exclude others at will regardless of the havoc it wreaks on other peoples lives and careers. Just so that their little kingdom isn't upset is all that matters to them. Then you, a victim, just shrug them off as being of a funny makeup or ill-natured and do and say nothing further about it. Come on Leo," urged Gilda, obviously moved to deep feeling on the matter, "put it into words. You can do it. Let's get to the root of the matter and bring it out into the open. Describe to us those funny, those ill-natured, those screwball, if you wish, actions and attitudes. We'll help you," she added, now beaming with excitement. "Come on, let's do it!"

Leo was held in amazement by Gilda's challenge. After a brief pause he looked around at the other group members. There was no response from them, for they too were somewhat amazed, but more than that, they stared at Leo, as if in support of Gilda and her demand that he take up the challenge. There was silence.

"Describe with words a screwball's attitudes!" repeated Leo slowly and thoughtfully—then after a pause added quickly, "sure, sure why not."

"As you tell of your experiences with this professor throughout the year," came back Gilda, "Let's try to describe his attitudes toward you; I can help you with it, and I'm sure some others present can as well."

"I think I can help with that" agreed Owen.

"I can too" responded Collin.

"I'll try" joined in Brett Culver, "but it's a brain drain. I usually try to ignore or avoid such mind boggling exercises, but this case can be an exception."

"I guess it is possible" pondered Donna Coyne aloud. "I've never bothered, but it would be an interesting experiment among friends. I'm for it."

Albin Anders and Dr. Eldren remained silent. This was unknown territory for them. *Hopefully Albin will learn from it; but more important if Dr. Eldren will take a positive attitude towards it*, thought Collin again to himself, *then we will all come out unscathed.*

Everyone in the group looked toward Leo, waiting for him to try. Leo began, "The outstanding thing that comes to my mind concerning the remainder of the year in that course is his behavior towards me in class. I'll try to illustrate that behavior throughout the year, then between us maybe we can describe it more fully, and make some sense out of it."

"There won't be much sense to it," quipped Collin, "mostly nonsense, NON-SENSE, he spelled it out, emphasizing the hyphen.

There was a chuckle.

"But we can describe even a weird attitude enough to better our understanding of the matter," insisted Gilda. "nonsense isn't always easy to understand. It can drive you right out of your mind if you let it. But if you learn to take it in your stride, then understanding such behavior in other people can be a great asset in enabling you to cope with them. At least you can cope with them after a fashion."

Collin shifted uneasily in his chair, but said nothing.

Brett shook his head, "understanding is one thing, coping is another."

He intended to continue on that aspect of the matter, but Collin interrupted, "maybe we can extend our format here to accommodate the matter of coping. Earlier we decided to leave the 'whys' and 'wherefores,' the analyses, until later. Perhaps now the coping aspects can come after that again."

"That sounds reasonable" offered Dr. Eldren, "we certainly need the full story from each one before we can adequately cope with coping," he said amusingly. "Of course," he added more seriously, "there is bound to be some overlapping of the three. However, if we find at any time during the relating of the experiences that we are getting off too much on the why and coping aspect, let us check ourselves and leave these matters until later when we have the grounding on which to base them."

There was general agreement.

Leo continued to tell his story. "After the unproductive interview with the professor, I was uneasy about my standing with him. During the next class this uneasiness was substantiated by the professor's attitude toward me. As he lectured he looked everywhere around the classroom except in my direction. I felt somewhat self-conscious about it. I struggled not to let it interrupt my concentration. On reflection after class I recalled he had avoided looking at me in the class that was held before the interview. As time went on I came to feel he didn't like me at all."

Gilda perked up in her chair. "You came to feel he didn't like you?" she asked, placing much emphasis on the word 'feel'.

"Yes—-well, he did things throughout the year to make me feel that way—-I mean it wasn't feelings only. It became obvious to me and to some others too, that he didn't like me," replied Leo nervously.

"Ah, good" sparked Gilda, "that's what we want to hear. We want you to describe the things he did, the actual actions of his that made you feel the way you did. These actions are not as intangible as one might think."

"You're giving me a tough assignment Gilda," remarked Leo, "but I see what you're getting at now, and I think I can respond sufficiently to bring out the points you are after."

"If you don't" responded Gilda, amusingly but meaningfully, "Dr. Eldren here will think you are imagining these things; reading into your professors actions and attitudes persecution against yourself, a feeling, just a feeling," she emphasized, "brought on by your first unpleasant encounter with him."

"Oh-h-" replied Leo, looking apprehensively to Dr. Eldren, then back to Gilda as though looking for further clarification. Collin could not help but join in on what in the past he had seen to become a fray between doctor and patient. It was against his better judgment to get involved in such an issue as this, but he was free to walk out if he pleased, he reminded himself.

"Paranoia?" Collin queried, before Gilda had been able to continue.

"Yes" said Gilda, unabashedly, even defiantly, "that's been my experience."

Tension mounted quickly throughout the group. Dr. Eldren looked with concern at Gilda, then around at the others. Collin wondered whether Dr. Eldren would tip his scale in favor of or against Gilda's position. At any rate he would not wait to see before stating his own.

"That's been my experience too Gilda," he said coolly and reassuringly.

Dr. Eldren, unruffled, responded in his usual graceful manner, "Your point is well taken, Gilda, and Collin. You have brought out a point which, I expect, we will have to watch carefully—very carefully," he reemphasized, "as we pursue our discussions; paranoia verses unexplainable or intangible attitudes."

The group was at ease again.

Leo struggled in his mind. He grimaced a little as he sought to proceed. "The professor's attitude towards me in general is very difficult to put into words, but usually he ignored me. Most other students were asked a question occasionally, I never was asked. When a general response was sought from throughout the class, someone else's response was always taken over mine. Then one evening when we were discussing an author, his works and his critics, all of which I had studied thoroughly, I decided to enter the class discussion whether he wanted me to or not. I watched for an opportunity when it was appropriate for me to enter the discussion in a mannerly way, without crowding out someone else, and without giving him the excuse of listening to another person rather than me. I offered the opinion of a well known critic on the matter under discussion.

"I stated the position of this critic, which I knew to be a leading, valid, scholarly and accepted position, and I stated it in such a manner as to infer that it is the position I would take. At the same time I was fully aware that among several other critics there was another one whose view was runner up for top position. This critic had taken a different view altogether. But before I could state that second position and compare, as I had intended to do, the professor jumped the gun on me, stating the second position and inferring that he favored this position. He inferred but without substantiation, that this latter position was much superior."

"How did he actually infer that superiority," pried Gilda.

"Well," strained Leo again, "mainly by the emphasis of his voice and the expression of his face, and somewhat by the gestures of his hands. He spoke of the position I had stated in a disdainful manner, and of the position he had taken in superior tones. Both positions are logical and scholarly positions. But worst of all, after openly showing his bias toward the position he favored, he very subtly made a mockery of the position I had favored."

"How did he go about making that mockery," asked Gilda. Leo broke into a brief uncontrollable smile. "Your point is well made by now Gilda," he said, "yes, these attitudes can be described in words can't they?" Then he continued seriously, "he trivialized it with a chuckle and a grin and a wave of his hand as though brushing it aside as if what I had said was of no consequence. I knew differently, but nevertheless he drew several chuckles from around the class. That's when I began to lose control of myself. However, I did manage to hold myself together somewhat until the class was over. Then I went immediately to his desk, being sure I was the first there.

The professor was standing pleased, poised and proud. He had belittled me before the class. It was obvious he counted it a victory for his ego. Without waiting for him to either receive me or brush me aside, and it probably would have been the latter, I opened out at him in a somewhat uncontrolled manner.

"Sir," I said, "you know as well as I that both of the positions we discussed before the class are accepted positions with regard to the author we are presently studying.

The professor smirked, obviously still on a high from his victory over me before the class. And as I look back now, he was in complete control of himself, and I was not."

Coolly he said, "There are many positions taken on the matter, by many critics over many years." Then he said sternly, "It is as I told you before, it all depends on your ability to discern."

"I fumed as he proceeded to gather his books from his desk. I knew he was about to walk out and I couldn't let him do that without letting him know I could see through him. 'You hate my guts, don't you?' I said rather vigorously and contemptuously as I stared him in the face. He paled and his smirk left him. He was brought down from his high, and was actually frightened — I think he was," said Leo, now lifting the tone of his words to a lighter vein. "Yea, I think he was actually frightened by my affront," continued Leo in wonderment.

"A coward in the crunch?" interjected Collin.

Leo paused briefly, "Yea — yea maybe that's it."

"But he found a way out!" came in Collin again.

Leo looked at Collin with surprise. There was a pause.

"They always do." came in Collin a third time.

The pause continued until this time broken by Leo. "Yea, he found a way out. Although shaken, he somewhat kept his poise and in a subdued manner said, "I don't have to take this from you, you'll be hearing more about it." Then he walked out of the classroom.

Albin had been listening intently and wide-eyed.

"Leo," he said excitedly, "your experience in that class is similar to the one I had in a philosophy class last year. Did you drop out of the course?"

"No way," replied Leo, "I stayed to the end."

"Oh-h" responded Albin, "I did, I mean I dropped out of my philosophy course last year. Didn't think there was any use hanging in there if they were against me."

Dr. Eldren's eyes glanced toward Albin at the sound of that statement. Collin noticed the glance.

"Albin," said Collin, "I'm going to ask Leo some further questions about his class experience. I would like for you to pay particular attention to them and to the answers. O.K. with you Leo."

"Sure," said Leo.

Collin asked, "Leo, when the professor brought chuckles on you in the lecture room, did everyone in the room chuckle?"

"Oh, I don't think so," said Leo, "a minority of them really."

"Did anyone openly show support for you," asked Collin again.

"Well, there was no opportunity in the class, but after it was all over and the professor gone, a chap who had remained behind came forward, gripped my shoulder real firm and said, "Hang in there boy. He doesn't like you, but hang in there." Then he went on his way.

Collin asked further, "Were there any others there who showed support either by word or implication."

Leo smiled. "We're getting into attitudes and intangibles again aren't we?"

"Yes, but they work on both sides," reminded Collin kindly.

"Right," said Leo, "Yes, you're so right, and there were some positive attitudes around that evening. After the professor had gone, there were a few students standing around the lecture room, and also some lingering outside the door who gave me what I would interpret to be sympathetic looks and glances, a few smiles, as I gathered my things and left. Of course these gestures meant so little to me at the time. All that was on my mind was the confrontation itself, and I was so upset."

"Thanks Leo," said Collin as he now turned his attention towards Albin. "Albin, I just want to ask you a simple question; first, you stated that you dropped out of your class last year because 'they' — 'they', he repeated with emphasis, 'were against you.' Now, I haven't heard your story yet, but I would assume that your professor for that class, and some of the students no doubt, didn't like you, and took a negative attitude towards you, or, as you say were against you. But I would like to point out to you, using Leo's example, that although those who were negative towards you absorbed your attention, and certainly a negative professor would produce that effect, there were also, no doubt many there who were silent supporters."

Albin nodded.

"These silent supporters are not always of much practical help, but they do give a boost to the morale when we are up against it," said Collin.

"I see what you mean," said Albin as he now seemed pleased rather than shy about being included in the procedure. He added, "When I was a soda-pop salesman it was easier to distinguish the good ones from the bad. In that less complex environment most of them were good and showed it openly, but that all seems to be crowded out now by the bad experiences.

Collin turned his attention to Dr. Eldren. "Dr. Eldren, I have parted from the story telling, but I figure if I just planted that thought in Albin's and indeed in all our minds, near the beginning, it would help us to keep in mind the positive side of our experiences."

"I think it's a very good point you brought in there Collin, very good," nodded Dr. Eldren, obviously pleased.

Collin turned to Leo, "Your professor's parting remark that evening was 'you'll be hearing more about it,' and we assume you did. But since you finished that course, I can only assume one of two things: either the department tried to cover up for the professor, brushing under the carpet the wrong he had done, as though nothing much had happened. This would allow you to go back and finish under a sort of truce between the two of you; or, he was oblivious to that whole aspect of human behavior and in his naïveté just passed you on to a counselor thinking automatically that you had a problem, that the problem was yours and yours alone."

Leo looked wide eyed at Collin. "You seem to know my story before I tell it," he quipped with a smile of amazement, "are you psychic or something?"

"No, not psychic" answered Collin, "just experienced; been through the mill many times in various spheres of life."

"Of course there are other possible scenarios but to my mind, these are the ones most often used." Then Collin came abruptly from his reflection. "Sorry folks," he apologized, "I've interrupted Leo's story, and delved into speculation. Guess I just couldn't resist sharing as though at long last I have found people like myself; but tell me Leo, and then I'll let you be free to continue, since you did complete the course, which of the approaches was it?" "It was the second Collin, as you will see when I relate the happenings to you."

Owen now spoke up. "I just knew from the beginning you'd be a great help to us Collin, and its showing through already. You show that you have insight into our problems."

The other group members passed varying positive remarks, in support of Owen's statement. Collin cautioned them soberly, "Understanding a matter is one thing, coming out on top of it is another, as you shall find out. Leo should tell us what happened now, and we shall see."

"Sure Collin," Leo continued with his story. "The unpleasant incident in English 2002 took place at a Tuesday night lecture. On the Thursday night following I attended my weekly class in English 2007. I arrived for it about ten minutes early as usual. Shortly after my arrival the professor came in, a very pleasant person indeed, and he handed me a letter, saying he had been asked by the department head to deliver it to me. The letter was sealed. I opened it and it was a request from the English Department Head that I make an appointment to see him. So next morning I phoned his office, and arranged to see him that afternoon. I got off work early to keep the appointment."

Leo went on without interruption, "I arrived at his office on time, and entered the outer area where I was greeted by his secretary. "He's expecting you," she informed me, "I'll take you right in."

I followed her through the open door.

"Mr. Aidan to see you sir."

"Yes," he replied as he began to size me up and down. "Yes," he said again, hesitantly, "yes, thank you." The secretary left the room, closing the door behind her.

"Sit down, sit down," the department head said, his hesitancy now coupled with a puzzled facial expression, as though almost bewildered.

"You're getting good at describing the intangibles," said Gilda joyfully. Other group members supported her with similar remarks.

"Why was he bewildered at the sight of you Leo?" asked Albin again. Leo paused to search for words for his answer.

Collin, now more glad than ever to be in company of his own kind, could not refrain from answering for him, "He was expecting a rowdy and a ruffian, was he not Leo?"

"Right on Collin!" remarked Leo excitedly, "right on. He had been expecting a tough character, and when it didn't turn out to be so, he was on unfamiliar ground, and puzzled by it."

Gilda probed once again for descriptions of intangibles. She would leave no room for misinterpretation or wrong diagnosis if she could help it. "Can you substantiate with something concrete, your supposition that the department head was puzzled, and that he had been expecting a rowdy?"

Leo smiled at her, "yes, I can Gilda, I think I have the hang of it now."

Leo continued, "I sat down, and he said, 'you're having some problems in English 2002 class. Can't be much I'm sure." He looked me up and down, obviously favorably impressed by me. "Can't be much," he repeated. "I'm sure this matter can be easily rectified through our Student Counseling Department. I'll make an appointment for you there", he said as he reached for the phone.

"But sir," I replied.

"Oh don't worry, we have a very good department there. You'll find them to be a good bunch, very helpful and effective, and they won't hurt you; strictly confidential of course, no need to worry about anything."

"I knew," said Leo soberly to the group as he shook his head, "I knew I was talking to the wrong person about my particular problem. He was a scholar and a gentleman to be sure, but it did seem clear to me already that he would have not the slightest insight into my problem with my professor. "Maybe," I thought," if I go to the Student Counseling Department, someone there would understand. So I offered to go. The department head proceeded with the call to Dr. Eldren, and made an appointment for me. After the call was made and arrangements completed, I asked, 'Sir, may I continue in English 2002?'"

"Oh yes, by all means," came his reply. The instructor of that class is a very good teacher you know. He has been with us for some time now. I'm sure this little matter can be straightened out; and don't worry, you're counseling is strictly confidential. The counseling department is kept entirely separate from other departments of the university—no problem there."

"Although disappointed in my overall interview, I was relieved by his last statement," remarked Leo to the group. "I was now convinced that my English 2007 course at least would not be affected. That was a major comfort to me. Of English 2002, I was skeptical, but I would hang in there, as a class supporter had urged the evening of the trouble. However, I decided to put my trust in the counseling department, and here I am."

"How did you make out in English 2002 afterwards," inquired Collin.

"Well," answered Leo, "surprisingly enough, in the two assignments I had after the skirmish I received a B and a B plus."

"He was being cautious," interjected Collin, "and what was your final grade for the course?"

Leo responded with a measure of disgust, "a B minus."

Gilda joined the discussion, "What grade did you get in English 2007," she asked sharply.

"An A," replied Leo."

"What did the course in English 2007 consist of?" pried Gilda again.

"Shakespeare," came the reply from Leo, "Shakespeare's Tragedies and Romances."

"What did the course in English 2002 consist of?" Donna probed further.

"The Nineteenth Century English Novel," responded Leo.

There was silence in the group, and a mixture of silent expression. Flashing thoughts were evident in revealing eyes. A head or two shook in dismay. There was puzzlement. There was astonishment. Leo had done far better in the more difficult course.

Collin Seldon eventually broke the silence with a question, "Why, Leo, did you not go to university immediately after high school graduation? Why wait 'till now?"

"A-w-w." replied Leo dejectedly, "I got turned off from studying by a couple of obnoxious high school teachers. "Then raising his voice in determination, "the same way as I'd get turned off now by this professor, if I'd let him, but I'm not going to let him do it to me. That's not going to happen this time. I'm older now."

"Tell us a little about yourself and your family," suggested Collin.

Leo began without hesitation, beginning with his father for whom, it soon became obvious, he had much respect. "My father was a judge, a good one too, and a good all around man. That was a blessing for me in one way, but in another way it was a problem. You see, my father was an outstanding public figure, and some people used to pick on me for it. I used to get it slapped up to me."

"Do you have brothers and sisters, Leo?" pried Collin again.

"Yes," replied Leo, "one brother and one sister. They are both older than me."

"Did they go to university after completing high school?" asked Collin.

"Yes, they did, and both graduated and have done well," said Leo, heavily, then as though to make light of his burden, he added jestingly, "now I'm trying to catch up."

Some group members smiled, but Collin remained serious, and inquired further, "did your brother and sister get picked on because of your father's position?"

Leo blushed and got nervous. "Well some I guess," he replied awkwardly and with embarrassment, "but not as much as I did. I was younger I guess."

"Did you have a group of friends Leo?" asked Collin again.

"Oh yes," replied Leo, now relieved with this less bothersome question." I had some good friends; but also many enemies, mostly members of what I regarded as questionable peer type clusters of students. Out of respect for my father, I wouldn't associate with them so they would shun me."

Collin kept up the questions, "Did your brother and sister have similar trouble with peer groups?"

Leo's face flushed and he stared at Collin with complete fear.

Collin spoke again. "What I'm getting at, Leo, is that there is another reason other than your father's position why you were picked on by some teachers and peers when you were in high school, and now again by a professor in university." Then Collin quickly and reassuringly added, "this other reason is not something that is your fault, and not something you could have avoided. It has to do with you, your makeup as a person, exceptional in some ways, that causes some people to like you real well, and others to hate you profoundly."

Leo nodded in agreement, then added a little excitedly, "I think I know what you are getting at, Collin, but I couldn't dare discuss it myself for fear of being labeled conceited. It has been in the back of my mind but I have never brought it out into the open."

"I know how it is," replied Collin, sympathetically, "to discuss it is to leave yourself open to all sorts of labels and misunderstandings so it gets pushed into the subconscious, or at least way back in the shadows somewhere. Your brother and sister didn't get picked on to any extent but you did. It wasn't because of whose son you were, although that would definitely be the outwardly indicated reason, the alibi given by your tormentors. It was because you, fine person that you were and still are, too nice a person for their kind to tolerate. You stood out among others, not only in appearance, but also in character and intelligence. They were envious of this and held it against you every opportunity. We can explore this later, together with their ways and means of putting you down, as we proceed with the stories.

Collin looked around at the group members for possible response. Their faces were bright with expectation as though they knew what was coming over the horizon and into this group; all except young Albin who was overwhelmed by the intimation of so much new knowledge to come, and the elder Dr. Eldren, who appeared mystified for the same reason.

"Just one more question from me for today, Leo," spoke Collin again. "You haven't mentioned your mother, how does she fit into your life?" Leo replied, "My mother in her lackadaisical way, sees me according to her own concept of me. She just makes such casual remarks as, "Leo won't get as far ahead as the others. He just doesn't have the drive," She means me no harm, but could never help me to better either."

"I see, thank you," responded Collin. "That's all I wish to ask you this evening, Leo, thanks for your co-operation."

"And thank you, Collin," he replied with enthusiasm and enlightenment.

"Very interesting, indeed fascinating," replied Dr. Eldren, and since Gilda had considerable input to this evenings discussions, I think it would be helpful to hear her story next week, if she will agree."

"I'll be prepared to do so next week, Dr. Eldren," Gilda volunteered.

After parting courtesies Dr. Eldren left for other commitments.

Owen brought to the attention of the others that there was a nice student gathering place, The Corner Coffee Shop, just down the street next to the parking lot. They all decided to go there for coffee and snacks, and socializing in a lighter vein before driving home.

# Chapter Three

Quilibet University was now into the second week of its fall semester. It was, on the whole, a good institution, not world renowned, but domestically respected, and generally considered to be a good place to go. Many successful careers would be fashioned here — careers that would do much good in a sometimes erratic world. Such a world seemed to be symbolized in the routine activity of students as they poured out over the campus on their way to classes, criss-crossing this way and that, to one building or another, many hundreds of them all at once. Most of them are exuberant and lively, some smiling, others serious looking, many chatting, others deep in thought; altogether giving the campus the sensation of being fully alive. As students enter the lecture rooms and classes begin, then for an hour or so on the grounds outside, all is quiet, except for only an occasional person criss-crossing here and there. There is a quiet, a lull, until it is time to go to another class in another building. Then, on the outside, in outward appearance, all is alive again.

Of course, the meaningful activity takes place in the quiet of the lecture rooms. This is where the work is done that eventually makes the whole world blossom out into vivid aliveness. For graduates it is as though the world becomes a huge campus with people going happily, meaningfully hither and yon, after work well done in the classrooms. The world will be a better place because of Quilibet. Many careers indeed will be fashioned here to help make a better world. Some careers will be lost here too —lost because of irresponsibility or incompetence, in one way or another, on the part of the loser.

But there are some good students who will lose their careers through no reasonable fault of their own. These will be victims of an underestimated evil, sinister and subtle, at work all around them. They will fall by the way unnoticed by most people. They will receive token gestures of friendship and encouragement from those who did understand to a degree. Rarely however, would anyone be willing to step in and take up their cause, because to do so would be very difficult and dangerous. It would be dealing with intangibles. The facts, although not altogether elusive would be difficult to pin down in concrete terms. In the clearest cases of injustice it is often difficult to find someone willing to champion a cause. More so, in cases like these, it is virtually impossible to find anyone willing to ripple the waters or churn up the waves on such intangible issues. So the victims fall largely unnoticed by the wayside, and the culprits continue on in their own domains, their brutal deeds also largely unnoticed, or if noticed, brushed aside.

This problem is relevant not only to educational institutions. It is an affliction in every walk of life. Yet it is in educational institutions that it can probably best be noticed and brought into the open. Collin Seldon was fully aware of this, and he hoped and prayed that this support group which he was attending, could somehow come up with some answers.

As for the psychology class he was attending, Collin was playing very low profile there. Except for routinely attending classes and doing the prescribed work, he would lay low and refrain from activity in question periods and class discussion. He also avoided personal contact with the professor. Professor Yates seemed satisfied with this. Except for drawing his eyes and his face to himself and pulling his lips together all in a snobbish manner whenever he accidently met Collin at close range, there was no further problem. Both Collin and Professor Yates were avoiding close confrontation of any sort. Maybe they could get through the whole course this way. Collin Seldon would aim in that direction. The course wasn't crucial to his career in any way, as it would be for some, but his continuation with it would qualify him to stay in the support group.

So Collin had attended his class on Tuesday evening. Now on Wednesday evening he was heading again for Room 405 and the support group. He was very anxious to learn how Gilda Emerson was finding her way successfully through university, when for all intents and purposes she should have been among those who fall by the wayside, unnoticed, and through no fault of her own.

The members were all present in good time that evening, including Brett Culver. Dr. Eldren remarked that he thought that was indicative of the interest building up in the group. He himself was enthusiastic about it. Although still looking pale in appearance, he was not lacking in vitality. Success seemed to be the order of things concerning this particular assignment of his. That was a welcome and inspiring situation in the world of psychiatry, where so often measurable progress is so slow in coming, or is utterly elusive. It was evident this evening, that Dr. Eldren was pleased.

The group members stood around chatting for a while, moving about, exchanging greetings and information as to the week's activities. Albin Anders, although still plenty shy, was doing much better. He seemed to relax more with Owen Winslow than with anyone else. Owen paid him friendly attention, and carried on a conversation with him. Collin joined the two of them in their small talk.

"Things going well so far this year, Albin?" asked Collin, as he boxed Albin on the shoulder in a friendly gesture.

"Not too bad," said Albin in reply. "I somehow think I'll have a better year this year than last."

"Great," remarked Collin, "keep up the good work, and remember, you have friends behind you!"

"Right," added Owen assuringly.

Leo Aidan was well dressed as he had been the previous week. Apparently he and Donna Coyne had been heading towards a close relationship ever since they had met at the University. Now he was taking her out evenings following the group sessions as well as at other times. This explained Donna's well dressed appearance also, although she was a person who would look lovely in almost any clothing.

Donna Coyne, a young lady of average height and build, had about her an air of gracious modesty which was reflected in her general being. Her light black hair was as though a shingle cut had grown too long, yet it was intentionally kept that way, with the front, unparted, over an average size forehead, swept upwards some before it swept back over her head, slightly and irregularly waved on the way and trimmed neatly at the bottom. Her complexion was tinted only slightly dark and helped to highlight the slight natural rosiness of her high cheek bones. Her face, a little long, was pleasant and soft looking, beset with a little larger than petite, slightly upturned nose, moderately thick lips and average width mouth. She wore a deep red lipstick in a modest proportion. Her clothes were in good taste. This evening she wore a charcoal dress, with subdued floral patterns throughout the top, covering her moderate busts. Stylishly it tapered in to show a well proportioned waistline, then flared out again in the same stylish manner to complement her well figured lower body. Her jewelry was a small silver necklace and matching earrings. Her shoes were black patent leather.

Donna Coyne, at age twenty eight or so was an unassuming lady who unintentionally stood out among others under any circumstances. The way she kept herself, her choice of clothes, her jewelry — and more especially so, her character and general manner of behavior showed her to be a truly fine person. Yet Donna was always just herself; likable, by many at least, pleasant to know and eager to be friends with friendly people.

There was a sharp contrast between Donna Coyne and Gilda Emerson. If ever anyone thought that to be two fine ladies was to be two alike, they would have to think again when in the company of both Donna and Gilda together.

Gilda Emerson could best be described as a lady in her naturalness — sophisticated, yet totally unpretentious. She stood out in tasteful decorum at all times; lovely to look at with the bright light complexion of an overall rounded average size face. This was complemented by hair, deep golden through and through, and which set her facial features in an air of dignity. Her facial expression was one of determination — a slightly protruding chin below the somewhat thin lips of an only moderately wide mouth. Her straight bridged and little larger than usual nose added poise to her profile. There were lovely average size blue eyes under trim eyebrows of a little lighter color than her hair. She wore only a modest hair style of medium length an inch or two of permanent around the ends. The curl feathered out as it extended up the sides of her face. Her golden hair, parted on the right side, showed on the crown of her head its true color, sheen and beauty. Her only visible make-up, just a trace of light red lipstick contrasted remarkably with her complexion and her very unpretentious hairdo.

Her clothes were equally plain and simple, though it was evident she had an eye for quality. An all beige sweater with a pattern of raised same color flower petal stripes lengthwise, although worn loosely revealed a little more than moderate bust size. Her adequate slimming at the waist line was revealed by a patent leather belt worn with a plain brown felt skirt with sweater tucked inside. The below knee skirt flared over her nylon covered legs. Plain beige small heeled shoes of medium height daintily covered her feet. Her extra height had an overall slimming effect on her well built, well proportioned solid looking body. She wore a minimum of jewelry — a small golden cross hanging from her neck by a fine chain, and small plain circular earrings of matching metal. Yes, Gilda Emerson, unpretentious hairdo and all, would stand out in any crowd— because of her fine appearance. She would stand out also because of her fine character. It wasn't difficult to observe that her behavior also was unpretentious. She too was just herself. She had that much, and more, in common with Donna Coyne, regardless of the contrast.

As the group members stood around the room exchanging greetings and chatting on this their second night of meeting for the season, Dr. Eldren seemed to be enjoying the social activity as well as did the others. But time was passing by. He looked at his watch, motioned towards the chairs, already placed in a circle by the early comers.

"It's time to get started folks; a few minutes of socializing warm up is a good way to begin, but there will be a long day again tomorrow for each of you," he said caringly.

After all the group members were seated, Dr. Eldren set the

stage for the evening's discussion.

"Leo told us last week of how he came to be here in this group," remarked Dr. Eldren, "but I also take note that Gilda pried deeply and brought to the forefront some very significant details of Leo's experience. Gilda has said she would relate to us this evening some of her own experiences so that we may be able to compare and contrast the experiences of each of them."

Gilda replied positively, but with qualifications. "I think," she said, "that in my case I had better start earlier in life, and then in the light of that, my university experiences may have more meaning for you."

"Good, Gilda," responded Dr. Eldren, "begin where you think would be most appropriate."

"Well, first I'll mention my home life," Gilda began. "It was satisfactory for the most part. I was close to my parents and well thought of by both of them, in my younger years at least. As time went on my father and I drifted further apart than we had been, but I'll leave that matter till later. As I grew up I had a good circle of friends, drawn from various walks of life, both boys and girls, with whom I feel I socialized well in the usual ways that young people do — sports events, parties, outings, visiting in one another's homes, and congregating at nice teen age meeting places. I feel I was well thought of by most people."

Gilda then paused for a moment as if reflecting more deeply, "Of course, not everyone thought well of me, I had enemies too," she remarked more slowly, as though it pained her to say so.

Dr. Eldren interjected, "perhaps Gilda, as you tell your story it will reveal to us some reasons why you had these enemies.

"Oh yes, yes," replied Gilda, now becoming fully alert to the present again. "No doubt about it, Dr. Eldren."

"You see I have always done well in school," Gilda proceeded. "Right from my early grades I was usually the leader of my class academically. Although I wasn't intentionally competitive at all, I received a great satisfaction from it. I was simply doing my best and was well pleased with myself. It wasn't till grade five I ran into problems. There I had a teacher who disliked me, and was determined to put me down. She resented me because I came from a well-to-do family, and she favored several other children over me — one in particular who did well and who usually came second in class. I had come up through the earlier grades with this girl. We were not close friends, but there was no animosity between us either. In fact we often helped each other by discussing the more difficult math problems together.

But this grade five teacher drove a wedge between us by her discriminatory attitude. For example, once when I made an error in answering a question verbally, this teacher said to me in a seemingly polite yet cutting tone of voice, 'see Gilda, just because you come from a rich family doesn't mean you have all the answers.' At times when I didn't give a satisfactory answer, which wasn't very often, she would turn to the other girl and of course often receive the right answer. Then she would remind me that other people can come up with good answers too. Such open abuses as this were not frequent, but often enough to confirm in a tangible manner her general attitude towards me.

As young as I was I could not help but sense the teacher's dislike for me. This dislike was shown almost daily in more subtle ways. For example again, when a question was asked and several of us put up our hand to answer, I would always be the last one chosen to answer. Again when the teacher singled out one student to answer a question it was seldom me she asked, and then only when it was a very difficult or tricky question to answer; one in which it seemed she wished to stick me, which she occasionally did in such a manner as would embarrass and discourage me greatly."

Gilda paused, as if reliving the experience for a moment.

Collin Seldon broke the silence. "How did this affect your school year Gilda?" he asked.

The question alerted Gilda again. "I gave up trying" she said. "I was discouraged and no longer had the desire to do well. I slipped to seventh place in my class that year; still not too badly, but I just sort of got by on what I already knew. I didn't work hard like I used to."

Collin asked another question, "How did it affect the girl who had been coming second?"

"It turned her into a rival," replied Gilda, "and naturally she came first that year. She and some others held me in disdain because I was no longer out front. I'm sure though that they at that age were innocent victims as I was, and were led without being aware of what was happening to them.

Collin probed with still a further question. "Was your family wealthy Gilda?"

"At the time my father was in an upper middle income bracket, Collin. We were well-to-do but not wealthy. My father was moving up in a very well known corporation. Some people therefore assumed he was wealthy. Presently my father is Vice President and General Manager of this medium size corporation. He has worked hard and done well. I still wouldn't say we are wealthy even now, but definitely not when I was in grade five," was Gilda's reply.

Dr. Eldren came in with a question. "Were your parents aware of this difficulty you were having in grade five, Gilda?"

"No," she replied, "at that age I didn't fully comprehend what was going on. It is only as I look back on it now that I can see clearly what was happening. I did complain to my parents at times that the teacher didn't like me, but they took the position that if I kept up my work and did it well the teacher would be pleased with me again. They tried to encourage me in various ways but that only added to my frustration."

Gilda's face was flushed. The telling of this old story that had long been pushed out of memory brought painful feelings to her now. "My parents didn't understand," she repeated, "and I was too young to explain!"

Owen Winslow picked up the matter sympathetically so as to share Gilda's burden. "Your parents had no way of knowing Gilda, so they took the effect to be the cause and the cause to be the effect."

"Yes," she said, "that's just it Owen."

"Gilda, I would like to ask more questions if I may," said

Collin as he leaned forward in his chair in eager anticipation.

"Yes, certainly, go ahead Collin," she replied.

"Do you have any brothers or sisters," asked Collin. The question seemed irrelevant, but Gilda answered it questioningly, "Yes I have a brother, two years older than I."

"Did he attend the same school?" Collin came on again.

"Yes, he did," was the reply.

"Did he have similar troubles as he went up through that school Gilda."

"Well, nothing much," replied Gilda thoughtfully. Then as she puzzled she added slowly, "He being a boy I suppose must have made a difference."

Collin questioned again, "Were there other well-to-do children in your grade five class?"

"Yes-s," responded Gilda, now puzzled even more, "there were three or four who were at least as well to do as my family. In fact," she retorted more quickly, "there was one whom I would say was from a much more wealthy family that I."

"Did she do well in her school work, Gilda?" Collin kept probing.

"Oh-h she did average; not really a student you know," came the reply.

"Was she a nice girl?"

"She was all right — friendly, but didn't keep herself well in appearance. She wasn't a pretty girl if that's what you mean, but she could have looked all right if she bothered to look after herself."

"One more question, Gilda. Did the teacher put her down too that year?"

At that question Gilda became perturbed. Her voice quivered and strengthened alternately as she responded to Collin's probing. "I'm not sure what you're getting at Collin. Are you suggesting that it was somehow my fault because that teacher was discriminating against me?"

Collin shook his head slowly but emphatically, as Leo came ahead of him with a verbal response, while visibly fuming.

"No way was it Gilda's own fault that she was picked on that year," he shouted angrily. "That dirty slink of a teacher should never have been allowed to teach young children. She should have been whipped and put to work in Antarctica somewhere where she couldn't do anyone any harm."

There was silence for a moment as some of the group struggled between apprehension and smiles at this vigorous but well meaning remark.

Owen finally broke in with soothing words. "I don't think Collin meant by his questioning to place blame, Gilda. In fact I'm sure he didn't. You were heading for something else weren't you Collin?" he asked as he turned from Gilda to Collin.

Collin nodded. Then looking at her in a prying manner, "Gilda, Gilda, don't you consciously by now, recognize the problem after hearing Leo's story. You were discriminated against by that teacher, not because she thought your father was rich. That was only her alibi. It was because you, yourself were a fine, well kept, well cultured person.

"People like that teacher cannot allow themselves to admit that a person like you is too good for them to tolerate. They tell themselves that if they were rich they or perhaps their children would be just as good as you. The fact is, whether they were rich or not, they don't have what it takes to develop it within them as you do. So they turn on you to destroy you, knowing that they can get away with it because so many people hate the rich ones. The fact of envy never comes to the surface. That teacher was envious of you, and used your father's riches as an alibi motive for treating you badly. The other girl in your class who was from a well-to-do family apparently was not a fine person and had no desire to be so. The teacher didn't treat her badly. But she continuously put you down, fine all around person that you were."

Gilda was astounded as this idea dawned on her consciousness after being tucked away in the background of her mind since childhood. "Yes, Collin, yes," she said, "that's it. I should have known. I guess I really did, but somehow couldn't face up to it."

"Couldn't face up to it," questioned Collin, "because of your fear of being labeled conceited about yourself?"

After pausing for the longest time, Gilda replied softly, "Yes, that's it, that's it again, Collin. It's a fear all right — a fear that can lurk there and affect your whole life. I'll have to think about that some more — a whole lot more as time goes by."

Collin said sympathetically, "It is a warranted fear, Gilda. It is another ploy—a mind-game used by our adversaries. In their self-centeredness, and sometimes with projection involved they like to make us and others believe that if we become anything or do anything they cannot, then we are thinking too much of ourselves, conceited and over ambitious. In their warped minds this justifies their putting us down.

"Another ploy closely related to this is that some of them make believe — yes, they just pretend — that they think we think too much of ourselves, and that they are treating us as they do, abusively that is, in order to knock the conceitedness and haughtiness out of us. Of course they know the difference full well. Collin then added emphatically, "Please take note of that, friends, because it is one of the deadliest and frequently used mind-games that our adversaries resort to. Try openly to defend yourself against it and they will point the finger at you and say in effect, 'see what I mean. He thinks we are picking on him because he is smart, or good looking, or a better person than the rest of us.' In their warped minds this justifies to themselves, and they hope to others, their putting you down in every way possible that they can get away with, because you think too much of yourself and therefore deserve what they are doing to you."

Gilda pulled herself together, even smiled. "That bit of knowledge will help me in future for sure."

Dr. Eldren tipped his head towards Collin, "I think you have something there all right, Collin."

"Sorry I blew my stack," said Leo remorsefully. "This incident is a big help to me as well as to Gilda."

Dr. Eldred turned to Leo. "You really feel strongly about these matters don't you Leo. It's upsetting to you in a very measurable manner."

"Well, yes sir, it is very upsetting, but you'll have to excuse my flipping my lid. It's a part of me at times."

"No harm done," replied the doctor, "you're entitled to let out your feelings." Then turning his attention to Gilda, he asked, "Gilda, did you have any similar troubles through the remainder of your school days, or was this just an isolated incident?"

She continued with her story, "It wasn't an isolated incident, but I did have a good year the following year in grade six. Although I began grade six with lots of apprehension and not much ambition, I was blessed with a friendly, unbiased teacher who really thought well of me and whom I eventually began to trust. Over a period of two or three months I became an interested and hard working student again, doing well but intentionally using restraint so as not to come first in my class for fear of being turned on again. The main rival of my grade five class was in another grade six room now, so that was a great help, but I really worked at it, or didn't work at it would be more accurate I suppose, to intentionally stay behind another girl who had not been in my grade five room. I purposely let her hold first place. However, it was a great healing year for me, but it wasn't the end of my troubles, for beyond grade six came grade seven."

Gilda paused in reflection again.

"More troubles there?" Dr. Eldren queried, gently and sympathetically.

"Yes," in grade seven we had a different set up. We were no longer under the one teacher only, but now had subject teachers, which as you know meant several teachers to get to know and cope with. Most of my teachers I found to be good and helpful and fair in their attitudes. There were two, however, whose attitude towards me was similar to that of my grade five teacher, except that they were less open in their discrimination. One just showed a continuous dislike for me but made no attempt to discriminate concerning my school work. The other made every attempt to keep my grades low, but I was two years older now than when I began grade five, so it was here I began to get wise and do battle for myself."

"You began to cope?" asked Dr. Eldren.

"Yes, that's it, I guess. I began to cope as best I could at that age."

"To cope with such things at all at that age is quite notable, I would say," replied Dr. Eldren. "Perhaps in this instance it would be in order to take exception to our planned format about coping and as you tell of your junior high school experiences, you could at the same time tell us how you coped with these experiences."

All present agreed to that innovation and beckoned Gilda to proceed with her story.

"It isn't really so much an intriguing story from here on, as much as it is simply a continuous struggle, sometimes a battle to keep moving ahead."

"Keep moving ahead or go under," interjected Collin, as though he knew her story already.

Leo became excited. "Hey," he said to Collin, "you're able to foretell her story too."

Owen, with a smile on his face, raised his eyebrows towards Collin, "hardly that, I think, but I'm sure glad I persuaded you to come to our group, Collin." Then turning to Leo, "Collin isn't psychic, Leo, just experienced."

Gilda picked up the conversation again, "I expect it is experience that has taught Collin such things. Experience has taught me that if you don't forge ahead, one way or another, you will go down. When people are trying to put you down, that's just where they want you to go — down. The only effective defense against this is to go forward regardless. There are various ways to forge ahead. I chose and learned to handle well the method that has worked for me. However, I can see where it would not work for some others."

Gilda, now visibly exuberant, perked up in her chair. She continued speaking: "There were two things that spurred me on to do well regardless of what may come. First, I did not want ever again to feel that I had lost the respect of my parents, as I felt I had when in grade five. This thought not only spurred me to do well in high school, but gave me a concrete desire to go on to university as

I knew this is what my parents wanted for me. Secondly, I was inspired to go on by the thought that things would be much better in university than in high school. If only I could win the struggle in high school, there would, so I thought, be smooth sailing in university."

Gilda settled back in her chair now. "Of course, she continued, "I'll explain later what finally happened to that bit of philosophy when I tell you about my first year in university. Nevertheless, it did give me incentive to try hard in high school, and continuing with my high school experience, I did have one or two things in my favor there. One was that I was good at mathematics, and unlike as in Leo's case, I was not dependent on 'my ability to discern,' as Leo was told. Rather it was a case usually of working out a mathematical problem by the method prescribed by the teacher or the text book. At that I was able to do well. Secondly, I was a quick thinker, and developed well the ability to argue my point thoroughly, continuously and forcefully, without losing my patience.

"Work in my science courses could also be defended in the same manner, since they did not have about them the 'ambiguity' that Leo was reminded of in his English course last year. Many times though, before certain teachers, I had to defend my method of working out a math or science problem. Some times I lost; most times I won, thereby building a reputation for myself as being a keen student whom my adversaries held in dread and disdain. I did well in some of the 'ambiguous' subjects too," she said with a smile, as she emphasized the word ambiguous, to the amusement of the group. "This gave me protection to a point, although all through my high school years, there was always the discriminatory teachers to do battle with, or to cope with if you wish. It was a continuous, most strenuous struggle but I did get through high school with honors."

Gilda then turned thoughtfully to Albin Anders. "Albin, throughout my school years, I did have several obnoxious teachers, and I do not to any degree minimize the misery they caused me, but, I want to emphasize also that I had some very wonderful, helpful and friendly teachers as well. Without them I wouldn't have gotten through. I want to be sure you see both sides of my story."

Albin blushed, but only a little. His self esteem was improving already. The broad smile into which he broke, was the predominant feature. "Thank you Gilda," he said somewhat confidently, "I do see both sides of your story, as you tell it now. I also see similarities to my own experiences through the years, of which I was not aware, or of which I had only a semi-awareness at the time, but of which I am becoming fully conscious as time goes by."

Then looking around at the whole group, Albin continued, "In the midst of all the discrimination and hostility, it is difficult to feel the friendships. One can see them there, and that is alright as far as it goes, but it is so difficult to really feel that you are in a sphere of friendship. The friendliness is so often subdued and implied. The hostility is so predominant and upsetting that when it is in sufficient quantities it easily dominates the mind."

"Exactly," said Owen, as he placed his long arm protectively around the shoulders of Albin who was sitting next to him. The friendship is there Albin, usually in larger quantities than the hostility, but it is often so silent, even dormant, that all we can see is hostility. I'm happy to see the awakening of your awareness to a higher degree.

"I think," Owen continued, "that the saving grace for Gilda is that she had a friendly teacher in grade six. That brought healing for her. Had she been unfortunate enough to have had a disagreeable teacher in grade six also, it would have spelled disaster for Gilda. Furthermore, I think that this rather unique experience of her having vivid exposure to the two extremes of hostility and friendship in two consecutive years was a very valuable awareness experience for her. The pleasant sixth grade not only renewed her perspective, but opened the way for her to learn to cope so well at so young an age."

"Yes," replied Gilda, "in those two years I learned both sides of life. As I proceeded on through school, there were to be more bad experiences similar to those of grade five, but, there also were many in the category of my good grade six experience. This better side was a great encouragement to me."

There was a brief silence. Dr. Eldren showed no visible expression of wanting to pick up the conversation at that point. Owen looked to Collin.

Collin had no desire to continue with the analytical aspect just now but he broke the silence with another probing question. "Gilda, if we require you to go through the ordeal of relating to us your whole high school experience, which you have already described as a continuous struggle it might be repetitious. Could you tell us of any outstanding incidents that might reveal something more of the nature of our problems?"

Gilda paused for a moment as she intentionally put a wide eyed expression of wonderment on her face. "Outstanding incidents?" she drawled, "yes-s-s", then quickly, "yes, sure. The one that comes most quickly to mind is an incident in my final year of high school. We had a new science teacher that year. One day, early in the year, in science class we were discussing the capabilities and limitations of aircraft when I brought into the discussion information I had heard of when on a trip abroad about a new, yet unpublicized invention. The science teacher had never heard of it, since news of it had not yet been released to the media. Immediately the teacher's nose was out of joint. He ridiculed me and trivialized my information before the whole class as if I was fantasizing. 'Who ever heard of such a thing,' he scoffed, "except Gilda Emerson.'

"He put me down, and put me down hard in a very hostile manner, denying the accuracy of my statement most emphatically, in order to save face which he felt he had lost. Most of the class could see through him I'm sure, but the damage between him and me was done.

"After outshining the teacher in this manner in a discussion before the whole class, I was to be on his bad books for the remainder of the year. From that time on he was cold and distant towards me. It was another burden to carry that year, and I must say it affected my overall performance. Nevertheless, I had what can be described as a good year, passing with honors. The thought that this was my final year of high school and just months away was my freedom from pettiness helped me to struggle on to do well. In university things will be better than this, I told myself; and then there was my parents — they so wanted me to go to university, and I wanted to please them. Of course I did want to go on to university myself also," she hastened to add at the end of her statement.

Owen gave his head a quick twist of admiration. Then he asked, "Gilda, how did your parents figure in your high school years? You mentioned earlier how they misinterpreted events in your grade five experience, but in high school, being much older, you were probably better able to explain."

"Yes, I was better able to explain, and I talked to my mother a great deal about it. She developed a sense of sympathetic understanding about the matter. I talked to my father about it some too. My mother suggested to my father that perhaps I should go to a private school. He didn't agree. He is a self made man who came up the hard way. He felt it would be good for his children to do the same. My brother had done all right. I should harden myself to the knocks and keep pressing on. That was his philosophy on the matter. I didn't push the idea of private school with him, because I knew it would be a financial burden for the family. We had a good standard of living all right, but I wouldn't say we were wealthy. My father had not always received the salary he was getting at the time of my high school years, so he was really just then getting financially established at this point in life."

"Thank you Gilda," said Owen.

Collin asked, "And you really did think, Gilda, that there would be none of this pettiness, as you called it, in university?"

"Oh boy! was I mistaken on that one," replied Gilda. "Should I tell about that phase of my life now?" she asked Dr. Eldren.

"Yes," replied Dr. Eldren. "It's all very interesting, go right ahead."

"Well," said Gilda, "I went into university like a butterfly that had just been freed from the cocoon. Little did I know that butterflies have their problems of survival too!"

"Same problems, just in a different setting?" queried Collin.

"Yes," answered Gilda, "the cocoon even with the protection of camouflage often gets trampled under foot and crushed into the ground. But the butterfly with all its openness can just as easily be attacked in flight, brought to the ground again and crushed mercilessly into it."

"With all its openness — and color," added Collin, emphasizing the word 'color'."

"A butterfly is colorful all right, and easily spotted," responded Gilda as though she could now find meaning in Collin's statement.

Gilda proceeded with her story. "The big disappointment of my life came when I was only a very short time into my first semester at university. Where I thought I would be free, I soon learned I was in for more of the same, in some ways even worse. As the semester proceeded, this butterfly was attacked more and more by a hostile hawk who knew every sly trick in the book, and many that weren't. He tried to down me at every turn.

Then there was the second one. She wasn't bright enough to be tricky. She knew her subject well, but not much else. She just brooded and snooted in my presence, pushed up her lip in rejection, sneered in scorn, ignored me passively trying always to make herself feel superior to me. Here was a person whom I would say had spent her years specializing in her subject, the professional student type, earning her degrees, but with little contact with the active world. She was a characterless, socially inexperienced scholar, whom as I said, knew her subject but not the world in which it had its setting. And she had a chip on her shoulder because she wasn't always the center of attention."

"What was her overall appearance like, Gilda?" asked Collin.

Gilda blinked and puzzled a little as though once again, she was struggling to grasp the full significance of Collin's question. "Oh, she wasn't too bad that way," remarked Gilda casually again. "If she would buy some sensible clothes and care for herself a little more, she'd look quite okay, but you know, she never got out of grade school as far as choice of clothes is concerned. Anyway, I pity her more than anything else, but she and the other guy, the hawk, each in their own separate ways, sent my spirits down so much that towards the middle of the first semester it happened. I felt I couldn't take any more of this. The disappointment of having to take more of the same in university sent me into despair, and I had a nervous breakdown, if that's what you can call it; I was totally exhausted from working so hard and under so much stress, a combination of the two," she added.

A momentary silence followed. It was broken by an emotional remark by Leo. "Oh-h Gilda, you didn't let them do that to you, did you? he asked as tears became noticeable in his eyes.

"I'm afraid so Leo. The butterfly was attacked in mid-air and brought low, but," continued Gilda in a firm tone of voice, "not for long, not for long."

Leo's face brightened. The other group members perked up.

"Not for long?" repeated Owen.

"No, just for three weeks. That's all I was out — just three weeks," said Gilda confidently, "and that brief period was the big turning point in my life."

"You briefly mentioned this to me before, now tell us more," urged Owen.

Gilda pursued her story, "Our family doctor recommended me to a psychiatrist, who in turn recommended that I be admitted to the psychiatric ward of a general hospital. I followed this recommendation, and while there was on moderately heavy medication and started psychotherapy sessions with the same psychiatrist."

"It did you good?" asked Owen.

"Ugh" retorted Gilda with such an emphatic rejection of Owen's statement that it seemed to be almost out of character for her. "It got my back up," she said firmly.

"Oh-h-h," said Owen.

"Yes," affirmed Gilda.

"Why? asked Owen.

"It was the whole tone of the therapy that did it," replied Gilda, now more calmly. "The whole approach of the therapy was to the effect that I wasn't approaching these people properly; I wasn't diplomatic enough with them; I was letting this and that disturb me; I was allowing myself to be too easily upset; I wasn't very effective at coping; I was making mountains out of mole hills; these people weren't all that bad."

"He told you that?" asked Owen.

"Much of it he inferred. Some he told me outright," replied Gilda, "but in the course of the therapy, that was the kind of thinking he was steering me into. There I was, after a young lifetime of rather successfully doing battle with these warped characters that always appeared on my horizon, being told now it was all my fault."

"What did you do about it?" asked Owen, now with hushed tones of astonishment.

"One day, after nearly two weeks of therapy, and when I could take no more of his inferences, I screamed at him. I screamed good and loud, with tearful anger saying, 'Don't you see what you're doing to me, you madman! Leave me alone and let me go home."

Owen glanced at Dr. Eldren, but then quickly back to Gilda, and in tones even more hushed asked, "What happened then?"

"He put me on heavier medication," Gilda replied coolly, "so heavy I couldn't even think. I did nothing much but sleep for two days."

"And?" Owen questioned further.

"My parents came to see me. I begged them to take me home, and after another two days they did so. It took that long for me to become fully coherent after being taken off the heavy medication."

Gilda then turned to Dr. Eldren. "I'm very sorry sir for being so harsh on your colleague in psychiatric practice, but that's how I felt about him and the whole approach."

Dr. Eldren smiled. "You're entitled to your opinion," he said. It seemed he wanted to make no more comment on that particular experience, at least for now. He was interested though in hearing the remainder of her experience. "It seems you have somehow survived your ordeal very well. You are here with us now and still going to university. It would be most encouraging, I'm sure, for everyone present to know how you did it, if you will share it with us?"

"Glad to," Gilda proceeded again. "Before my parents took me home they talked with the psychiatrist at the hospital. He told them that if they wished, I could go home. He suggested that a period of rest at home might do something for me. Also, unknown to me at the time, he had suggested to them that perhaps university was too much for me and that I should consider a career in some other direction. My parents were good about taking me home. They showed genuine care and affection, and I was so glad to be out of hospital, I felt so free now and relaxed at being home, that my original despair lifted.

"The next day after arriving home, my mother and father and I were having the evening meal together and we discussed my situation at length. Both parents assured me that I need not continue with university; that they would not be disappointed if I were to look for a career in sales or office work or whatever I chose. My father said he could get me a promising job in his corporation, or, I could be more independent and seek employment elsewhere."

Gilda paused in her story telling for a moment of reflection, then spoke again, "you know, you could never imagine the burden that was lifted from me in that discussion with my parents. I didn't have to go to university in order to retain their respect. I told them I'd sleep on it and think about it. Actually, it was late before I slept that night, because I did much thinking beforehand. I lay there, with my light on. I was looking at the ceiling as though it was the sky. I felt so light and free again. My parents loved me no matter what! No obnoxious teacher would ever again make me feel they didn't. I felt like a butterfly again — for whom the sky was the limit."

"*Indeed the sky is the limit* I thought to myself again and again, until abruptly another thought penetrated deeply into my mind. *The sky is not really the limit if I can't go to university. I didn't only go to university to please my parents. I wanted to myself. And if I can't do what I want to, then I'm back in a cocoon of sorts again. No way,* I thought. I mulled it over in my mind some more. For the first time since my grade five days, I was fully conscious now that I didn't have to do well at studies to retain the respect of my parents, but, and it was a big *but* — I wanted to go on to university myself.

It seems at that point I became fully aware that I had always wanted to study and do well academically because that is the life I liked for myself and now wanted to continue. The fact that it pleased my parents was just an added bonus, and would be in the future as well, no doubt. That's what I wanted for myself, regardless, to continue my education. *If I can't go on to do what I really want for myself, then the sky isn't the limit. I'd be letting those hawks drive me right out of the sky, and I can't do that. But then, there are obstacles. Oh Gilda it's late and you are tired now,* I told myself, *go to sleep and think about it tomorrow."*

"I slept late next morning, and all that day I just sat and lay around the house resting my body and letting my mind go through the process of restoration. When evening came, my father was home in plenty of time for dinner at seven. This wasn't always so with him, but he was making a special effort now to be with mother and I in this time of difficulty.

"It was mostly small talk at dinner and around the house that evening; talk about how nice it would be if my brother was near home to join us, incidentally he is doing post-graduate study at a university far from home; how when my father was just another accountant in his firm he had more time at home, carefree time; how hard work and promotion had brought prosperity to the family, but also brought its responsibilities, and these were not left behind at the office at five o'clock but tagged along with him. We discussed the pros and cons of this life of responsibility and decided it was very worthwhile overall, because it was fulfilling.

"Because of the spontaneous way that conversation evolved that evening, I feel sure there was no intention on my parent's part to spur me on to higher goals, yet it did set me thinking about fulfillment. As we watched television together that evening it kept popping into my mind. However, mostly I wanted rest and relaxation, so I kept it to myself. I slept well that night and well into mid-morning. I awakened feeling refreshed and restored, almost fully restored. My mind was active again now, and thinking about the problems of life. The thought foremost in my mind all day long was the dreadful thought of defeat that would come over my life if I did not return to university. I became more fully conscious that day that I had had two incentives spurring me on to university. One incentive was the example and desire of my parents all right, but, a second was that I really and truly wanted to for myself. I pondered and came to the conclusion that the second reason was indeed the more important to me. Whatever influence the first incentive had over me was gone. It didn't matter whether my parents wanted me to or not, I wanted to go to university for myself, and not to go would be a dreadful and shattering defeat. As I look back now, I see it would have been a very traumatic defeat.

"I surveyed my high school performance in dealing with problem teachers — and students — and felt that, contrary to what the psychiatrist at the hospital thought, I had done well. My downfall had been that I had let down my guard because I had led myself to believe there would be no need for such guard at university as there had been in high school. Now I was becoming reconciled to the fact that it may be the same all the way through—through university, perhaps through life. I was now prepared to dig in my heels and press on through university as I had through high school. Not to do so was to let those obnoxious ones rob me of life as I wanted it for myself. The thought of allowing that to happen was devastating to say the least. I thought over these things again and again all day long, and the more I thought of them the stronger my desire became to return to the fray at university.

"That evening at dinner the conversation was light for awhile, as it had been the previous evening. It was mostly my father talking about some of the interesting things happening in his business nowadays. I did wonder, at the time, if he had a hidden motive in this, trying to arouse my interest in a business career. He told me later it was not so, it was just sociable conversation.

Nevertheless at a convenient time I interrupted that conversation with a rather abrupt and excited statement. 'Mom and Dad, I've decided what I am going to do from here on! I want you to know.'

"My father was always the first to take me up on anything I came out with in the line of ideas and suggestions. "You've decided already?" he asked. Have you thought it through carefully, whatever it is?

"'Yes,' I said, 'I've thought it through carefully, and I'm going back to university, next week.'

"'O-h-h-h!' replied my father in a non committed manner. But then after a brief pause he added in positive tones, 'You feel that well already?'

"'Yes,' I said, 'I do.'

"'You don't have to go back you know,' my father said affectionately. 'There are plenty of other roads in life to choose from.' He paused, then continued, 'but if you want to....'

"'But dear,' my mother interjected, 'the doctor says that perhaps you shouldn't go to university, it may be too much for you.'

"I looked at them in wide eyed surprise at that statement. Then I felt determination asserting itself in my mind. 'Mom,' I said, very emphatically, 'I do not intend to listen to that doctor now any more than I listened to him in the hospital. I'm going to university, and in four years time I am going to graduate!'

"My mother was awestruck. My father arose from his chair, walked around to my side of the dining table to the back of my chair, put his hands firmly on the sides of my shoulders, squeezed them together, placed his cheek against mine for a second, then kissed me on the face and said, 'Gilda, you go right ahead if that's what you want to do, and any way I can possibly help you I will.'

"'Thank you Dad,' I said, 'but this is something I have to do on my own. Your morale support is welcome. You're financial support I will need, and I want to live at home and commute as I have been doing. Other than that, the struggle is mine. I have to do it on my own.'

"My father rubbed the palms of his hands together with

enthusiasm as he returned to his place at the table and began eating his dinner in hurried excitement. It was not often I had seen him that way. My mother was stuck for words. 'But your health, Gilda — the doctor —.'

"My father spoke up to reassure her, 'Mother dear, in this case, I have much more faith in Gilda than I have in the doctor. The doctor meant well, but he doesn't know Gilda like I know Gilda. I think she can do it.'

"Mother quivered a smile. 'Okay,' she said, in rather musical tones that were in complete submission to my father's persuasion.

"I was on my way in life again — like a butterfly. Only this time I would be wary of the hawks who are ready to peck me out of the sky and send me crashing to the ground.

Gilda paused, took a deep relaxing breath, as though a marathon had just ended. Telling the kind of story that most people, including psychiatrists, are not familiar with is stressful indeed. Gilda had no idea of how Dr. Eldren was taking her story. For all she knew, she could, as often happens, be labeled for life for simply telling it as it was to people who may know little or nothing about such matters.

Finally she asked, "can I tell you the remainder of the story now?"

"If you wish," replied Dr. Eldren quickly, "but your face is flushed with tension. We can wait until next week or you can tell it now."

"I prefer to do so now if I may," said Gilda, "while it is all fresh in my mind."

"Okay," said Dr Eldren, "but it isn't easy on a person recalling an unpleasant past. We can have a five minute break to allow you to simmer down."

They all stood around chatting until Gilda was much more at ease. Then she continued with her story.

"On the Friday of the third week of my absence from university, which was the day after I had revealed to my parents my plans to return to university, I was up and away from home early and heading toward the university offices. I went directly to the office of the dean of the science faculty and asked to see the dean. After a brief wait I was granted an interview.

"He was a neutral sort of man, a scholar no doubt, not unpleasant but neither did he impress me as one who would be in command in a difficult situation. Nevertheless, I told him I had been absent from classes for three weeks with a mild type of nervous breakdown; that I was ready to return now, and wondered whether this would be satisfactory to the faculty. He asked questions concerning my past scholastic record, and seemed pleased with what I told him.

"I would suggest." said the dean, "that you see each of your professor's individually. If they each are of the opinion that you can still benefit by continuing after this absence, then I also will agree to your return. You can ask them to contact me."

"'Thank you, sir,' I said, 'that's what I'll do."

"First I went to the three professors who had not taken a dislike to me, and with whom I had been getting along quite well. They wholeheartedly agreed to my returning, and we discussed ways and means as to how I could best catch up on the work. They were very helpful. Secondly I went to the professor who hadn't really tried to put me down as far as my work was concerned, but who, you may remember my telling you, had just by her attitudes and related actions, shown a great dislike for me, and had, as I said, snooted and scorned and that sort of thing.

"She was cold towards my approach. I think she thought I was gone and out of her hair for good. When I explained to her my problem, however, she quite suddenly took on a very pitying attitude towards me, which I soon learned was coupled with a very superior attitude on her part as well. Now she had reason to feel superior to me, so she accepted me back, open arms, so to speak, but with an approach that was to not only belittle me in her eyes, but before the whole class as well throughout the remainder of the year."

"She could look down on you now!" exclaimed Collin.

"Yes," replied Gilda, "that's it. From then on she felt she had reason to look down on me because I had been sick. I received fair treatment scholastically throughout the class, but her attitude was always one of pity towards this poor thing who now needed help so badly. She became the pitying mother of this poor helpless girl. Needless to say, it was very humiliating. However, I learned to take her with a grain of salt."

"What about the professor you referred to as the hawk?" inquired Owen, "how did you make out with him?"

"Oh that's quite another story," responded Gilda as she perked up in her chair. "I purposely went to him last. I told him my story, as I had told the others. His response was cold. 'Well, that's too bad I'm sure, about your sickness,' he said, 'but this is a very difficult course, and I would strongly advise you to forfeit it and perhaps try again next semester. No, you should not try to catch up on this course at this time.'"

Collin asked, "Was that course really a difficult one, Gilda?"

"Not really," replied Gilda. "Actually it was one of my better math subjects. I felt sure I could catch up, and there was tutoring available."

Gilda continued, "I insisted to him that I could, and wanted to continue with the course this semester. He took offense and stated that he didn't want anyone telling him what could or couldn't be done in his classes.

"Well," I said, you are telling me what I can and cannot do. Can I not even express what I feel I myself can do and am willing to do?"

"The professor fumed. 'You are the student, and I am the professor,' he said, as he stretched his shoulders upward. 'I have made my decision,' he snapped, 'and it is final.'"

"'We'll see about that,' I snapped back, and I turned and headed straight for the dean's office again.

"I told the dean how four professors had accepted my return and one had not. I told him how the fifth professor had been cold and snappy.

"'I am sorry about that,' replied the dean, 'but he has made his decision, and you will have to abide by it.'

"'Abide by it!' I retorted, in a mixture of surprise and anger.

'Abide by it? You mean you won't even take the matter up with him?'

"His eyes shifted from side to side, avoiding mine. He was either a fence sitter or a coward. Whichever it was, I wasn't going to be the same way.

"I would have to learn now to cope in university, as I had learned to do so in high school. Coping here wouldn't be quite the same. It was on a different level. I would upgrade my coping too, I decided then and there.

"'You won't take the matter up with him?' I asked again forcefully.

"He hesitated as he stumbled for words.

"I couldn't wait. 'Look here, sir,' I said, 'that professor has been very discriminatory towards me ever since the beginning of the semester. Now four other professors are willing to accept me back. Only one is not willing, and when all is boiled down, cut and dried, the only reason the fifth one has not accepted me is because he is prejudiced against me. I don't intend to be pushed out of university, and out of my career, by a person like that. Now sir, do I get re-admitted, or do I get a lawyer to take up my case for me and fight this matter right to the very end.'

"There was a pause.

"Then I continued, 'There are people in that lecture room who know I was discriminated against by the actions and attitudes of that professor.'

"The dean kept his outward composure. 'Miss Emerson,' he said, 'there is no need to go to such extremes. The same course you have been barred from is being taught simultaneously by another professor. She is a very good person. I will speak to her, and I am sure she will be glad to have you in her class.'

"'Why can't you speak to the professor who has rejected me?' I asked, pointedly.

"His eyes shifted from side to side again.

"'Listen,' he said, 'you will get the same instruction in this class I wish to get you into. Why go through all the fuss of trying to get back to your former class?'

"I knew then and there," continued Gilda, "that I would have no support whatever from the dean in any effort I may make to get into my former class. I thought the matter over briefly. Since there was an opportunity to join another class in the same course, I decided to take that opportunity. But I didn't let go easily. 'All right sir,' I said with a tone of dissatisfaction, 'I'll transfer to the other class when you make the arrangements, but I would like you to know I am not very pleased at having to do so. I have made some pleasant acquaintances with students in the former class. That will be a loss to me now. Also, having to change classes is a further disruption to my work and just adds to my problem. Nevertheless, since there is another class open to me, I will take it. But if there was no other class open to me I would fight the matter to the end by all possible means.'

"The dean's face was expressionless. He was covering up his feelings. I was to learn, as the years went by, that he was not alone in taking such an attitude in matters such as these where there is a real sticky problem involved. Some do not recognize the problem. Others fear the perpetrators of it. Still others avoid involvement in such circumstances, simply because there has never evolved a victorious way of dealing with it. With the dean I suspect it was the latter case. He was afraid to get involved because it is so difficult to deal with all the intangibles of it.

"As for me, I made up my mind then, that I would never be in the first two of these categories. As for the last one, I decided, come victory or defeat, I would never be found avoiding a battle with such people as the hawk, whenever a battle was necessary to fair play.

"And that folks was the experience that gave me the know-how to fly and glide and battle my way through to an undergraduate university honors degree. There would be other hawks in subsequent years, all somewhat different in approach but in actuality motivated in their misbehavior by the same type of faulty character. They were always in the minority, but for various unavoidable reasons they nearly always managed to dominate life's experiences. However, I battled my way through them, and came out on top."

Gilda paused, then added lightly with a smile, "A butterfly has survival problems too!"

Owen smiled back at her, and asked, "What was your final grade in that course, Gilda?"

"Oh," she replied gleefully, "I got an A," and then added mischievously, "I made sure the hawk knew it too. I purposely encountered him in the corridor and showed it to him on paper."

"What did he say?" asked Owen curiously.

"He pushed up his lip, half contemptuously, half approvingly so as one couldn't tell for sure which way he meant it, and remarked, 'I guess you were lucky,' and then went on his way. I figure he will keep on going his way — of discrimination against those of whom he is envious, with nobody ever really challenging him."

Collin spoke next. "Gilda, by flying, gliding and battling your way successfully through university here, no doubt you have ruffled many feathers. Where do you intend to go from here?"

"'Where' is the right word," replied Gilda. "It is true I have ruffled many feathers. In fact I am known in some circles here as a terror, throwing my old man's weight around, etc. etc., although, I never once called on my father for help. In fact, neither of my parents know of quarter of my battles. So, Collin, from here I will go far away, to another university to do post graduate work. At present I am taking some extra courses here, necessary prerequisites to take care of a minor change in the course of my future studies. But to stay here to either study or to make a career would be a mistake. I was successful in gaining a degree all right, but in the process of fighting my battle and defending my rights two things have happened which must be left behind. First, as I said, I am known as a terror, simply for standing up for myself. Secondly, this prolonged battle has been detrimental to me in that in some very real ways I have become a battle axe of a sort. I hope to go away to new surroundings to do post graduate work, which is a wise move academically anyway, but, also to make a career in a new environment where I can again become the pleasant person I was and really still am."

"You will have to be careful where you choose to go if you want to accomplish these things," remarked Collin.

"Yes," said Gilda, "I have thought about it a great deal. I have reason to believe that in post-graduate work the flying will be smoother for various reasons, although I will never drop my guard again. Usually, not always though, the professors in post graduate work are the higher caliber ones. That will help. In addition, when it comes to choosing a place for further studies, I will have a varied selection to choose from, so I am very encouraged about the prospects."

"Gilda," spoke Dr. Eldren, "you have contributed quite substantially to the session this evening. No doubt you have had this matter on your mind all week, keeping you up tight. All the members, I am sure, will find your experiences to be of real value. It isn't easy I know to recall and relive those things. It is a tiring and burdensome task. Thank you very much. I would suggest we hear from Donna Coyne next week. As you know, in our later sessions we will want to refer to your experiences again, as we will those of the others. For now though we will let you relax and unwind."

"Thank you, Dr. Eldren, I agree, I need to relax," said Gilda with a heavy smile.

"I would like to mention," said Collin, "that one of the predominant things I see in your story is the way your whole life has been altered by people who are down on you simply because you are a nice person and they can't tolerate it. That illustrates the whole purpose of this support group — to bring such unjust realities out into the open. Even more striking, of course, is that you are succeeding regardless."

The group as a whole sat momentarily in admiration of Gilda Emerson, complimenting her on her successes before it dispersed for the evening.

# Chapter Four

Collin Seldon, as his custom was on occasion, was lost in thought. *Yes*, he mused to himself as he again approached Quilibet University for a support group session, *Gilda Emerson did make it through. That feat is not merely the result of good work from a hard working person. It is not just an accomplishment of another person who had used her above average talents to the utmost. Rather, it was an extraordinary achievement against the odds. Of course, most people wouldn't see it to be any more than another success story — the kind of story one would automatically expect from a person of Gilda's caliber*.

But Collin was aware, from his own experience, of the deep and prolonged anguish, the times of excruciating stress, the sheer mental agony that Gilda had been through to attain her goal. To retain the stamina and keen powers of concentration it takes to earn an honors degree, while at the same time bearing that burden, was a remarkable achievement indeed. He mused further, *with such a background of academic attainment, and experience, she may someday well take her rightful place at the top of the ladder somewhere, not here, but somewhere else*. Most people would not think of that as being out of the ordinary either for a fine person like Gilda Emerson. They are not aware of the difficulties of the upward road, and of how many like her drop by the wayside, or settle for lesser summits. *I wonder*, he thought to himself, *how many in this group, have settled for less, because of these sometimes overwhelming circumstances!*

Collin expected he would find Donna Coyne's story equally as interesting as Gilda Emerson's. No doubt about it there was contrast in the setting of the lives of these two women. Collin, in his varied life, had gone the way of the business world also, for a time, so he handy about knew how the essence of Donna's story would go. He was glad for her though, for at a young age her awareness had grown and come to full flower; not at the exceptionally young age that awareness had come to Gilda, but still relatively early in her life — in time to avert a catastrophe.

That is what Collin pondered in his mind as he sat in the foyer on floor one of the university arts building. He had arrived early this evening for another support group session. Having been out on a lengthy pastoral call, he had gotten himself a snack somewhere between his pastoral visit and the university. Now he had time to spare. So amid the tranquil setting of the appropriate benches and indoor trees, and the early evening quiet of the area he sat and meditated on the latest happenings of the support group.

Awareness, semi-awareness! Collin well knew from experience what was meant by the terms, but it is very difficult to put into words a definition of them. As Gilda Emerson would say though, "it can be done you know" — and so it can.

To Collin, awareness in its various stages is a characteristic that a person just grows into as life progresses. As we go through life's experiences they make imprints on us which greatly affect our behavior, particularly with regard to our reaction to those events which may affect us heavily.

When we are very young persons, as with Gilda in Grade Five, before she had the unusually early and awakening behavioral learning experiences of Grades Six and Seven, these experiences may affect us with our having little or almost no consciousness that they are doing so.

With an older person, such as a university student, or a person in the work force awareness or consciousness of the social influences become more predominant in the mind. If only a semi-awareness develops, then thoughts of these influences take a secondary place in our total thoughts. People on this level of awareness generally try to just automatically avoid events that they sense to be unpleasant. Their reaction is, to a great extent, unconscious and unpremeditated. Many people go through life this way. And so they can, and get by — perhaps — depending on what category of people they are. People such as are in the support group, they being assailed in life so much more than average, need a more highly developed consciousness of what is happening to them in the kind of world in which they are compelled to live.

So awareness, more complete awareness, is to be fully conscious of the influences, good and bad, other people are having on you, on your very being, and your response to these influences. It is to be not only fully conscious of, but to be able to discern and understand the influences of others upon you; to be able also to discern and understand their motives as they take their various attitudes toward you, friendly or otherwise, or as they try to either manipulate or befriend you; to be fully conscious of other peoples effects upon you. To be able to discern by keen observation of speech and action another persons motives is not an easy task but one that can be developed with time and experience.

To have also honest understanding of one's own motives, actions, and reactions, and coping methods, is another element of more complete awareness. All of these together are the things that bring awareness to its full fruition. Surprisingly few people master this trait.

*But for people such as us, it is a necessity*, mused Collin. Then as he looked up and saw Albin Anders and Owen Winslow approaching from a distance, he thought again, *yes Albin Anders will have to master this if he is ever to make the grade. How can we best help him? It is really something you grow into but first you have to be introduced to it by oneself, or by others, or by a combination of both. Yes, that's how we can best help Albin, by continuing to introduce him to awareness, but for heaven's sake don't smother him. He has to do the growing himself.*

"Hello Collin," said Owen and Albin, as they came and sat beside him. "Enjoying the tranquility before you face the problems of life once more?" quipped Owen.

"Yes," replied Collin, "just having a period of peace and meditation, before our session begins."

"Are you glad you have joined us in the group, Collin?" asked Owen.

"Oh yes, I really am," he replied. "If for no other reason than just to have the assurance and support of other people like myself."

Then Collin turned to Albin, "Your awareness is beginning to blossom more fully. Am I right on that?"

"Yes, Collin, you are right, I am beginning to understand about awareness and about many other things many of which I am not sufficiently aware yet to discuss them intelligently, but it's coming."

"Good," continued Collin. "I would like to point out to you that as your awareness grows, so may the awesomeness and difficulty of the fuller life it opens up to you. But don't ever let that despair you. As time passes, and you master the art of living in this new sphere, you will gain new confidence, and in years to come you will be able to look back at these more difficult growing years and smile. Will you remember that Albin? It's like learning to swim. Once you have mastered it to a point, you are at ease in the water."

"I will remember," responded Albin, as his boyish smile broke over his face. "It's like swimming, difficult at first, then later you are buoyed up by the water and its much easier. I swim quite well Collin. Maybe I can do likewise in this realm of life."

Then Albin surprisingly took the initiative of the moment, looked at his watch, and remarked, "it is time to proceed to our group session. Perhaps we should go now."

"Sure, sure," Owen and Collin responded, as all three got up to move toward Room 405.

*Great*, thought Collin, as they walked down the hall towards the elevator. *Albin is coming on good. He's not afraid of us any more. He is even showing some initiative among us, although we are very much his senior age-wise. That's a beginning for him. Just great!"*

They entered Room 405 to greet and be greeted by other group members and Dr. Eldren.

"In my opinion Dr. Eldren," said Collin as the time drew near to begin, "it will be good indeed to hear now from Donna, the other woman of our group. There might be an interesting comparison or contrast to Gilda's experience. If you don't mind my saying so."

"Not at all," replied Dr. Eldren. "If Donna is agreeable to that and I think she is, it will be an excellent next move. What do you say, Donna?"

"I'm willing, if you people can take it," she responded, "but there will be quite a bit of contrast between my story and Gilda's as we compare them. Basically though there will be likeness, I mean the same underlying problems."

Dr. Eldren was enthusiastic again this evening. "Sounds like it will be plenty helpful to hear your story also," he said.

Donna Coyne began to tell the story of her life as she had lived it thus far, and as she saw it now at twenty-eight years of age.

"I wasn't so fortunate as Gilda," she began "in that I didn't have a vivid contrast between my grade five and grade six, that would teach me at so young an age one of the main lessons of life for people such as us. Surveying my school years," she continued, "I see now that from the beginning I was greatly affected both favorably and adversely by my teachers. Many of my teachers I remember affectionately. The remembrance of others still brings a cloud over my life.

The earliest I remember now was in grade two where I had a teacher who put me down throughout the year. I am still not sure why, but it seems she was envious of me for some reason, so her attitude towards me was always negative. In her attitude towards the students of the class generally, I was always at the bottom of the ladder. It was an attitude only, and as in Gilda's case, difficult to describe, but not impossible, I suppose. It was mostly her way of noticeably ignoring me while paying noticeable and friendly attention to the remainder of the class, sometimes some specific student in particular. I got through that class with only a minor sense of isolation, and no other particular harm done.

Throughout the remainder of my schooling there were similar experiences with teachers, and students. The students that were of the same type as the obnoxious teachers did me considerable harm over the years as did the teachers. Since these students had some teachers as their example in this regard it sort of gave them license to be down on me too. It also caused them to be more numerous. The students of that type did affect me considerably. This was partially offset by my living in the sphere of my own friends as much as possible. However, when I consider now the overall effect of the teachers who were obnoxious in their attitudes towards me, and they by their poor example, in turn, leading some students to be down on me, I believe they affected my life a great deal. The goodness, and the kindness, even the affection of the good teachers was not able to overcome it."

Dr. Eldren interjected, "Donna, from Leo's and Gilda's stories we now have a good conception of what we mean by the attitudes of obnoxious teachers. Is your concept in that regard, the same as theirs."

"Oh yes," she replied, "exactly."

"Perhaps then, Donna," he added, "we can spare you the pain of relating in detail your experiences in school days. This will enable us to avoid being repetitious in relating experiences. If there are any further really different experiences, or outstanding events which would be of significance in making a particular point, we should hear these. Otherwise I think it would be sufficient now for you to describe to us the overall effect you believe your teachers had on you."

Collin added, "and then perhaps we could hear from her, in more detail, her experiences out in the business world where she has worked for the past several years. These would be very revealing too, I am sure."

"If you wish!" replied Dr. Eldren. "If it's all right with Donna."

Donna smiled. "Collin must be reading my mind."

Leo was mildly ecstatic. "Collin is psychic," he quipped.

"No, No," replied Collin, "just experienced."

"Can't wait to hear *your* story," came back Leo to Collin.

Donna then continued with her presentation. "I had only a semi-awareness of the social and psychological forces that influenced my life in its younger years. By younger I mean in this instance right up to the age of twenty one or twenty two; around that age, as well as I can place it now. I think I was in the realm of the majority in that regard. I find that most people do not really understand such things, even at a much older age. Some never do. Yet they get through life in various ways, depending on their personal makeup and other circumstances.

"Referring again to me personally, in retrospect this semi-awareness wasn't sufficient for me to learn to maneuver my way through life. I just pressed on with perseverance, patience and firmness. I would say, I developed a high degree of stability, a stability that stood, regardless of the circumstances. I took what came, high marks or low, acceptance or rejection, affection or scolding, fair treatment or unfair, all in silent forbearance, always pressing on to do my best, regardless of circumstances. Needless to say, the burden of this influenced my life greatly, both favorably and adversely; favorably in that I became hardened considerably, with regard to my sensitivity to criticism or unfriendliness. I developed, and rightly so, I would say, a sense of confidence in my own character, and felt that generally I was a good, pleasant, and likeable person. I was well liked by the right kind of people, and this helped to somewhat offset the effects of the others.

"These others, however, did affect my mind-set and consequently my career. Even though I graduated from high school with very good grades, I had not the slightest inclination to go on to university. When I look back at that, I can now see that I was unconsciously steered away from it by the unpleasantness of academic life caused by the obnoxious characters, both teachers and students. It was a case of the obnoxious minority overshadowing a majority composed of both friendly and neutral people. For survival purposes I handled the circumstances of the time by becoming hardened. But I coped with the future in advance, by saying to myself, why go through more of this, when it doesn't mean that much to me. As I look back now, that was my semi-conscious reaction at the time."

"There was also another factor that had an equal influence on my steering away from a university education. It was family circumstances at the time. Up to a year before I graduated from high school, my father had been a car sales manager in an auto dealership. Then in the year previous to my graduation, the owner of the dealership retired from business. My father bought him out and became the new owner. It was a crucial time for my family, and although some financial help would have been forthcoming for me to continue my education, and in addition I could have earned some myself, I turned it down. I felt it would be an extra burden on my family, not only financially but in other ways as well. 'Why put my family through all this?' I thought, 'just for me to have to take more of the basically unpleasant life I had through my school days."

"Collin spoke. "Donna, may I for a moment, change the emphasis of the conversation from the influence circumstances had on your mindset, to the circumstances themselves in your final two years of school?"

"Well, yes," Donna replied, questioningly, just what do you have in mind?"

Collin continued, "I have in mind the fact that in the year before you graduated from high school, your father became the owner of a car dealership in your home town. What I am curious to know is just what change of attitude took place towards you by teachers and students because of your father's change in business status from employee to owner."

"To my friends and friendly acquaintances, it made very little difference, Collin," replied Donna. "They were generally happy at my father's success, and thought it was just great. For the neutral ones it didn't seem to make much difference either. But for the obnoxious ones it did make a great deal of difference. They had been nasty to me before, but now more so. But most notable of all, now as I look back, was the change in their motivation for being that way towards me. It was a change, and yet in a sense it was the same, basically at least. What it amounted to was that when my father was just a very successful salesman, I was snubbed for *trying* to be a big shot. When my father became the owner, I was snubbed for *being* a big shot."

"You were being discriminated against because of your father's success?" queried Collin.

"Yes, oh yes, that's it," replied Donna.

Collin questioned and pried further. Her father's success was only one factor. There was that other affecting element too. He would like to bring it out to increase Donna's awareness. "Donna, were you not also discriminated against because of what you were yourself? You were and are what we are calling a fine person."

"Yes," replied Donna. "I wasn't aware of that at the time, but when I reflect back, I can now see that it was so. There were some other 'big shot's' children around who were not picked on. But when my father became owner of the car dealership, that seemed to give them all the more license — they could now more openly pick on me because I was 'a big shot's daughter,' so they inferred with their side-swipes and innuendo.

Collin led Donna back on course again in the telling of her story. "So you abandoned the way of the academic life for the business world, did you Donna?" he asked.

"Yes," Donna replied, "I prepared myself to be a stenographer and went to work eventually in the offices of a large manufacturing company."

Collin smiled at her sympathetically, "was it any better there for you, Donna?" he asked.

Donna shook her head as she returned the smile. "Not really," she replied, "not for me." The place where I worked was known as a reputable company. My experience there was quite different in essence than I had in high school, but no Collin, it wasn't any better for me," she said with an emphasis on the 'me' at the end of her sentence.

Dr. Eldren came in with a suggestion. "Perhaps Donna, you could tell us in detail something of your experience in office work that would be helpful to furthering the understanding of the group members. That could be the main thrust of your contribution, if you wish."

"All right, Dr. Eldren," Donna replied. "I will try."

So Donna resumed her story, now in the sphere of her career in office work. "I went to work as a clerk-typist," she said, "and as usual when a person is new in a place, you neither know people nor are known by them. Apart from the feeling one gets from being eyed by other people who are trying to figure you out, you are in a kind of pleasant vacuum where you haven't yet come into close association with anybody. There are people all around you, and in the course of their synchronizing their work with yours and showing you how the system operates, there is an all around almost perfunctory friendliness.

"Only as time goes by does this preliminary friendliness become enhanced or marred as people figure you out in their own way and either accept or reject you to varying degrees on the basis of their speculative opinion of you. So for approximately my first three months with the corporation I had no unpleasant experiences to speak of. During that time I learned my job well, did very well with my work, and was gradually given more responsibility. At the end of the first three months I was given a substantial increase in salary on the merit of my work.

"However, one cannot be involved for a prolonged period in any organization without being eventually caught up in its social joys and trials. As time passes you find out who are your friends and who are not."

Collin asked, "Donna, do you not find that out as you do your work better and better and perhaps get a promotion or raise in salary?"

"You sure do, Collin," Donna replied, "but I was fortunate in my first year in that I was in a department where the supervisor appreciated good work, punctuality, and decorum."

"Don't all supervisors appreciate these qualities, Donna?" asked Albin.

"Many supervisors do not appreciate decorum at all, Albin, and often these same supervisors appreciate good work and punctuality only to a degree. I am glad you asked that question, however, and if you will keep it in mind, I am sure that it will be answered for you as we continue through our discussions. In the meantime, in the department of my first year, I did make some enemies because of these favorable attributes, if I may say so without sounding conceited or presumptuous."

Collin cut in, "that is something a person like you always has to be careful of when you make an honest assessment of yourself, isn't it, Donna? I mean being careful not to be accused of conceit or presumption."

"Oh yes indeed, Collin," said Donna, "there is always someone ready to accuse people like us of that. However, in this group I feel free to express my thoughts without restraint."

"That is good, Donna," interjected Dr. Eldren. "It is sometimes very difficult to make an objective assessment of one's own experiences, but you are doing well. I think if we all keep in mind that the more open and objective we are in our analysis of ourselves and each other, the more beneficial it will be to our learning experience."

"Well," said Donna, "I think I am being objective and factual in stating that my enemies were made because of my good work." She then quipped with a nervous smile, "Of course, Dr. Eldren, I made many friends there too, so I wouldn't want you to think I came out of there paranoid or with delusions of grandeur or persecution."

"No such thought entered my mind Donna," Dr. Eldren replied, "feel at ease and continue."

Donna continued with her story. "It was there in the year one department, as I will call it, that my semi-awareness began to grow into a more complete awareness. There I learned the art of maneuvering among and coping with the many and varied personalities one finds in life's experiences. In semi-awareness I had been led into a mind-set that made me feel I was to be an underdog anyway, and just grin and bear it. I thought then that if I just plodded through in a somewhat stoic manner, I would in the end average out a good distance up the ladder. But now, on my way through year one, all that changed.

"There were a few newly made friends who dared to befriend me regardless of the hostilities of some others. Also, there was my supervisor with her absolute fairness, and her appreciation of myself and my work. This led me to break out of my youthfully formed mind-set, to begin my years of awakening and growing. Why this awakening didn't happen to me in school is a matter of speculation. Of course I was older now, and that was a contributing factor. I rather think it came about in year one at work, because there I was in an entirely adult situation. Among adults both friendship and unfriendliness are more pronounced, and people are more openly reactive to my response to their overtures of either friendliness or unfriendliness. This made it easier for me to discern and know who was my true friend and who was not, and how to react to, even utilize friendship, in an ethical manner of course."

Collin asked, "did you have more time to contemplate these things now Donna, even dwell on them for periods?"

"Yes, —yes," replied Donna. "During my school days, I recall now, it was the custom to brush all troubles aside so as to participate in and enjoy extra-curricular activities or to do home work. Now that I was working, I often had some evenings of inactivity. As I watched television, or read, or did some craft work or helped around the house, there was time to reflect, to think, even to dwell at times on the activities and happenings of the day. This certainly was a contributing factor to my awareness, and a tremendous aid in the process of my growth, provided I didn't let it bog me down. To be active in the world, with ones feet planted firmly on the ground, and to have not too little, nor too much time, to meditate on life's experiences as they happen is, I would say, an invaluable aid to growth and development."

"So getting back to my story," continued Donna, as she stirred herself to new thoughts evidenced by her stirring herself in her chair, "year one was a learning year. I came through it well, but I owe a great deal to my supervisor. She realized that some other employees discriminated against me mostly by their attitudes. There was little she could say, but she very graciously counteracted these attitudes by openly befriending me in front of them, by taking time to pause and talk a minute or two with me on occasion. This was always in sight of them, but often not within their hearing distance, just to show support for me, and to keep them at bay. She did this for some others too. It seems her policy was to show open support for the better employees in this manner which she had developed very skillfully. I will always remember her as a very helpful and kind lady whom, may I say with truthful modesty, appreciated better type people."

"At the end of year one, on her recommendation, I was promoted to a more senior and larger department. Now, having been awakened from my semi-awareness, I was to have opportunity for experiences that would make me fully aware indeed of the harsh realities that exist for people like me in the realm of life out in the market place."

"I was placed in charge of a section of work that had previously been poorly organized and carelessly carried out," Donna related. "This isn't just my summation of the situation. It was generally felt in the department that there were things gone wrong with the overall efficiency of what was now to be my section. It would now be my responsibility under the supervision of a department supervisor and assistant supervisor.

"As often happens in industry, I was given only a vague introduction to my work, its general structure, and how it is to relate to other work sections in the department. From there one finds the way partly by asking others, such as the supervisor, or those to whose section certain aspects of your work relates. But most of all the way is found simply by digging in and figuring things out for yourself and building on the preliminary introduction. This method one accepts as a norm.

"So, I dug in — challenged, eager and anticipating. As I look back now I still agree there was a challenge beyond a doubt. But as for my eagerness and anticipation, they would over the three year period I spent there, become largely dulled and disillusioningly unrewarded.

"My particular work within the department was designated a job to be handled by one person. However, it seemed that, in the recent past at least, one person could never keep up with the work load. So at periods when it was crucial that the work be more up to date, temporary help was brought in from outside the corporation.

"In a brief and broad outline, I will describe the work as consisting basically of receiving from the billing department a copy of billings going out to numerous customers across the country, and recording them. Also receiving records of payment of accounts by customers. Breaking these payments down and particularly keeping record of the various taxes collected for the different levels of government. Also separating shipping charges for a variety of products, as well as payment for products from other branches of our corporation. By the way, this was at a time before the corporation had computerized this part of its operations. Records were kept and requisitions were issued for either payment of accounts, or transfer of money or credits to other branches or departments as the case may be. This was to be my work. And I recognized it as being a job vital to the well being of the corporation.

"Also I soon recognized that my predecessor on this job had not taken her work seriously. The system was sloppily cared for; records so carelessly entered that a person other than the one who did the work could at times scarcely decipher the nature of the transaction or the date it took place. In time, it also became noticeable to me that many transactions were not recorded at the proper time. Postings were sometimes omitted for a period. Then caught up on later. These items could all be accounted for in time, no doubt, but as it was they now lay in a jumble in the drawers of the desk I had inherited for the job. This caused delays in the corporations financial transactions. Delays cost money. In addition, the system was poorly organized. If there was any chance at all of keeping up with the work load there would have to be changes to the routine. With the procedure streamlined, I felt, then the thousand and one items requiring special attention would be reduced to a minimum."

As Donna spoke now, her glowing expression seemed to indicate deep satisfaction with her accomplishment in re-organizing the system of her vital work section.

"I was purposely cautious at first," she continued, "but as I learned more assuredly the details of my job, I began to point out to the department's assistant supervisor the deficiencies in both the system and its implementation. Also, as I began to see ways of improving both of these matters, I made recommendations for change to the assistant supervisor, who in turn would take them to the supervisor for his consideration. He always approved them.

Only very occasionally, however, did he come by to speak of the implications of these changes to me personally. The assistant supervisor was nearly always his liaison. This I simply took for granted at the time, as I figured he had many other matters to think of.

"It was shortly past the beginning of the new financial year when I had taken on this job. As its end approached things were running very smoothly in my section. Many innovations had been made to enable the work to be done more efficiently. This required changes not only to the immediate system, but also in its interaction with the other departments from whom I received my work and to whom I sent the end results. The assistant supervisor was showing a great deal of satisfaction in having this corner of his work operating so smoothly, and consequently, much more speedily. Now, even as the year end approached making it so much more expedient to have all accounts up to date, there was no need to bring in extra help. I too was pleased with the accomplishment. It gave me a sense of satisfaction. I felt it on the inside, but I dared not show it."

Dr. Eldren broke into the narration of the story, "there is nothing wrong with showing your feelings, Donna. Why hide them?"

Donna paused. She was stuck for words for a moment. Then she responded, with a pronounced emphasis on being courteous, to Dr. Eldren. "Maybe we can discuss that further after I've finished my story, Dr. Eldren?"

Collin, sensing her embarrassment of the moment, came to the rescue again. "You've told us the rosy side Donna. The other side is yet to come, is it not?"

"Yes Collin, that is right," Donna replied.

"Experienced again, eh, Collin!" quipped Leo.

There was a chuckle throughout the group that put everyone at ease once more.

Collin would now alleviate Donna's embarrassment by purposely steering the conversation into focus on year two of Donna's industrial life, and thereby away from an analysis of

Donna's hiding of her feelings. "Year one was a success, Donna. I'm awfully anxious to hear more about the end results of year two," he remarked.

"Yea," quipped Leo. "It's like watching a mystery unfold. I can hardly wait for the next episode."

Donna was relieved, and pleased to continue with her story. "First, let me say again that during this year two I accomplished a great deal in streamlining the processes of my section. In doing this I worked very, very hard, with my 'nose to the grind-stone', as the saying goes, almost continually. But as the year drew near to an end, the system was running so smoothly that I could take things a little easier —that is reduce my effort to what I would consider to be a normal and reasonable pace.

"It was a great relief to be able to do this, as I had worn myself down quite a bit during the year with the continual concentration, changing this, eliminating that, and adding something else. It had been heavy going. There was much relief and joy for me at the end of the financial year when the annual department audits proved my renovated system to be quite efficient. Now, I thought, I wouldn't have to work any harder than those around me.

"To add to my relief and joy, one day the general manager stopped by my desk and congratulated me on my work. He had heard from other departments, he said. Payments and transfers were able to be credited punctually, adding immensely to the efficiency of these departments. He encouraged me to keep up the good work.

"He left my desk and went to the supervisor's office. As he stood there besides the supervisor's desk talking, they both looked out at me periodically. I could tell they were talking about me. I could also tell that pleasant things were being said, at least on the general manager's part, since he was smiling and looked pleased.

"My relief and joy were short-lived. One day, before I was very long into year three, the assistant supervisor came by and informed me that since I had had plenty of time to learn and become familiar with my job, the supervisor would now expect me to also do some work in the next section to mine. This entailed helping to collect overdue accounts. The collections section was, in a vague manner, connected to mine in that once the accounts were collected, they were handed over to me for recording and relevant distribution to proper departments. But it was a different type of work altogether than that of my section. It looked as though I was to become a 'jack-of-all-trades. I was deeply let down by the request, but in time became reconciled to it and thought, well maybe this is another stepping stone — maybe, but I had misgivings about the matter.

"Nevertheless, I went into the work in this new section as energetically as I had during the past year in what I will call my own section. In this collections section there were four other people working. Collecting overdue accounts was part of the work and obviously a time consuming task. However, I soon formed a favorable opinion of the system used there. The work was usually running a little behind, but occasionally the employees would work overtime in keeping the related paperwork up to date. This would leave them free during regular hours to do work that could be done only during business hours, such as contacting other business establishments.

"There were two girls of average efficiency in the new section. Then there were two who usually dragged behind, often coming in late, taking time for gossip and for personal telephone calls, and extra time for coffee breaks. But the two efficient ones kept the system rolling along at a satisfactory pace, somehow motivating or prodding the other two along with them, thereby keeping the whole process moving.

"I soon became friends with the two efficient girls, or young women I should say. They were both in their thirties. The other two, approximately the same age resented me. As annoying as that was at times I tried not to let it cause me any great concern. I enjoyed my job, and contrary to their attitudes continued with my usual punctuality, decorum and hard work. The two efficient girls were pleased with this and in some instances endeavored to copy my ways of working, dressing, being punctual and pleasant.

"As was usual by now, and almost expected by the group

members, Collin interjected with a question: "were you able to keep up on the work in your own section while working part time in the other section Donna?"

"Well, therein lies the crux of the matter, or at least one of them, Collin. At first I obligingly speeded up the work in my section so that I could spend time in the other section. I was working very hard again now. As weeks went on, eventually things got turned around. On direction from the supervisor through the assistant supervisor to me, I was now to spend time 'as needed' in the collections section, doing the work in my own section as time permitted after that. The outcome of this was that I was eliminating the need for overtime in the collections section and practically killing myself to keep up the work in my own section. I did this for a while until I realized what I was doing to myself, and what was being done to me. Then I reduced my effort to a pace which allowed me to survive. The result was, work in my own section went behind, thus requiring overtime on my part to keep it up."

The group members looked around at one another in silence, then still in silence looked to Donna, astounded, and eager for her to continue.

"If there can be two cruxes to a matter," continued Donna, "Then the second one happened a few months later. I just told you the first one. I had now been employed there for nearly three years. In all that time I had not been late for work any morning. In fact I was usually the one who arrived early, turned on the lights and got things humming in the department.

"One morning I finally was late. It was a very wet morning. It had rained heavily all night and it was still raining in the morning. As I drove to work in this rain I had not noticed that a section of the street ahead of me was flooded up to sidewalk level. I drove into the flooded section at a good city speed for that kind of weather. Water splashed up over the vital parts of my car engine and it stalled, leaving me sitting there in my car surrounded by water. I tried to restart the engine, but to no avail. Before long another car stopped slowly beside me. The driver asked if he would get help for me from a service station a half a mile or so down the street. I said, 'yes please.'

"About fifteen minutes later a tow truck arrived. The driver drove up behind me and pushed my car out of the water to a higher elevation in the road. Then he explained to me that with my car just sitting there with a warm engine, it has probably dried out some on its own. However he would check and use some ignition spray to be sure. After drying and spraying the ignition parts, the car, with some sputtering started up. Soon it dried completely and was running smoothly. But I was now to arrive at work fifteen minutes late, whereas I was usually fifteen minutes early."

"As I walked in through the department with my raincoat still on, I met, part way, one of the more friendly girls from the collections section. She was surprised to see me late. 'What happened to you?' she asked in a loud whisper of disbelief. I was explaining to her the difficulty I had on the flooded street, when the supervisor, who usually kept his distance from me and communicated to me through the assistant supervisor, now came charging towards me. He roared like a lion, "Don't you know we start work here at 8:00!"

"But sir," I replied quietly, trying to calm the situation, "I had trouble with my car on a flooded street."

"You're not on a flooded street now," he snapped, "you're just standing there talking."

"What could I say," said Donna as she threw up her hand to the support group. "I took off my coat and went to work, with no time even to properly wipe the rain off my face. There was a deep silence around the department as everyone worked away. Eventually the girl to whom I had paused to speak on my way in, had work to do near where I was working. She couldn't get over what had happened. "He turned on you for being late," she said, "you, you of all people. I don't understand. Do you?"

"Well, yes I do, sort of, as much as something like that can be understood," I replied. "But we'd better not talk now till this thing cools down."

"Okay," she said, and moved away.

Donna's face was flushed as she related this story to the group.

Obviously it had been a traumatic experience for her. She was now reliving the event, and it hurt badly. In one way it would have been easier on Donna's feelings if the session for that evening had ended there. However, although it had been an intense session it had not been a long one. "It is so painful to recall all this," said Donna. "I'd just like to end the session right now, but I know it will be just as painful next week."

"Perhaps, Donna," Collin said, "if we pursue this discussion to completion this evening you will not have to relive it again next week, nor would it be heavy on your mind during the week. Would this be too hard on you this evening?"

Then without waiting for an answer, Collin turned to Dr. Eldren, "what do you think, doctor?"

Dr. Eldren responded, "my observation is that this was a very profound and disturbing experience in Donna's life. Further discussion may relieve some of the obvious trauma. So I think it would be beneficial, not only to the group but to Donna as well if we proceed with it further while the matter is open. Then she can put it behind her again to some degree and hopefully with some resulting relief of pain.

"Yes," replied Collin, "I agree. Its been my experience that when such profound experiences are left dangling in mid air so to speak for a period of time, it leaves the person in a mental turmoil for that period, in this case it would be a whole week."

"Would you like a five minute break, Donna, as we did for Gilda?" asked Dr. Eldren.

She agreed, and after the brief period of relaxation said she was able to recollect her thoughts and continue.

"It doesn't hurt beyond my endurance," she said, "and I would prefer to discuss it more fully now rather than have it dangling all week, as Collin said, and have my mind in a turmoil until next group session."

"Good," said Dr. Eldren.

"May I question you more, Donna?" asked Collin, eagerly.

"Sure, go right ahead," replied Donna.

Collin asked, "Donna, did that supervisor who chastised you

for being late ever chastise other employees in the same manner. Was this a regular way with him?"

"Not to my knowledge," said Donna. "In all the time I was in his department, I never saw nor heard of it happening to anyone else."

"Were there other people late at times," asked Collin further.

"Oh yes, lots of them," said Donna, now becoming more calm and settled, as she began to realize she had in Collin a friend who understood.

"Were there some who were late often, perhaps habitually late," Collin pressed on.

"Sure there were, Collin," Donna replied. "One of the girls in the collections section, one of the draggers, I call her, she came in late nearly every morning. Not only that, after she did come in and make an appearance at her desk, she would leave again for the washroom where she would spend ten or fifteen minutes putting on her make up and fixing her hair, things she should have done at home."

"And to your knowledge nothing was ever said to her?"

"That is so."

"What kind of girl was she, her character I mean."

"To put it bluntly, she was coarse and tough, sometimes getting impatient with her work and using bad language to describe it. She often complained about other employees behind their backs, running them down, supervisors and all. At times when a supervisor or other employee would complain about her work, she would lash back at them with tough defensive talk about the faulty system, thereby putting an end to their complaints. Does that give you some idea, Collin?"

"Indeed it does," replied Collin. "Were there others of her type in the department?"

"Several," said Donna, "but she was the worst, I would say."

Collin's questions became more crucial to the point he wished to bring out.

"Was the supervisor afraid of that tough girl and the others like her?"

"Yes, yes indeed, replied Donna, breaking into a smile of relief. "That's it Collin, he was afraid of them. Come to think of it, I heard her tell him off one day when he questioned her about something pertaining to her work, and he walked away like a beaten man."

"Coward!" remarked Leo boisterously and contemptuously.

"Yes, Leo, a coward all right, but more, a bully also. Bullies are always cowards," added Collin as he turned to Donna again. "The supervisor was afraid of those other girls, but he lashed into you for being late. It may seem this was because he was not afraid of you. But there was more than that churning up in this man.

"Yes," replied Donna, "I think you are right, much more."

"Do you care to put it into words?" asked Collin.

"I'm not so good at that especially on the spur of the moment," she replied. "Would you help by expressing your views on the matter?"

"Okay," said Collin. "The way I see it is: this man hated you because you were too good for him. He didn't know how to look up to and respect someone he perceived to be a cut above himself. He worked you hard as if that was expected of you in *his* office; and as if you wouldn't know the difference that you were being overworked. It is another mind-game such people play on people like us. If you had cracked up or quit because of this overwork, he would be able to say you weren't up to the job. He would make himself believe that, and hopefully other people too. Your enemies there, the draggers and so on, would be only too glad to believe it.

"This man hated you because he was envious of you. The more you beat him to his game, the more his hatred was stirred. Sooner or later, such people, when they can't stand any more of your fine character and exceptional abilities, explode at you in some way. Or, they may take some other rash retaliation in return for what they perceive you are doing to them just by being what you are, a fine, gifted person.

"This man's envy could have been stirred for various other reasons. Maybe he could see in you what he would like to see in his wife or his daughter, or his mother for that matter. He may have been deflated because he himself couldn't get as much work out of the other employees under his supervision as you were able to do. Either way, he was envious of you and hated you surely for unintentionally deflating his ego. It was his problem, not yours."

"That sounds like the way I would put it if I could have," responded Donna. "Thanks for your help."

A noticeable look of relief came over Donna. She expressed gratitude to the group that the supervisor who had caused a trauma in her life was, to her present frame of mind, now out in the open and exposed for what he was. At last some others, the group members, understood in a friendly, supportive manner.

There was a momentary silence, as if the members were waiting for a direction by which to proceed.

Collin broke the silence. "Donna, it may seem relentless of me to ask more of you at this time, but I am anxious to know how things went for you generally during the remainder of your time with that corporation."

"All right, Collin," responded Donna, "I think in the time that is left this evening I can give you an overall picture of the remainder of my final year with that corporation." Then, as if to release her long time pent-up feelings some more, she interjected, "first let me say further, you have been a great help this evening in expressing for me what I find difficult to put into words, mostly because of the trauma involved. And it makes a tremendous difference to talk to a group of people who have had similar experiences as I am sure you all have had; people who know the world out there and who can truly and realistically empathize. To talk about such things to someone who doesn't know or care what it is all about has a negative effect on a person to say the least.

Collin was curious. "Have you tried previously to talk to someone about your experiences?" he asked. Donna blushed slightly as she cast a glance at Dr. Eldren, then back to Collin.

"Yes, Collin," she said, "sometime after the shaking experience with the supervisor, and as tension continued to grow there in the office, I went to talk to my clergyman about it one evening. I told him I was under a great deal of tension because of conditions at my place of employment. He made arrangements for me to see a therapist, which I did and which after a few sessions I discontinued."

Collin's curiosity was aroused some more. "May I ask, Donna, why you discontinued with the therapist?"

"Well Collin," she replied, "with all due respect, it was really futile. There was very little response except once in a while a brick came tumbling down from the wall, knocking me on the head. I was having enough bricks tumble on me at work."

Some group members were puzzled at Donna's statement. But Gilda Emerson smiled a broad smile of acknowledgment of familiarity.

"Would you clarify that statement for us Donna, please," she asked.

"Yes Gilda," replied Donna, "what I mean is I talked and talked and talked. As I said, there was little response except that once in a while when I would relate to him a particularly upsetting experience he would say, 'and that bothers you does it?' or, later he started saying something to the effect, 'well why are you working there if it bothers you like that?'; and later still, 'well why are you working in a place like that?' I found it to be deflating to say the least. So I stopped seeing him.

"The therapist had no idea or understanding of the world in which I had to live. Even if he had, I think the approach towards which he was heading me was just futile. It seems he was going to impress upon me that I was too sensitive, and that he was going to help me change my mind-set so that I could take all that the obnoxious people threw at me without it bothering me, or that if it did, then I should move elsewhere.

"When the hatred and hostility are so intense, and your job, your working credibility and capacity, and your personality are being destroyed, how can you not let it bother you. No person is that insensitive. How can you go somewhere else, when you know chances are it will be just about the same there? And why should I have to forfeit a good employment opportunity with future promise just because some obnoxious persons can't stand to have me around?" said Donna with disgust.

"Can't stand to have you around because you are too good for them," emphasized Collin.

Donna nodded in agreement.

"It is a fact everything is stacked in their favor and to our detriment," Collin commented further, "and psychology is keeping it that way and supporting it. Psychology has done nothing to discover and expose the raw side of adult life. They only try to soothe the pain of it for us. That may help us sometimes, and only sometimes, to survive after a fashion, but it does nothing to help us live life fully as we ought to be able to do."

"I'll say amen to that," added Gilda vibrantly, "your therapist was sending you in a similar direction my psychiatrist was sending me. I'm mighty glad I got out of hospital and away from him."

Dr. Eldren shuffled uncomfortably in his chair.

Collin thought to himself, *we'd better get off this track quickly, and onto another. Sometime later, much later, we will somehow have to get back on this track again. I myself will want to express some very strong concerns in this regard. But for heavens sake let's get off it now until a more appropriate time.*

"Donna," Collin shot quickly and emphatically, "your point is well taken by me. It is very understandable, yours too Gilda. But now I wonder can we have Donna wind up her story as she had planned in the time that is left this evening?"

Gilda, having sensed Dr. Eldren's uneasiness, caught on quickly.

"Yes," said Gilda, "I think it would be a relief for Donna to get through with her story this evening. I'll try not to interrupt again."

"Well," said Donna, "to describe my later experiences briefly, it was a time of almost continuous tension. I was working hard at two jobs. From a distance, the supervisor kept an almost continuous eye on me. For the remainder of my time there, I had to be near perfect to avoid criticism. I was fast becoming high strung and a nervous wreck. By being so nearly perfect, I was able to protect myself from any open and severe criticism. I never left him room for complaint, although I could sense he was almost continually looking for an opening to get at me. But his attitude towards me was negative from that time on. Hard looks came my way often. There was never a cheerful word or greeting when, on occasion, I was in his close vicinity. From time to time, through the assistant supervisor, and never directly, he made inquiry concerning my work, asking why was so much overtime necessary in my section. Why could I not spend more time in the collections section? Was I spending too much time away from my desk during the day? The pressure was really on. I didn't feel free even about going to the washroom any more, although I did when necessary. But even that was a nerve wracking experience. And the most hurting part of it all was that others were just as free as they pleased to be. Most of them were doing a normal day's work with time out for chatting, and coffee, etc. etc, a reasonable touch of those things that keep a person human as you work through the routines and intricacies of commerce and industry. Some others of them were doing less than a good day's work. None of them were being disciplined."

"I began to feel very strongly and much to my disappointment that I wouldn't be able to stay on working with this corporation. However, there was one thing I could try. I could perhaps appeal to the general manager. It would take nerve. It would take tactful explanation, and certainly it would be a long shot. The supervisor had been with the corporation for a long time. So had the general manager. They were long time business associates. I would be sticking my neck out, but I had nothing to lose. I just couldn't stay on under present circumstances."

"I watched for an appropriate opportunity. One day when the general manager was circulating through our department, as he occasionally did all departments, I maneuvered myself to be in his pathway. Being in a jolly mood he greeted me cheerfully. I asked if I could speak to him for a minute about a personal concern.

"'Sure,' he replied, 'what's on your mind?'

"'Well,' I said, 'I have tried very hard since I've been working here to do my work faithfully and well. My own summation of my efforts in this regard is that my work is efficient, if I may say so myself. However, the department supervisor seems to be down on me. I get the impression that he doesn't like me. I am under a great deal of unnecessary pressure here.'

"'Oh come now, Miss Coyne,' he responded, as he patted me cheerfully on the upper arm, 'your supervisor has been with this corporation for a long time. He has gotten more work done for us over the years, than anyone else I know. You'll get to know, in time, that he's a good sort. Don't worry about a thing, Miss Coyne.' He went cheerfully on his way. My problem hadn't reached through to him to any depth. As capable a manager as he was, he was apparently unable to recognize my particular problem. My hope for survival in that corporation was diminished greatly in one brief conversation.

"In the weeks that followed, I made a brave effort to keep up and keep going. Occasionally, an added quandary would creep in on my mind. I would wonder if the general manager told the supervisor of my complaint against him, and if so would he be vindictive, or, would he improve his attitude towards me?

"As the weeks went by, I observed no change in the supervisor's attitude towards me. I came to the conclusion then that the complaint had not gone further than the general manager, and also that with him it was just a frivolous matter that warranted no further attention.

"As disappointed as I now was, I decided to make a good stand, and hope that something would change. But nothing did. I surmised that, yes, I could stay on there and become hard as iron, insensitive and consequently characterless, if I wished to choose that way. But I decided against it. Like Gilda in her experience, I believe I am entitled to be free to be the pleasant person I really am, and prefer to be. Therefore I would leave this place and search for fulfillment elsewhere. I put in a month's notice of leaving.

"About a week or so after my resignation became effective and all my ties were broken with the corporation, I received a phone call at home one evening. It was the supervisor of my first year department, as I have called it. 'Donna,' she said in earnest tones on the telephone, 'I heard that you have left our corporation. I'm very sorry that it became necessary for you to do so, but I don't want you to feel too badly. Similar has happened previously. Good people like yourself just don't get past that supervisor. I have promoted others to his department, but for people like you it becomes the end of the line. I am very sorry indeed that lovely people like yourself have to be treated so. And since I am the one who has to promote such people as you into such a booby-trap predicament, I too am leaving the corporation.'

"'Wait a minute,' I frantically replied to her, 'it isn't your wrong doing. You don't have to take the blame for what happened to me. You did well by me. You gave me a promotion that I welcomed and looked forward to. What happened afterwards wasn't your fault.'

"'No,' the first year supervisor replied. 'It isn't that I shoulder the blame for what has happened, neither in your case nor that of others preceding you, Donna; rather, it's the futility of the matter. I train and promote top quality employees only to have them turned away later. You see, Donna, it's a dead-end for me too. I've been contemplating for some time now, whether to look for a position elsewhere. I've come to the conclusion that it's past time I did.'

"'I think I understand,' was my more positive response. 'I'd like to thank you for calling me and for all your kindness to me in the past,' I said, 'I really did have a valuable experience in your department you know.'

"'Good,' replied the supervisor. 'I hope you will have every opportunity to put it to better use in the future, and, lets keep in touch,' she continued, as she gave me her phone number and address. 'I would like to keep contact with you and to hear of what you will be doing in the future.'

"'Great,' I agreed. So a lasting friendship was formed."

Collin was quick to say, "this is another of many examples I could give of businesses being deprived of their better employees by obnoxious people in their midst, and how the wayward ones manage to stay in there. The matter is practically unrecognized." Then he continued, "One question, Donna. What was the assistant supervisor's place and attitude through all this?"

"He was young, Collin, a whiz at his work, but with very little understanding of people and their behavior. To him, the second year supervisor was a man who knew his work but who simply got into a bad mood once in a while. I doubt if he ever paused to think it through more deeply than that."

As if to spare Donna from more grueling questions after so long and arduous a session, Leo came to her rescue with what he meant to be the conclusion of the story in a sentence.

"And now Donna works in her father's business where there is both challenge, and appreciation for her response to it, and where she can be the pleasant person she really is meant to be."

*Yes, Yes indeed,* pondered Collin to himself. *There is a lot to be said for being secure and comfortable in a family business. But also to be in business brings its own problems, and that is something else again. The independence of owning one's own business does offer a measure of security to people such as us, provided we get wise to the obnoxious ones in that sphere as well, and can stay afloat in the learning process long enough to master the art of survival and success. This area of life rings a familiar bell too, and would make for meaningful discussion. But Donna has had enough. It isn't easy reliving the unpleasant past, and also the evening is about gone. Brett Culver could best tell us about being in business for oneself.*

"Brett," said Collin, aloud. "You are in business for yourself. May I suggest you tell your story next session; what led you to where you are, and how you find things on the road of independence."

Brett smiled slightly as he shook his head. "Okay with me, Collin, but I warn Leo and any others who may have a rosy conception of life for people like *us* in business for oneself, that I am not going bald without reason!"

There was laughter, and the group session adjourned in a relaxed mood, as the members gathered around Donna to express appreciation for her contribution to the support group. It was obvious they all were by now more at ease with each other and most of the time with Dr. Eldren. This would be of great help in their future story telling and analysis.

Dr. Eldren left for another appointment. The group members decided to proceed to The Corner Coffee Shop for refreshments and relaxation. Brett Culver asked to be excused from that. He and his wife had work to do at home pertaining to the next day's operation of their family business.

## Chapter Five

Another week had slipped by, and Collin Seldon once again approached Quilibet University to participate in the support group. His wife walked with him this time as he proceeded towards the now familiar doors of the Arts building from the parking lot down the street. It wasn't easy on the mind of a man in late middle age to have thoughts of a difficult, sometimes torturous past revived each week by listening to the experiences of others.

He appreciated the words of St. Paul the Apostle, ".......forgetting what lies behind and straining forward to what lies ahead, I press on toward the goal..." (Philippians 3:13-14 R.S.V). There certainly were times to forget the past. Collin had done so many times in order to survive. But now in this support group, it was a time to remember. As stressful, disturbing and pre-occupying as it might be for all concerned, here was a time to remember in order to help someone else; in order to help each other. Some good would come of it surely, for the younger ones at least. Collin, at his age, was reconciled to his lot in life. But these others in the group, they are still on the edge of things, young and looking for an opportunity to break into life and find fulfillment. Yes, there is a time to forget, but this is a time to remember.

It is a dangerous game to say the least. One of the mind-games posing the most danger to fine, but besieged people, is when the players of the games try to keep us guessing for answers and solutions when there often is nothing tangible to base our ponderings on. They would love to wear us out. Over the years, however, Collin had played along with their games sufficient to figure them out, and after protecting himself from them as much as possible, just turned it off and shut it out of his mind. Now though, it was necessary to have it on his mind more than usual in order to make something worthwhile out of the support group's project.

So to help alleviate the after effects of the strain of remembering, Collin brought his wife along. They had planned that she would wait for him in the library, an entrance to which was located on the first floor of the Arts building, from where an enclosed ramp type passageway had been built to the library building next door.

Collin accompanied his wife to the library where she would browse through books while the group was in session. Afterwards she would do the driving for the evening while Collin relaxed beside her. Instead of going directly home he would from now on, at times after a group session, go out somewhere with his wife for the remainder of the evening. At times she would accompany him to the coffee shop with the others; or they would seek diversion at a pleasant restaurant, a drive by the lake on a moonlight night, a suitable movie, anything enjoyable and soothing to put the mind at rest before bedtime. Collin's wife had always done things like this for him. They had continually been very close. She understood, for not only had she been through much with Collin, but she too was the same kind of person, one of *us*.

So Collin left his wife there in the library and headed for Room 405. No sooner had he started out, than his mind began to toss around the happenings of the last session. It had been obvious that remembering had been strenuous, though beneficial for Donna Coyne. What had been a burdensome experience bearing heavily in the back of her mind was now a burden shared with, and understood by others. And although this is not the same as something lurking in the sub-conscious, it does have a similar, though often heavier effect. A burden in the subconscious may have an unconscious effect on the person; but to be conscious of a burden is to be conscious also of its effect. Therefore it can be all the more heavy to carry. There are often times when we cannot eliminate such burdens. Nevertheless, a burden shared is usually a burden lightened, when it is shared with friends.

There were things Collin would like to discuss with Donna concerning her story. One thing in particular at this time was the pros and cons of her move into the family business. Was it withdrawal into a cocoon, there being assured of survival, but forfeiting the right to be free to fly as a butterfly. No, I hardly think that of Donna Coyne. Here she is studying at University now.

Then again, a family business, because it may bring Donna a measure of security a person such as she wouldn't have at the corporation, by no means indicates that it is short of challenges, troubles, and the opportunity for fulfillment. On the contrary, a family business is one of the greatest avenues there is to personal growth and a sense of accomplishment in life. Collin himself had experienced that.

Or again, perhaps this was a tactical withdrawal by Donna in order to do better in some future advancement. Generals of armies have often withdrawn to regroup their forces only to make a new approach under a new plan of attack altogether. This perhaps is Donna's design, a wise maneuver rather than withdrawal.

Collin decided against questioning Donna any further now. She had been through enough for the present. Anyway his questions would be answered in time as the group members got to know each other better. Already, Donna was showing evidence of being a person game for life.

As meeting time approached, enthusiasm was evident as usual. All the group members were present. Dr. Eldren, the enabler of the group, was as vibrant over it as were those seeking help through this unusual, experimental gathering. His manner and interest showed no lack of enthusiasm. He was an aged and much experienced psychiatrist, yet this event in his career seemed to be an adventure which was pushing back his horizon. He truly was being caught up in it.

As the group members still stood around chatting before the formal session began, Dr. Eldren approached Collin Seldon and Owen Winslow who had been talking together.

"I'm really pleased with the way things are shaping in the group," said the doctor. "I do believe we are isolating a rather peculiar fact of life that has never been really brought out in the open sufficiently to explore it and enable people to grasp its significance and deal with its impact on persons and society.

Owen spoke in response. "Personally I am deriving a great deal of benefit from simply hearing the stories of people who have had similar experiences as I. Perhaps after we have all shared our stories you as a psychiatrist can shed more light upon our problems for us."

"I think I can help some," replied Dr. Eldren, "but since this is turning out to be such an unconventional case in the history of my experience, I rather believe we will have to help each other." Then, as if losing himself in his own thoughts for a moment, he added slowly and in a low voice, "where the matter goes from this room when we are finished with it, I am not sure yet, but — but," he dallied, then bringing himself and his thoughts back to the present, he turned to Collin, "would you like to see things proceed as is, or do you see some other course we might take?"

Collin replied, "All is well as is sir. Specifically I would like to hear Brett Culver's story this evening. When he is finished, I would suggest we hear Owen Winslow's experiences. After that I would be interested in hearing from Albin Anders. Albin is young, but with the understanding I believe he is deriving from the other stories, he will certainly be able to tell of his experiences very well."

"And what about you Collin?" Dr. Eldren caught him up quickly as though eager to have him included. "Can you help us help each other?"

"I certainly can help to bring a measure of understanding to these matters, doctor, but I assure you, if you view us and our cases as unconventional now, you will view them that way much more so when I am through."

Dr. Eldren smiled at Collin. "I think we can take that in this group. In fact, I would say its what we ought to expect — unconventional explanations for unconventional problems. We will hear you out." Then smiling to Owen, he asked, "Okay. Owen?"

"Seems to me, doctor, that it's just what we've been looking for. I'm all for it!"

Good!" replied Dr. Eldren, his vibrancy becoming obvious as he turned to Collin again and earnestly requested, "But you will tell us your story also, won't you Collin?"

Collin paused, as his eyes moved about, revealing a mind in

gear. Then he replied slowly, thinking as he spoke, "We are becoming more relaxed with each other and with you, Dr. Eldren. By the time we get to my story we will have delved into analysis, and the whys and wherefores enough to make my story more believable. Then, when all that is said and done, and we have a fair understanding of our problem, hopefully we can find ways to help each other, and people like us."

Owen was pleased. "It was a providential meeting the evening I met you in that classroom, Collin," he remarked. "I knew you could help us."

Collin shook his head. "Don't get your hopes too high. Only so much can be done under the circumstances of a problem mostly unexplored in society as a whole. But I think I can be of some help. However," he continued in a now lighter manner, "you are one of the older and better educated members of this group. Much will be expected of you also, Owen."

Owen smiled and responded with a remark that befitted two clergy people talking to each other, "Every one to whom much is given, of him will much be required; (Luke 12:48. R.S.V.) is that it, Collin?"

"Indeed," came Collin's reply, "there are people to be helped. Albin Anders is only one example. He needs our help badly. We just have to help him somehow!"

As Dr. Eldren looked at his watch he remarked, "we have a good thing going here." Then he called the group into session.

Brett Culver began his story with a brief verbal profile of himself and his family. He was a quiet unassuming type and people generally would not associate such a modest and seemingly reserved person with such business accomplishments as he was about to reveal in the telling of his experiences.

"I am in my early thirties," he stated. "For some time I have been the owner and manager of a chain of gas stations and automatic car washes spread over a wide territory. More recently I have become involved in a manufacturing or more accurately, a re-manufacturing business as well. My growing business interests account for my being enrolled in an evening course in business administration here at Quilibet University, and consequently my presence in this group. So you see it is easy for me to tell you in a few sentences how I came to be with you here in the group. But if you were to ask me how I arrived where I am in the business world, that would not be so easy a matter. Perhaps I can more accurately reveal that as I proceed with the story of my life's experiences as a member of what now seems to be known to those present as the *us* group."

There were chuckles throughout the group.

"You really have joined the club," remarked Owen.

"Yes, I've truly joined your club, Owen, with the hope that people like us can somehow find a better way," responded Brett.

Leo Aidan interjected admiringly, "seems to me that you have, at least for yourself, found a better way already, Brett. Your apparent accomplishments in business certainly indicate success against the odds."

"It may seem so, Leo," said Brett, "and I suppose in a sense I have succeeded, but in another sense I am a misplaced person."

"Oh," said Leo, puzzled.

Collin sought to relieve Leo's perplexity. "Do you mean by a misplaced person, Brett, that you originally intended to enter into some other occupation in life, but somehow circumstances put you into the business you are in now?"

"Yes, that's it, Collin, as you will see for yourself as I tell my story," answered Brett.

Leo's amazement was aroused again. He cracked a smile and quickly twisted his head in a gesture of wonder towards Collin. Then to Brett, "I can't wait to hear this one."

His action and remark instilled expectancy into the minds of all the members. Interest was running high in this unconventional group.

Brett was now at ease among his friends. As he prepared to pursue his story, the lines of strain left his forehead, and the furrow disappeared from his brow. Now a bright, wide eyed facial expression revealed the kind of person good people take to very quickly, and a certain type of bad people hate vehemently.

As Brett had mentioned at the end of last session, he was losing his hair. It was thinning back from the temples on either side, the centre part remaining a little thicker, but showing some thinning there also, even though it was combed high and to one side. Offsetting this scarcity of hair on top, was well groomed, comparatively thick hair on the sides, combed back in a sweeping manner to meet the equally thick hair of the back in a very loosely and irregularly formed duck tail. This black hair was augmented by a well shaven, yet shadowy facial beard area, the darkness of which was highlighted all the more by a white complexion. Below his slightly high forehead were two wide open innocent looking eyes, then a majestic, chiseled shaped nose, beneath which were larger than average lips that often and easily broke into a relaxed looking uncontrolled smile. All of this together with a body that was only a little less than average height, yet well within a satisfactory weight for his size, and despite the hair shortage, gave Brett the appearance of a person with appeal to well cultured people. The clothes he wore, although inexpensive were an indication that he had good taste. Yes, Brett was a fine looking person who stood out among others in public. It had already become evident to the group members that he was of fine character as well.

Having known Brett now for some weeks, the group members could not help but surmise he had been brought up on the better side of life, that is, with good grooming, culture and manners; also with appreciation for the good things of this world. His story was soon to confirm this.

"My father," he began, "was a retail business manager employed by a large corporation with department stores across the country. He had a solid reputation with his employer, so much so that he could pretty well ask to be placed where he wanted to be and expect to have his request met whenever it was possible for the corporation to conveniently do so. So we moved several times during my school years. I mention this now and ask you to remember the fact because it will be of some significance in my story.

"My father was a good man," continued Brett, "and my mother a genuine woman. I was their only child. I loved them both, and they loved me and did extremely well for me without spoiling me, contrary to what some people automatically expect with an only child. Our family ties were close. Small family though we were, we fulfilled each others needs in that regard. This aspect of life was invaluable to me as I faced the kind of world that lay in store for the kind of person I was. I learned very early in life what it was like to be one of *us*.

"One other aspect of life that was and is indispensible to me is my religious faith. That I could not have survived without either, nor could I now. I was brought up in this faith and in the Christian Church. My father and mother were ardent Christians, active in both church and community affairs, choosing and giving priority to those activities they considered to be most helpful to other people, particularly underprivileged people in various areas of life, including the sphere in which you and I frequently find ourselves."

"We were living in a large city when I went to kindergarten. Although I had attended a nursery school mornings for a year before that, as far as I know it is of no special significance. To my knowledge things went well for me there, and I must have benefitted from it. But it was in my year of Kindergarten that I learned my first hard lesson of life. I remember it well to this day. It started me on the road to awareness early in life.

"My kindergarten class was double the usual class size, but we had two teachers who worked together as co-teachers of the class. I soon found out that one of these teachers liked me immensely. The other hated me just as intensely. At the time I didn't understand why she hated me, or for that matter why the other teacher liked me. But, as young as I was, I did become fully aware of my circumstance, and learned in a childish way to cope with it, simply by associating myself more with the teacher who liked me and who treated me with respect, and, by avoiding as much as possible the teacher who hated me. Regardless of this effort of mine, she was able to put me down quite often; that is, to ridicule me in front of the class at every opportunity, to trip me up on an answer whenever possible, to enlarge the least bit of misbehavior into a major infraction of rules. If I had had this one teacher alone in my kindergarten year, I may have been damaged for life."

Collin remarked, "Ah-h, Brett is a person who already knows the score. Indeed, he really could have, and probably would have been ruined or badly affected for life had it not been for the fact that he had one favorable teacher present that year."

Brett continued, "The kindergarten teacher who was good to me made enough of a favorable impression to tide me through the year. In various ways she assured me that I was a good and likable child. She encouraged me in my work and into good behavior. She included me with the other children in her general comments about favorable class and individual accomplishments. She made me feel a part of the whole, whereas the other teacher was more inclined to isolate me as an unsatisfactory element in the class."

"For clarification purposes, Brett," asked Collin, "were you in any way an unsatisfactory element in the class? I mean was your work shabbily done, or your behavior terribly bad?"

"Oh no," replied Brett, "my work was among the best in the class, and my report card showed it to be so, for which I am thankful to the good teacher. As for my behavior, I was really a child who made a very concerted effort to be included among the well behaved. It was my nature to do so. I remember that many times I tried to win the liking of the obnoxious kindergarten teacher by behaving well, but to no avail. Of course, like any child, I was a bit mischievous occasionally and went the wrong way once in a while, but my infractions, though minor, were treated as major by the teacher who didn't like me."

"So the good teacher, as we call her, really did stand up for you, Brett?" Collin asked again.

"Yes Collin," said Brett, "she really knew how to stand her ground in a tactful way. I wish there were more like her."

"And Brett," Collin continued to question, "what is your opinion as an adult, as to why the crummy teacher disliked you?

"That is easy to answer now," replied Brett. "I know from reflecting on the friendly teacher's attitude, and that of later teachers and other acquaintances that I was a very nice and likeable sort of boy. Maybe I stood out better than a son or brother of hers, or something like that. She was envious of me."

"Thank you Brett," said Collin. "I would say you are one hundred percent correct. No more questions for now."

Leo Aidan interjected with his wit, "Man, what a judicial inquiry this would make. My father would be pleased to be on the bench for this one."

Hearty laughter rang out.

Brett continued with his story, "so as I was saying at the beginning, I learned early in life, in kindergarten, to discern the good ones from the obnoxious ones and to deal with them. I learned from the good kindergarten teacher that there are good people in this world, and that good people liked me because they believed I too was a good person. This experience at so young an age gave me a healthy self-esteem for life. This self-esteem is still with me. Had I only the obnoxious teacher in kindergarten, I can see how, at that young age, my self-esteem may well have been shattered for life, and other damages done to my mind-set as well."

Albin interrupted, much to everyone's delight, "Brett, when it is my turn to relate my story, would you remind me please of what you just said concerning your self-esteem and mind-set. It will be very helpful to me in explaining my situation. In fact it is a great help to me in my own mind now."

"Will do," replied Brett, exuberantly, "will do, Albin. I think I see what you are getting at. You're going to do all right, I'm sure."

Collin added, "The issue of the presence of, or lack of self-esteem in our lives is a major issue for us of this group. We should bear that in mind at all times."

"I agree," said Brett, and continued. "So after coming out on the top side in kindergarten, I had, with the exception of grade two, good school years up to and including grade five. My grade one teacher was good to me, as she was to everyone else. This confirmed my self-esteem and my confidence and belief in good people and the good side of life. Scholastically I was among the top ones. I grew in other ways too becoming an all around child, mixing well and participating in all satisfactory activities that opened to me.

"Although this grade one year at school of which I am speaking now, stands out in my memory as a wonderful year, the event of that year that is most outstanding is not related to school at all. One of the executives from my father's corporation, together with his wife, used to visit us at our home from time to time. It seemed he paid more attention to me as each visit went by, getting to know me, and taking a liking to me. One summer evening such a visit was taking place on the patio in our back garden. I had been playing with a couple of my friends within view of my parents and the visitors. In the course of our playing, we had occasion to run from the back garden, past the patio, out around the front of the house, temporarily out of sight from my parents and their friends. As I ran around the corner out of their view, I caught the words of my father's executive friend. With excitement and sincerity he said to my father, 'that's some boy you have there!'

"I wasn't supposed to have heard that remark, but I did. It astounded me so much so coming from a man whom I held in such high regard in my boyish mind, that I continued on out around the house to sit on the front steps for a few minutes to ponder and absorb what I had heard. I was pleased and humbled and assured by it all at once. For a moment or two I felt too self-conscious to return to their company, but soon my friends were tugging at me so I brushed it aside and ran with them again to the back garden to play. I never forgot that incident. It reassured me many times in life, but it never made me conceited.

"In grade two, again I had a teacher who didn't like me. Her dislike for me, however, was passive most of the time. What I mean by that is, she ignored me more than she picked on me. Once though, near the beginning of the year she did try to downgrade my work. We had some drawings to do, underneath which we had to print captions. After correcting them, she handed them back to the class. On mine, she had entered a very low pass mark. I brought it to her attention before the whole class, telling her that I had received top marks for similar work in grade one.

"'But,' she replied, 'you are expected to do better in grade two.'

"I argued that I had received high marks for such work near the end of grade one, and that this was only the beginning of grade two. To my surprise and delight she agreed to look at my work again, which she did right away and revised my mark upward to the category I was accustomed to getting. I had won my first battle in the care of myself, even at so young an age. But tougher battles were to come in my older years, from which I would not evolve so victoriously. For the remainder of that year, except for being passive towards me, even out rightly ignoring me at times, that teacher did me no other harm.

"Buttressed by the remembrance of the good teachers I previously had, and, by the overheard remark of my father's executive friend, I knew I was a worthwhile lad. I persevered, did my work to the best of my ability, and behaved well. The result for me was a good year, coming out near the top again. I must add though, that although it turned out to be a good year, I did not come through it entirely unscathed. As the year neared its end I was beginning to feel the effects of the negative attitude of the teacher towards me, as passive as that attitude was. I was beginning to feel self-conscious about it, and at times found myself shying away from her. This she would have taken advantage of, I am sure, had she noticed it. But I think I was saved by the year coming to its end before the effect of it had injured me too noticeably. Happily, I am able to say that the next year gave me once again, a teacher who liked me.

"Continuing on now into grades three, four and five, I say without hesitation, they were three wonderful years, and I prospered. My marks were always high, and I placed first in my class approximately half of the time, taking second place at other times to another bright lad with whom I was on very friendly terms. There was no rivalry between us, nor was any generated by biased teachers, as sometimes happens. We were good friends with each other, and with our teachers.

"Other aspects of my life went well too. I was active in some school sports, although I had no interest in excelling in that sphere. I attended church and church Sunday school regularly and also Boy Scouts. One of the highlights of those years for me was attending church summer camp. There, more than anywhere else, I learned to develop leadership abilities. I was popular with most people there, including leaders and other campers. Altogether, my church life, both at home and at church camp was an enriching, growth oriented, and enjoyable experience for me. My religious faith became an integral part of my being. I was a happy, well-liked, young lad, growing in ability and grace and stature. I was well on the road to a satisfying life — so I thought.

"One evening when my father, mother and I were having dinner at home as usual, a discussion arose as to what might be in store for me in the future, and what goal I may have in mind as I pursue my studies through school. The occasion occurred as I had brought home an excellent report card that afternoon. My father examined the report card as he ate his meal. My mother had seen it earlier. After examining the card carefully, my father made some very favorable comments about it. My mother agreed it was a wonderful report card.

"Then, as if to arouse some worthwhile ambition in me, my father asked a very pointed question, 'Brett, what do you intend to be when you grow up? You are a very talented boy, and such talent should be put to good use. Do you have any idea yet what you would like to be when you grow up?'

"This is a very common question, I suppose, and no doubt most parents ask it of their children. But the way my father asked it that day stirred me on the inside, and almost instantly made me want to use my life to the very best of my ability in the service of my fellow beings.

"For some time prior to that I had been, in the back of my mind, toying with the idea that someday I may be a medical doctor. There had been class discussions from time to time concerning careers. 'To be a doctor', the teacher said one day, 'you have to be a top scholar. When dealing with peoples lives it isn't satisfactory to be right, for example, sixty percent of the time. To be a medical doctor you have to get top marks.'

"The teacher's remark stuck into my mind that day. I was getting top marks. Maybe I could be a doctor. From time to time after that, the thought of being a doctor would cross my mind in various ways. *Was I really able for the task*? I would ask myself. Also, it seemed so awesome at times. But as time went on the thought of it grew on me, until I became reasonably sure in my own mind that I was capable of such a career. But I had never told anyone.

"Then came my father's conscience arousing remark about putting one's talents to work, followed by the question, 'What would you like to do when you grow up?'

"It seemed to be just what I needed to bring my hitherto secret thoughts out into the open. 'Dad,' I said, hesitantly, 'I think I know what I would like to be when I grow up.' Then getting a hold on my confidence I blurted out more firmly, 'I am going to be a doctor.'"

"'Great, just great,' responded my father exuberantly."

"'Do you really think I am able for it Dad?' I asked with a mixture of joy and apprehension."

"'Of course I do' his reply came quickly and assuredly. 'Don't ever doubt it.'"

"'Thanks Dad,' I said gleefully, 'that's what I'm going to be Dad'. My assurance was now well established."

"My mother added, 'Being such a good student, Brett, I am sure you can become a doctor, provided you keep up your work over the years. And being such a fine all-around person, I'm sure the way will open up for you.'

Brett paused in his story telling, as though his thoughts had wandered far away, perhaps into the past. "I only wish," he said in a distracted manner, "that my mother had been right."

It was plain for all present to see now what Brett had meant earlier when he said he was really a misplaced person. They felt his pain with him, and they were more than anxious to hear the story of how so fine a person with such a promising start in life, could wind up so far from his original goal.

Brett pulled his thoughts together once more and as if mainly to remind himself, but speaking aloud for all to hear, he remarked, "during the course of the story telling in this group we have already had revealed many experiences concerning school and university and teachers. But that is only one sphere of life where our problem exists. And although that sphere is a major and critical one, I think we should be careful not to treat it as the only one. Nevertheless I will have to tell you many of my school experiences in order to show you adequately how I came to be where I am. I will endeavor to do this as briefly as possible, and hope it won't sound repetitious. In addition there is one brutal period in high school that I will have to bring out in more detail. From there briefly I will tell you of my university experiences, and then it will be into the world of business.

"And now to continue with the relevant experiences of my school days. Grades six, seven and eight found me in another school. My father had been asked to transfer and manage a store in a shopping mall on the fringes of another city. So we moved and took up residence in a pleasant little village within commuting distance from my father's work. I attended the village school, which was a moderately sized elementary and junior high combined; a modern, well equipped facility, large enough to absorb the students from a wide surrounding rural area. With regard to its program, it was as good as one could find throughout that particular school system.

"Grades six and seven were prize years for me in this school. I had no confrontations at all with obnoxious teachers. My two main teachers during this period were elderly women nearing retirement age. They were persons of the integrity of a passing era, classic teachers so to speak, skilled in their subjects, in their way of teaching them, and in their handling of students in all their diversity of character. There was absolutely no need for concern about fair treatment; it came naturally with these teachers. The principal of the school was also in this category. I had two enjoyable years at school there."

"Two," caught Gilda, "but you were there three years!"

"Yes," responded Brett, "but the third year was not so enjoyable."

"Oh, oh, wouldn't you know!" quipped Leo in his now familiar manner.

"What happened?" asked Gilda curiously.

"Just my luck," replied Brett, "the two older teachers retired, and the principal moved on to another school. So in grade eight, a young local man recently out of college and replacing one of the retirees became one of my main teachers. Also the new principal, although perhaps not too bad a sort as far as I know, was not so experienced as his predecessor. He was a younger man, also a local now come back home to fill the position.

"However, to get to the central part of the story, as luck should have it, this new young man was my teacher for two of my favorite subjects, math and science. He did his best to put me down, showing his bias towards me after our first exams, by giving me B grades in both papers. I had always gotten A grades, and was still getting A grades in my other subjects. After receiving back my papers in class and examining them carefully I went to the teacher after school hours to protest. I showed him how my math problems had all been solved properly. He replied, "yes, you have the correct answers but nobody's methods are perfect. I never give an A.

"Likewise I brought before him my science paper. He had a little more leeway here, for a large portion of the paper included English composition in the process of answering the questions. I told him I had always done better than that in both science and English. Again he repeated, 'I never give an A. Nobody, but nobody, deserves that high a mark.'

"I reconciled myself to his policy, as I thought it was at the time. Later, however, I was to learn that it wasn't really his policy at all. It was his attitude towards me personally. Over the months at this school I had become close friends with another boy in my class who was doing very well with his school work. He was a hard working student who deserved to do well, and he did. In fact he was doing better than I in math and science as in time I found out. One day, several months into my grade eight year, we were walking home together, my new found friend and I. We each were carrying home our report cards for parental examination and signature. In our friendliness we compared report cards, and there to my surprise I saw on his card A Grades for both science and math. I felt terrible on the inside. But I realized he was innocent of any bias. I congratulated him on his high attainments. The teacher was the culprit.

"My parents and I discussed this revelation thoroughly that evening. After exploring possibilities of error on my part, on the teachers part and on our perception of the occurrence as we talked, we could only arrive at one conclusion: that I had been discriminated against by the teacher in a very flagrant manner.

"My father, knowing what I was up against, as I was to find out later, did his best to sooth my pain that evening. I was still very young, and he wished to shelter me from the full realities of the situation. He reminded me that B grades in two subjects wasn't so bad, especially since I was getting A's in the remainder of my classes. He reminded me of the two very lovely and fair minded lady teachers I had during the previous years, and that overall, it is fortunate to have only one teacher who was not as friendly to me as he might be. That consoled me, and I accepted my lot in that school.

"'Nevertheless,' said my father, 'your mother and I will do all we can to see that you are treated fairly.'

"My parents didn't give me all the details of what they tried to do until years later, and what happened was this: they went to the teacher who had given me the B grades, presenting him with the knowledge that A's were given to the other boy, and why not to our son if he deserves it. The teacher made flimsy excuses that were not characteristic of the school. 'Well, yes, he did give A's to the other boy, but that boy has been in this school since the beginning of his school days. He knows how we do things here, and so does them just a little better.'"

"Not being satisfied with that, my parents went to the new principal whom, in his lack of experience they quickly discerned, was completely oblivious to the concept of prejudice or discrimination or favoritism in schools, and perhaps anywhere else. Trying to be the nice guy, he clumsily defended the teacher. 'Oh now,' he said, 'that teacher is a good man; doing real well for what little experience he has. He's a local boy you know, just out of college. I don't want to discourage him. He teaches very well, and your son is a nice boy. I'm sure they will get along well in time.'"

"My parents could have pressed harder and maybe could have won the battle but lost the war, by bringing bad feelings against us, and making school life even harder for me at my young age. They dropped the matter realizing it was a contest between the locals and us the outsiders. One way or another I would be going to a different school, high school, in the fall anyway.

"By coincidence, it was shortly after this limited protest, that my father announced at the dinner table that we would be leaving the community at the end of the school year. My father would be transferring to a city store in another part of Secundaterra. There I would be attending a much larger and very well equipped high school. All three of us expressed the opinion that this would be good for me. That's what we thought at the time anyway!

"During the remainder of our stay in that town I became very good friends with the boy who was getting A grades that, according to the teacher, nobody was supposed to get. I still did not get more that B grades for math and science, but I never did reveal the secret of the discrimination to my friend. I tried not to let it bother me. Most of the time it didn't, but I did have my moments of dejection with its temptation not to care about doing well in anything at all. There was an inclination not to respond to the better impulses of life, to say 'what's the use' and to slip down and into the company of those who didn't care, didn't try, and so went their way on the downward road of life. Such things happen to disillusioned youth. However, my love and respect for my parents, and their love and oneness with me helped me to hold the line.

"Shortly after the village school closed for the summer, we moved away to what appeared to be a better opportunity for us all.

We took up residence in an outlying suburb of the small city in which my father was to work and I was to attend school. We were once again in new surroundings. Here in my impressionable and critical adolescent years I would have to take what was in store for me, and make the best of it. My years here were to have a profound bearing on me, both at the time, and for years to come. Little do most people realize the far reaching effects of what they do to a person in his adolescence, or at any age for that matter. However, some certainly are aware of what they are doing, but pursue their course of mental abuse regardless."

With these words, Brett's face flushed. The presence of hurt was evident. He had referred earlier in the conversation to a brutal period in high school. It was obvious now that it was a time that had great effect on his life. The group members felt for him, surmising that a tale of great woe was about to be told. They tried to find ways of sharing his burden.

"Brett," said Owen, "would you prefer to call it an evening at this point, and continue with your story next week?"

Donna interjected, "if its going to disturb you too greatly, you need not stir it all up again for us, Brett."

"Oh," replied Gilda, "we just have to hear the story. It will give us such tremendous insight; I can tell by your approach to it, Brett. You can do it, I'm sure you can," she urged.

"Yes, Gilda," replied Brett. "I can do it, but you will have to put up with my extreme hurt at times, as I recall it. Some things are better forgotten. This does, however, seem to be a time to remember."

Collin, who sensed the nature of the story that was coming, spoke a word of encouragement. "It will be difficult for you Brett," he said, "but beneficial to us, perhaps to you also. We will appreciate this strenuous effort on your part."

Brett cracked a little smile. "No need to feel that way Collin. I appreciate being here," he said. "I can continue on with the story because I know by now that I am among understanding and trustworthy friends." It was as if a burden was already being lifted from his life by having the opportunity to share it with friends who understood. Even before the actual sharing was done Brett loosened up and remarked, "Oh well, I guess it is all a part of the battle of life. Sometimes you win, sometimes you lose, somehow you survive — and I have survived well," he said with a sigh of relief.

"But to get on with the story now: the corporation had opened a very large modern department store in this city. My father had been chosen to manage it, and it was a step up the ladder for him. Over the years he had been a faithful, cooperative and diligent employee, bringing prosperity to each store he had managed. He was humbly pleased at the opportunity and challenge this his latest appointment had brought him. As always he continued faithfully in his work. In addition, and as always, he soon became active in the local church and in the local lodge of the fraternity to which he had belonged for many years.

"My father was not one to try to be a high profile man in the general sense, yet just by his presence in a place he stood out beyond the average, and even more especially when people got to know him well. My father was respected mainly for his sincere, industrious, straightforward, above board approach to both his work and his extracurricular activities. He left the impression upon people that he was a good man; an easy going, dependable man of integrity, rather than the stereotyped, hard fisted business man.

"My mother, on the other hand, in addition to having the same integrity and sincerity as had my father, was a high spirited woman who appeared from one's first encounter with her to be an activity oriented person, outstanding among the crowd. Her main objective in life, however, was to make a pleasant home and home life for us. Both my parents seriously endeavored to live the Christian life in which they had a profound belief and hope.

"So in the city in which we now found ourselves, my father was at a new crest in life. His faithfulness to his work over the years had now been rewarded. He appeared to be very happy. My mother, as always, was close to him in all spheres of his life. They were both close to me, and I to them. They were pleased that I would be attending a city school with up to date facilities. I would do well here — so they thought. But life takes strange and unexpected turns.

"And now to bring you to the main thrust of this period of my life," said Brett, "I must tell you what I found in this school in which my parents and I thought I would do so well."

"Before many weeks of school had passed," continued Brett, "I was able to discern that there were two opposite elements at work in this particular school. These were spearheaded by two basic types of teachers, with both types present in large proportions. There were the good teachers, as we have been calling them to date, and there were the obnoxious teachers as also we have been naming them."

Collin intervened, "I hope that in later meetings we will be able to clarify and define more fully these inadequate designations, and to separate the characteristics of each group. They can, I believe, be placed into two distinct categories according to the basic behavior patterns of each. "I think we can do that between us all, Brett."

"I'd be glad to see that done," said Owen, "and I can help with it. I know what you're getting at."

"Good," replied Brett, "it will be interesting to do so.

"So there I was," Brett continued, "unwittingly and unavoidably caught between these two factions; the individuals of the one trying their best to help me and others like me; and the individuals of the other in all their obnoxiousness, trying to put us down, to varying degrees according to how much they hated each one of us. By individuals," clarified Brett, "I mean there was no organized support on either side of these opposing factions, and there was no planned strategy against me or anyone else. We mustn't get to thinking that or we will have Dr. Eldren after us for paranoia. But birds of a feather do flock together, and so by their loose association in this manner they did form opposing factions."

"Your point is well taken, Brett," said Dr. Eldren.

"Thank you, Dr. Eldren," replied Brett.

"Whew, we're saved," quipped Leo, to the amusement of all present. "No paranoia here today!"

"To make things worse in this school," continued Brett, immediately, "for the first time in my life I was now in a school where the members of the obnoxious faction outnumbered the better ones, among the teachers and down through the student body also. Obviously, one cannot have such an element present on so large a scale without it being reflected down through the ranks in large proportions.

"To add to my problem there was an element of pride throughout this school system, that it was the best there is. In my opinion there was no factual reason for claiming this. The system did have some favorable characteristics over some other school systems, but vice versa also. It was a very arbitrary matter. Nevertheless pride ruled on the matter throughout this school. I was to be caught up in this pride controversy as well, although I did nothing intentional to bring it on, as you shall see.

"This might be a good place to add and to emphasize," continued Brett, "that regardless of the difficult predicament I was to find myself in, and all the problems it would bring, I decided early in my first year not to say a word about it to my parents. I was under the impression that they were very happy in their new environment. My father was now at the threshold of new opportunity in his career. He talked of trips for us and university for me, and of having things we had always wanted but could not afford. I would not spoil that for all the world. I would fight my own battles and I would win I told myself with uneasy confidence.

"There were some things in my favor in this school, but not many. On the good side was my English teacher, also my French teacher, whose subject I took as a second language; the industrial arts teacher whose class I attended as an option, doing wood and metal work; and the business practices teacher from whom I took typing. Over and against that was stacked both my mathematics teacher and my science teacher — a familiar experience from my previous school; my social sciences teacher, of all people; my history teacher, so down went another of the subjects in which I had previously excelled; and the physical fitness director. The latter were later supported by the guidance counselor and the principal. In addition to this I was up against formidable odds from the students generally, only a few of whom I was able to befriend over the two year period I was there."

Brett paused and reflected briefly on the broad statement he had just made concerning the teachers at this school. "I guess," he then said, "the best way for me to relate to you my experiences there and their effects on me in a revealing and meaningful manner is to take one teacher at a time and describe his or her attitude towards me. As has been said before in this group, describing an attitude is not easy, but where possible I will try to illustrate it with specific incidents."

"It can be done Brett," reaffirmed Gilda, as she had on previous occasions.

"Brett can do it," remarked Collin supportively.

"Thank you for your assurance and confidence folks," replied Brett, "yes it can be done. Most people never bother to do so and its a pity they don't. That is something we can discuss more fully later on, and I am sure it will contribute to better awareness and more efficient coping."

Collin interrupted, "You know the score, Brett, you're going to be a terrific help to us."

"Agreed," added Owen.

"I can hardly wait," Leo quipped in his usual manner.

"At last I know I'm not alone in our particular type of struggle in life," said Gilda with a combined sense of relief and enthusiasm.

Donna and Albin remained silent, but were obviously perked up with keen interest.

Dr. Eldren also silent, smiled and nodded approvingly. Yet as experienced a man as he was, an elder of his profession, there was the wonderment of a child in his total expression.

Collin's thoughts summed up the feeling of the group at the moment. *Thank God*, he thought to himself, *we have a humbly matured, open-minded doctor overseeing our group. Otherwise we simply could not have it functioning as well as it is.*

Brett took command of the situation. "I will first relate my experience with my mathematics teacher. It seems I was destined in life to have problems in that field, and here in this school the problem was not only to continue but to be multiplied.

"My math teacher was a female in this instance. On the first day in her class my impression was that either she didn't like me too well, or, she was afraid of me. Since I was very young, and she was more than twice my age, I reasoned that the first impression was more accurate, that she didn't like me, although, as I know now, there may well have been an element of fear there as well."

Leo was alarmed. "A teacher more than twice your age, and in authority over a class, and you a harmless adolescent, and she afraid of you, I mean, I mean, well, ah-h. Well, from your previous revelation of yourself I assumed you were a well behaved type, not a rowdy or anything like that. Am I right on that?" he asked.

"Yes, Leo, you are right in that the teacher had nothing to fear from me in a physical way," replied Brett, "neither had I confronted her with hostile words or looks; nor did my appearance give her any impression of hostility, as it does not now that I am years older. What I had in mind was the fear that stems from insecurity. This teacher knew I came from a high caliber family. From observation, I could discern she was not. From further observation I would soon find that rather than learn better from high caliber people, she would turn on them."

"You are right, Brett," interjected Collin. "People fear for reasons other than hostility. She was insecure merely because of your high profile presence. I've seen it lots of times."

Brett agreed, "Yes, I think it is quite reasonable for me to suppose there was an element of fear present. However, it was soon overshadowed by another characteristic which for me was to be far more devastating. I sensed her dislike for me from the beginning. In a short time it became very intense and remained so for the duration of my two years at that school. What brought about its intensity was that before long she discovered from my work that having come from a different school system I was away ahead of the present class in mathematics. She was correct in this appraisal as I had covered a considerable amount of the work in grade eight in my previous school system. Here I was now in grade nine able to give the answers at a glance as the teacher requested participation from the pupils while she worked out a problem on the board for their observation.

"Before many days had passed, the teacher became noticeably annoyed at my coming up with answers so easily. She struggled to contain her annoyance, and then one day asked me before the class in an artificially courteous manner, 'Brett, did you go over this work last night at home?'

"I answered politely, 'No miss, but I covered most of this work last year in grade eight."

"At that she lost control of herself. Her annoyance now became very evident as her temper flared. 'There are no schools in which this math course is taught in grade eight. If there were it would be taught in grade eight in this school.'

"I was shaken by her near rage. It was difficult for me to collect my thoughts under such circumstances, but I tried desperately in broken sentences to emphasize to her that I had been in another school system. She knew what I was saying alright, but would not listen to it. She shouted me down desperately. 'Nowhere is this work taught in grade eight.—Nowhere.'"

Brett could not help but reflect for a moment. "It is surprising," he said in a monotone, "what pride can do to a person."

"Pride, and fear of having it shaken," added Leo, as he showed evidence of his improved grasp of the matter.

"Pride and fear plus, Leo," responded Collin. "There is also the element of envy. We will have to explore all of these thoroughly further along the line. But just recognizing them is sufficient for now."

"Getting on with the topic then," continued Brett, "I used much restraint for the remainder of that year. I was bored with my math and uneasy with my teacher. She was quite satisfied for me to sit on the sideline and refrain from participation. I kept up my written work, did well with my exams, and obtained an A grade which the teacher had no choice but to give me, since my work was well up with the other top students of the class to whom the same grade was given. I kept up my grades in other subjects in my first year at that school also, getting mostly A grades, and some B grades. But that was only my first year. My second year at that school was to be the beginning in earnest of the undoing of my goal in life, and nearly the undoing of me. There were several teachers involved, of course, but first I will continue with my mathematics teacher.

"During my second year in this teacher's math class, she was no longer content for me to sit on the sidelines in quietude. Now we were in a phase of mathematics that was new to me as well as to the remainder of the class, so she became vindictive towards me. She would repay me for her last year's sense of humiliation before me, so it truly seemed.

"She continued her practice of working out math problems on the board and asking for class participation. At first I refrained from participation as I had during most of the previous year. But now she wasn't satisfied with that arrangement. She began to ask me specifically for answers. I responded as well as any others in the class, but now I was into new work. I remember well the day she asked me a rather difficult question concerning a problem she was working out on the board for the class. I felt reasonably sure of myself in math, but in this instance I needed a second or two to think through the phases of the answer, as other students often did, so I had observed.

"But my span of thinking time was to be very short according to her. She quickly pounced on me with a verbal barrage. 'You can't do it can you, can you, Brett Culver?' she said in a rage, and then added with a sneer, 'it's too much for you isn't it? I knew grade ten math would be too much for you. You got by last year, but grade ten is much, much more difficult', she emphasized. Then coming toward my desk she leaned forward in her anger and repeated, 'You can't do it, can you? Can you? Can you? You can't do it can you?'

"I was shaken as never before," said Brett, as he shook his head before the support group. "Fear ran through me that day, as she came closer and closer to my desk, still in her anger. Still shouting, 'you can't do it, can you?'

"No miss," I finally said, utterly distraught.

"I knew it," she said as she backed away.

"My young body trembled. *What on earth was I in for this year*, I asked myself. I was really afraid. As I glanced around at the class for support, I found very little. I had a few friends there, but very few. Mostly there were smirked faces staring at me. During the remainder of the year for me at that school, my estimate of friends on that day was to be borne out. I was to have few friends there, very few indeed. Most would be glad to see this 'wheel' from that other school system brought low. Well, at any rate, that was the most apparent reason, the surface reason they had for bringing me down."

"I'm glad you added that part, Brett," interjected Collin, 'the surface reason'. You know, and I know there was another, the main reason, for bringing you down. Overall you were too much for them — too good and too nice a person."

"Right you are," replied Brett. "We'll discuss that main reason later on, eh! But now to briefly wind up the remainder of my year in this math class. For the duration of that year, this teacher, much to the delight of the majority of my classmates, put me down at every opportunity. Over the year she thoroughly instilled into my impressionable young mind that I wasn't a very capable person in mathematics. She did this so successfully, that it showed through the following year in another school system where I was fortunate enough to have a high caliber classic teacher for math.

"My parents were asked of this later teacher, 'Why is it, Mr. and Mrs. Culver, that Brett thinks he has a problem with math? Actually,' said this teacher, 'Brett is very good at math, but he really thinks he is not. He thinks he has a real problem with math, when he doesn't. I am sure,' he said further, 'with a little more work and some catching up to our system, he can bring his marks to the top category. I feel sure of that, and I'll help him in every way I can.'"

Brett paused for a moment, opening his hands in a gesture of futility. "You see what the obnoxious teacher had done to me, and she was only one of several. Needless to say," he continued, "in such an atmosphere my math marks went down, down, down, as time went on. I generally managed C grades towards the end."

Brett went right on with his story as the group sat in awe and silence. "To have such an unpleasant experience with one teacher was devastating enough, but on top of that were the several other teachers with a negative attitude toward me.

"You handy about know by now what kind of story I am going to tell you about these. You have already heard of the school experiences of Leo, Gilda, Donna and some of my own. So I think a brief outline would be sufficient to support a point I hopefully have already made.

"The science teacher's attitude towards me was basically that I was generally neglected in the laboratory. He was almost continually doing the rounds to the other students, helping them with the experiment of the day. He seldom came my way, and only then to pass a remark, usually half hearted approval, or very negative fault finding. What I gained from my lab period I gained by my own industry. I studied my work as well as I possibly could on my own, I was handy with my hands at doing things, and I was determined not to go under entirely.

"In the classroom this science teacher's attitude was much the same in essence. On occasion, when the class as a whole had been asked a question for anyone who will to answer, I would try to participate. If I gave a more accurate or more complete answer than another student, I was either shunned, ignored, or, at times even offended by the teacher pushing his lower lip out in contempt. You all know what that can do to any person, but particularly to a young person over a period of two years.

"Then there was my history teacher. History had previously been a subject in which I not only did well, but which I had always enjoyed immensely. Now came two years of being put down, mainly by the old trick of 'you have to have the ability to discern and interpret; or, your facts you remember pretty well, but —; and then your composition, that is something else, etc. etc.' In addition, there was the usual accompaniment of an attitude of dislike made evident by a general lack of approval for work well done; also quick criticism for errors, and more generally ignoring me in favor of other class members. You can imagine what happened to me and my history over these years.

"Then there was my social sciences teacher. She was so pietistically concerned about discrimination against the poor and the oppressed that she was unable to recognize the same oppressive malady in her attitude towards those who managed to climb above these afflictions. This is a topic I would like to discuss later, particularly with you clergy, but sufficient for me to say now, under this teacher also, I was put down, down, down.

"Last of all the obnoxious ones, as we are still calling them, was the physical fitness director. I was a thorn in his proud flesh as well. Concerning my athletic abilities, I was short for basketball and light for football. But I was extremely agile which enabled me to do better than many students of a more favorable size. In such an environment as I was in this didn't enhance people to me either. So with the exception of a limited participation in class basketball and some track events, I stayed away from team sports. I was above average, I would say, in some track and field events. Now to avoid repetition in describing attitudes, let me simply say of my years with this physical fitness director that, as with others of his type, so with him, I was put down, ignored and slighted, at every possible opportunity.

"So there you have it folks — a brief resume of my adversities during the critical period of my adolescent years. I think already you can imagine what it did to me. In my first year there, I stood up well, slipping only a little in some subjects. But two years of it was too much for me at my age. It nearly devastated me, but not quite. Let's save further discussion about its causes and effects for later.

"Just now," Brett went on quickly, "I must tell you of one victory among all of these defeats. It was a victory won in the physical fitness department." Brett cracked a very temporary smile as he approached this victorious item, then quickly returned to the sobriety of his previous story telling. The other group members were intent on listening. There was no interruption as Brett continued.

"It was sports day near the end of my final year at that school. I knew now I would be moving away before the next school year began. At a family discussion just a week or so earlier, my father, mother and I had discussed this matter in detail, but no one outside the family knew it at this time. I'm getting ahead of my story here, and will fill in the details of what led to our intention to move at our next week's session. There is just time to relate this one incident before I finish for the evening.

"So as I said," Brett went right on, "no one knew of our impending move. Consequently, my teachers did not know it, but I did and I was secretly elated by the thought of it. So on this closing sports day I was feeling real good amid my unfriendly surroundings.

"To begin this sports day, events were held indoors in the morning. Then in early afternoon the program moved outdoors. This was the physical fitness director's day of the year. He was in top form, carrying an air of exaltation about him all day. He made a point of praising each class team for their efforts, and more specifically of congratulating any individual participants who excelled in an event, all except me that is.

"I had played indoors in a basketball game and had excelled. I was short, remember, but agile, and moreover, I was now elated at the thought that my parents were to take me out of this sea of hostility in which I had lived for two years. I played extremely well that day, leading in the scoring, and leading my team to victory. When the game ended, the fans and the director came onto the floor.

"As I walked around in the usual manner of unwinding I kept the director in sight in the corner of my eye. He ran straight out to our team captain, a logical thing to do, I would say; then to some other players, offering congratulations with the usual back slapping and hair ruffling. I know he could see me, he couldn't help but do so, as I was in his line of sight several times. But each time he would cast his eyes away from me, either up or down or right or left. The self-consciousness of doing this was written all over his face. I walked away to the shower room; then to lunch in the cafeteria, and from there to the grandstand outdoors where I sat and relaxed as for an hour or more I took on the role of spectator, watching the track and field events of the day. As for myself, I would participate in only one event that afternoon. I knew I could do well with it, and I felt on the inside that I was going to. The morning snubbing hadn't dampened my spirit at all. In fact I felt victorious in the thought that no matter how I ended up in life, I would never be so small, nor such a let-down to humanity as was the person who snubbed me today. I felt good as I approached this coming event which was to become the grand finale of competitive sports for me."

There was an attentive silence throughout the support group. An air of wonderment prevailed noticeably as Brett kept right on with his story.

"A major event of the afternoon was the one mile race. I had entered my name for it some days before as previous registration was required. There were to be ten of us participating. At early mid-afternoon our time came. We proceeded to the starting line. The physical fitness director was there to see that we were properly in place. He went from one to the other, starting at the person on the inside, he placed the tips of his hands on the participants shoulders, remarking 'you are good as you are.' Then to the next, nudging him back an inch or two so as to be behind the starting line. Then to the next person, advising him of better starting posture, and on across the lineup with a word for each one, until he came to me.

"I was on the outside, the shortest of them all. As he left the person next to me, he paused only briefly in front of me, gave a very slight smirk, said nothing, then proceeded to the sidelines for the starting gun.

"A world of thought ran through my mind in that brief second when the director stood in front of me. I thought to myself, *yes sir, I know what you're thinking. I am the shortest of them all, I am standing on the outside, and you think I don't have a chance. Well I've got news for you. I chose this spot purposely so that when I do well in this race, perhaps win it, there will be no ifs or ands or buts, or excuses for the others. If I win I will win the hard way. I am not only standing on the outside but I am an inch or two from the starting line, and furthermore I am going to be slightly, only slightly tardy in starting after the gun fires. And even after that I am going to break with general practice. The usual is to remain just behind the lead throughout the major part of the race, conserving energy as best one can until the final stretch when I turn on the last ounce so to speak, take the lead and win the race. Well, mister director, I have devised a different plan for myself. I am going to take the lead not later, but just before we come out of the first turn. It is a difficult place, but I have a good pair of shoes and I have practiced my turns well. So early in the race I can surely put on a good burst of speed, and in that location no one will be expecting it. Then I will glide along for the next three and one half laps keeping just out in the lead. When it comes to the home stretch I will be able to make another burst. But in this burst also I will be unconventional. I will begin it not on the final straight but on the curve before the final straight. That maneuver will be a surprise also and will give a safe lead.*

*"Yes, mister director, I have practiced my turns well. Besides that I have something going for me that you do not possess. You have taken a lot away from me, mister director, you and some of your colleagues, but I possess something which you are not able to take from me, and it will be working for me today. I have it, and I have my plan of strategy, I've made provision for change in strategy as circumstances may warrant during the race, and I am going to run to win. Even if this is the last thing I ever do, if I break my body in doing it, I am going to pour my best into this race. Win or lose it will be my best.*

"Flashing thoughts can be quickly cleared. I cleared my mind and waited for the starting gun. It fired and the race was on.

"Going into the first turn there wasn't a great deal of distance between any of us. I was somewhere in the behind half of the group. Then I put my plan into action, poured on the speed and at the same time worked towards the inside. As we came out of the turn I surged barely into the lead. As I reflect back now, I figure my adversaries were stirred prematurely into action by the thought of me being out front. Some of them poured it on even on this first full stretch. This was the side of the track on the far side from the grandstand. I had to keep a sustained effort on this straight, more than I had anticipated. However, I would not contemplate dropping the lead, so on I went, and then into the next turn I used my personally planned maneuver and gained a more considerable lead as I strained my body forward.

"Only once more was this lead seriously challenged. It was when we were running the stretch up in front of the grandstand ending the first time around and beginning the second. The participant who was, I would say, expected to win the race, not inconceivably to play to the grandstand, from what I know of him, put out a vigorous effort to take the lead from me. I heard him coming up close to me. I was no professional. I glanced out of the corner of my eye and sure enough he was coming. My spirit surged within me, and my legs began to move me faster than I thought possible. At the end of the stretch I was out front by a few yards. Now, I thought, I will leave him safely behind. I poured on the energy around the turn. This unprofessional maneuver of mine was working.

"I took a safe lead, but in doing so had tired myself to a point where I needed to just cruise along for a period. This I did as I cautioned myself that this could be a point at which my competitors may try to take the lead. However, to my surprise no one gained on me. They too in their desire to keep up to or pass me had expended any excess energy in their earlier efforts. I could cruise for a while and hope to regain enough strength for a final burst. I had gained and retained the lead on the first round and into the second.

"Around we went a second time, a third time, and into the fourth and final round. Now I thought, as we near the home stretch in the final round, my competitors, those of them who can at least, will pour on the speed in a last ditch effort to gain the lead and win the race. So, I decided, I would begin my final spurt a turn and a stretch ahead — that is as I took the turn into the side of the field far from the grandstand. They will not be expecting that. It will be a long distance over which to keep up a sustained effort, almost a full turn around, but I can do it, I know I can, I have this something within me that says I can!

"So this I did, beginning at the turn shortly after passing the grandstand, on around the end of the track and into the stretch on the far side of the field. *This is it*, was my final thought out there. I put all thought of maneuvering or of winning or losing or anything else, clear out of my mind and I ran, and I ran, and I ran. My comparatively short legs moved as I never thought they could; my lungs gasping for oxygen to sustain a body that was outdoing itself by far. I neither looked, nor thought, but only ran — faster, faster — down the stretch, around the turn and up the home stretch. I saw no one, heard no one. I would keep up this pace if my body were to burst, until I felt the ribbon on my body. I had no idea where the competitors were now. I did catch a blur of a person holding the ribbon, and then felt it slightly as I crossed into the finish. I'm sure I could have gone around again at the same speed, so great was this feeling within me, this something that no one had been able to take from me. But after I crossed the finish line, I slowed to a wind-down pace for a very short distance. Then in a most unprofessional way, I stopped running, and simply walked around an area some distance past the finish line. I was able to see the others coming in. To my surprise I came in with a lead of about ten yards. Only two others came anywhere near that ten yards behind me.

"My only thought was, *yes, mister director, I have something you people haven't been able to take from me*. I had no sense of elation because of victory over others. I sensed no joy in having won a battle. My only satisfaction was due to the fact that I had assured myself that they hadn't taken everything from me. They had taken a lot maybe, but not everything — not my indomitable God-given spirit.

"The other participants eventually gathered near the finish line where the director gave his usual congratulations. With my heart still pounding within me and my lungs pumping furiously, I stayed a distance up the track towards the end of the grandstand, determined to make no effort to go to him. Neither did I want him to come to me. I felt he wouldn't, and he didn't.

"A whistle blew to signify the beginning of another event. I sat for ten minutes or so in the scantily occupied end of the grandstand. Then while others watched the sports events continue I slipped away to the showers, then out into the street where rather than waiting for the school bus I hitchhiked my way home. It was safe to hitchhike in those days.

"The next day of school was to be taken up with a bus trip to another city. The day following that was to be closing day with an assembly and good wishes for the summer. I hadn't the desire to participate in either. I went back to that school only once more, a week or so later, and that was to accompany my mother to pick up a transcript of my record she had requested from the school office."

Brett paused for a moment. There was no immediate reaction from any group members. They sat in awe. It was up to Brett to break the silence.

"That folks is the beginning of the undoing of one Brett Culver." He smiled and said further, "next week, I will tell you the story of his eventual salvation."

Then turning to Dr. Eldren, he remarked, "Dr. Eldren I have kept you for a long session this evening. I would like to leave immediately to be alone for awhile if I may, and then continue with my story next week if the group wishes."

"I'm sure that will be most satisfactory, Brett, thank you for your major contribution this evening. We'll certainly look forward to next week's meeting."

Brett stood, bade the members good-night and proceeded to the door. As he opened the door he turned and gazed inquiringly at Collin Seldon. Collin smiled and gave him a motion of approval via a quick twist of the head. Brett returned the smile, obviously feeling now the assurance he was seeking. He held up his hand, "Good night everyone," he said as he left, closing the door behind him.

# CHAPTER SIX

There had been no time at the end of the group session to question Brett Culver. In fact there wasn't any time to empathize with him, since he had made his exit so suddenly after winding up that part of his story.

Collin talked about this to his wife, Vita, as they drove down the city street that was aglow with flashing and dancing neon signs.

"Perhaps that's just it, Collin," observed Vita. "He left before anyone could empathize with him. How would you feel, telling your own tale of woe objectively and for objective purposes, and then having a bunch of people shed tears all over you?"

"I'd feel terrible," reasoned Collin quickly, "that's it!. The rascal skipped out on us before we had an opportunity to break him down with tears. Great maneuver, seeing the type of person he is!

"Yes," she replied, "from what you've told me of Brett Culver, that's it. It seems he is quite in control of his own life."

"Right," remarked Collin elatedly. "But now I think I'll just look at those dancing dazzling lights, and the people coming and going, and get all this off my mind rather than take it home to bed with me. Thanks for accompanying me and doing the driving," he added.

"At your service sir," she replied with a grin.

Collin's wife accompanied him again the following Wednesday evening. In fact browsing in the library of Quilibet University would become for her a regular Wednesday evening occupation for a while. She loved to read so welcomed the opportunity. When Collin was through a group meeting, rather than drive, he liked to be free to ponder the events of the meeting if he wished. He would rather not do city driving while pre-occupied with things that absorbed him so much. His wife was happy to come along and do the driving for him. So again Collin left her at the library and proceeded to room 405 for another group session, and to hear at this meeting, the remainder of Brett Culver's story.

The group members gathered early this evening. Brett surprisingly was among the first to arrive. This was in contrast to his tardiness at most meetings. It was to be his night again, so as soon as the group had gathered, he took command of the situation. It was evident to any discerning observer that when Brett decided to do something, he decided to do it his own way. He was his own man, and it was to be seen later that this was an attribute that would see him through to a substantial success in life.

"Dr. Eldren," said Brett courteously. "I would like to go on to tell the remainder of my experience in life immediately, if that would be satisfactory?"

As was his custom, Dr. Eldren asked the group as a whole to express their desires. Brett's plan was agreed to immediately.

Brett began with self-assurance. "Last week I took you along to the end of my two year period at the school involved in my life at that time. This evening I must take you back in time, in order to incorporate into my story some other incidents and family circumstances that were to bring about my departure from that school and my family's departure from that city.

"You may remember, near the beginning, I told you that I had decided to fight my own battles so as not to affect my father's happiness with his new position. But one early winter's day, a Sunday, in the afternoon, in my second year there, my father, mother and I were driving along a suburban road on which only a few people lived. The houses were spaced out here and there in a setting that was really still more country than suburban. To date that year we had had a great deal of winter already, with a heavy snow storm only the night before. Snow was piled high everywhere. It was still snowing some, and occasional drifting made driving somewhat hazardous. As we drove along we saw a car which apparently in its attempt to enter a driveway, had, in the drifting, missed its mark and the back right wheel was off the road and deep down into a snow filled ditch.

"My father decided to stop and help. We had snow shovels aboard and we could help the man who was already shoveling. All three of us got out to help the man, and his wife who was also present. As we observed the situation it was evident that a great deal of shoveling would be necessary, as the bottom of the car was also bogged down in snow that had accumulated in the driveway.

"We approached and my father offered our help, and at the same time started shoveling. Then to his surprise the man said hello to me, calling me by name, but doing so in a rather cool manner. My father remarked, 'you two know each other, eh?' 'Yes,' I said, 'this man is a teacher at my school.' I introduced him to my parents.

"As we all shoveled and furiously kicked away the snow, there wasn't much other conversation, except that the teacher let an almost continuous stream of oaths and curses out of him as he worked away. He cursed the snow some, and he cursed the car some, but mostly it was just cursing, period. It was enough to make your ears sore. My father said nothing. My mother stood by us. When the job was done, the man drove his car into the driveway, foul language still coming from him, but not any thanks. We got aboard our own car and drove on our way.

"My father was very quiet the remainder of the afternoon, and at the evening meal at home. Then shortly after dinner, he said to me, 'Brett, I think we should have a talk. Let's sit in the living room.' My mother was beckoned to join us and we sat down to talk.

"'Brett,' my father asked, 'that man we helped today is a teacher at your school?'

"'Yes, dad,' I replied.

"'And, is he typical of the teachers at your school?' he asked further.

"'Well dad,' I said, 'they don't swear at school like that. It wouldn't be allowed.'

"'No, I wouldn't think so,' replied my dad, 'he was just cursing and swearing like that to humiliate me, and your mother too perhaps. That's his type you know.'

"'I know what you mean dad,' I replied.

"'Oh, so you do! Well then in view of that, perhaps you and I and your mother had better talk some more. Is he typical of at least many of the teachers at your school?'

"'Yes dad, in attitude at least,' I responded.

"Then my father became openly frank with me. He told me how he had noticed that my school marks had gone steadily down, particularly in my second year at that school. He revealed how he and my mother had tried not to show any disappointment in me, but could not seem to detect just what my problem was.

"'Now I know what you're problem is Brett,' he said, with eyes piercing as though they were looking straight into my mind. 'You've been an underdog at that school, all this time, haven't you?'

"Tears came into my eyes, I was not sure why, but I think now it was mainly because I now no longer stood alone in my predicament. It would be difficult to reveal all that had happened to me since coming to this city and this school, but at last the door was opened so that my parents could help me in my dilemma. I would find it difficult to share my woes with them, because in my solitary battle I had become one who was very reluctant to cry on anyone's shoulder. However, my parents were able to understand without being told all the details.

"'How do you know, dad, that I have been an underdog at school?' I asked curiously.

"His answer surprised me no end. 'Because I too have become an underdog of sorts in this city. My experiences have no doubt been different in detail than yours, but in essence they are the same. There are a lot of good people in this area, some wonderful people, but the obnoxious ones have taken control, not only out in the work-a-day world, but obviously in your school as well. This is no place for people like us to be living. Eventually they will wear us down and out.'

"'But dad,' I stammered, 'I thought, I thought things were going wonderfully well for you, what with this ultra modern store and all.'

"'Not in this city,' my dad replied.

"'Oh dad,' I said, near crying, 'I would have told you how

school was for me here, but I thought you were so happy, I wouldn't spoil it for anything.'

"My dad shook his head. 'Not so, Brett.'

"We talked for about two hours. I couldn't bring myself to tell my parents all, nor nearly all I had been through, but I did tell them enough so that they were able to surmise the circumstances generally. I told them something of the discrimination by a large segment of my teachers, and how this was reflected down through the student body."

Brett paused, then addressed the support group. "This may be a good time to interject here that a great deal of the attitudes of the obnoxious teachers was passed down to the students, so much so that I had very few friends. The few students who did take a liking to me were fended off by my enemies. For example, a lovely girl about my own age, who came into the school during my second year, showed a liking for me. One day on the school grounds during lunch period, she came to talk with me. Soon a bunch of thugs gathered round, some of them walking in towards us, and then momentarily retreating again, looking tough and perturbed that I had found a friend. First she became puzzled, then scared. She courteously told me that she must go now. As she left, one of the gang made a sneering remark to her concerning me, 'he's a goody goody,' he snarled.

"That was not the only such incident. There were others who had tried to befriend me before that, boys and girls. They were all driven and frightened away in a similar manner. I know most of them remained my friends, but only at a distance. We would exchange friendly looks. Sometimes, but only sometimes, there was an exchange of greetings. But no one dared come near. With all due respect, I was the *white nigger* of the school.

"Furthermore, I had to ride to and from school on a school bus with some of these people every day. There, in close quarters, they tried to make life miserable for me in various ways ranging from simply shunning me to trying often to make it impossible for me to find a seat. Very often, seats that were meant for two, suddenly would be filled with one sprawling person.

"There was also much beer drinking on the bus. One day a bunch of them pinned me down and tried to pour beer into my mouth. I successfully fought them off. The driver was often unable to control the behavior on the bus. There did come some talk of having a second adult riding the school buses, but it never happened, probably due to the extra cost.

"Had I shown any fear on the bus, I am sure they would have found some way to do me in. But I defended myself after a fashion by losing my temper at them. This worked to the point where they dared go only so far.

"I need not tell you that two years in such an environment took a very grave toll on my personality. Just as Gilda Emerson revealed to us earlier how in her battle for survival, she became known as a crust and a battle axe, so I too became know as the guy with the temper. Of course no thought was ever given to the fact that I had to develop that characteristic in order to survive. But not only that, as controlled as my outbursts at them usually were, the smoothness and pleasantness of my character was all but destroyed.

"I would say now that the only things that saved a remnant of pleasant character within me was that during the summer I went to a church youth camp some miles away, where believe it or not I was quite popular, a good mixer and regarded by my camping companions as a leader. During the year, I also attended a church youth group where there was enough freedom from fear for some to befriend me. Without these glimmers of friendship, to say the least, I would not have come through as well as I did.

"Also I appreciate fully the acquaintance of the few teachers who treated me respectfully and fairly. I mentioned them earlier. The one that stands out in my mind most of all was my English teacher. She was a sincere well dispositioned teacher, highly intelligent, helpful, and a hard worker. I feel she paid a price for her fair and respectful treatment of me as she tried to do with everyone. The large majority of the other students in the class were almost continually trying to break her, as they openly admitted, with everything from mimicking to behaving stupid intentionally, to mixing up and hiding things on her desk when there was opportunity to do so behind her back. She too was in a hostile environment as was I. When I left she was in poor condition, having already had three weeks off for *nerves*. I have often wondered how she made out.

"Now back to the conversation with my parents on the night when this all came out into the open; my parents were dismayed at what I had been through. 'We should have known,' said my father disgustedly. 'We should have known when your marks kept going down and down, and on top of that, when I got to know the atmosphere at work and elsewhere in some aspects of the city activities, yes, I should have known.'

"Then my father revealed to my mother and I such things as the poor caliber of attitude of employees at the department store, obnoxious elements predominant in social life, and what he described as rivalry in some spheres of the church. He did not go into detail about these things but from my experiences at school, I knew what he was getting at. My mother understood too. We were a different caliber of people than those who were predominant in the area.

"As we talked, mother listened very intently, and talked very little except for an occasional question for clarification purposes. But when the discussion was winding down, my father sighed, with the remark, 'What, I wonder, should we do about all this?' He then brought my mother into it by questioning her, 'Should we move back to our home in Lower Secundaterra?' My mother's response was fast and firm. 'We should indeed move back to Lower Secundaterra so that Brett may finish his education in a reasonable environment.'"

"'I think I can get a transfer with the corporation,' my father quickly added.

"Then my father spoke to me of reasons he favored education in Lower Secundaterra. 'The school system you will find, will be quite different there, with advantages and disadvantages. But on the whole,' he said, 'I like the system better in Lower Secundaterra and would prefer you to be educated there. Over and above the education system, you will be in a much better social environment. In that area of the country, school children are still generally treated with a greater measure of care and respect. Almost the whole adult population takes a keen interest in the welfare and accomplishments of students. It may be fading some, but it is still there and predominant at present. There will still be some obnoxious people there, but they are not in control, not yet anyway, and not for a long time, I would forecast.'

"It would be a good environment for me, my father told me; a place where I would have a better chance to reach my potential.

"My mother reaffirmed what my father had said, then asked me, 'How do you feel about it Brett?'

"I pondered for a second, then questioned my mother; 'Are you sure the atmosphere in school will be better down there, Mother? If it isn't, I'd just as soon never go to school again.'

"'Oh don't say that Brett,' my mother said with tears. 'You must complete your high school education, and hopefully go on to university too. It won't be all roses for you down there, but for the most part it will, at least be a friendly environment for you. Life in some ways is not as sophisticated as here, but that has its advantages too as you will find out in time, and many parts of Lower Secundaterra have some very superior refinements about it also; far in advance of the average for many places.'

"'And mother,' I questioned again, with some apprehension, 'how different is the school system down there?'

"My mother explained, 'It doesn't synchronize with the system here very well. There are less years in high school there, so you will not pick up on some of your subjects there where you leave them off here. Except for some overlapping, the curriculum you go into there, in some subjects at least, will be farther advanced. You will have a gap to fill. There will be a difficult year for you academically, and you will have to work hard. Then there will be an extra year in university.'

"'Do you think I can do it mom?' I asked.

"She responded with another question, 'If we stay here, do you think you can get through high school?'

"'Impossible,' I replied. 'A person needs a clear, contented mind to study well.'

"'Then what do you have to lose,' mother remarked with a ring of finality.

"A unanimous decision was made then and there. All three of us enthusiastically agreed we should move back to Lower Secundaterra. It would be a step down the rung of the ladder for my father but he was very willing to take it. My mother could be content wherever she was. Once the decision was made, I was delighted at the thought of going.

"There was still more than half a year to see through at my present school. My father decided he would try to make things better for me while I was there. He asked me to let him know, as early as possible, of some specific incident in one of my classes, in which I felt treated unfairly. That was easy to come by; a low mark in a history paper, the reason for which was given that my presentation of the subject, although factual was not of a good caliber composition. Ironically, I was still doing well in English composition. My English teacher had always been fair and friendly towards me.

"So with this specific incident in mind, my father, after first making an appointment, went to see the school guidance counselor. He talked to him of how I used to get high marks in history, and how my marks were down now. Then he referred to this specific paper, how the composition was said to be poor, but at the same time my English composition still brings good marks.

"The counselor replied that there was bound to be a difference between the ways two different teachers assessed a paper.

"My father then explained how I had done well in many subjects in my previous school, and now in this school my marks had gone way down."

"'I take it'", said the counselor, with an air of hostility, 'that you are not satisfied with the education your son is receiving at this school.'

"'Not really,' replied my father. 'I have reason to believe he hasn't been well received here, to say the least.'

"'How have your other children done here?' the counselor asked in a calculated manner as his eyes became shifty and he searched for an out.

"'I have no other children,' came the reply from my father."

"'Well then,' replied the counselor, 'there's your problem, and your son's problem. He's an only child, and most likely a spoiled child. But don't think for a minute he's going to get spoiled here. He has to take what he deserves the same as the rest of the students.'"

"'No,' responded my father patiently, 'he has never been spoiled. He's been disciplined, given responsibility and taught to live simply, and within our modest means.'"

"'I've heard all that before,' snarled the counselor."

"'I see I'm wasting my time here,' said my father finally, and got up and left the counselor's office.

"From there he went to the principal's office. The principal was out of the school at the time so my father received an appointment with him for two days later. At that appointment my father approached the principal in much the same manner as he had the guidance counselor, and also referred to his visit with the counselor.

"The principal's response was no better. 'I have every confidence in our guidance counselor,' he snapped coldly. 'In fact, he has already told me of his interview with you. I agree wholeheartedly with his summary of the matter.'

"This indicated that the principal too regarded me as a spoiled child looking for preferential treatment, or, at least he was using that as an out to cover for the treatment I had received at the school.

"My father got up out of the chair in which he had been sitting, placed his hands on the principal's desk, leaned over and stared him in the face and said sternly, 'I see I have also been wasting my time by talking to you, but listen to me now, very carefully. I do not expect my son to be treated any better than he has been in this school. But he has to finish his year here. And if for any reason, in the next seven months or so, we find he cannot stay here to finish, believe me, it will not go unnoticed; believe me, the matter will go much further than this office.'

"The principal sat dumb-founded in his chair, a reaction typical of his kind."

"'Do you hear what I'm saying,' continued my father. 'You had better, because this is the last time I will speak to *you* about the it. Next time, if necessary, I'll take the matter to a much higher authority.'

"The principal remained silent, his face white. My father walked out."

"May I interject a thought here," said Collin to the group. "It is one of the oldest of mind-games for these obnoxious ones to use on fine people; that we are spoiled brats, or we think too much of ourselves in some way — conceited — and therefore deserve to be trampled on — put down. Under this phony cloud, very little of society will sympathize with the victims."

"Agreed," said Brett, and continued, "the remainder of my year at that school was slightly improved. There was no aggressive hostility towards me from the teachers. Just a passive coolness and unfriendliness now. There was no change in the student body towards me. One could hardly expect a change in so large a number of people in any time less than years, even if some great impact were to be made on them. So I plodded through to the end, very much alone, except now with my parents understanding and moral support. I ended up the year as I told you earlier, with a one mile race, hitch-hiking home afterwards.

"There is one more incident I would like to relate to you concerning this school, because it amuses me so.

"The week after the school closed for the summer, my mother phoned the school office to ask for a transcript of my record to take away with us. She was concerned that I might not get a good one from this school so wished to settle the matter while we were still living there. She asked the secretary if we could get the transcript that same week. The secretary asked if we would come in following week to get it as their records had not yet been brought up to date. My mother just casually mentioned that we were going to Terraprima next week. So we were, but just on a few days vacation.

"'Oh,' replied the secretary, 'then come in tomorrow and I will prepare one for you in advance. It will take extra researching, but I will prepare it for you.'"

"What a surprise!" said Brett to the group. "You see we had planned a vacation to Terraprima before moving to Lower Secundaterra. The secretary thought we were moving to Terraprima to live. The point of the matter is that secretary now made out an extra special transcript for me, making sure that all the school curriculum was listed on it. Noting the grading system used, the high standard expected of students, and even implying that I had done very well considering the high standards set by this school.

"My mother was amused as she and I waited in the office while the secretary prepared this custom-made transcript of my record.

"When we got outside the office with this rather high profile record, I asked my mother, rather loudly and excitedly, 'How come she went to such great lengths to come up with a transcript like that for me?' I asked.

"'S-h-h-h,' said mother. 'She thinks we are going to Terraprima to live, and she just had to prove to them down there via this transcript, that this school is better than theirs. And so-o-o,' she said, as she raised her eyebrows in delight and smiled at me, 'after two very traumatic years in this school, you came out with a favorable transcript of record. It doesn't make your marks any higher, but it does make you come out looking as though you have done very well in an institution of very high standing. It is amazing, isn't it, Brett, what pride will make people do?'

"We drove to our home, still amused, even laughing. Yes, I had come away from that school for the last time, laughing, actually laughing.

There was an intermission of a few minutes in the story telling, as group members engaged in small talk. They speculated on how some good usually comes out of most everything, how a door usually opens for you if you persevere, and how where there is a will there is a way.

"I question the wisdom of some of these old sayings with regard to their validity for today's world," remarked Brett. "Doors may open for you all right if you persevere, but it's not always the door that's best. Sometimes you have to take an escape hatch instead of a door, as you will find out as my story proceeds. I should get on with it before it drags on too long.

"To make the next episode as brief as possible," Brett continued, "may I merely sum up my final year of high school. The corporation, at my father's request, transferred him to a nice though smaller store in Lower Secundaterra, my parent's home territory. We were all happy about the move.

"School for me there was a pleasure by comparison. The students were friendly; the teachers, also friendly, were interested and interesting. All except one obnoxious one. He had transferred from the school system from which I had also transferred. However, it was easy to put and keep him in his place since he was only one. I could do so simply by playing down the environment from which he and I had come, and praising the one into which we now were. This pleased the other students. To my knowledge the other teachers were unaffected one way or another by this imported teacher whose negative attitude towards me was nipped in the bud before it amounted to anything. Eventually, this one negative teacher, with so many better examples all around him, had no choice but to change his attitude. There was one other teacher who, out of his own feeling of inferiority, shied away from me in certain ways and attitudes, but he always treated me fairly.

"Truly, I now enjoyed the best year of my life to date. I was not only befriended by the better and larger part of the student body, but was accepted to the point of being popular at least in the circle in which I operated and it was a sizeable circle. The teachers of this school were not only friendly but fair to the utmost. Discrimination and prejudice were not to be found among them. I was especially encouraged by the math teacher who was concerned because, as he said himself to my parents, 'Brett *thinks* he has a problem with math, but really he is very good at it.' What a delightful year for me! I cherish it still. My marks soared, my personality became renewed. To quote Gilda, I became 'the person I was meant to be,' at least for a year.

"Just for a year, Brett?" asked Collin.

"Yes Collin, just for a year," replied Brett sadly."

"Don't tell me there's more trouble ahead in your life," blurted Leo in his now familiar manner. "I mean, how much can one person take?"

"Trouble never ends for anyone, Leo," responded Brett, "much less for people like us. But there are some bright spots ahead for me."

Leo responded sympathetically and soberly, "I guess I should have realized that by now, Brett, that there is more trouble ahead for a person like you. I'm glad that there are also some bright spots in your life. Don't let me interrupt you unnecessarily."

"No problem," said Brett, as he began the prelude to the next phase of his life.

"I graduated with honors from high school that year. It was a good year for me also in that I graduated to a new and more confident maturity in my outlook on life. In spite of all the difficult years I had been through, I was able, because of this one good year, to be completely salvaged and set on a successful road in life; not altogether the road I had planned to be on, for that is another story coming next. Nevertheless that one year was so good it lifted my spirit and enabled me, in the future and to this day, to cope well with obnoxious people without getting discouraged or worn down. To this day I am grateful to that school and to all my friends and acquaintances of that year.

"The following year I went away from home to university, still in Lower Secundaterra. I was undecided as to whether I would pursue my earlier desire to be a medical doctor. Much of that desire had been knocked out of me, temporarily at least, during my difficult years in high school. But now with this good year behind me, a spark of such ambition still remained within me. I talked about it with my parents, and tossed it around some in my mind. Time will tell, I told myself and them. I would hold off on the decision, until after my first, perhaps my second year of university. I knew I was going to an excellent university. Its reputation and credibility were well established far and wide throughout the country and in Europe.

"To make a long story short; this university after a period of tremendous growth, both in numbers and in curriculum, had attracted to its faculty people from various parts of the world. Inadvertently included among them were a sizable number of obnoxious people as we are still calling them in this group. They were experienced in their craft of dealing with people like us. Some of the locals were also in this obnoxious category, and although they were not as seasoned in their devious behavior, were nevertheless obstacles in the way for people like us.

"These obnoxious professors of lower to middle caliber, generally did not occupy the higher chairs of the faculties. These excellent higher chairs were occupied mostly by high quality, well charactered, people. As in almost any university today, so in this university to too large an extent, the lower chairs, teaching the pre-requisite and other required courses that enable a person to advance into a specialized field, were occupied by obnoxious professors from various parts of the world. They were keepers of the gate, so to speak, people thriving on their own personal power and control; and students they perceived to be of higher caliber than themselves seldom got past them unscathed. These students were either down graded so as not to have sufficient grades for admittance into a specialized field, or they were driven away.

"After my first year the only faculty I could find my way clear to enter was business administration. This department, perhaps by coincidence, or maybe by the maturity of its head professor, was in the hands of people who were always able to adjust to varying personalities, beyond what is the norm for themselves. I was able to steer my way through, with only a few scars, to an honors degree in business administration.

"Such a degree is not much of a prerequisite for studies in medicine. Having also learned much about business from a long line of successful business people in my family, I decided to aim at going into business for myself, feeling confident that I could do it.

"Before getting into that, I must tell you very briefly of how one person like us did get into medical school at that university. He simply faked his character through all his prerequisite and required pre-med courses, behaving like a strange clown or slightly out of sync character. He did his scholastic work well and was marked high according as his work deserved. At the same time, his desire to be a doctor was taken with a grain of salt by his would be adversaries. He being no threat to them, character that they thought he was, they allowed him to proceed on to success. When he was ready for medical studies, he put aside the facade, behaved as the well rounded personality that he really was, and went on to become a medical doctor.

"I would like now to go on to tell of my experiences in business if that is satisfactory to you and to the group, Dr. Eldren", said Brett, apparently eager to get the episode over with.

"*I don't blame him for wanting to get it over with as soon as possible*, thought Collin. *Anyone who is busy building up a business can't have his mind cluttered with the past, and to recall in detail such unpleasant and painful experiences is bound to cause the mind to dwell on it all for a period, perhaps for days. The harder times have been, the more difficult it is to banish them from one's mind.*"

Dr. Eldren spoke with an air of sincere interest. "Brett, my observation is that the group as a whole is most keenly interested. Am I correct in that assumption, folks?"

"Yes indeed, yes sir," came the reply from all around.

"Please continue then," Dr. Eldren nodded to Brett. "Your story is most interesting."

"As you try to make your way in business," Brett began again, "you bump into the same kind of characters as in school or university or anywhere else. People are people. But in the business world, in particular when you are in business for yourself, there is more room to maneuver around the obnoxious ones. They give you problems, often serious problems, but it is possible not to let yourself become as dependent on any one of them, as you are on say a specific professor or teacher in whose class you are placed or otherwise find yourself. In business, in a larger city particularly, if you don't like doing business with one person or company, you can take your business to another.

"Before venturing into business for myself I figured I needed to gain additional experience in the work-a-day world. I had had summer jobs ranging from farm help to office work. My greatest work experience asset to that time was extended periods of work in the offices of major European industries. These periods had been a part of my business practices total immersion. They had been valuable to me with regard to experiencing a wide assortment of people, as well as for the business experience. After graduation, I had the desire to gain more business experience.

"My first full time job after leaving university, was what I considered at the time to be a stop-gap arrangement. However, it turned out to be a valuable experience for me, considering the line of business in which I eventually wound up. This job was tending a very busy self-service gas station. I stayed with it for a while, but there was no opportunity there to gain experience in overall business management, which I was anxious to do, so I began thinking farther afield. Opportunity for employment was very limited in Lower Secundaterra, which for me I now considered to be my home. One day I set out for a far away city in Secundaterra. I knew life was going to be difficult there, perhaps even real tough for a person such as me. I didn't go alone however. By now I had had a serious relationship with a lady friend, for more than a year. She has since become my wife. She decided to go to the city with me, and having some relatives there was able to room with them, while I found accommodation a mile or so away.

"My girlfriend soon found work in a utilities company office. I wanted specifically to find a job in a business office of some sort where I could learn the inside track of business generally. I was interviewed for some such jobs, lost some of them due to inexperience, some because of being over-qualified and others I suspect due to obnoxious people, the same old story you know! With determination I kept trying to find what I wanted, and eventually came up with a job which was to begin in the stock warehouse of a large auto parts manufacturer. Keeping records of inventory for stock control purposes was my job, but I was all ears and eyes. This, I decided almost immediately, was a good business to know. My European business experience had included some inventory control. I had gained an amateur knowledge of car parts from working with my father in his hobby of repairing and servicing our own cars. Both of these experiences were of help in my obtaining this job. It was, by the way, before the time of computerized inventory control in this company.

"My two years in that business were good for me but there too, as I progressed in my knowledge and know how of the business I felt the sting of discrimination as did Donna when she was employed in industry. Everyone feels such a sting somehow in life I guess, but I had learned only too well that for people such as me, the sting would always be acute. I debated often whether I should gird myself and ride it out or at this time seek to launch out into business for myself. I believe now that I had at that point in my life developed an impatient attitude to having to put up with the sort of life that obnoxious people caused people like us to live. Somewhere in this world, I thought, there must be a place for me where I will not have to continually take such antagonisms.

"With an idea for my own business firmly in my mind I shared it with my girl friend. She agreed to my plan, and would also share with me in its financing, as much as her resources would allow. I would also need financial backing from a bank, and a preliminary exploration had shown the feasibility of this to be likely. The plan was that I would obtain a franchise with a major oil company for a self-serve gas filling station and accompanying automatic car wash. This was to be the beginning of a chain that I, or I should say we, my fiancée and I, hoped to eventually acquire.

"While still holding my job with the auto parts manufacturer, and my fiancée continuing with her position in offices of the utility company, we began to work on our project.

"The first major step taken was my appointment with an oil company executive. After telling him what my interests were in this field, he was skeptical. Although a very amicable person, for which I was more than thankful, having met so many obnoxious persons in my life, he wondered about my age. I was not only young, twenty four years of age, but I also looked younger than my years. He was concerned whether I would be able to manage with a good firm control over my business.

"I tried my best to convince him that I could handle it. He wasn't convinced, however, and remarked, 'I'm favorably impressed by you, and I don't anticipate any problem for you in raising the money to deal with this oil corporation. Banks consider us to be an excellent investment. But if only you were ten years older, even five years.' At the conclusion of the interview he said, 'I will have to think about it for awhile, and let you know.'

"As I left his office I was discouraged but still hopeful that somehow our plan could be brought to reality. Outside his office I passed by his secretary's desk, and there across from it, in the reception and waiting area sat a man whose face looked familiar to me. I knew immediately it was a man I had known many years before and had met occasionally over the years since. He looked older now of course, but I would know him anywhere. I couldn't help but remember him because he has always been openly and genuinely nice to me. It was the man who had remarked to my parents that day on our patio when I was only six years old, 'that's some boy you have there.' A person who has been kicked most of his life is bound to remember any kindly and affectionate person he experiences in life. This I did that day.

"Immediately, I went over and reintroduced myself to the man. He remembered my father well. He and my parents had exchanged Christmas cards all these years, and had crossed paths occasionally at business meetings, or on vacations, although they had not lived in the same city for many years now.

"This family friend and business associate of my father was more than happy to meet me. He asked about my parents, then about me. I knew he could be confided in trustworthily, so I told him my business plans, and also how the oil company executive to whom I had just been talking, was skeptical because of my age.

"'I have an appointment with that same executive now in a few minutes', remarked my new found friend. 'I know him well, have been dealing with him for years. I'll speak to him,' he said with a smile and a twinkle.

"I lit up like a Christmas tree. 'Would you,' I blurted out."

"'Oh yes, sure,' he said, 'I'd be happy to. Now you just give me your phone number so I can follow this matter through if necessary, and here, take my card, and don't hesitate to call me anytime you wish.'

"A sense of elation came over me immediately, but in a moment it was replaced by a deep and sober sense of assurance. I felt now, even though the deal had not yet gone through, that a door was opening for me. My renewal of acquaintance with my father's friend, I felt, would be an invaluable help to me. I appreciated the fact that he had connections, but more than that, he would, I felt, be a sincere and helpful friend who knew my side of life. After thanking him for his interest in me, I departed barely in time so that he would not see the tears well up in my eyes.

"My deep sense of assurance of that afternoon was substantiated that same evening by a phone call to me at my apartment from the oil company executive who informed me that I would be granted the gas station franchise. He had taken the trouble to phone after hours."

Then Brett chuckled aloud before the support group. "My fiancée and I went out and celebrated that evening — at a nearby restaurant. It was a real treat for us. We had been saving money for our business so stringently that very little went for entertainment or recreation. As humble as it was we enjoyed the evening, and over our modest dinner made preliminary plans to be married when our business was far enough advanced. Things were definitely on the upswing for us, but just around the corner was another obnoxious person waiting to put me down.

"The next phase necessary for the procuring of our business franchise was to arrange a loan from our bank to go along with our savings, as the initial outlay of capital to get us started. I had not anticipated any problem with this. My fiancée and I had both built up impressionable accounts with this bank, established a satisfactory credit rating, and had become fairly well known at the local branch. A lesson I learned at that time though, and which I have had confirmed many times since, is that friends one may make when on the lower plains of life, do not necessarily remain friends when you attempt to rise to a higher plateau.

"Ours was to be a sizeable loan, but not outside the means of our combined salaries, let alone the income expected from our business. As I talked to the bank branch manager about our desire to get a loan to take up a franchise on a gas filling station and automatic car wash, I was puzzled at first by the coolness of his reception, especially when it was at a period in time when banks were bending over backwards to lend money. Ours was a sound proposition, and I was able to present concrete figures from the oil company to support it. In addition, my fiancée and I were both still working and would continue to be able to do so until our business was expanded to the degree that it needed my full time management; that is, until we acquired other stations, and established a chain according to our long range plan.

"At first, however, I did not want to tell the manager of our plans for future expansion. It was unnecessary, I thought, and I would keep our plans to myself. Having told him of plans for just this one initial outlet, he balked and said, 'I don't think you are on the right track. You should be buying a service station with a couple of bays, one for routine servicing and one for repairs. Then you could build a sound business for yourself.'

"Even though such businesses were common at the time, I protested, 'but that's not the kind of business I wish to get into. Besides, I'm not a mechanic. I wouldn't know that aspect of the business sufficiently.'

"'Well then,' he said, 'you should be taking training in mechanics, instead of being here looking for money to start a business of which you know very little.'

"'Look,' I said, 'if I was interested in going that way I would get a service station with three or four bays and I would hire mechanics. It's a good business, but it so happens that it is not the kind of business I have in mind.'

"I was getting exasperated, but held my patience. 'Look,' I repeated, 'I'm not interested in that kind of business. Neither do I want to be a mechanic.'

"The manager cut in sharply, 'what's wrong with being a mechanic?'

"'Absolutely nothing,' I protested, 'for anyone who wants to be a mechanic, but it so happens that I do not want to be one, and I do not want to get into that kind of business.'

"The manager looked at me contemptuously and spoke haughtily, 'my son is a mechanic, and he has his own service station, and he is doing quite well with it.'

"There lay the crux of the problem.

"I remarked emphatically, 'I'm sure your son is doing quite well, and I hope he continues to do even better in the future, but that just isn't the kind of business I am interested in getting involved in. Let me explain further,' I said. 'Listen, I want to take over this one franchise for the present, filling station and automatic car wash. Now the way I have it planned I know there isn't a great deal of work in that for me, except for management which will be part time. But in the near future I plan to expand, by establishing other such outlets. When my business has grown sufficiently, I will give up my present employment and manage my business full time.'

"*Surely he can see that*, I thought. But he simply pulled down his mouth and pushed out his lips in contempt. He didn't want to see what I was getting at. It was just too much for himself and his son. His nose was out of joint, as we would say, and it was like talking to a brick wall. People like that just don't want to see. They quite literally put up a wall, and you can't get past it. The manager sat there staring daggers at me.

"Now I was getting out of patience with him for his attitude and also disgusted with myself at having bared myself and my plans so fully before such a bigoted and prejudiced clod.

"'Well,' I said, pointedly, 'do I get the money or don't I?'" He shook his head as he pushed up his lip again. 'No, your proposition is not sound,' came the reply.

"It was a devastating blow to me, and at the moment, I hardly knew what to do. From experience, I knew that to coax or beg from such characters, only enhances their already puffed up position. These types just love to see you squirm before them. *I would never stoop to that*, I told myself. I never once did in all my brutal years of high school, and other difficult years of school and university, nor since. *No, I would never do that*, I repeated to myself. I thanked him for his time, got up out of the chair and walked out.

"You did right, I'm sure you already know," remarked Collin. "There in that bank manager you see the essence of the self-centered man— what is good enough for me and mine is good enough for anyone; and no one who doesn't think so gets past me, unless they are willing to come down to or below my level. Such a person should never be dealing with the public."

"Agreed," said Brett, and continued. "The two miles to my apartment from the bank seemed a long way that day. I had covered them by bus to come to the bank. I walked them now to return to my apartment. Having been given time off from work to keep the appointment, it wasn't necessary for me to return to the plant that afternoon, so I strolled along the sidewalk slowly and dejectedly. The disappointment was severe, but, I kept thinking there must be some way. If only I could come up with another approach or plan of action before I saw my fiancée that evening, to save her from disappointment as well. And then there was my father's friend, who with full confidence in me, had put in a word on my behalf at the oil company. What would I be able to tell him. He had gone out on a limb for me, and now I couldn't even come up with the money.

"'My father's friend!' I repeated to myself. 'Yes, I'll let him down too, my father's good friend and mine; hey, that's it! My father's friend and mine.'

"I had his card in my wallet. He had told me to call him if I ever needed help. Pausing and looking around, I thought, *there must be a telephone nearby*. My eyes scanned the area, but there was no phone in sight. *I know where there is one*, I remembered, *just two blocks and around the turn, in the foyer of a department store*. My steps speeded to a near run as my hopes came alive again. Once more I felt an assurance that this man could help. He was a very astute business man with a lot of connections, and a helpful type of person generally.

"'Hello Brett,' he said, as his secretary put him on the line to me after telling him who was calling. 'How is your business venture going?' he asked in a manner that made me feel as one of his closest friends.

"'Not very good sir,' I replied. 'I'd like to thank you for recommending me to the oil company. That part of it is all right. But to my surprise, I'm having trouble raising money at the bank.'

"'That surprises me too,' replied my friend. 'Did you talk to your bank manager about it?'

"'Yes, I did sir,' I said, 'but his response was negative.'

"'Tell me just what he said about the matter, Brett, if you will please,' he asked.

"So I related to him the whole conversation with the bank manager. My friend's response was without hesitation. 'You have to get established with another bank, Brett.'

"'But sir,' I mildly protested in my inexperience, 'I thought if perhaps you could put in a word for me to a bank authority higher than the manager it might help. I've been established at that particular bank for two years now.'

"'No good, Brett,' came the reply. 'If a person like that is a manager in that organization, chances are there are others like him up through the system, and down through too for that matter. Birds of a feather, you know,' he added, then continued, 'tell you what Brett, I'd like to suggest another bank to you. I will phone the manager, if you wish, and tell him of you and about you and that you will be in to see him first opportunity. That will be a satisfactory substitute for being an established customer for a period of time. I would suggest you place your proposition before him, and be willing to transfer all your accounts to his bank. He can tell you how to best do this, and I think things will work out for you there.'

"'Thank you, sir,' I responded, still hesitantly. 'Do you think he will approve a loan for my business venture?' I asked, seeking assurance.

"'No doubt about it in my mind,' came my friend's reply. 'It's a sound proposition. However, talk it over thoroughly with him, before you make your move. It will make you feel better about what you're doing.'

"'Okay, great, sir, I'll do just as you advise. And thank you again,' I said gratefully.

"'And by the way,' came back my friend, 'call me again to let me know how it all turns out, and let's keep contact.'

"'Be very glad to,' I said. As we ended the telephone conversation, I thought with deep gratitude how wonderful it is to have a friend.

"Things went well from there on. My friend's advice and help proved to be sound. In due time my fiancée and I were in business. That business expanded, to include eventually several outlets spread over a wide territory that was to progressively take more and more of my time for management. At the opportune time I resigned from my job at the auto parts plant. In time also my fiancée and I were married, and we are very happy."

That seemed to be the happy ending to Brett's story. However, before anyone else could speak, Brett indicated that he wanted to continue. He quickly said, "There is one more incident from my business career, a recent one, which I would like to relate to you before I conclude my presentation. I will try not to keep us too late. Is that all right, Dr. Eldren and group members?"

Leo remarked in amazement, "still more! man, are you sure you are still alive?"

"Very much so, Leo," answered Brett, "but I suspect there are many like us who don't come through it as fortunate as I."

"That's for sure," remarked Collin, "but for a fiancée and a true friend eh, Brett!"

"Right," agreed Brett, "how true! Now this latest incident will have further bearing on the matter," he said as he kept his story going.

"About six years after I started with my gas station and car wash chain, and with that business by then solidly established, I became interested in an auto parts rebuilding plant. The work of this plant was the rebuilding of alternators, generators, regulators, and starters. Having once been a thriving small plant doing a good business in the local area only, it was now, under a different owner, not doing very well for various management reasons, and was up for sale again. The prospects enthused me tremendously. I investigated the business thoroughly; the history of its productivity and financial position, employee-employer relationships, market potential, and the reasons it was for sale. My estimation was, if I became the owner of this plant I could overcome the deficiencies in the business and do well with it.

"Having had by now several years of successful business experience, and having had contact with business management and financial consultants, and having taken extra courses in business management here at Quilibet University I felt I was ready and capable of safely expanding my horizons in the business field. Also, I became convinced that this auto parts rebuilding business could not only be rescued and put on a sound financial basis, but in time could be expanded considerably. I felt confident I could do that safely and soundly.

"There was low interest government guaranteed aid available for the establishment of new industry, or, for the renewal of existing industry. I first took out an option on the business, then went to the government agency to seek financial aid. Here again I ran into you know what by now."

"Again, eh!" remarked Collin. "It gets to be a part of life doesn't it?"

"Yes it does, Collin, and I expect it now. However, by then I was in a position where I could usually get around it somehow or other."

"Good," said Collin.

"Well," continued Brett, "this time it was the government agency officer. His nose was out of joint almost from the beginning of my approach to him.

"This middle aged officer sat in a rather cold silence as I told him of my plan to purchase that ailing manufacturing plant, and through improved management over a period of about a year or so make it a viable and profitable business.

"The officer's first response indicated by its tone that a negative reaction was coming. 'What makes you think you can turn this business around and make it profitable?' he asked curtly.

"From previous experience I had a pretty good idea that I was beaten on this matter already. However, I had to be sure, so I pursued the discussion further. I explained to him how I had already built up one business, and in addition to that I had experience in a related field of the auto parts business. Furthermore I explained that as well as having my degree in business administration, I had taken extra business management courses, and in addition had access to business consultants.

"It was obvious to me immediately that coming from a person such as me, only near thirty years old and looking even younger than that, this was all too much for this middle aged man. His shoulders lifted as he straightened back, pulled himself higher and higher in his chair. Then he set about to let me know that he knew a thing or two about business also, and wasn't to be outdone by this young smarty.

"'I think,' he said with an air of proud authority, 'the trouble with this manufacturing business you have in mind to purchase is that it is not large enough to survive in today's business world. Now if you were to borrow money enough, not only to purchase the business as is, but to double its capacity almost immediately, then, I would say this business would be able to survive.'

"My reply to him was contradictory," Brett continued to the group. 'To my mind, sir,' I said to him, 'there are two reasons why I would not agree with you. The first is that before this plant changed hands three years ago it was prospering under its original management. It was sold at that time for reasons other than financial. Only under its new ownership and management has it gone downhill. The market hasn't changed enough in these three years to make this plant obsolete because of its size or otherwise.'

"'Secondly, sir,' I continued, 'it is much too soon for me to borrow additional money now to double the production of this plant at this time. The plant as it is has lost many of its good customers. It will take time to rebuild a reputation and build up a clientele large enough for its original capacity. It will be some time before a market can be built up to handle increased production. Consequently, if I were to borrow that extra money at this time the interest and principal payments would be an obstacle in the way of the successful rejuvenation of the business. Either that, or my present business would have to carry the needless load for some time. Sorry sir,' I said, 'I can't agree with you on that.'

"The officer began to look shifty, but I knew he would have an out, and he did.

"'The government,' he said, 'through the funds available through this agency is interested primarily in producing jobs. Now if you were interested in borrowing enough to double, yes even triple the capacity of that plant, I can see how we could let you have the money. But as it is, well, you can fill out an application, and I will place it before the committee when we meet next week, but I can tell you right now your chances are slim unless you aim to drastically expand that plant.'

"My mind was appalled at what I was hearing," said Brett. "True, the government is interested in creating jobs, but look at what I was being offered. I would be turned down if I insisted on leaving the plant at its present size for a period. If I agreed to immediately enlarge, I knew that doubling capacity would be bringing an unnecessary and risky burden on my present business. Tripling the capacity would ruin me. I suspected, and I feel, correctly, that he knew this too. He was leading me into a trap.

"Immediately the words of my father's friend came back to me from the time he had advised me concerning the bank. 'It's no good, Brett, you have to change banks,' he had said then. I thought to myself, *this is not a bank, and there is no other government to go to, but I have to get out of here*. I made a quick decision that I would turn the agency down, before they had the opportunity to turn me down. To be turned down by the government is not the best reference. So just in case it may somehow make a difference in the future, I decided not to put in an application.

"'Sir,' I said to the government officer, 'I have decided to pursue other means of financing instead of bothering the government.'

"'You will pay higher rates of interest,' he shot back quickly. I simply smiled and rose from my chair.

"'Where will you look now for the loan,' he shot at me again snappily and obviously bothered that I might succeed elsewhere.

"'That will be my concern now sir, thank you for your time and good day,' I replied as I left his office.

"Setbacks such as this were very familiar to me by now, so I did not despair. I was in a favorable position to borrow my needs from my bank. The interest rates would be higher, but I could obtain smaller, periodic loans suitable to my needs as I saw them coming. However, I did not forget my father's friend, but went to visit him at his office that same day. Upon my explaining to him what had taken place at the government agency, my reaction to it, and what I now proposed to do, he whole heartedly agreed with me.

"'Be your own man,' he said, 'do your thing. That kind of people will lead you down the garden path, and when you end up in the mire, they turn and walk away leaving you to wallow for yourself. Then when the finger points at you for being so stupid and naive, they put themselves in the clear as though they had nothing to do with it. Yes Brett,' he spoke assuringly, 'you have the hang of it now. Always exercise caution, and you will come out on top. And by the way,' he said to my surprise, 'I've heard via the corporation grapevine that your father is coming back to Secundaterra with the corporation. Not sure just where he will be yet, but there is to be a store management position for him somewhere. I guess the compelling reasons for which he left, whatever they were, have been taken care of and he's free to move again. He's a good man you know, I'll be glad to see him back in the mainstream.'

"I felt a smile go right through me and reflect on my lips. 'I hadn't heard yet. I'm very happy,' I said. 'I know he will inform me of the move when his plans are finalized.'

"As I left my father's friend's office that day, he expressed his usual and sincere, 'Keep in touch.' I walked away feeling good about the business assurance I received again from this good friend, but also ever so much more because my father would pursue his career in the mainstream of life again, where there would possibly be more fulfillment for him too, as well as for me.

"Getting back to my business now," continued Brett, "my bank financed my takeover of the auto parts rebuilding plant. As I had estimated, in a little more than a year it was operating profitably. Having access to money from the bank as I needed it, even though at a higher rate than if it were through the government agency, I was able to borrow gradually, and increase production gradually, until now, three years later, the plant's capacity and output are nearly doubled, and increasing steadily and soundly.

"Furthermore, I have recently landed a contract to rebuild these parts for a large national auto parts chain with water pump rebuilding and brake shoe relining added to the list of electrical parts. This contract will help supply their stores in the eastern part of the country. With this expansion taking place, I am changing the plant from a bench type of production to an assembly line production. This will necessitate some enlargement in the size of the plant also.

"In addition to this I presently have my eye on what may or may not be a good opportunity in the manufacture of ignition parts. Through a connection I have with a young auto engineer, an ailing ignition parts plant has come to my attention. This plant hasn't modernized to keep up with electronic ignition systems. There is still some business in the old type ignition parts, but it is getting less and less. The plant is ailing for obvious reasons. The young engineer is a whiz in his field. His abilities have not been recognized by his superiors for the same reason yours and mine are often not recognized. He thinks that he and I can modernize this plant and make a go of it, perhaps expanding into some lines of auto accessories. At present I am still exploring the possibilities. It raises questions such as how much do my wife and I wish to expand our business, and is this the only way we could help the young engineer who is a person like us, with much the same problems in life.

"So-o-o-o-, ladies and gentlemen," said Brett, after a brief pause, "there it is, my tale of woe and survival."

Leo spoke next. "Brett, you describe your story as one of woe and survival. The woe part of it is apparent. But survival! You have done more than survive, you have built up a little business empire for yourself, and it continues to grow. Is this mere survival?"

"Surprisingly, in a sense it is," replied Brett.

"When someone is trying to put you down, Leo, they are never content to hold you down to where they think they have you already. Rather, they are always looking for a way to send you down further. In the process they put you down by spoiling on you that which you already have. So if they spoil it and you jump to something less, then you are playing into their hands. If you want to live victoriously, you have no alternative but to jump to something better. So I keep climbing in whatever direction opens to me. Yes in a very real sense it is a matter of survival."

"I understand," remarked Leo.

Collin then asked, "Brett, originally you intended to be a medical doctor. The doors to this career were closed to you by others. Now you have made a successful career for yourself in industry. Are you finding personal fulfillment in your present work, or do you still sometimes wish for what has been taken from you?"

Brett answered with assurance, "You've put your finger on the key, Collin; in the words 'what has been taken from me.' I am happy in my present occupation, and I am, not in the least, bitter about not having become a medical doctor. I do not need to be a doctor to find fulfillment. Yet every time I go to a doctor, I am reminded of the injustice done me. Injustice always hurts — always.

"On the other hand, fulfillment for me is doing something worth while with one's own life in such a manner that it not only brings a good life to oneself, but is also beneficial to others. Certainly, being a medical doctor, would bring opportunity for that kind of fulfillment. However, as I am now situated in industry I feel I am doing something worthy with my own life in such a manner as to provide products and employment for the benefit of others. My businesses have to pay their way, and I like to see them pay their way by a safe margin. That is only good and safe business. But I have no desire to accumulate great wealth. Each venture in business or industry is a challenge to create, and to build something worthwhile and beneficial to the better side of life. I find personal fulfillment in that.

"I also find personal fulfillment in not only providing employment for people, but in helping employees to find a happy and fulfilling better side of life within the scope of their own horizons, whether they be larger or not than what I can provide for them. My employees to me are a family for whom I, in cooperation with them, am responsible. I care for them and treat them well, within the limits of the opportunities I have for them. If and when they outgrow these limits, these horizons, they are free to search for a higher fulfillment elsewhere with any help I can give them.

"But this something that 'has been taken from me,' is another matter. It is an injustice done against me by others that will never even be recognized by most people. There will never be any correction or punishment for their robbery, and that is what it is you know, robbery. I never brood over it. Heaven forbid that. But I will never forget the injustice of it either, as it has left deep scars on me. However, life has ways of compensating."

Dr. Eldren remarked, "We are running very late, Brett, and you look very tired. But it has been most interesting to say the least. I am sure though you would appreciate a break at this point. May I suggest we adjourn to meet again next Wednesday evening. If we continue to follow our plan, Owen Winslow will be called upon to relate his experiences next. Will that by okay, Owen?" he asked.

"All right with me," said Owen.

Leo remarked, “With Owen being a clergyman, I don’t suppose there is any of that kind of skullduggery going on concerning his life.”

Collin chuckled aloud in contradiction.

Owen smiled. “Don’t count on it, Leo,” he said. “See you next week.”

## CHAPTER SEVEN

Collin Seldon and his wife Vita arrived in the foyer of the first floor of the Arts building of Quilibet University in order that Collin might attend this next support group session in which Owen Winslow was to tell his story. They arrived a little earlier than necessary.

Looking at his watch Collin remarked to his wife that they were twenty minutes early, and suggested they both sit on a bench in the foyer for a while before Collin went to the session in room 405 and Vita to the university library to pass the time while waiting for him.

As they relaxed there the conversation between them drifted around to the subject of how best might Owen, and indeed Collin himself later on, handle the delicate matter of being critical of the church. They would have to do so as they each in turn told of experiences affecting their life within the church. Such criticism would be necessary to the authenticity of the stories, they mutually agreed.

They had not been sitting there long when Owen Winslow came by on his way to the support group. Collin motioned him to join them on the bench.

After an exchange of greetings, Collin said, "Owen, my wife and I were just discussing the matter of criticism of the church on the part of you and I as we tell our stories."

Owen broke in, "yes, I've given that a great deal of thought myself during the past week. I realize there is an unwritten law in the church that open criticism is taboo, and that the person who practices it is likely to be branded a fault finder or even worse. Furthermore, I know that this unwritten law probably came about for a good purpose originally; to keep the church's public image one of high spiritual profile despite the fact that it is made up of imperfect people. But it has gotten out of hand."

"Yes, I know," said Collin, "that's the way I feel about it too."

Vita asserted briskly, “Any rule that has gotten out of hand needs renewed attention. I would say that is so, more particularly in the case of the church if that law is being used, or misused, as a cover-up for things that should not be. Under those circumstances you have every right to criticize. In fact it is high time someone did.”

Collin and Owen, both clergymen, looked at each other. Collin put up his hands in an open gesture, raising his eyebrows as he stretched his face in a questioning manner, “there you have our opinion,” he said to Owen, curious to know what his reaction would be.

“Yea,” replied Owen, “and in all good conscience that has to be my opinion too. I’ve given it a great deal of thought during the week, and I have come to the conclusion that the truth never did any harm yet. Are you with me Collin?”

“All the way,” said Collin with a smile.

“Then let’s get up and at ’em,” said Owen, lightly, as he stood. It’s time to go to room 405 is it not?”

“Just about,” said Collin as he also stood.

They bade farewell to Vita Seldon as she departed to read in the library while awaiting her husband’s return from another group session.

The group members stood around room 405, chatting for a few moments before starting time. Owen Winslow stood tall above them all, his broad shoulders and heavy set, yet trim body somewhat dwarfed the other members. He had a good head of medium brown straight hair, parted at the left side and combed very simply back with a slight natural rise at the front where it looked to be still of average thickness for the age of middle thirties. He was dressed in a pin striped navy blue suit, with appropriate shirt and tie. His kindly facial expression exemplified his character. It is difficult to imagine that such a large manly body could house such a firmly gentle personality with a serious and searching mind. Such was the unusual make-up of Owen Winslow. Despite his size, you would not expect to find him on the football team. He was not the athletic type. Yet he would stand out with a pleasant distinction, in any crowd. He too had this in common with the other group members.

When the group had assembled, Owen took command at once. "Group members," he began, "I would ask you not to be any more appalled at what you hear concerning my experiences as a minister of the church. People who are active in the inner circles of the church are often aware of the shortcomings of some of its people. Generally, however, most people either regard the church or its ministry at least as being very near saintly perfection, or, they tend to gloss over any faults they may see. Consequently the institution in which they try to keep faith does not often become tarnished in their sight and in the sight of others. The hard fact of the matter is though, the church including its ministry, is made up of people, nice people, obnoxious people, all sorts of characters and personalities, just as in any other sphere of life. You may wonder at this point whether the church should be better than other areas of life in this regard. I would ask you to leave that question open for the present. Collin is a minister also. After we have both told our stories we should all have a picture of the church as it exists for you and I and your question may be answered."

"That complies with our general format, Owen," remarked Dr. Eldren.

The group members agreed that they were interested in hearing about the church with regard to their common interests.

The usual, and now expected quip came from Leo Aidan, "brace yourselves folks, your faith is about to be shattered, but remember we have a psychiatrist present as a viable alternative!"

When the laughter over that remark had subsided, Owen spoke in serious tones once more, "really folks, there is no need to lose your faith. God is perfect. Have faith in Him, remembering that His church is made up of sinners."

"Redeemed sinners, though," interjected Leo.

"Yes mostly, but not all," answered Owen. "the wheat and the weeds are there together as the Bible says, (see The Gospel of Matthew 13:25-30 R.S.V.), and that makes a difference. Then again, there are far too many who haven't matured much at all since becoming Christians; growing in grace is still largely something foreign to them. Hence people like 'us' have our problems in the church as well as anywhere in the secular world.

"Now to begin my story," Owen started, "I grew up mainly in a small city not far from here, where my father was minister of a medium size church, medium for that part of the country. We moved there when I was ten years old. I was the youngest of the three children, three boys in the family. My mother was a good sort of woman. In my estimation, my father was the problem causing person of the family. My father's long stay at this church saw my two older brothers and I through high school and away to university. Even after that my father stayed on there as minister for several years.

"Being the younger of the three brothers put me in an unfavored and unfavorable position in the family and consequently in much of later life. This was due to my father's philosophy in life, that a younger brother must not be ahead of, in any way whatsoever, his older brothers; as though a younger brother could turn his mind off at will, just to remain dumber than his brothers. Or, of course, when he doesn't turn it off, the obnoxious ones try to turn it off for him. You might see immediately the absurdity and the impossibility of this philosophy, or rather this ill-born concocted notion in my father's head, as it is in many other peoples heads in various ways and degrees. It is surprising how many people do adopt such a problem creating policy as this for the raising of their families.

"In addition to a younger brother or sister in some families, not getting ahead of an older sibling, some parents have the concoction in their heads that some, or all of the children, as the case may be, must not get ahead of their parents. What's good enough for the parent is good enough for the children. None of them must get ahead of their parents.

"This notion of my father's is just one more way some obnoxious people have, in their minds at least, of keeping people they deem a threat to their pride, including family members, where they can be looked down on rather than looked up to. I realize other such obnoxious parents sometimes are quite willing for their children to do better than the parents, sometimes in some other occupation, provided the parent is able to feel in control and take the credit for it somehow. Again, other such parents set up in their minds rivalry with people outside the family only.

"Getting back to myself, you can see that as I was growing up, one of my greatest problems was right at home; my father's continuous effort to keep me behind my brothers and himself so that I would not hurt their pride, stir their envy, or ruffle their feathers in any way. Strangely enough though, the middle brother sometimes quite noticeably outdid the older brother in something or other, but that was always overlooked.

"In time it became obvious to me that I was the one at which the policy was aimed. Through the years, my father kept this policy into effect by continually showing favor to my brothers by making them out to be superior to me, and making me feel inferior to them. One of the resulting consequences was that it made me, in my younger years, feel inferior to most other people with whom I came in contact outside the family. So I was damaged at an early age.

"The attitude of my father towards me was manifested also in his life and dealings with certain other people. He scorned people he deemed to be a cut above himself, continually looking for their faults and flaws to justify his feelings towards them. Ironically enough, he befriended and praised those whom he felt were beneath him. This, by the way is a common characteristic of the kind of difficult people we in this group are dealing with. It is obvious to me now in a more mature retrospect that in my father's eye, perhaps unconsciously, I was in the realm of those he considered to be a cut above him. My two brothers he considered to be on the other side of the coin. Feeling they were no threat to him, he could talk down to them and nurture them through life within the sphere of his own stifled and unopen mind set, at least until they were on their own. Then they had opportunity to outgrow whatever they might have absorbed from this erroneous parenting. I might interject here, that from observation I have learned that in some cases it is the mother who leads her family by this error ridden philosophy.

"As you hear my story it may seem odd to you that a man educated in arts and theology would have such a personality make-up. On the other hand he supported these characteristics with various wayward interpretations of the Bible and Christianity that are not at all uncommon throughout the church; interpretations, or misinterpretations to my mind, that cause untold prejudices and widespread misery.

"You know how it goes, 'Christianity is a religion of the common people.' My father was so down on anyone he perceived as uncommon, and yet he was continually trying to be like them and be in their sphere himself, never being able to figure out why he couldn't attain it. Then there is the sometimes sentimental, sometimes nostalgic, always supposedly humbling factor that Jesus was 'just a carpenter,' brought up in the home of Joseph, also a carpenter. Furthermore, Jesus' chosen disciple Peter was just an 'ordinary' fisherman.

"True, Joseph did own a carpenter shop, and in all likelihood Jesus learned the trade and the business and worked at it until he began his ministry. Yet Joseph, and likely Jesus, did not work in someone else's carpenter shop, he owned and operated one himself. That is something different. Joseph was in the carpentry business, which was a substantial business of the time. He didn't own, for example, a furniture factory as we visualize a furniture factory today simply because that wasn't the way it was done then. He didn't own a construction company and mass produce housing. Neither the houses nor the building of them was done in that way at that time and place. But Joseph, and likely Jesus, did own and operate a carpenter shop, a substantial business of that era. Given Joseph's financial means to raise a family, and to travel, it seems he did quite well with this business. He wasn't turned away from the inn that night because he didn't have money, but because there was no room.

"Then there is Peter, the 'ordinary' fisherman. There are many ordinary fishermen in the world today. No doubt there was then.

There are many very well-to-do fishermen in the world today. I have known some of them whose yearly net income for one season of work would give many ministers and some executives an inferiority complex. People often visualize the occupation of fishing as a hook and line occupation lived out in a tiny boat. The fishing business can be big business. No, Peter didn't own an ocean going trawler or a dragger from which most of the business is done today, but he was in the big league of his time. One scholar has written, 'Although his occupation was a humble one, yet it was not incompatible with some degree of mental culture, and seems to have been quite remunerative. (*Unger's Bible* dictionary, P. 847. The Moody Bible Institute, Chicago 1957).

Collin could not help interject a thought. "Owen," he interrupted, "I know a great deal about the history of the fishing industry of the past several centuries. For many, many people, at some periods more so than others, it was big business, creating barons of the seas; people not only making money, but becoming people of social, political and cultural influence; also, often branching out into other avenues of business, or as we would say today, diversifying."

Owen beamed a broad smile amid the misery of telling his story. "Collin," he said, "that's the best support I have ever had for this bit of my theology. Thanks."

"I suppose," interjected Collin again, "Your father's and your own views on *The Magnificat (The Gospel of Luke 1:46-55)* are quite different too, are they not?"

"How did you ever guess that one," said Owen. "To my father The Magnificat meant that God would not rest until he had brought down all the mighty and the rich and exalted all who were not presently in that category. There were some things he chose to overlook, however, the first of which is, after God exalts all the lowly, does He then whittle them down too, the way my father continually whittled me down? Not at all. God is not like that, except in the warped minds of those who whittle God down to their way and level of thinking. The second was that my father himself, in his own way, and within his own life's sphere, was continuously trying to be among the mighty and the rich, as well as wishing to be exalted by God. Thirdly, there was no one more proud than he, yet the thought never daunted him that he might be among those to be scattered by God.

"This all seems so trifling, yet The Magnificat so misunderstood can cause widespread prejudice and hardship. My personal belief on the matter is that of traditional Christian theology which says that wealth and position are not sinful in themselves, but can be sinfully misused. This theology has been all but lost in the church of Secundaterra today in its biased and frantic passion for the poor. I recently attended a seminar conducted by very prominent church officials. There The Magnificat was quoted, and interpreted to imply that all the rich were automatically condemned, and all the poor were automatically saved simply because of their station in life.

"My father's attitude towards me, and towards many others in whose category he placed me, was much influenced by this commonly accepted and deep-rooted bias in the contemporary mainline churches. By this same bias, he placed my two brothers, and the remaining segment of society in another category, the category of the common people. Through this envy ridden, erroneously scripture supported, prejudiced oppression, I was to suffer all my youthful years. Were it not for my mother's skillfully concealed and usually silent love and support, I would never have made it, for everyone needs someone, and more.

"Such was my father's way and attitude, down with the rich and the mighty, up with the common people. The ironic part about it as I have already indicated, and which in turn indicates that his erroneous theology was motivated by envy, is that he was continually trying to climb up to the sphere of the rich and the mighty himself. Although there was no opportunity to become rich in the ministry, his frame of mind was conditioned to take every opportunity to make or save a dollar where he could. Not a penny was to be overlooked when it came to settling accounts with the church board concerning everything from salary to postage stamps. I know he needed money to provide for his family, but, he practiced his personal financing in such an exacting way, one wondered at the priority importance it seemed to play in his life.

"All clergy of our church had to be good managers and thrifty people in order to make ends meet with their often small salary, comparatively speaking. But there was an almost intangible element present in my father's attitude towards money that placed him in the category of those whose only aim in life is to make money and more money. For example, when a couple would come to him to arrange a wedding, he would come away from the interview with no such thought as, 'what a lovely couple' or 'this is another couple heading out on the adventure of life together.' Rather, his remark would be, 'that's another twenty dollars coming in,' or 'I should get fifty dollars out of that one,' or, 'maybe even a hundred dollars for this big one.'"

Owen shook his head sadly, "there was no need of that in our family. We were comfortably well off. Our needs were cared for to the degree of average for the people around us."

There was a silence as Owen, for a brief moment stared in a fixed gaze. Then, as if to shake off the sadness of criticizing his own father so, he stirred himself in the chair. Toning up his voice to firmness he remarked, "It's as Collin and Gilda say, we should bear these attitudes in mind throughout our discussions, and put them into words when possible."

"Moreover," continued Owen, "over and above the financial climb, there was in his life the ambition to have a large city church. He did get up to a medium size; the one he had when I was growing up, as I told you. He figured that would be the stepping stone to something even larger. But the larger one never came his way. So there he stayed in the medium size church; year after year, long after his welcome there had worn out. He had reached his peak but wouldn't accept it. He muttered about the big shots in the larger churches, yet that's where he longed to be himself. Not possessing the character for higher echelons, perhaps being already further up the ladder than he should have been, he now had nowhere else to turn, except to an appointment in a smaller parish. This his pride would not let him accept. My father held on to what he had until his retirement. He died a few years later, mellowed some, at least to the point where he could shrug and say, 'Oh well, I did the best I could.' On the other hand, as though still struggling with his problem to the end, he occasionally continued to mutter about those big shots; something he had never been able to become nor understand why. It was simply because of his misled personality, and he was minister in a church area where such personalities as he were not predominant, and so did not often get their way.

"Such is a brief outline of the story of my father. I tell it to you because I feel it has a profound bearing on my life, and may figure in our later discussion. But now I must go on with the story of my own life.

"On the way up through school I had my trials and experiences with some obnoxious teachers and students, as many of you have already revealed you have had. I will not go through them in detail. You already know what kind of experiences they are. I would like to point out though, because I think it is a matter of relevance, that most of the open hostility, shunning, and discrimination against me in my school days took place in my younger years. There I had a mixture of the good and the bad, but much to my good fortune the good side was predominant. Added to this I had my mother's love, care and concern to encourage me on.

"Regardless of my mother's genuine concern for me, and her loving expression of it in the way she treated me, she was never one to understand the kind of thing I was up against in life. She was a good woman who believed that as long as I remained on the good side of life, well behaved, good mannered, studying hard, keeping good company, there would be a good place for me in life. I appreciate that atmosphere in which she placed me, since it gave me the incentive to keep on the good track, at least most of the time. Any time I wavered from that track that atmosphere served also to bring me back.

"On the other side of the coin, my mother did not know, let alone understand the darker side of life. She was well aware, of course, that there is evil in the world but like many others, evil to her was made up of the kind of things that often make the headlines in the newspapers, things like stealing, shooting, gangsterism and the like. She had no conception whatever of the kind of evil I had to contend with either in our home or outside it. Consequently, my mother was of no direct help to me in contending with obnoxious teachers, and other such acquaintances. My father, you have well surmised by now, was in the category of the obnoxious himself, so I could expect no help from him in that area of life. I had, therefore, to fight my own battles to a very large degree.

"As I said earlier, in elementary school, although there definitely were battles and struggles, the good side was predominant and I came through in good condition and with mostly good marks. Also, as I said earlier, my mother's love, care and concern, though naive in some respects, was a definite inspiration to me. Strangely enough, as I see it in retrospect now my father was inadvertently a help to me too in one sense. For although, as a person, he was well known in the small city in which we lived, he was not known as a big wheel but rather was associated in the minds of the people generally with the common people. Therefore I was not discriminated against at school for what my father was. At least that excuse could not be used to discriminate against me. This, I think helped soften the blows some, but I was still put down plenty because of what I myself was.

"Coming to senior high school," continued Owen, "this is an area in life where one can experience the most outward and vicious type of put down, as I will call it and as Brett so well exemplified in his story. But I am very thankful, that although I was far from popular among the obnoxious ones in high school, I was spared much of the agony that normally would have come my way. In retrospect again, I quite seriously, and with much thought and experience to support my belief, attribute this welcome relief to my physical size. I had grown to be quite a big person in size by now."

"You mean to tell us," blurted Leo as he broke into the story, "that they laid off you because of your size?"

*Owen is breaking new ground here*, thought Collin. *I'd better give him some support*. Then aloud, "remember, bullies are cowards, Leo!"

"I see," said Leo, now appearing a little goggle-eyed."Well-l" he pursued the matter, "did you get to be a tough guy, I mean did you flex your muscles and threaten them or anything like that?"

"No, Leo," replied Owen, "I probably would have been expelled for something like that. It's just that I grew tall and broad, not fat, but generally big and masculine. As absurd as that may seem, it had a profound subconscious psychological effect on them so they wouldn't pick on me. They didn't like me either, and they kept aloof. The tension was there, and the estrangement, but at the same time being spared the agony of being picked on enabled me to do well with my studies."

"Well I'll be!" said Leo in amazement.

"I was not only able to do well with my studies, graduating from high school with honors," continued Owen, "but in contrast to Brett's experience I was able to enjoy the fellowship of a circle of friends. There was always present the stress of having so many silent enemies, people just waiting for me to fall into misbehavior of some sort, which I am sorry to say, I did, a few times. These were periods when in dejection, having been put down hard and long by peers, or teachers, or by my own father, and taking the attitude 'what's the use', I dropped away from my own well established, but not yet sufficiently consolidated code of behavior. At such periods in my life, the pressure being very great, I swung over into the company of less well behaved people. I can fully understand how so many potentially good youth are prone to go astray. However, the lesson I continually learned from such action, and which eventually permanently impressed my developing mind, was that the people whose company I slipped into at these times, never really became my friends. They delighted in seeing me come their way, but only so that they could send me further down the road towards destruction. Whatever their bad habits were, they expected mine to become worse. If they took one drink, I was to take two. If my parents expected me to be home by eleven on a

Friday night, they would see to it that it was first eleven thirty, then twelve, until I was in deep trouble at home. I was eventually to detect that in this they delighted.

"Then again there were periods of isolation for me. These were periods when in between the swinging from the well behaved group to the poorly behaved group and back again, it seemed to me I belonged nowhere. Many promising youths, I suspect, get lost in that category of belonging nowhere. Being rejected by sufficient numbers of obnoxious ones with a degree of constancy can lead one to feel rejected by all, and by the world. It leaves a void in one's need to be included as a part of humanity. To fill this emptiness, I remember that at such times I used to spend my money too freely — money I had earned and money I received as an allowance. My savings would diminish. I would seek out more money from family sources. I would, in my dejection and aloneness, fill my time with movies, restaurants, and hobby materials. I remember one place where I spent a great deal of this time was in a billiard hall. Playing billiards was the thing that could keep my mind off my troubles best of all. It was a respectable type establishment I went to, where, thankfully, I was in good company. However, all of these things took more money than I was accustomed to spending. Altogether though, this trend did serve to keep me from slipping into idleness and despair, which would have been even more harmful to me.

"By the grace of God, I eventually fully recognized the futility of resorting to any group except the well behaved. I recognized too, that my father's discrimination towards me was instrumental in periodically affecting my mind-set, and causing me to go down the wrong road. Having become wise to his ways with me, I decided I would not let him and others like him do it to me anymore. I consolidated myself with my circle of genuine friends with whom I was able to be, to do, and to grow all in a manner for which no one would have legitimate reason to put me down, and for which I would have no regrets.

"I mentioned that by the grace of God I came out on the right side. It was at that period in my life, the period when I was definitely coming out on the right side, that I developed a healthy respect for God. My convictions were separate and apart from the rather doubtful conception of God I had formed from my father's teaching, preaching and witnessing in his ministry.

"If God is like my earthly father, I used to think at one period in my life, then I have some very grave doubts about the merit of making a place for God in my life. But as I grew, I recognized and came to realize more fully that there was, in reality, a good God whom I would now come to know in my own way instead of in my father's way. It was to be much later that I would decide to be a minister of the church, but as I was going through my final year of high school and my early years of university, I struggled with and eventually made a firm decision to live the Christian life as I saw it for myself.

"By the half-way point through my undergraduate degree, I was solidly entrenched in the better side of life. This brought with it its problems as well as its blessings. Nevertheless, I was free now from preoccupation with my own inner self, free to, among other things, learn to cope, as best one can, with those who would put me down.

"In this I did not do as well as Gilda, in that I did not get out of university a degree in the subject I wanted, but like Brett, an honors degree I did manage amid the usual treatment for people like *us*.

"So the outcome of our struggles are many and varied," remarked Collin.

"And our personalities too," added Gilda.

"It seems each of us did the best we could according to our circumstances and the possibilities that opened up to us," said Donna, "but in essence it all amounts to the same kind of life for all of us."

Albin at this point became discouraged, "doesn't look as though there is a very bright horizon in my future," he remarked, "I'm only just beginning the battle."

Leo's emotions were stirred again, this time to tears, which he successfully struggled to hold to a minimum. "There will be some way, Albin, there is always a way," he said in a kindly effort to implant hope and encouragement.

Collin looked approvingly at Leo, but inwardly his heart was heavy as the thought of Albin's future loomed before him, *yes, there will be a way, Albin*, he thought to himself, *but I am very much afraid that for you, it is to be a long, arduous up-hill road, with many detours and down-hill dips. But there is always a way if we can help you learn to find and travel it*. Then aloud for all present to hear, "yes Albin, as Leo says, there is always a way." He said it in as kindly and as determined tones as he could, and he sincerely felt it was true, that there would be some way for Albin. But Collin ably concealed his many and troubling apprehensive thoughts concerning the route Albin may have to travel. Collin repeated again, "there is always a way for us all."

Dr. Eldren remained silent through this discussion. *For why, one can only speculate*, mused Collin to himself, *but I think mainly it is because the doctor is awed and overwhelmed by the magnitude of this problem that has scarcely been recognized by his profession and by society. It remains to be seen what position he will eventually take but I think he is right in remaining silent for the present.*

Owen took over the conversation again. "There is one main area I wish to emphasize concerning my undergraduate university years, and that is to explain why I did not get the degree I first aimed for, but rather a degree from another faculty."

"Next case please," interjected Leo joshingly, mimicking his father's court procedure. "Ladies and gentlemen, this too is bound to be a thriller," he added. Then his joking manner giving way to a hurt based quiver in his voice, he continued, "skullduggery to the nth degree, and all that. Stay with it folks." Then he tossed his head in dejection of himself and smiled. Everyone smiled with him.

"Yes Leo, skullduggery it was again," said Owen as he continued his story. "I had hoped to gain an honors degree in English and American Literature. Not only had I over the years, become very efficient in this subject, but had also become creative to a significant degree. As you might guess by now, this ability was to lead me into more trouble, in fact the major problem of my whole education process.

"You know pretty well by now how these stories go. But to fill you in on the details of this one, let me first explain a characteristic that I was to find present in two of my Literature professors. This element may be found, as you know, in persons of all faculties, but I think I am right in saying it is particularly present in some wayward literature teachers to a very developed degree. Leo's experiences will support me in this. To illustrate what I mean first, there was this professor of Contemporary English Literature who, as one would expect was very knowledgeable about his subject, and not a bad teacher of it for that matter.

"This professor was not creative himself, but he recognized my creative abilities. However, rather than helping and allowing me to develop my own style of creativity, he instead wanted to dominate me, be my creator and master, and press me into a mold of his making. This mold, in turn, was a mold copied from past master writers who had long since been acclaimed for their own personal and unique style and content of writing.

"Before I became completely wise to the mind-set of this professor, I had on a few occasions been waylaid into his way of thinking. At times when I presented a written paper, or responded verbally in class, I eventually detected he was expecting me to quote, quote, quote the writers and their critics, fluently and in colorful words. He obviously regarded this as my creativity in the making. His response would be to stretch up and strut about the classroom talking and intimating the role of the professor is in molding creative people. 'We professors,' he said one day, 'are the people who keep creativity and art alive.'

"I realize fully the benefits of knowing the creative people of the past, and the basis such knowledge can lay in another budding writer. The major problem with this professor was made evident at times when I dared to do a little original thinking and creativity of my own. Then, with his nose noticeably out of joint, he would lose his temper, go almost into a tantrum at times, and shout, 'no, no, no, that's rubbish. No one has ever said that before!'

"Whether or not what I said was rubbish is debatable, I suppose. It wouldn't have bothered me at all to have had honest criticism about my own thoughts. However, the reaction of this professor was not one of logical criticism, but was an illogical putting me down. This professor wanted to be able to take credit for anything I may accomplish, either in the classroom now or elsewhere sometime in the distant future. This was his way of staying above me.

"On top of that there was the head of this literature department from whom it was necessary for me to take what for my intended program would be key courses. This department head, in the estimation of many, including myself, was very proficient in the teaching of his subject. He too was very knowledgeable about his subject, extremely widely read, I would say, and with exceptional retention abilities. This professor could discuss freely, any author within his field, and most outside it. But in addition he was able to quote quite accurately, any critique of significance over a period of centuries. This is wonderful for teaching. However, this man had a major flaw also.

"Before I tell you of this man's flaw, first let me tell you of an ability he did not possess. I told you he knew his subject, extremely well. Quote, quote, quote he could, and make sound scholarly decisions on the merits, or lack of such, regarding the authors and their critics, but alas he lacked sound creativity himself. All his speaking and quoting was, one way or another, a repetition of the critics.

"Occasionally he would bring before his classes, some of his own works, a short story, an essay, a poem. I heard several of them. They were all very narcissistic, containing no real objective in purpose, nor objectivity in style, and nearly always including some aspect of sex, either personal or as it affects society. It seems he thought this latter aspect would make his work appealing. He would present these works proudly, yet underneath it all one could detect his own sense of shortcoming in this field of work he knew so well. That was not his flaw, rather it was the cause of it.

"This second professor's flaw was that he resented any student who did show a genuine creative ability. Unlike the professor I just previously described, who recognized my creativity, but wanted to groom it after other of his favorite writers and their critics; this man simply refused to acknowledge openly that anyone in the room except himself possessed creativity. I do have the opinion, however, that either consciously or unconsciously in his private mind, he did consider me to have such talent, for before very long he was resenting me both openly and privately; not my work altogether, but more so me personally. He had similar resentment towards two other people in the class. Neither of us received the marks we would liked to have had and felt we deserved. All three of us had done well in some other literature subjects.

"So you see, with two key professors down on me, and one of them the department head, it was not quite the environment I needed in order to not only get an honors degree in the subject, but to excel in it. I wanted to do this, and knew I had the ability, so as to some day go on to a top caliber doctorate in the subject. I was put down hard and could find no way around them. So becoming discouraged and gradually having my creativity destroyed within me by an often upset mind, I turned my attention to the history department where things were going well for me. Having always done well in history, and being fortunate enough at this time to have a trouble free environment there, with the exception of one professor of minor significance in my program, I changed my major to history. There I did extremely well, graduating with a very good honors diploma."

"Another case of getting what you can, instead of what you want," remarked Leo in his now familiarly candid manner.

"Yes Leo, that's it," replied Owen. "Nevertheless it opened a door for me to something I did want. You see, by graduation time I had decided to go on to study to be a minister of the church. An undergraduate degree in history would certainly be an asset to me as I moved into the field of theology."

"So you decided to be minister even with the example of your own father to discourage such a course in life?" remarked Leo.

"Yes," replied Owen. "You may remember, Leo, and everyone, I mentioned earlier how I had begun to form a conception of God for myself, apart from my father's influence, while still in high school. In addition to that, during my university years I found my best fellowship in the young peoples group of a church near the university I attended. This group, in a mainline church which seemed to take the middle of the road in its theology and practice, fitted my way of thinking wonderfully well. In that group, and in that church generally, there was a good atmosphere for and emphasis on a personal religion that prepared a person for the world, rather than take him from it. It was a religion that sought to prepare Christians personally, before expecting them to go out to help shape the world. This was in sharp contrast to my own father's inadequate ministry and that of many others like him, who are trying futilely to make the world a better place when they themselves do not have their own house in order. These have neither the correct direction nor adequate know-how for improving the community or any segment of the world.

"Here in this church I saw what for me was the better side of Christianity, a side which promoted life on a high plane, as my mother thought it was already. Having developed a desire to promote this kind of Christianity, I went into the ministry, deeming it to be the most worthy cause one could pursue. I have found since, that although this worthy side of Christianity does exist, and is sometimes on top, the christian church is often, all too often, plagued with a serious malady that in some geographical areas more than others, affects people, more particularly people like *us*. It is so adverse to our way of thinking that it is only with extreme difficulty we can function properly within such a church."

"So," murmured Leo aloud, "people like us are no better off in the church than elsewhere!"

"I regret that is so Leo," responded Owen. "In fact there are situations within the church where it can be much more difficult for people like us to make our way there than in secular life."

"I agree," added Collin, the other minister of the group. "If you ever get to thinking that a career in the church will redeem you from this malady by which people like *us* are afflicted, think again, and consider some other calling for your life's work."

"I can support that thought with some of my experiences, merely as a member of a congregation," added Brett.

"Good," said Owen, then took the lead in the discussion again "So we have established two points, namely, first, what motivated me towards the ministry in spite of my father; secondly, in the church, sometimes more so than in secular life, there are troubles for people like *us*.

"Taking you to theological seminary with me, let me say that these three years were good for me, among the best of my life. There were problems there, but making allowance for the fact that people are imperfect people, on the whole it was a pleasant three years. There were no obnoxious professors there. I attribute this to the principal who, being a sound person himself, would choose similar people for his staff.

"Among the students at seminary there were segments of genuine christian fellowship, in which I was able to participate with a sense of belonging. There were a few would-be belittlers there, but they dare not practice their antics in an atmosphere like this. In this environment where the better side definitely prevailed — the obnoxious ones would stand no chance with their damaging nonsense. It goes to show how, with sufficient awareness of the problem, the good side of life could prevail, even for people like us.

"Altogether I did well academically and also grew personally in many worthwhile ways at this theological seminary, graduating with honors, was ordained, and sent to the pastorate. Soon I was to find there are pastorates and there are pastorates, there are churches and there are churches, there are ministers and there are ministers, and amid them all are many obnoxious people.

"Here I would like to draw your attention to the fact that the church generally recognizes that all types and conditions of people are drawn to it. People who are not wanted in, or are unable to get along in other fellowships, fraternities, clubs and so on are able to come to the church, find a 'home' for themselves, a sense of belonging, and a closeness to people as well as to God. I have no argument with that. It is one of the worthy purposes of the church to gather the lost and the lonely into its fold. But it is seldom this kind of people who cause the problems that people like you and I have to contend with so much. Rather, it is another segment in the congregations, who cause our trouble, as you shall see as our group discussions go on.

"So now to relate some of my experiences in the pastorate," continued Owen as he went on into his story. "I was placed in a pastorate made up of two churches ten miles apart with congregations each consisting of people who earned their livelihood in small town industry, or farming, or in public service with the local utilities, and schools.

"These two congregations were as different as chalk and cheese as the saying goes. They were at opposite ends of a line of expectations. The congregation at the better end of this line was looking for leadership in all their church business and spiritual matters. Having had thorough training in all church related matters, I made myself available to them in this regard. I had by no means the last word on any issue, nor did I pretend to have all the answers. I am a person who is able to come up with practical ideas however. I was able to also guide the church officials in church policy, practices and beliefs. In addition, I was made to feel free by most of them to put forward ideas of my own; to point to goals toward which I would like to lead the congregation; goals founded as a result of my years of training in all aspects of church work, and also as a result of having participated in the work of larger churches with a more developed program before I had become a minister. Most everyone, including myself, participated in the decision making. There were only a very small number of obnoxious ones, and they didn't have the upper hand, so only caused minor concern.

"This congregation prospered. Their prosperity, made possible by their favorable attitude, led them to appreciation of their minister's services of leadership and spiritual nurture among them, which in turn fostered the minister's creativity and energy. As they allowed his work among them to take root and grow, and as they helped him to cultivate it to mature development, they came to appreciate the time and effort that must go into such work. They realized their minister was a very busy person, so they themselves took on a helpful attitude towards him in a desire to lighten his obviously heavy load. As I said, there were some exceptions to this favorable attitude, but here was a church where people of good-open-above-board character, and not the obnoxious ones, were predominant.

"At the opposite end of the line was the second congregation whose general attitude towards the minister was that he is the one we are paying to do our church work for us, so do it he must, and we shall see to it that he does it our way and does plenty of it.

"There was an element in the administration of this church with an attitude that 'since we are the church board we are the boss and the minister is our employee who is to do as we say.' This was augmented by the additional element in their thinking to which I will refer as a dollars and cents attitude towards the minister; that is, we are the people who are paying him so he must do our church work in return, as we see it should be done. With such attitudes overriding the atmosphere of this church, there was no thought at all that the minister was there as their leader, except to lead as they commanded or implied.

"The people of this church also pitched in but for a different motive altogether in that for them it was only a power trip, an ego trip to boost their pride and feed their self-centeredness. There developed a definite attitude of the people verses the minister; only the board members' ideas get put into action, and they get the credit for them, make no mistake about that. The minister works as their employee. Their attitude allowed them in their minds to look down on, rather than look up to the minister.

"Such an element as this in a congregation is not uncommon throughout most protestant church denominations. In a congregation where the people, for the most part are uneducated, such characteristics are generally attributed to ignorance, or, to an immature congregation. In a congregation where there is a more educated caliber of people, it is attributed to personality clash. Such congregations establish their own reputations. Needless to say, this second congregation did not greatly prosper. The reason they came up with for this lack of prosperity is that the minister isn't the right type, neither is he working hard enough. These were the problems I learned to cope with early in my ministry. However, through diplomacy in this congregation and prosperity in the other, I came through the experience with the reputation of being an effective minister.

"One thing common to both these congregations, however, was the obnoxious ones in the sense that we have been talking about in these group discussions. As I have said, they were present in both congregations. In the one they were able to have their way, in the other they caused problems another way.

"Let me speak of these obnoxious ones in the congregation that did not prosper. A few of them had been well entrenched in offices of the congregation. One in particular was the self-appointed leader. The others supported him, not all together in every single suggestion he came up with, but overall as leader of the church. The trained minister was treated as his employee and subordinate. Before long I figured out it was expected that any idea the minister came up with was to be presented to him privately. He would then pass his judgment on it, and if he considered it a worthwhile idea, would adjust it here and there so as to make him feel he was improving on it over the minister. Then at a board meeting, he would present the idea in a now fixed pattern. 'The minister has suggested such and such, but you know if we do it that way such and such might happen, so I say we do it this way.' His two accomplices would almost always agree with him, or, occasionally suggest some minor alteration of their own, with which he was certain to agree in return. In effect they patted each others backs, and that of as much of the congregation as they could carry along with them. I could do little work of progress with this congregation.

"The only way I could survive this ordeal and not earn the name of an ineffective minister was to concentrate on appealing

Sunday worship services, funerals, weddings, and baptisms. Then after all my preparation for these was taken care of, as well as the numerous routine administrative duties, and the sick and elderly were ministered to, I did a larger than usual amount of family visiting. There was never enough of this to satisfy the powers that be, nor would there be if I kept at it night and day. This was their one sure way they could always complain and keep the minister beneath them. However, they usually passed off their complaints with the thought that minister's just don't visit nowadays like they used to.

"Next, let me speak of the obnoxious ones in the congregation that did prosper. Here, they were not in command of the situation. Although they obviously tried to show authority and superior knowledge of church work, they had not successfully entrenched themselves as leaders in authority.

"Other well motivated people of the congregation spoke out freely, knowing they had a right to do so. But over and above that, they developed a deep respect for me as their minister and would consult me openly at meetings. Often I was able, by interpreting church polity and practices, to open up ways for them to accomplish things they hadn't tried before. Sometimes too, I would make suggestions of my own, which they either accepted outright, or to which they openly offered amendments. The rapport between minister and congregation was excellent, except for two or three cases where noses were out of joint because the minister was the leader and facilitator, and not they.

"So what do such people do when they are not on top? They pout and murmur and complain, often behind your back. They watch, oh so carefully, just waiting for you to make an error so that they can pounce. This can put the minister under tension if he let it do so, because it doesn't take too many errors, minor or otherwise, not too many awkward decisions or ideas and they will use it to try to whittle you down in the people's eyes. In turn there is a tendency for you to become cautious, and only put forward an idea when you have figured it to be very sound and so not likely open to criticism. Therefore, these people, if obnoxious enough and numerous enough, can destroy the atmosphere in which free, open and speculative dialogue is possible. However, in the congregation that did prosper, such people were by far outnumbered by more compatible people. For the most part I was free to pursue my own ministry. There was by far sufficient support there by the well adjusted people.

"You can see then that on the one hand in the congregation where the obnoxious ones were in control I was blocked almost entirely from enabling a congregation to prosper and grow. On the other hand my efforts were only minimally stifled in the better congregation by having to at times exercise caution against being ridiculed, for unworthy ideas.

"I draw this comparison between the two congregations to illustrate the effects obnoxious people have; also the varying degrees to which it exists and by which it has its effects.

"An ordinands first pastorate is unofficially considered to be a continuation of training, or at least a place where he can bring his training to experience. So after learning these two opposite sides of ministry in the church, and after developing to some degree by now a way of diplomacy among people, boards and congregations, I moved after a few years, to a larger, single church pastorate. Here, I had hoped there would be an all around maturity. If so, then as I have been able to do in the better of my two previous churches, I would now be able to do to a greater degree in this larger, and I had hoped, mature church. I was confident in my ministry now, and looked forward to developing a full program for Christian nurture in this larger, more challenging congregation. I thought for sure I was on my way in life. But life takes strange turns for people like us.

"I was moving to this larger church with, as I said earlier, an established reputation of being a good and able minister. My new congregation, having heard this, were in a state of expectancy when I arrived. Within a few weeks it was evident their expectations were being met. However, that happens before one gets caught up in the nitty grittys of closer association with personalities. There were many nice people in that church, as well as the usual number who swayed with whatever seemed to them to be the going thing at the time. There were also the usual number of obnoxious ones including a retired minister who did not know how to retire, or, to remain active for that matter because he did not know how to look up to and respect a minister whom he perceived in his mind to be cut better that he himself.

"Usually, when a minister retires, he plays low profile in the congregation to which he becomes attached in his retirement. That is an unwritten and widely accepted rule and practice of the church. This retired minister of whom I speak, may well have been able to abide by that rule, at least to a greater degree, had I been a minister whom he did not perceive to be a threat to him, but apparently I was.

"Also, the active minister of the church which the retired minister attends is usually very happy to have a well charactered retired minister around. It is someone to help out in a pinch, or even to take on a definite roll of leadership in usually one or two aspects of congregational activity. My attitude was one of delight when I heard there was a retired minister in the congregation who was willing to help out. Before the first year had ended, however, my delight was turning to grief and pain, for this older minister wanted to father me in a very strangely condescending, possessive and envious manner. Because of him my sojourn with that congregation was changed from immeasurable joy to a deep and hurting misery. Let me tell you how it happened. It was as if I hadn't had enough of this type of trouble with my own father.

"I went through my first year as minister of that church with my youthful vigor and outlook and my sincere wish to minister to all age segments of the congregation. I was able to stir the interest of many people to assist me with their time, talents and general support in establishing spiritually oriented activities for all. This together with my well accepted still improving worship services, and sincere pastoral care gave this church a burst of enthusiasm. Toward the end of my first year there, attendance at services and other activities was at an all-time high. I had the very unusual circumstance of always having enough and more volunteers for any task that needed doing. Likewise, there was never a shortage of money to finance any project that would normally be taken on by a congregation of this size. The church treasurer reported at meetings that the finances of the church were in excellent condition. No longer was the church treasurer waiting for money to come in to pay church bills. Rather, we were keeping ahead. There was always sufficient on hand to pay each expense as it occurred. The people were delighted, all except the retired minister that is. As things got better and better in the church, he showed increasing obnoxiousness, as we might continue to call it for the present.

"Since coming to this pastorate this retired minister had suggested many times that I should feel free to visit and talk with him any time I felt I needed someone to talk to about my work or any problems I may have. For various personal reasons I viewed this invitation with caution. I had a very capable and understanding wife to confide in. There was a fairly extensive church system open to me whereby help, information, programs and resources, were available for the asking. I availed myself of these from time to time, and their help was considerable. I was quite willing also to include the retired minister to be among those whom I might consult occasionally, and I did. It did not satisfy him.

"In time I became aware that this man wanted to possess me totally, to be my father figure and confidant, and to take the credit for all I did. His attitude now appeared to be that I the younger minister should consult him, not just occasionally, but in all matters, even personal ones. I was to become a dependent, forfeiting my own initiative and self reliance in doing so. This I was not prepared to do. It would not be healthy. Whenever I showed a negative response to these overtures he would scoff at me and push up his lip, indicative that he considered I thought too highly of myself to avail of his services.

"I was and am today a person who is willing to accept advice and assistance from any person or persons provided it is offered in a healthy context. The help this man was offering, was not in such a context. Furthermore, such help was not needed. There were no church problems I wasn't willing to learn to cope with myself.

"However, I did try to cope with him, not because I needed him, as he thought I should, but rather as a means of trying to fulfill his needs, to a point at least, without forfeiting completely my own freedom and initiative. I not only went to him occasionally to talk, but in a further effort to include him more actively in the life of the church I asked him to take on a job or two in the organizations of the church. This he did, but used it only to assert himself over and above me in the congregation. The actions and attitudes he portrayed in the process of this self assertion made it appear to many of the parishioners that there was hostile rivalry between us. There was rivalry indeed on his part, but none intentionally on mine. I continued to do my work faithfully and well. In my opponent's mind this was taken as rivalry against him. As always happens in such circumstances people take sides. My congregation began to polarize.

"In a further move to try to contain and quell this rivalry before it was full blown, I asked the congregation to appoint the retired minister to attend a church conference with me. This was a further effort on my part not only to eliminate the rivalry, but to increase his activity to give him a sense of usefulness as he had implied many times was his reason for wanting to be involved so much. The congregation appointed him without question or any notion of the further trouble it would bring. So we both went to the conference. While there we mostly went our separate ways, as each of us had our friends with which to associate and renew acquaintance.

"Upon return from the conference, I invited the retired minister to join me in the pulpit on Sunday morning, when each of us could present our views of the conference events. To this he gladly agreed. I thought I was making progress in human relations, but alas it was not to be so.

"At the appropriate time during the worship service, I gave a brief summary of the conference agenda, and spent a few moments talking on two or three events which in my opinion were of major interest.

"One of these events at the conference had been a controversial lecture given by the guest speaker of the day. As I spoke to my congregation now about this issue, I spent a little extra time, stating first the essence of the speech, then expressing my own disagreement with a point in it, as well as opinions, both for and opposed, expressed at the conference by others.

"Then, as previously arranged with my colleague, I turned to him and asked him to express his views of the conference. Immediately he picked up the issue to which I had expressed opposition. He stated to the congregation that I had misunderstood the whole thing; that really it was an excellent lecture which he found to be exhilarating and forward looking. He made no attempt to examine the lecture either in content or meaning, or to give reasons why or how I was wrong in my assessment of it, or how he arrived at a different opinion. The essence of his shorter than I had expected talk, five minutes at most, was that it was an excellent conference, and only those who could see through to its finer points could derive the most benefit from it. This obviously was a slur aimed at me, openly before my whole congregation.

"After that experience, I came to the conclusion that one cannot befriend by appeasement such a person as my new found adversary. Being a minister of relatively brief experience I hardly knew what to do. I thought of turning to someone in authority in the wider church for help, but felt hesitant about it. My adversary was often mentioning big names, and also associating with some of them at church meetings and conferences. I wasn't sure yet whether he was just a name dropper or if he really did carry weight with these people.

"One day not long thereafter I was attending a seminar for area clergy and lay people. Among the fairly large crowd of perhaps a hundred people, I spotted a church official to whom I thought I might be able to turn for help or advice in my predicament. I did not know this man well, but he was occupying an office of leadership in the wider church establishment as well as being minister of a large congregation. I thought to myself, *perhaps if I approach this man casually, here among the crowd during the coffee break, rather than in the formality of an appointment at his office, I may be able to share my problem with him more effectively. Or, if the results of my consultation with him are not favorable it will be easier here to drop the matter and find a way out.*

"By the time of the coffee break I had decided definitely to do that. I watched as he went for coffee. Then I approached him quickly but casually before anyone else took his attention. We started a friendly conversation about the seminar. It became evident as we talked, that we both found it interesting and educational. We were on common ground and off to a good start. When the rapport between us going well, I tactfully changed the conversation to the problem I was having on my pastorate. I began to explain the problem to him but when I was only part way through he seemed very surprised at hearing my complaint.

"'Well' he broke in, 'I'm surprised at you. Your retired minister friend tells me things are going very well in your church. He has told me all he is doing out there to help out. You should be glad to have him with you. He is trying to help you.'

"I protested gently, 'whether its help or not depends on his motivation. And if his motivation is to possess me and keep me under his thumb, that is not help but hindrance.'

"My prospective counselor brushed it off lightly. 'Aw, he may be interfering a little. Retired ministers sometimes like to tinker around to have a feeling they are still involved. He won't hurt you. He means well. Just take him under your wing and be nice to him," he said as he walked away.

"My heart sank. I sat through the remainder of the seminar but took little of it in, as my mind was very troubled."

"Your retired minister friend had himself well covered," said Collin to Owen sympathetically.

"Yes, I'm afraid so," replied Owen.

"They always do," added Collin.

"Yes, I know, Collin. They cover themselves and their motivations well."

Owen continued, "after a few days of nursing this wound, I was able to regain my composure. I decided then I would neither fight nor appease this man, but simply ignore him, going on to do my work arduously and as I saw it should be done for the benefit and betterment of my church. Two months or so of this proved to be fruitful. The prosperity of my church and its work continued, until the next fateful episode, which marked a turning point in my stay at that place.

"A turn of events was brought about by the resignation of the church treasurer due to failing health, and, of course, the necessity to replace him. The resigning treasurer gave us considerable time to find his replacement, so before calling a meeting I discussed the matter with various people of the church board and congregation. By meeting time, I had names of competent people willing to take on the job if requested by the board. I would place these before the meeting for open consideration, together with a request for names of other nominees, so I thought.

"Immediately as the matter of a new treasurer came before the meeting, a member stood on his feet and nominated my adversary, the retired minister, to be elected to the office. 'But', I protested, with little time to collect my thoughts, 'he is a retired minister. I would prefer that a lay member of the congregation be given the job. Not only is it good,' I said, 'for the congregation to handle its own affairs, but it is good for individual people to have a turn at being involved in a church office. I have other names to put forward.'

"'What's wrong with our choice,' came a shout from the obnoxious person who had made the nomination.

"Some others chimed in, to the effect that he was their choice too.

"'I will ask you to excuse me from the meeting for a few minutes,' I responded, 'and I will ask my colleague in ministry to meet with me for a brief discussion in the next room, if he will, please.'

"My colleague and I went into another room where we could talk privately.

"'Listen,' I said, 'one of my pet theories in ministry is that of developing people into something more than they already are. That is done, by nurturing them in the way of God's grace, and by involving them actively in the functioning of the church. They thereby gain a confidence in themselves and a mastery over their immediate surroundings and all that it entails for them in life. They are then able to be of greater service to the church and their community.'

"My adversary just stared at me as though such a policy confused him.

"I continued, 'Look,' I said, 'I am only a young minister, and I have never been pastor of a big church as you have been, but…'

"I was interrupted, 'This is a big church,' he said, glaring at me, 'and being treasurer of it will make me feel useful.'

"Then the crux of the immediate matter dawned on me. I had known for some time that this man had to feel he was up on top looking down on me. Now he was showing yet another characteristic in common with my father, in that money, one way or another, was important to his sense of position in life. If he could control the presently affluent treasury of the church and take credit for our excellent financial standing, he, and he would hope many others also, would feel he was responsible for the flourishing of this church. Time was to prove me out in this thought. Later research also showed me that this retired man had never really been minister of a church as large as this one. In the meantime I continued to try to get through to him with my sincere view on the matter of involving lay people in church offices.

"'Listen,' I said again, 'even in my brief ministry, I have seen tremendous change for good in people who being properly motivated and directed have taken on a church office. They grow and become capable church and community workers, mature Christians out in the world in positions of leadership. As a vital part of my ministry I would like to help produce as many such people as I can, a force for good in society.'

"I was sincere in this pleading. It was only partly a maneuver to keep the man out of this office, because I knew he would somehow be a pain to me if he were there. I had long ago truly come to the realization of the value to personal growth of holding an office of responsibility in the church. That was one sincere motivation for my protest to him. It was above his head. It wasn't working, so I put my second motive into action. 'You are a retired minister,' I said. 'Most retired ministers out of courtesy take on honorable yet more minor roles in the church they attend in retirement.'

"'Not this minister,' he replied very curtly. 'I'm not ready to be shelved yet.'

"My pleading was of absolutely no avail. My adversary just glared at me with disturbed eyes, pushed up his lip in a now familiar gesture of contemptuous rejection, shook his head and remarked, 'I don't see any point in all this lecturing. I was asked to take the position of treasurer, it will make me feel useful, so I'm taking it.' At that he walked back into the meeting hall. I had no choice except to do the same.

"As I took my place again in the board meeting, I informed them that my colleague wished his name to remain standing for the office of treasurer. Chuckles of victory came from a section of the floor, chuckles that were meant to belittle me and vaunt my adversary over me. I sensed then that lobbying concerning the filling of this office had been going on behind my back and a decision had been reached before the meeting. Why this man wanted to hold this office so badly, many of them did not understand, but I felt I did. I could see too, now, that my congregation was being split by rivalry despite my efforts to prevent such a thing happening.

"It was easy for my adversary to obtain the votes necessary to put him into the office of treasurer. His supporters of course were for him. Those who couldn't see through the situation thought it wonderful that this retired minister would still expend himself in the service of the church. That gave him the majority. The minority remained silent. He was now in the foremost office of the business affairs of the church."

Collin interjected, "The retired minister kept telling you he wanted to feel useful. My opinion is it was more than that. He was envious of you. In his case he wasn't seeking to destroy you.

Rather, he was seeking to control you so that he could take the credit for all you did, and thereby have power over you, in his own mind at least. Such people do not appear to be powerful in the usual sense of the term, but they would like to be. So they revert to power and control tactics to make themselves feel that way, and to hopefully impress upon others that they are powerful and have control over what is being done around them. This man was now in what he saw as a position of power and control in your congregation and no doubt will try for even more of the same."

"I think you are right," agreed Owen. "But at the time I still wasn't wise to the ultimate motive and goals of this man. This I was to learn gradually. I began to realize it more fully as he took the next step in his intrusion into my ministry. It wasn't long in coming.

"One saving grace for me amid the administrative turmoil in which I was becoming involved in this church was that I had a record of preaching good sermons. I had received many favorable remarks concerning my preaching each Sunday without fail since being there. My adversary would now attempt to make inroads on this aspect of my ministry.

"A few weeks previously, in a private conversation between the two of us, he questioned me about my practices in sermon preparation.

"'I suppose,' he asked, 'you read quite a bit, do you?'

"'Yes, I do,' I replied, 'a great deal as a matter of fact.'

"'I suppose,' he asked again, 'that a great deal of what you read is reflected in your sermons?'

"'Yes,' I replied, 'it is.'

"He looked at me with a grin.

"I continued, 'I am a young minister with very little experience. I expect I will have to depend heavily on my reading for some years yet in order not to be repetitive in my sermons. However, I give credit where credit is due. Furthermore, as time goes by and I gain experience and insight, I find I can be more and more original.' His grin was quickly replaced with a sober face.

"I thought very little more of this incident until one evening there appeared at my door, my adversary in the company of a prominent member of the worship committee of my church. I invited them in. They soon advised me that they had in mind a special type of service for a particular Sunday of the church year which was just a week and a half away. They wanted to know if I could come up with a suitable sermon for the occasion, a sermon relevant to the kind of service they had in mind.

"Immediately the thought struck me that this service had been preplanned without my knowledge, without me the minister of the church being consulted. I was simply now being asked if I could produce a sermon for it. Sensing an ulterior motive, I quickly replied, 'Yes, I can, no problem.'

"And really, there was no problem, with that part of it at least. Although not yet an extensively experienced minister, I had every confidence in myself that I could produce a good sermon on any reasonable topic or text I chose, or, as in this case was chosen for me. With effort and extra work I could come up with a very special sermon for a special occasion when necessary.

"Not only had the format of this service been planned without consultation with me, but the tone of the request I was now receiving indicated to me that I was being put to the test by my adversary. His companion of that evening, I believe was an innocent accomplice to the act, who didn't in the least realize what he had been led into that evening. His continuing friendship towards me in the months that followed confirmed my belief of his innocence.

"The reaction of my adversary to my sermon on the following Sunday, and at times thereafter, confirmed my notion that I was indeed being put to a contrived test. On that special Sunday I preached my well prepared sermon. There was a positive reaction to it from nearly the whole congregation. Several people were quite vocal with their compliments, some of whom said it was my best to date. My adversary could not help but hear their remarks. I kept him in my eye as well as possible. As people mingled with each other and I circulated among them, my adversary stood alone at the rear of the church, his mouth drooping downward, and obviously bothered. Finally he did notice me eyeing him, so putting a broad smile on his face, and springing forward towards me, he shook my hand vigorously and complimented me on my sermon. I could not help but feel it was all so artificial.

"My feeling was substantiated the following Sunday for which, although it was not a special occasion, I did prepare another special sermon. It was a follow up of the previous one which had gone so well. I thought it a good idea to keep up the momentum for another week. I spent extra time in preparation, then preached it well on Sunday. It went well again, and again there was a positive reaction generally from the congregation. The people, as the custom was in that church, stood around the sanctuary visiting and talking with one another, and I circulated among them on my way to the exit to give a final greeting as they left. As I proceeded down the aisle, stopping to speak here and there, my adversary being in my path, and as though struggling greatly with his problem, made the two or three steps towards me, and with mouth drawn noticeably downward, eyes dripping tears, held out his hand to shake mine, and whimpering like a small child said pathetically, 'your sermon was good again this morning.'

"'Thank you,' I replied, 'I appreciate your remark.'

"For a moment I thought perhaps this was a moment of insight and repentance leading to reform for my adversary."

Collin shook his head in disagreement.

"Right Collin," said Owen, smiling. "I know now it was simply very badly hurt pride, hurt enough to make him cry. Soon the old self dominated once more as he quickly got hold of himself, raised his chin high in a contemptuous gesture of superiority and walked away.

"At the time though I thought even if repentance had taken a good hold on him, a leopard doesn't change his spots overnight, as the old saying goes. I still must beware. *And beware I must*, I very soon thought again, as I watched his supporters from the treasurer episode gather round him, patting his back, shaking his hand and conversing with him chummily, but making no effort at all to be friendly to me in any way.

"I had saved myself in this instance, but my church was becoming divided by rivalry. 'What shall I do?' I asked myself, but could find no answer. As the weeks went by the troubles of my church became more obvious. At meetings, there was now a pronounced coldness towards me by my adversary's friends and supporters. Any ideas or suggestions I put forward were received with coldness by them, and many times quickly shot down. I was really in trouble, and my problems were to be compounded more so in the future.

Collin, as though already knowing the answer to it, asked a pertinent question; "I suppose Owen that via the grapevine, news of trouble in your pastorate reached the clergy and lay people who make up the area governing body of your denomination?"

"Yes, Collin, it did." Owen said as he smiled painfully. "You know how it is eh?"

"And no one from that governing body ever came to ask you about that trouble at your church and to get your side of the story, Owen?" asked Collin again.

"Right again, Collin." replied Owen, "I know though, that it was being whispered by some behind my back. When I attended meetings of that body I could feel it and sense it."

Owen looked at Dr. Eldren warily, "It wasn't my imagination, doctor, I could actually feel it and sense it, yet it is so difficult to describe."

Collin came to his support, "I agree with you, Owen, that without doubt it was there. The reasons I asked those questions that led you into this was to point out again that there is no tangible help available in such circumstances for people like us. Almost nobody except ourselves are aware of the conditions under which we are compelled by obnoxious people to continually live. Therefore, there is no appropriate help available. To make matters worse, most psychiatrists do indeed take the position that we are imagining things, or misinterpreting events, or, that we are too sensitive to what they interpret to be minor hurts in life. A total awareness of this problem is sorely needed."

Dr. Eldren responded, "I'll keep an open mind on it. I have

every confidence in this group, and each member of it."

Owen was able to crack a smile. More confidently now he was able to continue, "you know how you can sense when a group of people are talking about you, how they look at you as they talk to one another, then suddenly look away, and when you approach them their guilt makes them scatter as though you had the black plague! There was an undertone there. I could sense it but I couldn't get hold of it. I wasn't able to find out how my church troubles were being interpreted by others, but I felt sure it was being talked about."

"Yes Owen, I know," Collin reassured him purposely, because Dr. Eldren, a psychiatrist, was present and he might misinterpret Owen's analysis of what he *felt* at the governing body meetings."

Owen added, "there were sympathizers there also. They smiled to reassure me, but also kept their distance from me, as if keeping away from trouble."

Collin further supported him. "Again this affirms what I said earlier, that there is no tangible help for people like you and I in our peculiar circumstances. Even in the church there is not much practical help, Owen," remarked Collin in a supportive manner. "But you look tired now, and its getting late. Maybe at the next session you could tell us how you got out of that jam and arrived where you are today."

"Yes, I am exhausted really. All right Dr. Eldren, if we end it there for this evening?"

"Yes, of course," replied Dr. Eldren. "I can see you are very tense, and it is a good time to break and dismiss for the evening. See you all next week," he said cheerfully.

As the group members stood around for a moment to bid one another good-night, Collin asked Owen, "can Vita and I drive you home, Owen? You have had a lot on your mind this evening, and you are no doubt very tired."

Gilda stepped forward with a long quick step and smiled. "He is taken care of for this evening, in that regard. I will be doing the driving for him."

"For us," Owen corrected her. "You see, Collin, Gilda and I are going to dine late this evening at a restaurant we both like, so that will take my mind off things."

"Good going," responded Collin as he bade them all good night and went down to the library to find his wife.

He thought to himself on the way, *I'm glad for Owen, that he, I hope, I hope, may have found some genuinely capable and understanding support for the first time in his life. Yes*, he mused to himself, *Gilda Emerson would be good for him, yes indeed, they would be good for each other. They are going out together. Well, I'll be*!

# CHAPTER EIGHT

During the week that followed, Collin Seldon did a great deal of reflection on Owen Winslow's revelations, particularly those about his experiences in the church. They were familiar. Collin had been a minister for many years now. His experiences were similar in nature.

*It seems ironic*, he thought to himself one day, *that such happenings though they are so unchristian, can occur in the church, unnoticed by many, and unchecked in any effective way by anyone. They are sins that are spelled out for us in the scriptures: envy, jealousy, rivalry, slander (that means spoken or implied,) hatred, pride; they are all listed there. Christian scholars across the ages have written about these sins. Still they are practiced openly and widely by 'Christians', more especially so in geographical areas where they are taken for granted. It should not be as though they are some deep, dark characteristics of which humanity has yet to become aware in its gradual evolution toward maturity. They have been before our eyes from time immemorial, yet have not been subdued. They have been tackled at times in the pages of fictitious literature, and have thereby been relegated, to a large extent, to fictitious life. Only seldom have they been recognized as a vivid part of present reality.*

Collin's view of the matter went this way: the Apostle Paul in his letters to the churches indicates very strongly that such people existed in the church in his time, and that pride, envy, jealousy, rivalry and strife, which he includes with a list of other sins, were very prevalent in the early church. If there is any change in the church in this regard, after two thousand years, it has gotten worse. Furthermore, it is a problem the church seldom tackles. It is there, and many people know it. There has, however, never been a method devised to bring it out in the open and deal with it. The church either appeases the perpetrators of it, or, gets rid of the person of whom these obnoxious persons are envious, and brushes it all under the carpet in some way. In this manner they keep up the appearance of a church at peace and fostering that peace in the remainder of the world.

In contrast to that a minister has dared to write, "that throughout his ministry he had had more trouble with other ministers, than with any other group of people." {Pulpit Digest — May-June 1981 page 36}. The church is by no means exempt from such people. They are to be found in all walks of life. They have caused untold havoc throughout the centuries, yet still today they go unchecked. They damage or destroy the mental health, and ruin the careers and dreams and hopes of countless people. Yet, strange as it may seem, modern psychology and psychiatry scarcely has them entered in its books.

"In fact many psychiatrists and psychologists confuse this issue with paranoia. A psychologist writes, 'Persons who constantly feel belittled and misjudged, and who bear grudges because they feel thwarted by others who they believe are against them, are often termed paranoid.' {The Person, LIDZ. Page 553. Basic Books, Inc., New York, 1976}. He then places the fault with the victim and the victim's projection of his own feelings on others. I cannot deny that the kind of paranoid so described may exist, although I have never experienced it. But neither can I confuse it with the very realistic circumstances people like *us* find ourselves in, the damage it does to us, and the more damage it could do to us if we were not wise to it and coping with it as far as is possible. The present limitations of recognition of the problem makes it near impossible to deal with it adequately.

Such were the reflections of Collin Seldon throughout the week as he awaited the time of the next support group session so that he might hear the remainder of Owen Winslow's story.

The reflective week passed and Wednesday evening again found Collin at Quilibet University accompanied by his wife who again went to the library to read while her husband proceeded on to Room 405. It was nearing seven o'clock when Collin entered the room, finding only Leo Aidan and Donna Coyne present. Dr. Eldren had been paged to take a phone call at his office, they informed Collin.

Just then Owen Winslow and Gilda Emerson arrived together. Collin was pleased with that. Owen was going through a difficult time these days, bringing to mind the unpleasant side of life. It is not easy. *A person needs support at such a time*, he thought to himself. *And Gilda is good support for Owen.*

The five stood around and talked while waiting to get the session started. Albin Anders and Brett Culver had not yet arrived.

"Strange for Albin to be this late," remarked Donna. "It had gotten to be so that he was often the first member here. He seems so eager to get to the root of his problems."

"I do hope he succeeds," added Owen, "and I hope we can help him, but he has a long way to go"; then to Collin, "do you think the prospects look good for him, Collin?"

Collin thought briefly, then replied, "the way I see it is that he has a steeper hill to climb than any of you. I think he can climb it, and with the proper help, hopefully from us, he will be able to climb it in good time. Left alone, he is in for a long hard haul."

Gilda looked curiously at Collin. "I'm glad you have an optimistic outlook for Albin," she said. "It isn't entirely favorable, but nevertheless quite possible with our help. And we are certainly here to help. But I am wondering about the way you worded your statement that 'he has a steeper hill to climb than any of *you*'. That I would take to include all the group members but yourself, Collin. Did you mean to say it that way?"

Collin hesitated, smiled self consciously, and searched his mind for a way to evade, at least for now, the issue he saw coming. "Well yes, it came out the way I meant it," he eventually replied. Then after hesitating once more, awkwardly added, "I'm older than you people you know, and that means I've had more years of life's experiences to cope with."

Gilda looked at him questioningly and with a prying smile. "Come now, Collin, you're holding out on us. We all know that the length of a hill and the degree of incline of a hill are two different things. Were the length of the hill and the degree of incline both greater for you than for the rest of us?"

"You are too smart for me, Gilda," Collin bantered back to her.

"You are right, they were both very great."

"We shall be very pleased to hear your story when the appropriate time comes," she replied.

"I will do my best," said Collin modestly, "but now Dr. Eldren is returning, and we have lost much time. He will probably want to get started immediately."

Just then Brett Culver came rushing in behind Dr. Eldren, and apologized for slipping back to tardiness again. The chairs were quickly put in place and the members were seated. Dr. Eldren apologized for keeping them waiting so long.

"Albin Anders will not be with us this evening folks," he said. "He has not been well the past few days, and is at present under observation in the psychiatric ward of General Hospital. His condition is not serious. I just had a lengthy conversation with his doctor, and he has decided that since Albin is getting help from this support group, he will discharge him with some medication by weeks end on condition that he continue to attend our group sessions."

Collin drew a deep breath, and in a sigh of relief let out a very audible "whew, thank heaven."

Dr. Eldren turned to him. "What was that for, Collin," he asked curiously and courteously.

"Well," replied Collin, "first, I'm relieved that his condition isn't considered to be serious. Secondly, I'm relieved that he is being discharged with medication."

Dr. Eldren appeared puzzled and looked to Collin for further explanation.

"What I'm getting at sir," continued Collin, "is that if Albin went into psycho-therapy at the hospital, where they don't know him and his specific problems as well as we do, he might, depending on the psychiatrist he has of course, be diagnosed as paranoid. Heaven knows where his case would go from there."

In response, Dr. Eldren raised his eyes and nodded his head in a kind of approval that still had some questions to ask, then said, "You really are careful with the paranoid issue aren't you, Collin?" replied Dr. Eldren.

"Extremely so, sir," said Collin, "I have always had to be."

"Will we hear more about it in time?" asked Dr. Eldren.

"Sure will, sir, at an appropriate time," answered Collin.

"Good enough for the present," replied the doctor. Then shifting the emphasis of the discussion, "now Owen, what do you have in store for us this evening?"

Owen took the lead in the discussion again. "Perhaps," he said, "I could wrap up my contribution now in a summary of the effects of these experiences upon me and how I handled them as best I could. "I must say that the very enormous pressure that came upon me as a result of my being caught between these polarizations in my church that were not of my own making eventually affected my performance adversely. Creativity came to be at a low ebb, and of course this is what the obnoxious ones delight in. My personality was gradually being eroded as well. Prior to the culmination of my troubles, I had been a person of patience and diplomacy. Now I was becoming irritable at times, and this of course is what the obnoxious ones also take pleasure in. If there is one thing in this world they would like to prove about you, it is that you are not the good character you appear to be. They hammer away at you, and when you make one mistake, or they find one flaw, they point the finger quickly and accept that slip as proof of all their other conceived and contrived ideas about you. Two or three times I lost my temper and told some of them off as the saying goes."

Collin Seldon interjected quickly, "They turned that one around on you!"

Owen gave a single chuckle, "How well you know, Collin," he said. "Yes they turned it around on me all right, and their accusation then was, 'look what he is doing to us!'"

"No thought of what they were doing to you," remarked Collin?

"Not in the least," replied Owen.

Owen continued, "there was an occasion or two also where I purposely used a controlled outburst in defense of myself. Being stern to a high degree, I guess you could call it. The reaction to that was essentially, 'oh my, he really is getting big in himself isn't he,' or, 'oh boy, be careful of that big man', all meant to be derogatory of course. I must admit, though, my outbursts did help a great deal. You no doubt remember how this method became a part of Gilda's defense and strategy, and it saw Gilda through to attaining her university degree. I admire her greatly and agree whole-heartedly with her approach to the problem. But in the ministry I think if used extensively it would have been different. If I became known as a terror, as was Gilda, and had to get there by making people afraid of me, then I am sure that as justified as I might be in being that way, no congregation would want a minister with such a reputation. In addition, the obnoxious ones would quickly pounce on a clergy who has become angry, labeling it as unbecoming of a christian pastor."

"It was as though you had no rights at all, was it not, Owen?" suggested Collin.

"Yes," replied Owen. "I found myself in the position where I had to take everything that was hurled at me, but could use no defense at all without it also being hurled back and attributed to my bad character.

"Being thus boxed in, there were only two alternatives open to me. One, become as hard as nails, as the saying goes, getting so that nothing bothered me. The second, get out while the going was good.

"On considering the first alternative, I found I could not visualize a minister being a hard as nails type, so callous, so insensitive, and still being successful in ministry and wanted by a congregation. There was a way for me to get out while the going was good, and I took it. Gilda in her circumstance stayed and stood up for her rights, earning the name of a terror in doing so. Now she is planning to go away somewhere where she can be her pleasant self again. I went away before that process was fully forced upon me. I admire Gilda for what she did, and I think it was definitely the right thing for her, but I do not think it would have worked for a minister.

"I had a friend far away, south of the border, who was able to recommend me to and put me in touch with a church official through whom I was able to obtain a pastorate there. It was one of the more favorable areas of the land south of the border. I've heard of areas where it would be very difficult for people like *us*.

"I'd like to tell the group later about one such area I call Terraprima", remarked Collin.

"I think it would be important for us to hear it," responded Owen. "But where I went I am glad to say it was in a different atmosphere altogether. Oh there were some obnoxious ones there too, as I had expected. I wasn't fooling myself on that. And, I must say, they have some peculiar antics of their own down there, some of which I didn't get figured out during my limited time there. But in this location of my new environment, luckily they did not have the upper hand as one would say. There I had three pleasant and effective years of full time service where both my church work and myself were very well received by the congregation and church government.

"During this time my whole being was renewed, and more than that, I grew in mind and spirit immensely, becoming a new person almost entirely. It was a wonderful liberation of spirit for me.

"During this period I also accumulated enough money so that it, together with earnings I would have from week-end church work, enabled me to leave the full time pastorate to engage again in full time study at a university. I chose a university where I had gotten to know beforehand most of the faculty I would be dealing with. They would be of a compatible type for me. Of course it was easier to find this compatible faculty on a post graduate level. After studying for three years and earning a doctorate in Church History, I decided I would like to teach on a university level. Openings were not plentiful for beginners in the field. After searching diligently, an opening here at Quilibet University was the better opportunity that opened up to me.

"You may be surprised that I took it and came back to this land where my troubles had all begun. I did so with the thought in mind that with a few years experience here I will then go away again.

"It was a chance I took, and it is working out. I am not only keeping on top of things here, but I have done some writing and have been published in some significant journals. Now there are doors opening for me in either teaching or the pastorate. In either of these I would be happy, but with a preference towards teaching.

"So I don't want to be entirely gloomy about prospects for people like us here in Secundaterra," added Owen, as an after thought. "With my more experienced perspective now, I am of the opinion that I, and all of us here can learn to successfully steer ourselves through to some kind of a good career. There will always have to be forfeiting here and there, but we need not go under."

Collin asked, "Owen, was not the fact that you had made good away, of some help in protecting you when you returned?"

"Right, Collin, it was a tremendous help," answered Owen. "I am of the opinion that once a person has successfully made it to the top or even to a reasonably high level south of the border, this serves to keep the obnoxious ones here at bay. They may murmur behind your back, but will seldom come out in the open against you. Some may even make close acquaintance with you if it serves to boost their pride to be associated with you, but beware of them. Yes, Collin, we are much safer and more sheltered when we reach a certain position in life. It is as if we are then beyond reproach."

There was silence throughout the group. Collin glanced around at each member. It wasn't a sad silence, he noticed. Their faces were bright.

*I wonder*, thought Collin to himself, *are their faces bright with hope? Is it that they know now that out there somewhere is a place of freedom for each one of them? Owen is finding his place. Is there a place somewhere for everyone? Heaven knows though, sometimes these places are so difficult to find, but there has to be a place for everyone*!

Leo confirmed Collin's thoughts when he broke the silence with a question, "It is possible then, isn't it Owen?"

"Yes," replied Owen assuredly. "It was for me, Leo, and I'm sure it is for all of us. Sometimes though, through no fault of your own, you have to take what you can get, instead of getting what you originally aimed for and justly have a right to attain."

Owen, as if clearing his mind of the tumult caused in it by his bringing to remembrance the unpleasantness of the past, reshuffled himself in his chair and remarked lightly, "there is my story, Dr. Eldren. I hope it turns out to be of some help. It took very little time this evening. If Albin had been here, we could have heard his story now perhaps."

"Thank you, Owen. It has been most interesting, and you have done well for us I am sure. It is Albin Anders' turn next to tell his story. If all goes as planned, he will be with us next week. We were late getting started this evening, but we are through early."

Leo quirked, "Forget your troubles, folks, and spend the remainder of the evening in blissful liberation."

Donna checked him, "So long as it doesn't take you too far from your world of reality," she said as she laughed with the others.

"Aw-w," retorted Leo, "I have to escape sometimes you know; diversion is a better name for it I suppose, and by the way, we can still make it to the late movie at the Town Cinema, Donna. Care to go with me? It's a good one, I hear."

"Sure, that would be lovely, Leo," replied Donna with obvious pleasure. "I've heard about that movie, and have been wanting to see it."

Owen spoke again on a more serious vein. "Before we disperse for the evening I would like to suggest that at least a couple of us visit Albin in hospital before his discharge at week's end."

"Splendid idea," said Dr. Eldren. "I would suggest only two of you go, and you would be wise to check with his doctor first to find out if it's in order for him to have visitors. But to show such an interest in him at this time may help put him at ease when he returns to us."

After it had been decided that Owen and Leo would be the two to visit Albin, Dr. Eldren spoke again on matters of planning for the following week. "I would suggest that next week we meet as usual, and if Albin feels well enough we can proceed with his story according to plan."

Collin added, "may I suggest, Dr. Eldren, we keep in mind that Albin is the younger member of the group, with, to date, a limited awareness. He may need help with his story and his understanding of it."

"Yes, yes," pondered Dr. Eldren aloud. "We can help Albin simply by asking questions that will keep his story coming and steering it in the right direction. It will have to be well conceived questions. Yes, I think that should be our approach in this instance." The group members agreed.

Leo and Donna left hurriedly to get to the movie on time. Dr. Eldren left for his office. Gilda, Owen, Brett and Collin proceeded together down to the foyer.

"I would like for you people to meet my wife," said Collin, "if you can wait till I call her in from the library. Owen has met her already, of course."

They all agreed to wait.

Collin was gone only a few minutes. He found his wife sitting in a reading area near the religion stacks engrossed in a classic devotional. This was her favorite type of reading, from which she had over the years, developed a wonderful faith and spirit. This enabled her to help her husband, herself and her family through all the ill-conceived fury they had been forced to come through in life at the hands of the obnoxious ones.

"Hi," he said, arousing her from deep concentration as he approached. "Reading something interesting this evening?"

"Yes," she replied exuberantly, "I was just reading this book of devotions with writings from the great theologians and preachers of the centuries. They say some wonderful things about good and evil, and about joy and peace. However, there is very little said about the kind of evil that destroys joy and peace for people like you and I. It says nothing about the many people who practice such evil."

"That's very interesting dear," responded Collin, "but come now, I would like you to meet Gilda Emerson, Brett Culver, and also Owen Winslow again. They are waiting in the foyer."

Collin and his wife Vita proceeded without delay to the foyer, where after introductions and greetings the five stood around to talk.

Collin asked, "Owen, how do you feel now having reviewed your past experiences with the church; what is it that comes to the forefront of your mind about the whole thing?"

Owen replied, "Collin, it makes me feel terrible to have to criticize the church before others. Had I been speaking to you alone, clergy to clergy, and with you already experienced in and understanding these situations, it would have been easier. But now that it is done, I feel I did what, under the circumstances, had to be done. There are people to be helped, and one cannot protect even the culprits of the church, when that would mean denying help when and where help is needed. And besides, as Vita inferred at our last brief conversation here, it is indeed high time these shortcomings in the church, as in other fields of life, were brought out in the open and faced squarely.

"And that, Collin, brings out another thought that is among the foremost in my mind. Many of us in the group have revealed our problems in the sphere of education. Brett has told of his troubles in business and industry. I have told of mine in the church. It seems to me," continued Owen, "that although these problems of which we speak in this group, have in all spheres of life a basic common source, these same problems take on a different cloak, so to speak, in the church. There people are expected to be good to one another, always forbearing one another in love. Yet because of the mind-set of the obnoxious ones, the victim often becomes labeled as the one who is not loving while the obnoxious person who is putting him down is looked upon by the naïve ones as a pillar of the church. This, it seems to me, makes them more difficult to handle."

"Yes, I would agree with you, Owen," said Collin, "the basic problems common to all circumstances take on very unique characteristics and consequences in the church. Added to that it is the church you are dealing with; not with a commodity, not with the business of creating and selling a product, but with the intricacies of peoples lives."

"Perhaps," said Owen, "you had better wait until the appropriate time in our group sessions to bring that out, Collin. For there you would share it with all of us, and I would say all members should receive the benefit of it, since church life does affect all our lives. I remember Brett saying there are some things he would later like to share concerning his church life. Right, Brett?"

Brett nodded agreement.

"Good," remarked Collin, "I agree, it is better I wait, and first we have to hear Albin's story. Give him my regards when you visit him in hospital. Tell him I am looking forward to having him present next week."

"Will do," agreed Owen, and then asked the other three, "Do you busy people have time to accompany us out somewhere tonight? We aren't going anywhere in particular, but maybe we could go for coffee?"

"Since tonight's meeting ended early I have the time," responded Brett. I cannot stay too long. As usual I and my wife have a business matter that needs to be taken care of in readiness for early morning."

"We can take some time," said Collin with Vita's nod of approval. I have an early rise in the morning to attend a church seminar forty miles distant from home, but we can stay for a while."

"We won't keep you late," replied Owen. "We too need our rest to help us bear the peculiar burdens of our lives."

The five spent an hour or so in the cozy little coffee shop just down the street past the parking lot. Collin, Owen, and Brett talked mostly small talk, purposely to save the more serious issues for support group discussions. Gilda and Vita found they had much in common.

After their pleasant visit the five proceeded to the nearby parking lot, with Gilda and Owen departing in one car, Collin and Vita in another, and Brett alone in his; all with their minds now eased, if only temporarily, from the heavy burdens such people as *they* usually carry.

# CHAPTER NINE

Albin Anders was out of hospital and pursuing his usual activities. He had been back to classes as of Monday, and now Wednesday evening was in Room 405 for the group session, arriving not only on time but earlier than usual. This shy, quiet young man was not shirking the challenges of life. He was eager and venturesome in his quest for fulfillment, even if stifled at present by life's little known cruel side.

As the members stood around the room in the usual manner before the session began, Dr. Eldren walked across the room, calling Albin apart to talk to him privately. "Albin," he said, placing his hand on the young man's shoulder, "I'm glad you look so well. I'm sure you feel well too, do you not?"

"Yes, Dr. Eldren," he replied, "I feel ready to go again. I am on a small dosage of a tranquilizer for a while though. I have found it a help in enabling me to get back to my classes right away, without having to take an extended rest. The medication does slow me down a lot but that's better than having to discontinue my studies altogether, even for a brief period."

"I would agree," replied the doctor. "Now Albin," he continued, "We want you to tell your story this evening, and as you tell it, would you agree to having Collin and Owen helping you by questioning you when necessary, in order to bring out points in your experiences that they feel would be beneficial. Does that sound reasonable to you?"

"That's super," replied Albin exuberantly, even while under the burden of his medication. "Though they may not realize it, they have both been a tremendous help to me already. I'd be glad to have help from them anytime. Both of them have the right motive and good attitude."

Dr. Eldren was pleasantly surprised at the insight Albin revealed in his last sentence. "You've come along farther than I had realized. You may not need as much help with your story as I thought," he said, as he patted Albin on the back and parted from him to inform Collin and Owen of his suggestion to Albin and Albin's agreement to their help.

"Albin agrees with you two helping him with his story," Dr. Eldren said to Collin and Owen who were still chatting together at one side of the room, "but," he added with a smile, "he has come a long way in these sessions, and may not need as much help with it as I thought." Then, after a slight pause, he continued again, "of course, he is not the only one who is learning from this. I must say, my own mind has been opened to new dimensions."

For a moment Collin and Owen both looked at Dr. Eldren with a measure of amazement, then at one another while breaking into smiles.

"It's good to have you with us, Dr. Eldren," remarked Collin.

"Yes," added Owen, "with us in empathy and understanding, I am beginning to detect, and that means a great deal to us."

"Thank you men, I'm very pleased to be a part of this," said Dr. Eldren, and then turned to call the support group into another session.

Albin Anders, young, wholesome, more wholesome than handsome in fact, could well be the idol of the dreams and desires of many flowering young girls. The type who would be attracted to him would be those who think of the man in their future as someone on a high plane of life; high, that is, in the sense of dignity and the pursuit of true and down to earth fineness. And although there were, no doubt, such girls thinking of Albin in this manner, his awareness of them was overshadowed by the darker side of his life which was robbing him of experiences that were rightfully his — experiences of growth and enrichment, offering the opportunity to maturity.

It wasn't as if Albin wasn't handsome to some degree. He was. His round full face was topped by a head of healthy blonde hair, swept back over his head without a parting. It was moderately trimmed at the sides, and the neck, and the remainder cut overall to a medium length so that it stood some and then flopped down on the ends, altogether in a sort of wind blown fashion, rather than lying flat. But there was his wholesome look, created by his healthy, fair complexion augmented by a tint of ruddiness in his cheeks. Then there were contrasting deep blue eyes. This wholesome look that far outshone any handsomeness was what made Albin Anders stand out pleasantly in a crowd.

Albin was of average height, and even though somewhat on the plump side, was of solid athletic build. He looked as strong and healthy and robust as could be. The troublesome darker side of life wasn't showing through at all in his still youthful appearance. That was most likely because he had always stood up to it relatively well for his years. Nevertheless, it had taken its inward toll, as was evidenced in his being painfully shy — a result of his almost complete lack of self-esteem, and seemingly more or less at sea in accomplishing goals in life. This was made even more emphatically evident in his being hospitalized in a psychiatric ward for a few days just a week ago.

Dr. Eldren spoke concerning the format for the evening just as another meeting of the group was to begin. He explained that Albin being younger and less experienced may need help in bringing out points in his story. If so, Collin and Owen would assist him by asking questions. On the other hand he pointed out that Albin has gained considerably since the group began, and that he may be able mostly to go it alone."

All agreed with this approach to Albin's story.

Dr. Eldren remarked further, "As I indicated earlier to Collin and Owen, I, too, am coming to a knowledgable understanding of you people and your problems."

Smiles flashed around from one to another. Albin perked a little higher in his chair, squaring his shoulders as a measure of new confidence set in.

"Perhaps, Albin," said Dr. Eldren, "you could begin by telling us about your family."

"Right sir," responded Albin, blushing only a little and then firming up to the task. "My parents live about thirty miles from here. They have three children, age wise I am in the middle of the three," started Albin. "My father, in my opinion, is a good man. He works with a large soda pop corporation as supervisor of distribution and truck dispatching. His job requires long hours of high pressure work, especially during the summer months, but also during the various holiday seasons such as Christmas. During the months of mid-winter the hours and the stress ease off and he has more time then for family, for social life, and for the church which is his main thrust in life, next to his job. He is an active layman in various spheres of church activity. Unlike Owen Winslow I have no quarrel with my father's character. He is a sincere, humble, confident, good-natured all around person. He has a small amount of university education, but family circumstances in his younger years didn't permit him to study further. He is able to take his place well in that sphere of the world in which he lives, and I know he is capable of stretching up to any new challenge. He is a good man and I like him."

The group members were pleased with Albin's adequate description of his father. It would help indeed, that he obviously would not be stuck for appropriate words, though he might fall short of the mark in human understanding. Even in that category he seemed to be outdoing himself, and Dr. Eldren expressed the feelings of all present when he interjected, "you have described your father very well indeed, Albin. We have a very good picture of him."

"Thank you, Dr. Eldren," replied Albin appreciatively, then in a disturbed manner, "but sir, it's my mother who puzzles me. In her character make-up she is something like Owen's father. That's the nearest I've ever been able to compare her to anyone else. Yet, of course, not being a minister of the church, she has to show her obnoxious characteristics within the framework of her own station in life."

"You are right Albin," came Collin Seldon's words of encouragement. "It is quite possible, and from what you say, quite likely, that your mother, in many ways is the same type of person as Owen's father, the obnoxious type as we can continue to name it for the present."

Owen smiled, "I'm glad I have some company, Albin. Can you

just pin-point for us, two or three of her characteristics that cause you to compare her with my father."

"Well-I-I, yes I can, at least to some extent," said Albin. "She is always trying to keep me beneath my two brothers, just as your father tried to keep you beneath your two brothers." At that Albin paused, looking puzzled, and then somewhat losing control of his composure, blurted out, "but that confuses me too. You see, unlike you, I am not the younger of the three of us brothers. I am in the middle. I have an older brother, and a younger brother. Yet she tries to keep me beneath them both."

Collin, always sympathetic to Albin's plight, was more than glad to come to the rescue again. "That one can be explained too, Albin, but lets wait until we hear more of your story. Then we may all be able to see it better. In the meantime, don't worry about not understanding it. For me it took many years of experience, and I was much older than you, before I came to understand such things myself."

Albin was reassured. "Thank you Collin," he said, "I will be patient and wait, but it won't be too long, I hope!"

"Not too long," said Collin, and added, "Often, learning the hard way through experience consumes too much of one's life. It steals away and takes the place of the more wholesome experiences of life that otherwise would have contributed to the kind of growth to which I and everyone is rightly entitled. But I feel sure now that we can spare you some from having to learn the hard way, Albin. One does not master all these things overnight. However, we can plant the seeds here, which will enable you to grow into a more understanding perspective of your own plight in life."

Albin cracked an honest to goodness, heartfelt smile. "Well, you made the grade, Collin, so with your help I should make it too."

Collin responded with a caution, "Please don't use me as your example of success, Albin. You haven't heard my story yet. But I do see a way whereby you may fare much better than I."

"I'll remember that as you tell your story," said Albin. "In the meantime I must take up Owen's suggestion and try to explain what causes me to compare my mother with his father in their character make up."

"As I said," continued Albin with his story, "my mother has always tried to keep me beneath my brothers, but she did it by means of her passivity towards me. I was always as well fed, clothed, and supplied with material needs, as anyone else in the family. My mother was a good home maker, and I was included in her care in that regard, as were my brothers. But, for example, when it came to response to our accomplishments in life, i.e. in school work or any extra-curricular or home activities, anything for that matter, my brothers always received her heart warming approval and praises. If I received any comment at all, it would be a very casual and passive, 'Oh yes, I see, very good.'"

At that Albin paused, not knowing where to continue from there. Collin helped him along with some pointed questions. "Was your mother's attitude towards you like that when you were a small child, Albin?"

Albin puzzled for a moment.

Collin asked further, "Can you recall if she was like that in the earliest days of your childhood that you can remember?"

"A-h-h-, I think somewhat," said Albin slowly, straining to think aloud. "Yes," he continued, and then his speech quickened, "yes, I can remember instances in my early years of elementary school when she was passive towards me. Sure, I can recall now when I was in grade three. I came home from school one day elated that I had been awarded the leading role in the Christmas concert. This award particularly pleased me because of my extreme liking for the particular play I was to be in. It had caught my young fancy. Overjoyed, I went skipping home to tell my mother. Her response was so devastating to me that it lingered with me for years. In late years it had slipped into the background of my thoughts. But as I recall now, when I told her of the part I had been chosen for, her response was very passive indeed. 'Oh, do you think you can do that?' she remarked in a negative tone. 'How come they chose you?' There was not a word of congratulations or encouragement. Then, a few days later, when I had learned my part well and was enthusiastically practicing it at home, and having mastered the part already and was doing it well, my mother remarked, negatively again, 'Your brothers could do that part too you know.'

"As far as I can recall, the occasions when my mother took such an attitude as that towards me were rare and subdued at that stage of my life. However, on thinking it over now on the spur of the moment, I would say as I became older and involved in more activities, her attitude although remaining basically the same, became more intensified. That is, her remarks of passivity became more frequent and cutting."

Collin asked again, "How were you doing in your school work in these first few years of elementary school, and how were your grades in comparison with your brothers'?"

Albin strained to recall. "I was doing very well indeed," he finally answered, doing top caliber work, but so were my brothers, as well as I can recall. I think though I was doing a little better than my older brother, and perhaps not quite as well as my younger brother. But there was no vast difference between us at that time."

"As you got older, Albin," pried Collin again, "did this scholastic pattern change in some way?"

"Yes," said Albin immediately, as he brightened up considerably.

"You're right Collin, the pattern did change. As time went by, both my brothers showed less and less interest in excelling in scholastic attainments. They continued to do average or perhaps a little better, but their inclination towards studying waned considerably."

"I see," remarked Collin, asking further, "and did your interest in studying wane as well, Albin?"

A pained smile came over Albin's face. "Your questions are difficult to answer, Collin. They require some very precise recollections of the past, but no," he said, as he strained through the burden of his medication and his hazy past combined, to come up with an answer, "No, my interest in academic work as such didn't wane. I did become discouraged in my later years of school, especially in high school. And this affected my performance noticeably in that my record was erratic, or to put it more precisely, it was up and down according to the kind of year I was having with regard to my shyness problem, and my lack of self-esteem and sense of inferiority. Some years I did very well. There were other years when my performance was down. I can observe in retrospect now that these were years when I was most plagued by the problems we are endeavoring to help each other with in this group. But my desire for a higher education remained. Does that answer your questions satisfactorily, Collin?"

"Yes, good," said Collin. "Very well indeed, but another question, Albin, can you recall if perhaps your mother's passivity increased noticeably as your brothers' interest in academics diminished, and yours continued?"

"Oh, yes," replied Albin, unhesitatingly, "I am sure it did. It increased gradually, of course, but I feel sure it gained momentum as the academic picture changed."

Albin paused for a moment, and then repeated a previous observation, "But I am not the younger of the brothers. I am in the middle of the three, and that doesn't jive with Owen's predicament."

"I know, Albin, but another question," Collin continued. "When in grade three you were chosen for the leading role in the Christmas play, think back now and try to discern: Apart from your academic performance, were you chosen for that role because you were well liked as a person? Did some of your teachers, and perhaps many fellow students too, think highly of you then?"

There was a long pause. Albin blushed, but gave no answer. Collin smiled sympathetically, and pried further, "You had never thought of that before Albin, that you might have been popular, in some circles at least?"

Albin shook his head hesitatingly. "Never before, Collin." Then after another brief pause, "but you may be right," he said wonderingly, "yes, the teachers who chose me, liked me a lot come to think of it. And many of my classmates were glad for me, though some wondered about it."

Collin questioned again, "Albin, is it as if your mother's passivity and that of many others towards you overshadowed any sense of joy and fulfillment you may have derived from being so popular among some as to be chosen for the leading role in the Christmas play?"

Albin paused again, his face still flushed and no answer coming.

"I know, Albin," said Collin, "that such questions often require a great deal of thought, especially for a person like yourself who hasn't yet explored his past analytically. I would ask you to think about that area of your life in the weeks ahead. In later sessions we may be able to discuss them further, and I feel sure you will derive some benefit from it. But I'll stop questioning you for now so you can continue with your story."

Leo Aidan, who had listened intently and silently came in with one of his now familiar quips — "The defense rests!"

Amid the chuckles that ensued, Owen spoke up jestingly, "I would like to continue to question the defendant," and then seriously, "that is if the defendant is in agreement."

"Go right ahead," replied Albin, "I need to get to the bottom of all this. I have never taken the time before now to go back over my past and to express it in tangible thought and form. What would you like to know about next, Owen?"

Owen replied, "I would like to delve into two areas of your life: first your father, a sketch of his life as it intertwines with yours."

"Where should I start?" asked Albin.

"I would like for you to tell us, Albin," suggested Owen, "something of your father and your family and its' social life, and your place within the same."

"Okay," volunteered Albin willingly, "I indicated earlier that my father was a very busy man at work during the greater part of the year. That left me and my brothers under the supervision of my mother most of the time. As I look back, I think I am right in saying that away back my father was, if at all, only vaguely aware of my mother's different, or indifferent, attitude towards me. His partial awareness of my problem came only after I had been afflicted by it for several years and had developed a very definite inferiority complex because of it. As the years went by, I came to feel very inferior and developed a painful degree of shyness. This became more acute in my early teens when I became terribly afflicted with the misery inducing malady of blushing whenever the slightest attention was drawn towards me in public, in class, in church group or whatever. As I look back now, I can see that I had come to feel inferior to everyone around me.

"My father could not help but notice my plight as I came into my adolescent years so very shy. He was not shy himself but neither was he the ultra out-going type. Rather, he stood in the middle, with no situation too much for him to tackle in his own unassuming mannerism. So, on occasions he would give me a pep talk on the need for me to overcome my shyness, and as he used to say 'give it all you've got out there in the world, and draw back from no one.' That was the essence of his exhortation to me, but in his own amateur way he also tried to probe into my feelings to try and discern what made me like I was. I was unable to help him in this because I had little insight into my own feelings. He was, however, optimistic that I would get over my shyness in time.

"During the winter months when my father had more time to spare from his work, he showed particular interest in me by taking me places such as sporting events, movies, church gatherings and so on.

I think now that he did this purposely to give me exposure to people in the hope that it would help me overcome my shyness. The trouble was though that my brothers and my mother too often came along, and by now I felt so inferior to all of them, that their presence negated any good the outings might do for me. It was always as if I was just tagging along behind them, and that I didn't really matter."

Albin paused there, as if not knowing where to go next in his story.

Owen Winslow broke the silence. "You mentioned that your

father was an active layman in the church, Albin. I would be interested in knowing how that affected you personally."

Albin replied, "It did affect me, Owen, in that it affected my mother, and this was reflected in her attitude towards me. Furthermore, our family church life is an area in which I can see some characteristics of my mother to be quite like those of your father in his attitude towards well-to-do people.

"You see my father chose for our family, a church which many well-to-do business and professional people attended. He chose this church mainly because it was near where we lived. The church was located in an upper middle class area, on the edge of which we lived, in a less affluent but good middle class area. So this lovely church was within a reasonable walking distance for us.

"My father said he liked this church because the people who attended there were genuine. 'There is nothing better,' he always said, 'than a solid upper middle class person who is also a feet-on-the-ground Christian.' There were many such people in this church.

We sat beside them. My father served on church boards and committees with them. We were one of them without discrimination of any kind.

"My father's character was unaltered by his church experience of serving with doctors, lawyers, corporation executives and so on. He remained himself, and was accepted as himself. For my mother, however, it was different. As I look back now, I see her making a conscious effort to imitate those whom she deemed to be above her, buying clothes which she felt would be up to the standards of theirs, being always careful in a social way to be 'just-so,' as she mistakenly thought she had to be.

"Now all this is not too bad in itself, even if unnecessary. In this church she could have been just herself and been accepted. But she was struggling to place herself in the upper middle class as she perceived it. The ironic part is that privately, and within the confines of our own family, she was generally down on them. Often, in her remarks, she would reveal her attitude towards them by, for example, referring to 'those big-shots', or 'those wheels.'

She would further reveal her attitude by picking up for the 'common people,' in which category she obviously placed herself in her less exalted moments. Strangely enough though, at other times she would place herself above the women of the upper middle class and in the privacy of our family we would hear such remarks as, 'that Mrs. So-and-So, if I was no better than she I'd hardly have the gall to put myself forward like she does, and she the wife of a big corporation manager.'

"My father asked her, on occasion, if she would like to change churches, but she showed no desire to do so. In fact, her attitude often revealed that she wanted very much to stay in the church she was in. In her social circles outside of church activity she made a point of letting people know she was a member of that church. She felt it gave her a great deal of prestige to do so and she used it often. I realize now there is a great deal of conflict and hostility going on in my mother's mind concerning her social standing. I do not understand it, but it is there.

"Like Owen's father, she continues to condemn the people she is trying most to be like. Likewise, as I perceive it now, she has always seen me, in my desire to do well in life, as trying to be like those upper middle class people of our church. She has shunned and slighted me for it, and by her passivity towards all my youthful efforts in every sphere of life, she has caused me to grow up with the feeling that I am an inferior type of person. Her overall attitude seems to portray that I belong on the bottom of life's heap, and for me to try to belong elsewhere is presumptuous."

Owen interjected with a thought. "I see some comparison between your mother and my father. I must confess with Albin though, that since Albin is not the younger of the children, there is much about this attitude that puzzles me." He looked to Collin.

Collin smiled and nodded, saying, "Yes, I'm familiar with that. I have formed my own opinions on the matter, and my years of experience have confirmed for me what I believe about it. It is a very important aspect of the problems of people like 'us'".

Looking at Collin, Owen asked. "Will you tell us at least briefly, what you think is the major difference between my father and Albin's mother."

"Yes I will," answered Collin. "It wouldn't be fair to keep you waiting, it being such a relevant point to you both, and besides, we are trusting of each other and of Dr. Eldren by now. We can feel more free to speak our opinions."

Collin then asked of Albin, "How did your two brothers behave towards this church your family attended?"

Albin answered, "Oh, much the same as my mother — making quips about the high society big-shots and so on."

"But it seems you liked the church, as obviously your father did," said Collin.

"Yes, we both liked the church," responded Albin.

Collin asked further, "Albin, are your two brothers more like your mother or her side of the family in appearance and character, than you are?"

"Oh yes," Albin replied, "they are indeed like my mother's side of the family."

"And what about you, Albin. Are you more like your father's side of the family than your mother's side?" asked Collin.

"Yes, yes," replied Albin, as he quickened his speech. "You are right, Collin, and my mother always favors her side of the family."

"Well I'll be!" exclaimed Owen.

"Yes Owen," explained Collin further, "Albin's case is different from yours. Your father's notion or excuse was that a younger brother must not get ahead of the older ones, or ahead of the father either for that matter. That is a frequent mistake made in families where an obnoxious person is present. Albin's mother's problem, I suspect, was that she set up in her mind a division and rivalry between her side of the family and her husband's side of the family. This is reflected not only in her dealings with Albin who is like his father's family, but also with the parishioners of the church Albin's father chose. This family division is also a frequent occurrence where an obnoxious family member is present."

Collin then paused a second or two, and added, "If that brief explanation will suffice for now, we can, if necessary, later discuss it more fully when we get into analysis further into the story telling or at the end of it." Owen and Albin both expressed relief at the enlightenment and agreed. Dr. Eldren suggested, "So now Albin, while your past is unfolding so well, tell us about your school life, then your break from studies, and leading us on into your present circumstances in university."

Albin, having had a good start in his story telling, was feeling more confident that he could continue on with it now, bringing out relevant experiences of his life. He went on with his story.

"As I mentioned before, I did well in my earlier grades in elementary school, very well in fact, and was usually considered a good student. As I look back now, I can see that as my confidence waned through the years, so did my academic attainments with it. As much as I wanted to do well, my shyness, brought on by my now fully developed sense of extreme inferiority was so pronounced that it affected my whole sense of well being. At times I was teased about my shyness and blushing by some classmates. But on the whole I was treated as being a person of insignificance by many teachers and fellow pupils as well. Of course this in turn added to my inferiority. It just seems the attitude of passivity toward me, begun by my mother, just followed me right down the line, gathering momentum as it went, and adding to my misery all the way along.

"Unlike Brett Culver, I was not really picked on by teachers in school. In retrospect, and in the light of what I have already learned from this group, I figure now that because of my extreme shyness, I was considered at the time to be too insignificant a character for anyone to bother picking on me.

"Again in retrospect, and in the light of Collin's revelation that I may have had a measure of popularity back around my grade three years, I recall now that throughout my school years there were teachers and students who tried to be kind and helpful to me. However, their efforts were far over-ridden by the passivity of those who didn't care about me. In later years though and indeed since this group has begun, it has been helpful to me to recall that I did have some supporters at that time. It has helped me to repair my thought processes so that I am able to fully appreciate that although everybody wasn't my friend, many were. This has come to a more full awareness for me since participating in this group. In addition, during my school years, I had some very good and faithful close friends, who were able to overlook my shyness and associate with me in a truly befriending manner. This I appreciate more than anything else that happened to me in my younger years, because it enabled me, in spite of all the odds against me, to have a sustaining measure of normality in the social life of my youth."

Albin was in command of his situation now, so he continued right on with his story. "As I have already indicated, my main problem right up through high school was, with some exceptions, the attitude of passivity towards me by many as though I was just an insignificant, no account, person who didn't matter too much to most people. But there were exceptions. On occasion I did try to assert myself as a person. There were periods in my youth when I made definite efforts in that direction. I was encouraged in this by the better teachers and some students, as I recall now. But I was so sufficiently, and sometimes I think now, intentionally treated with passivity by those whose attitudes served to keep me in my insignificance, that often I dared not try again for a long time. My periods of self-assertion would bring the same negative attitudes each time. Always the attitudes of the obnoxious ones would, in my young mind, override the more positive attitudes of those whose desire was to be helpful. Needless to say, with such a mind-set as that established deeply within me I looked upon school as something very unpleasant which I had to endure until I was through it, but which I would gladly disassociate myself with as soon as I finished the last grade. I had no thought whatever of continuing my education after high school.

"Having had various aptitude testings which showed I possessed exceptional abilities, and in spite of that, having graduated with only a very average standing, I turned my thoughts toward the work-a-day world."

"For three summers during high school, I had worked at the soda pop plant for which my father was a supervisor. For two summers I worked in the plant itself. The third summer I was a route salesman driving a distribution truck and on my own most of the time. At the end of the third summer, I had felt a little confidence coming upon me, a confidence that I had never experienced before. It was short lived, however, as I had to quit and go back to school. The thoughts and experiences of it lingered with me. When, after graduation, I was ready for a job I decided to try this same work again, except that instead of getting a job at the plant in which my father was supervisor, I decided to apply for a job at an affiliated plant some miles away, to which I could commute, and perhaps in time have my own apartment away from home. Therefore, I figured, I would be on my own and would have the opportunity to make my own way, which, because of my favorable experience the previous summer, I felt I could do.

"I landed a job as a salesman without difficulty, taking over a route that was already into its summer busyness. My shyness was an obstacle, and I wondered how customers would take to me. Most were courteous, but some were skeptical about me and that bothered me immensely. I soon noticed, however, the big advantage of being out in the work world. There people were much more open in showing either their hostilities or their affections, whichever any given persons were inclined towards. And here, I learned to more distinctly discern between enemies and friends, and accordingly better deal with the former and appreciate the latter. I was able only half consciously at first, to take on a positive attitude towards the friendly people I met and to be encouraged by their more openly shown friendship. As I became more conscious of this I could see a way opening for me to please my customers, the friendly ones at least.

"The salesman who had the route previously to me put very little extra effort into his work to meet the demands of the busy summer season, and usually headed back to the plant by five or six o'clock in the evening. He managed to keep his customers supplied with some kinds of soda pop all the time, but seldom did they have a full assortment on hand.

"The corporation in the summer months allowed and

encouraged its driver-salesmen to voluntarily stay out on the road late in the summer evenings to make extra sales, requiring only that they be checked in at the plant by nine p.m. This policy I practiced to its fullest extent on my route. Sales began to increase, slowly at first, but then more rapidly as I kept a full assortment of our products in all stores on my route. In addition I asked that a sales promotion person spend a day on my route, distributing promotion materials on our products. This request was granted. Sales soared.

"My efforts endeared the customers to me, with only two or three exceptions. For a change there was an obvious positive attitude towards me in my life. The attitude generally was: here was this shy young person, just a lad really, doing a better job than any salesperson they had had for some time. They liked me for it. I became popular among my customers on my route. For the extra business I received extra bonuses and commissions, and respect from those for whom I was working. I was no longer insignificant, but treated now as a real person, and my confidence grew immensely."

Albin paused, looked at Brett, and remarked, "Remember, Brett, in your story you told of getting your first great boost of self esteem from your father's friend who visited your home when you were a small boy. You overheard him remark that you were a great boy. You were fortunate Brett, to get such a boost at such a young age. I didn't get a comparable boost till I was working and in my late teens."

"I remember you took note of that when I told my story," replied Brett. "Without some verification of your self-worth, life must have been very uncertain for you throughout much of your childhood and youth. I see more fully now the value of that friend's remark, and the experience of self-esteem it gave me early in life."

"And I know what was missing in my younger life," answered Albin, "thanks for your help. Now to continue my story.

"I stayed in this occupation of soda salesman for a little more than two years, during which time I was becoming a new person.

My outlook on life and my approach to it was changing during this time. I became confident enough that no situation could arise that I would not immerse myself into whole-heartedly. Shyness no longer held me back. It was at a minimum by now, and still diminishing. And just as important, I was now able to look back over my past, and see what had been done to me; how I had been oppressed by the attitude of my mother and others towards me, and robbed of the better side of the formative years of my life.

"Without bitterness or any bemoaning of the loss of opportunity in my youthful years, I decided that now a new world was opening to me. I had confidence. I was overcoming my shyness. Surely, this would open new doors to me and I could put to good use the exceptional abilities that testings had shown I possessed. At last the world was open to me as it is to most other people, so I thought — but I was wrong!"

The support group members listened attentively as Albin, now having obviously mastered the art of telling of his past in the manner required for the purpose at hand, went on with his story.

"Toward the end of my second year as a soda pop salesman, I announced to my parents that I planned to go to university in the fall. My father was delighted. My mother took her now usual hum-drum attitude towards anything I might want to do. The difference now, however, was that I was wise to her and would no longer let her discourage me. Her attitude hurt me deeply at times, but I was now able, with effort, to stand up against it. When over a period of weeks I pursued my plans and made preparations to attend university in the fall, she found that her passive attitude was no longer working. Her reaction then was one of outright refusal to do anything for me. My other brothers, the older one who was now working and living away from home, and the younger one who was working but living at home, always had received her help. Whatever they set out to do, she helped with things such as the preparation of clothing for work, or for going away, as the case may be. For me, she now absolutely refused to help me prepare for university.

"I had saved considerable money over the two years previous, however, and could now be quite independent. My father offered both financial and moral support, so that gave me a measure of security and a sense of belonging to the family. But I decided that rather than commute to university, I would, in order to be independent of my mother and free from her obnoxious attitude, go to live in residence. The university was indeed considerable distance from home, so there would be other advantages to living on campus. I was game to be out on my own, but the world wasn't through dealing its blows to me yet.

"In the fall I started at university. I am sure I need not tell you in detail about my troubles and good fortune there. I had a mixture of both, and you have already heard of similar experiences from the other group members. The troublesome side created a particular problem for me though in that I had had only two short years of freedom, as I will call it, two years only in a pleasant environment, in which to rethink my whole outlook on life. It was a comparatively short time in which to rebuild my personality into one which was outgoing enough to truly take hold of life and its opportunities.

"Now, at university two major problems confronted me. To give you a brief outline of the first, I had one very obnoxious professor, who didn't like me and who seemed determined that I would not get ahead. He found every fault with my work that was possible at all to complain about, gave me no encouragement at all, and took every opportunity to pounce on me concerning any or every aspect of my work; the structure of its presentation, the composition of my sentences, the untidiness of my writing. Incidentally, from what I saw, my writing was much better than that of many others. He popped tricky questions to me in class. If I answered wrongly he chuckled at me as though I were a joke. If I answered correctly he always found some way to improve on my answer. I had no chance with him at all. In addition I had another professor who was just plain cold towards me personally. For the most part I think he was fair to me concerning my work, but it was always obvious to me and others that he didn't like me.

"Secondly, I was living in residence. Although I was able to make some friends there, I also had around me several who did not like me. This was all the more upsetting because here I was living in the same building with them. Unlike in my years of high school where I could go home at night and forget them and in the privacy of my own room be to myself at times, here in university residence I was living side by side with them continuously. So as I said, with these two major problems looming before me it was difficult for me to keep up the confidence I had gained in myself the previous two years.

"I have to say that I regressed considerably during that first year of university, not totally, but life did become miserable for me. During the winter I had what was termed a minor break-down, having to take a week out of university for rest, and having to take medication for a while longer. The doctor did not delve into the cause to any depth, but rather made a quick decision that my break-down was from overwork. I did, however, finish out my year, getting credit for four courses, three in which I did very well, just getting average in the fourth from the unfriendly professor, and failing in the course from the professor who was down on me."

Collin spoke up. "Albin, I have some questions to ask you at this point, if I may?"

"Sure," replied Albin.

"Was there still the attitude of passivity towards you at this time in your life, Albin?"

"No," replied Albin, "that was all past now and the attitudes toward me were more like those described by other group members previously, attitudes of hostility or outright shunning."

"Interesting," said Collin, "As long as you were an insignificant youth and later soda-pop salesman, your assailants treated you only with passivity. Then when you tried to improve your lot in life, they turned on you with attitudes of hostility and unfriendliness. It too is a frequent reaction of the obnoxious ones. It is as though it is more than they can stand to see you get ahead. Their mind-set on the matter causes them to come down harder on you. But now, another question, Albin," he continued. "What was the attitude of your parents to your fortunes and misfortunes in your first year at university?"

"My father's attitude was satisfactory," replied Albin. "He was sympathetic about the week I had lost and the course I had failed. But he thought I did well on the whole, especially as he reasoned, after having been away from studying for two years. He was pleased with my attainment. On the other hand, my mother's attitude was very negative. 'Better to be a healthy soda pop salesman than to lose your health trying to get to the top,' she remarked. Her overall attitude seemed to be that my ambitions were greater than my capabilities. Then of course, I end up in hospital for a few days again this year, and that to her is support for her claim."

"How does your mother's attitude affect you, Albin?" asked Collin curiously.

"It's not my mother's attitude that hurts the most," replied Albin. "I can easily overcome her obnoxiousness now. But it's those like her that I have to deal with in the present as I try to make my way out in the world. They, in effect, are blocking me from overcoming my mother, and are sending me back to her, broken. That's the part that hurts."

Albin then paused in a moment of dejection. Shrugging his shoulders, he said, "maybe she is right. I don't know. I have had two breakdowns now, minor though they are."

Collin spoke quickly and encouragingly, "No, no, she is not right Albin. You received high marks in three courses. There is enough indication that you have the capability. It is your mother's problem, not yours."

Collin looked at Dr. Eldren as though he was hesitant to say what he was thinking. The doctor nodded back and remarked empathetically, "That is a very heavy burden to bear, to have your own mother taking such an attitude, and then, in effect, she being supported by others in crucial places of your life."

"But the mother problem isn't insurmountable Dr. Eldren," Collin affirmed. "Albin has shown by his previous successes in life that he can overcome the loss of his mother's affection. The real problem is that these other people like his mother, whom he has to face and deal with every day are causing him to lose the old, old battle with his mother and send him back to her in defeat. Am I right or wrong on that Albin?"

Albin spoke slowly and affirmingly, "Yes Collin you are right. If I could study and work my way into the kind of successful life I wish for myself, I could leave my mother and her attitude behind me where it wouldn't hurt to any significant degree. The fact that others with an attitude similar to hers are sending me down to defeat before her in the present time, is what hurts the most."

Collin spoke to Albin again, as Dr. Eldren looked silently on. "Albin, you received above average grades in three subjects last year, and did average in a fourth. That proves you have the intellectual ability. It is the interference with your capacity and stamina from the troublesome people of your life at present that is bringing you down. I can bring this out further at our later meetings, when I tell my story. In the meantime can you tell us briefly now about your predicament in this your second year of university?"

"Well," replied Albin, "it's much the same as last year. I think though I'm doing a little better. I am not staying in residence, but instead I have a private one room apartment off campus. That is a help in that I can retire to privacy and peace whenever I wish. That's a great help to me. I am struggling, successfully I would say, to gain what I have lost in confidence. I will not give in to my shyness ever again, even though I am up against a negative professor again this year which is causing a great deal of disturbance in my mind. But still I ended up in hospital again this year, as you know."

"Yes, I know," said Collin. "Do you mind, Albin, If I state it the way I see it, subject of course to Dr. Eldren's correction?"

"Okay with me," replied Albin.

"Me too," added Dr. Eldren.

"I see it simply this way," said Collin, "You have a professor down on you. You might fail not only in the course you are taking from him, but if he upsets you enough you will not be able to study your other courses sufficiently either, and fail at least some of these maybe. If this happens, it will be a victory for your obnoxious mother and she will ridicule you again. At least I will use the words obnoxious and ridicule for now, but I have what I think is a more accurate word that I will use in our later meetings. But, Albin, is it the present stress of studying hard under such a crunch as you are in, in between the obnoxious professor and your obnoxious mother, that caused you to go to pieces for a few days?"

Albin paused and puzzled, his face red, not with blushing now, but with the flustering extreme stress. "Yes," he said slowly. "That combination is bringing a terrifying stress upon me, as though if it happens, it will destroy me; destroy me as a person, I guess I mean."

Tears came into Albin's eyes as he added further, "During my early teens when I would find myself in a crunch like that, thoughts of despair would come upon me, but I overcame them with thoughts that God really did have a place for me and somewhere, someday I would find it." Then he shook his head sadly, "It's a long time coming!"

Collin looked to Dr. Eldren who nodded in agreement.

"Let me help you find a way out of this Albin," suggested Collin.

"Sure thing," said Albin, a little more hopefully.

Collin asked, "Albin do you think that despite this professors attitude, if you can keep your health, you can at the end of the course write an exam good enough for a pass mark or better?"

"At least a pass mark," replied Albin, "I think I can write a paper good enough that he wouldn't dare fail me. I can do it if I can keep my health, that is."

"If you feel at any time you are getting overtired from the stress wearing on your nerves," said Collin, "can you have some of your present medication on hand to take in time of need, then drop it off when your feel rested?"

"Yes I can," replied Albin.

"That should get you through this year," said Collin. "It is a make-shift way, but I'm sure for next year we can do better for you. Okay Albin?"

"Super," responded Albin.

"There is another alternative," Collin continued to Albin, "You can drop out of that course altogether for this year, if you think it will be too hard on you. Then you can concentrate on the remaining courses."

Albin responded immediately, "I would prefer to follow your first suggestion. I will be able to make it through."

"Delightful," added Dr. Eldren.

Then with a heavy sigh, Albin remarked, "Oh but I'm so tired now. Can we end it here for this evening. This sure is energy sapping, recalling all the unpleasantness of the past and present, and even peering into the future."

"You've done very well, Albin," remarked Dr. Eldren. "That I would say is quite sufficient for the evening. In fact, I think we are ready to move on to Collin Seldon's story at the next session."

The support group meeting was over for the evening. But the members were reluctant to let Albin go out into the night alone after just finishing the unpleasant task of recalling all his life's misfortunes. All members, except Dr. Eldren who had another appointment to keep, decided to accompany Albin to the coffee shop down the street. There, refreshments and merriment would take Albin's and indeed everyone's mind off the problems of life and relax them for the remainder of the evening. They were joined in the foyer by Collin's wife,Vita. At the coffee shop they asked the proprietor's permission to put two of the square tables together so as to seat all eight of them in a group. There was good food, and light and humorous conversation.

Even Leo's reference to the next group session had an air of lightheartedness about it.

"Don't miss the next episode, folks," he bantered, "when Collin will offer the ultimate proof that those who are locked away should be out, and those who are out should be locked away!"

"That is a very old cliche, Leo," responded Collin, "as old as time itself. It has been repeated by the educated and the ignorant of the ages, yet never taken seriously enough to establish in a tangible way the near truth it portrays for so many people. One cannot take that expression literally and say that *all* who are locked away should be out and vice versa. But it is true in so many cases that the toll is enormous, not only in loss of health to individuals, but in loss of time and talent to the culture, industry and commerce of the world."

These words brought Leo back to seriousness for a moment. Then Collin made an effort to bring the gathering to a more positive frame of mind. "But," he remarked, "None of the keys have been thrown away yet, Leo, so who knows, someday there may be a grand deliverance, when what is now obvious to us may become recognized by others."

"Like I said, folks," rallied Leo again. "Don't miss the next episode. It may save you from the bogies."

Amid the laughter that followed, the conversation turned to a lighter vein concerning everything from the latest movies to the price of cars. The fellowship refreshed them all before they departed for their homes.

# CHAPTER TEN

Collin Seldon pondered all week as to how he would go about making his presentation to the group. Some weeks ago, at a group meeting, a general idea of his presentation was formulated. But after hearing the others, was it still satisfactory? There were factors pertaining to his role to consider that were not applicable to the other group members. For example he being much older than the others, therefore would, if he told it all, take up much more time than the usual one or two sessions. On the other hand, the group members were expecting much more from Collin than simply story telling. They were looking for explanations, reasons, and causes; and, as would anyone who was having problems of any kind, they were looking for answers and solutions. On these latter items Collin fully realized the magnitude of the task, especially since he would be breaking new ground. *Not all of the problems of the world have been solved*, he mused to himself one day, *and this is one that hasn't. Hope I can make a beginning on it anyway.*

So having considered several approaches he might take, Collin came to the next support group session with his mind still in the process of deciding in detail which approach would be most effective. He saw his wife Vita to the library as usual, and proceeded to Room 405, deep in thought on the way.

A burdensome wave of heaviness engulfed Collin's whole being. *Good heavens*, he thought quickly to himself, *I have spent years mastering the art of forgetting and putting behind me the miseries of life. It was a necessary tactic for survival. But now, do I have to recall everything? Well no, but most everything, in order to be effective. I don't need to go into detail about my growing up years. The pitfalls of these years have already been covered by the other group members, so I will just give a brief summary and comparison of them. My story will truly begin in detail starting with what I consider to be the main bridgehead of my life, when I launched out into the wider world. The recalling and telling of this story will burden my mind for weeks, far too many weeks, but it has to be done, and done effectively. I could lessen the time of agony by telling only specific instances, but that's all it would be. The story has to be told sufficiently to portray it as it is, a way of life, rather than occasional incidents in a life.*

Collin would now also lead them more into the whys and wherefores, the motivations, the causes and effects, bringing in a new point here and there, bit by bit. If necessary he would then give a comprehensive summary of the whole problem at the end of his presentation. His mind was now made up on the issue. The details of a previously generalized plan were now in place.

Entering the open doorway of the meeting room he saw that the other members, including Brett Culver who was usually late, and Dr. Eldren were already present, standing around the center of the room talking to one another. They welcomed him with smiles and greetings and continued with the topic of their small talk. On the surface Collin was with them on it. But the back of his mind was still deep in thought. As he pondered he scrutinized the others. For as long as he could remember it had been a custom of Collin's to discerningly size up people, both character-wise and physically, often being fascinated by the comparisons and contrasts between the appearance and the character of any given person.

But at this moment as he glanced around he simply thought of their present station in life. Owen Winslow and Brett Culver were still in their thirties and the other group members only in their twenties, and all of them still in the process of carving out their careers. Collin's career, on the other hand, had long been established. Well past his middle years he was now at a point in life when he, at times, wondered whether it would be better to settle for what he had already attained and glide along until retirement, when he could spend more time enjoying life with his wife, children and grandchildren. There were also the things he wanted to do but never had the time and freedom to pursue. This is a longing common to many people looking forward to retirement.

Then again, at this point in life he may still have enough drive left to set new goals, to keep forging ahead to new vistas of service and fulfillment. *It depends some on the person*, he thought to himself, *and it also depends on the opportunities that arise. Then yes, there is that other factor that affects people like us*, he pondered, as he lost himself in deep thought again for a moment, but quickly pulled himself out of it again. *But I must not dwell on that now. So I'll keep an open mind on the subject, remembering not to allow myself to be drawn too close to the rocking chair in the meantime.*

And Collin was right on that. Considering the present good state of his physical health he could so far hold a healthy outlook for his future. But there is that other factor of being a fine person amid, at times, a sea of hostility. How well would he be able to stand up to that as he grew older? So far, so good! Yet he often had hoped to retire at as young an age as possible in order to preserve himself for old age.

However, though Collin was older by years than the other members of the group, he still had this in common with them, that even now in his aging, as in his youth and young manhood, he stood out among others. He had an air of distinction and integrity about him, a clean cut and assuring appearance, plus a gift of keen insight and discernment; the kind of person good people look to with respect and affection and trust. But not nearly all of the people of this world are good.

So when the group members had pulled the chairs into place in a circle, they sat down to begin another session. Immediately Collin took the lead. "I trust you will find my approach satisfactory folks," he started.

"To begin my story from childhood and pursue it to the present time would be not only long and laborious but some of it repetitive of what you have already revealed in telling your life experiences .Nevertheless, I would prefer, if it is satisfactory to Dr. Eldren and the group members, to tell, not all, but enough of my life's story to establish that these are not isolated incidents, but rather a way of life for people like *us*. As I narrate this story, I would like for us to probe as deeply as our understanding capabilities allow us, into analysis and the causes and effects of our problems — the whys and wherefores we have only touched on in past sessions."

"So this is it!" remarked Leo Aidan in wide-eyed excitement.

"Yes, this is it, Leo," responded Collin, "the analysis, the whys and wherefores you have so patiently waited for. But even now you must work for them, Leo," added Collin with a smile. "As I tell of a relevant experience I would like for the members to join in with a recollection of an appropriate incident or an explanation that you may or may not have already told to this group. This may support, or contradict for that matter, our general summation of the experience, its causes and/or effects and so on. Then at the end of all presentations perhaps we can do a complete overview of our whole problem.

"Over the years," Collin continued, "on the basis of repeated experiences common to people like *us* I have spent much time in objective observation, objective observation, I say, of the people with whom we have problems. In our whys and wherefores, I will analyze and explain, as best I can in a layman's language, the psychological behavior of our adversaries as I have observed it over and over again in the experiences of my life. These explanations are not based on projection and transfer, to use these psychological terms, but rather it is derived from outward observance of people over and over again throughout many years — objective observation. When I am finished, I believe you will have been helped to a better understanding of your own problems. I believe you will also find that many of the explanations I give will be at odds with modern psychology and psychiatry, or, will reveal knowledgeable opinions that they haven't yet professionally taken into account. As unscientific as my observations may seem to professionals, I can only believe what I have seen and experienced."

Collin was dead serious now. So were the others, even Leo. There was silence for a moment. Then Leo revealed the other side of his personality. Instead of his usual and now familiar jesting, there was a quiver in his voice as he spoke with utmost sincerity. Looking first to Collin, then to Dr. Eldren with apprehension, and back to Collin he said, "whether your story and explanations are professional or not, Collin, if your experiences are anything similar to ours, and we already know well enough to feel that they will be, then we are solidly behind you, aren't we everyone?" he asked looking around at the members.

"All the way!, one hundred percent!, no doubt about it!" came the answers.

"Dr Eldren knows you too by now," said Leo further as he stared Dr. Eldren in the face.

"Yes, I do, and with much respect," responded Dr. Eldren. "The floor is yours Collin, when you are ready."

"Thanks, Dr. Eldren, Leo, and everyone," remarked Collin.

"I wish to begin," Collin started, "by giving you only a brief summary of my childhood and youth. From there I will take you into my twenties and onward to the present time. It is notable that most, if not all of you present have come to the bridgehead of your life, and therefore of your present troubles, while in your twenties. It seems to me that it is generally at that age when we try to establish ourselves by launching out on a career in life. It is then we seek to make a place for ourselves in this opportunity laden but sometimes turbulent society which we find ourselves facing as we set out in life more or less on our own.

"It is natural then that at that period in our lives we begin to find out what we are up against in our pursuit of fulfillment as useful persons. After all, just taking note of yourselves here now participating in this group, all of you, are in your twenties or thirties. It is the problems you are encountering now that have caused you to be here. Yes, some of your problems may have had their beginning in your young and formative years of childhood. Somehow you survived the later, crucial adolescent stage. But at that time you were within the physical security of your parents homes. There comes a time when you have to make it on your own. You have to establish your own bridgehead in life. In that regard our twenties, for some a little earlier, for some a little later, is another crucial stage. Much attention has focused on the formative early years and the later adolescent teens. Little or no attention has been given to the bridgehead of life, the twenties or thereabouts.

"In that regard our twenties is another crucial stage. It is here we begin at least to learn and experience what the world is truly all about. We learn then from the inside track what it has to offer, and also what it will do to us, especially what it will do to people like us. As I previously indicated, here usually in our twenties sometimes in late teens, sometimes in early thirties we are initiated into the open world. Before I tell you of the bridgehead of my mid twenties, I will take a little time now to summarize my life leading up to that time."

"I grew up as the rather insignificant younger member of my family. Any wrong attitudes towards me by some family members were passive in nature, mostly low keyed incidents, such as passive acknowledgement of my accomplishments. At times there was also a mild trivializing of me concerning my accomplishments, as though it was really something that I could do such things. It was somewhat similar to that which Albin Anders experienced from his mother, but coming from a different motivation. This motivation was as Owen Winslow experienced in his family; the concept of some members of my family that a younger family member must not be ahead in any way of the older members. This impossible notion was also present to some extent in the society in which I lived, so they came by it sort of naturally. I was kept in check by a significant number of people, through their passivity and trivializing towards me. Needless to say, this was indeed damaging to my young mind, and to my self esteem in my childhood and youthful years.

"During my school years, both elementary and high school, I had experiences similar to those expressed by other members of this group, including much passivity. You are already quite familiar with such entities, so I need not relate more of them to you, except to say they certainly did add to my psychological discomfort in life, and affected adversely my youthful and formulating mind-set at the time, causing me, among other things, to have an extremely low self-esteem and much shyness.

"Also damaging during my growing up years was my station in life in the town in which I lived. As was Leo, I was labeled by a substantial number of people in the town as the 'son of a big shot,' and treated negatively by those obnoxious ones. This also greatly damaged my youthful mind-set and brought my self esteem even lower. It affected me in that, instead of making me feel good that I had a successful and loving father, it made me self-conscious, shy, and feeling apologetic that I belonged to a cultured, fairly well to do family in comparison to many around us. From what Donna, Gilda and Leo have told us they too experienced similar labelings, and have experienced similar feelings. Like them also, I was not at the time conscious of the fact that I was being picked on mostly because of the kind of person I myself was — a fine young person. Being the son of a big shot was the excuse, the alibi, for their negative treatment of me.

"Neither did I realize in those years the significance of my father also being a person like us, a fine, honest person, generous to those less fortunate than himself, a keen, highly intelligent, hard working man, in business for himself. The better people respected him. For me however, this was overshadowed by the implied and spoken attitudes of those who actually despised him for his success, and for his generosity to others according as his moderate means allowed. The overshadowing by this very pronounced negativism toward my father, and towards me as his son, affected me enormously, especially in my teens. Out of this ill-induced sense of apology, self-consciousness and low self-esteem, thrust upon me by the obnoxious ones, for being what I was and belonging to a well cultured, well to do family, I began, in my teens, to blush severely, actually apologetic of my good station in life.

"Incidentally, my father, being assailed as all here in this group have been, fended off the obnoxious ones, those seeking to tear him down, by asserting himself strongly and forcefully, often with a seemingly bad temper. Much earlier in his life he had been very severely assailed by highly seasoned obnoxious ones, in another land where he had once lived. This caused him to be overly wary of some people at times, and consequently he sometimes made mistakes and blasted the wrong people. It is easy to do under such circumstances. Much later in our sessions I will be telling you of the severity of the obnoxious ones in that other land, and what it might do to a person. But for now staying with our present stories, as in Gilda Emerson's case, my father became known in some circles as a terror. He actually was, as many will agree, a good person of exemplary character, but obviously chose to part from it sufficiently to protect himself. I will refer to him at times in the remainder of my story.

"All was not lost for me in my youth, not by any means. I had a circle of good friends, both at school and outside it. They saved the day for me, by giving me a sense of the true reality of life. There were several boys my age who were the best of friends. With the exception of some common boyish mischief occasionally, we had a life of good clean fun together. I remember, even in my pre-adolescent years, some very nice and well meaning young girls of my own age, but as girls often are, more mature for their age than boys, taking me under their wing in a good natured and affectionate way. It was a great help to me in standing up to the personal difficulties I experienced in my school years.

"Regardless of the difficulties of my young life, there were enough bright spots in it to enable me to see both sides of life. After a very average or less high schooling, and contrary to my father's wishes, I refused to go on to further education. I gave no reason for this, but knew in my own mind that for me to continue further studies under the stress caused by the obnoxious ones would only lead me to a nervous breakdown and failure in life. Like Albin Anders, on my own accord I chose, at least for the time being, a less troubled road in life for myself. By age eighteen or so, I was able to see, though not understand fully, what I had been up against in life to date, learned to accept it and cope with it as best I knew how at that age. Before long, in my own mind I threw off the barriers that had been thrust upon me by family, by school experiences, and most of all by far by my station in life, and my concept of it at that time as to why I was being treated negatively as the son of a big shot.

"At that young age I had largely freed myself from all of it and took command of my being and doing, feeling more confident I would do well. As the good book, the Bible would say, 'I had overcome'. With confidence and efficiency I held very responsible jobs both outside and within the family business and did well with them. However for me the bridgehead of life was still to come. Previous experiences would be mild compared to what I would still have to go through. Adult experiences can be harmful too."

"So I will begin now to lead up to an incident in my middle twenties, for the reason that it describes a bridgehead in life, but not for that reason alone. I lead up to this incident mostly because it is the most dramatic, the most traumatic, and certainly one of the more devastating and life altering experiences of my existence; far more damaging than anything I had experienced in the formative years of my childhood and youth."

There was awe and wonder on the faces of the group members as they listened with suspense. Dr. Eldren was as intently drawn to the coming revelation as were the others.

Collin went into his most traumatic story. "I was in my middle twenties, and had been married approximately two years. Already I had made some worthwhile accomplishments in the business world where, in spite of problems, the nature of which you may surmise by reflecting on the stories told us by Brett, I gained a fairly good confidence in myself. Also I gained the confidence and respect of many business contacts. In my years prior to this business experience, I had been, as I said earlier, a very shy person, similar to Albin, very hesitant and blushing easily and frequently. In retrospect I can now see that there were periods when I was more bashful than at other times. These were times when I was picked on all the more by my assailants, and I can now reflect objectively on the causes of this. On the other hand, much of the time, and especially under certain favorable conditions, I was relatively free from shyness, did very well, and would now consider that I was at those times on a par, at least, with the average for my age and environment of that time.

"My accomplishments in business, however, were matched by unpleasant experiences with the obnoxious ones, as we have been calling them; a term which I hope shortly to replace with a more descriptively accurate name for those with whom people like us have trouble. These unpleasant experiences, when severe enough, sometimes caused me to regress to varying degrees into shyness again.

"Now all of this to date, took place in a far away part of this land. At that time, due to what would now be regarded as backward transportation and communication means, this land to which I refer was considered to be a comparatively remote and isolated part of the North American continent. In future discussions I shall call this land Lower Secundaterra; 'lower' because it is a smaller and less populated part of the land I shall later refer to as Secundaterra, the Latin word for second place, the rating usually given this land in North America. In actuality, Secundaterra and even Lower Secundaterra, both by the way, distinctive parts of North America, are in some ways more progressive than that part of North America I will be calling Terraprima; for Terraprima as I see it, is no longer Terraprima but rather Terraprima fallen, and I will later explain to you why I see it as having fallen from first place on the continent and also within its own nation.

"Due to its geographical location however, to at that time live in such a place as Lower Secundaterra was to be living on the outer fringes of the real world. With today's communications fully available, such places have now been placed more in the mainstream of life.

"My wife and I both grew up in this land I'll call Lower Secundaterra. We each had separately experienced trips abroad, which gave us a taste of life in its more cosmopolitan aspects. About a year after we were married we decided, for various reasons, not the least of which was the obnoxious persons reason, to move away from home, to venture out into the wider world, and to carve a new life for ourselves. We would be no more on the geographical fringes, but in the midst of where the action was. We chose to move to a part of the land that, at the time, was popular to both migrants and immigrants. The region was growing immensely, and there was an abundance of employment opportunities there for both skilled and unskilled workers in almost any occupation one may wish to choose. We could see no reason why we should not fare well, so off we went to the land I shall call Secundaterra, which as I said before, is the Latin word for a second place land. From some points of view the residents of this land could later claim first place indeed as time went by. They were fast catching up to Terraprima, even surpassing it in a few ways. However, at the time my wife Vita and I took up residence there, they were still lacking greatly in many ways.

"After moving to a large city in Secundaterra, my wife and I, both young and vibrant, set out to each find a job. I remind you this was several decades ago. Much to our dismay, we soon learned that in Secundaterra, people from Lower Secundaterra were at that time automatically expected to take more menial types of jobs, even though that has since changed drastically. This we could not accept. True, we had not as much exposure to the wide open world as the people who had always lived in Secundaterra. But yet we knew we had, even if on a smaller scale, experienced all of the things of life that they had. We had come from families of good social bearing, had lived in modern homes in surroundings that had most every social benefit to offer, but, as I indicated earlier on a smaller scale than in the outer world.

"It was argued by prospective employers that we came from a different education system. So we had, but we had both attended modern, well equipped schools, and felt we were at least as capable as those people we now met in our new surroundings. Our school grading was different, and did not synchronize with what they were accustomed to in Secundaterra. Our high school graduation grade being lower than theirs, even though the standards in that grade were of higher quality in some ways than the same grade in their system. Despite our explanations it baffled them, so that time and again they turned us down. We persisted.

"One day my wife, Vita, by far the more persistent of the two of us, applied in person for an office job with what was one of the larger corporations in the city. She knew they needed employees, so went there determined not to leave until she had landed a job. She was also exasperated with the attitudes shown us thus far in our search, and on the more practical side, we were getting desperate for money to live on.

"Upon examination of her completed application form, Vita was granted an interview with the personnel officer and in a matter of minutes was told she did not qualify to work in these offices.

"Why?" asked my wife.

"Because you have not completed high school," she was told.

"Oh yes I have completed high school," responded Vita firmly.

"Not according to this application form you have filled out," argued the personnel officer.

"There and then my wife fully realized that this supposedly cosmopolitan city, in which we at times felt so insignificant and obscure, was not so cosmopolitan as we thought it was and as it claimed to be. Her inferiority left her as she realized she was dealing with people who had not as much exposure to the outside world as she herself had. They had exposure to a larger city but to nothing outside it.

"'What you are implying,' said my wife, still holding very firm, 'is that since I do not have the same grade that constitutes high school graduation in Secundaterra, I am not a high school graduate.'

"The personnel officer began to speak in negative and hostile tones, but Vita broke in and continued, giving her no chance to turn her down at this time. 'Yes, it is true that in the education system from which I graduated, the graduation grade is different, but, may I remind you, that in the education system you have here in this land, the grading system is also different, not only from my education system, but different also from almost any other in this part of the world. Now lady,' my wife asked pointedly, and discretely lowering her tones, 'is this corporation only for locals, or is it also going to be open to people from all parts of the world who are flocking to this city?'

"The personnel officer sat in abject silence, struggling over her injured pride to control herself. My wife firmed up again and put in another tumbler: 'Different doesn't necessarily mean better or worse, it just means different. Who is to say which education system is the better just because of a grading system. In my land I am a high school graduate. Why not here?', asked Vita perturbedly, staring the personnel officer straight in the face. The officer tried to stare my wife down into defeat.

"'Not only am I a graduate," added Vita, all the more firmly, 'but I am an honors graduate!'

"Fuming, the personnel officer rose from her chair and strutted quickly across the large room saying as she left, 'I think we have as good an education system as there is.' She went to confer with a man, whom it seems was her senior. The two talked over his desk for about five minutes. As Vita watched, from outside hearing distance, the discussion closed with the man putting up his hands in an expression that implied he might have been saying, 'What else can we do!'

"The personnel officer strutted back in the same perturbed manner she had gone. As she sat down, she said curtly to my wife, 'We will hire you; but,' she added, 'I must inform you that you are on a trial basis for three months. If at that time you're work is not satisfactory we will have to let you go?'

"My wife smiled. 'Fair enough, when do I start?'

"'Tomorrow morning at our uptown office,' she said, still more curtly, now disturbed all the more by Vita's smile of confidence.

"To make a long story short, Vita went to work aware of the three month trial period. What she had not been told by the negative personnel officer was that if her work was satisfactory she would, in three months be promoted to another department with a better, more responsible job at a higher salary. So, my wife, one of the most determined people I know, did well — so well in fact that she broke all records in that corporation for the type of work she was doing, and was promoted after only two months. The job that was to take three months to learn took her only a few weeks to master. One of the better charactered executives of the corporation later told her confidentially that because of her the corporation had changed some of its personnel policies considerably, broadening the scope in their hiring practices to include equivalent qualifications. They would now also include married women, he told her, whom in the past they avoided hiring in this particular category of work thinking that married women would be so involved with family concerns that their work would suffer through absenteeism and other similar interruptions. Of course you have to remember this was many years ago. However, the outcome of the matter was that the corporation solved its employee shortage problem, my wife was on her way to a career in a kind of work that befitted her qualifications and abilities, and we had money coming in sufficient to keep us going for the present. Incidentally, that personnel officer never confronted or contacted Vita again in any way to make amends for her erroneous attitude."

Collin pursued his story as the group members listened interestedly. "Now of course," he said, "I as well was looking for a job. It is usually more difficult for a man than a woman to find a good job. In addition, I too was confronted with the problem of difference in education systems. But neither of these problems were the main obstacle to my getting a good job. I was soon to find out something new about myself. I told you earlier that back home I had been picked on because I was the son of a big shot, so I thought. Here now, in the big city, I was still being picked on, and discriminated against by the obnoxious ones, Why? Not because of who my father was, because nobody here knew him. I was a marked man because of what I was myself — a unique, fine, well cultured clean cut highly intelligent person who stood out among the crowd. It wouldn't be easy for a person such as I to steer around these obnoxious ones and land a good job. I had dealt with them fairly well back home in the small town. Here in the city it was quite a different matter. There were lots of them, with many in key places by which when they wished, could block a person such as me from employment.

"For example, I had an application in at the government operated employment agency, continuously hoping I would get a call from them some day. I had observed on my visits there that many others were being placed in jobs from that office. No call came for me however, and one day on approaching the counter after standing in line for a period, I remarked courteously to the interviewer on duty that I needed a job badly, that I had had an application in here for considerable time and could he please place me in a job. The big bullyish looking man leaned over the counter as far as he could towards me, stared me in the face in a hostile manner and roared, 'go look in the papers for a job.'

"I stood there frozen and stunned for what seemed like an hour but was only a few seconds. It was embarrassing to say the least, as I glanced around the large hall like office with several lines containing more than a hundred people altogether. There, for no valid reason I was singled out before them all as they stared curiously to see what the disturbance was. I somehow was able to retreat from the office without shriveling into nothingness, and never went back there again.

"A time or two, in different places, I tried the persistent attitude that had worked for Vita in getting her job, and also, as we know now, worked well for Gilda at various times in her life. But coming from a man, in contrast to a woman, it was taken to be rude and bullying, and so had a negative effect.

"When I would apply in person for a manual job, such as in a factory or similar, I would be met with a reaction such as, 'What do *you* want to work at something like this for?' This was all at a time when there was plenty, really plenty of employment for most everyone in this city.

You see folks," remarked Collin to the group members, "I was beginning to see more and more, that I was discriminated against, not because of whose son I was, but because of who I was in my own right.

"You may remember," Collin said to Leo, "when you were telling your story, that I asked you if your brothers were picked on or discriminated against as you were in your young days. Apparently they weren't, at least not near as much. You too, Leo, were being discriminated against not only for what your father was, but for what you were yourself, an exceptional type of person who stood out in a nice well cultured sort of way."

"I see your point," responded Leo, "and it is a relief to hear it from someone else."

Collin added, "Gilda and Donna both were reluctant, because of embarrassment, to acknowledge that they were discriminated against because they themselves were fine, well cultured people of integrity. We grow up thinking we are picked on because of who or what our parents were. In time we find that it is because of what we are ourselves. It is difficult to acknowledge that to others because of the high risk of being labeled conceited. If that were to happen we would really be put down, all the more."

"Thanks Collin," responded Donna. "It is indeed a wonderful relief to me to hear that from someone else."

"Same here," added Gilda.

Collin continued, "No doubt you will be able to understand that this continuous rejection and the difficulty it caused to my getting established in that city did nothing to enhance my self esteem. As with Albin in his struggles, so with me. Under the extreme circumstances, I regressed. More than anything else, my extreme blushing returned. This made me very self conscious and uncomfortable in public. I felt apologetic for what I now knew many people saw me to be — too fine a person for the obnoxious ones to tolerate.

"I was finally accepted in a job driving a delivery truck around the city. It was with a large reputable company whose supervisors officially treated me well. Some of them, however, and many of the fellow employees treated me as though I were a fish our of water — some sort of a curiosity they now had working with them, but who didn't really belong there with them.

"I emphasize again as Albin had regressed because of the experiences of his first year of university, so I too regressed, feeling my inferiority worse than ever, and taking on the malady of blushing so embarrassingly easy.

"My new found job on a delivery van did nothing to improve my confidence. It was a come down from manager of the family business back home to driving a delivery van in this city that in many ways was being so cold towards me. However, I did my work well and was given an increase in salary in a very short time. On the other hand, I was treated by the other employees mainly as a misfit; by some in a friendly way, by some in a demeaning way, but always as someone who didn't belong in a job like that. The remark would often come in a variety of words and inferences, 'Why are you working at a job like this?' This did not make me feel at ease, and neither did the job itself. As I said, back home in Lower Secundaterra I had been the manager of a family retail business. Now in Secundaterra I had been reduced to something less. My confidence waned, my sense of inferiority became more severe, and the painfulness of blushing so easily in public became agonizing.

"At that stage in my life, I had only a semi-awareness of my inner self. All of this took place more than forty years ago, before the full awakening of modern psychology to become a common source of self-knowledge among the population generally. Considering this I think perhaps that in my semi-awareness state I was on a par with most people of the time. I knew, however, that I had to somehow climb out of the unsatisfactory situation I was in and improve my lot in life. I did have a semi-awareness that if I could accomplish this, my personal being would improve with it.

"So I continued my search for a better job. One day, in answer to a newspaper advertisement placed by a very large manufacturing corporation seeking a number of employees to staff a major expansion program in the area, I went to the personnel office. There were scores of applicants there that day, being put through in assembly line fashion. I filled out an application form and was granted an interview with two men. One, a pleasant man, became interested in me, the other, an obnoxious man, took a dislike to me. I asked them about the nature of the several jobs they were offering, and pressed them to hire me, assuring them that I felt quite capable for what they were asking. The one intimated he wanted to hire me. The other withheld, saying, 'we're not sure what we have here, your qualifications are different.' In response to my pressing them, they said they would have to think about it and let me know. I asked them how long before I would hear from them. They said it would take about a week. That was something at least. I came away with some hope.

"More than a week passed and I had not heard from them. Remembering the name of the one who had shown interest in me, I phoned his office to inquire further and to remind him that I had not been notified one way or another as I had been told. He asked me to wait a few more days and he would see what he could do. I waited, then called again. This time he said that he hadn't come up with anything for me yet, but he promised to let me know, one way or another before the same time next week. This was a firm promise now. Sure enough, he phoned before the week was up, to tell me a supervisor had agreed to take me on in his department.

"I was grateful. And one would think this was the end of my troubles as far as a career in suitable employment goes. I remind you again, however, that by this time I had regressed considerably in my self-esteem, shyness and blushing. Now I was going to work at a good job, in a good place, but wondering whether I was really wanted there or had simply pushed my way in where I wasn't wanted. This feeling added to my inferiority complex.

"I went to work at my new job hopeful, but uneasy. Although I had now been in Secundaterra for more than a year, I had had almost no opportunity to adjust socially. My previous job had taken me each day out around the city by myself. Furthermore, because of my unsettled position in life and its effects on me, I had refrained from becoming active in any social organizations. In addition to my aggravated sense of inferiority there was also a lingering feeling of being a stranger in a foreign land; in a very realistic sense, according to the attitudes of many, an unwanted stranger, a misfit who upsets what is the norm for many people.

"Learning the job itself was not overly difficult for me. I had always been a technically inclined person, and this was highly technical office work at a time when business machines were the latest in the larger and more progressive offices. My mechanical mind thrived on this type of office work I was hired to do. I did well, and a in short time was promoted to a more difficult and more responsible phase of the same kind of work.

"I would like to make my life's career here, I thought one day, as I began to take stock of myself. I realized I was doing very well with my work, but, if only I could get over this inferiority, shyness, and blushing, and be more free to mix and associate with people!

"In retrospect now, folks," interspersed Collin to the group members as they listened to him, "I see that at that point I was beginning to have new insight into my life. My consciousness was awakening more fully. My semi-awareness was beginning to move toward a more mature awareness. I was beginning to grow and move forward again. There were very few obnoxious people working there, but nevertheless there were some, and they weren't helping my inferiority problem. Apart from that I hadn't adjusted to where I could feel at ease with the many nice people there. If only I could overcome these feelings, I thought, then I could really enjoy life here. It was indeed a time of awakening for me. A period of growth had begun. It was a beginning. If only I had simply persevered a little longer, I feel now in retrospect, I would have done well. As it turned out, I barely survived the catastrophe that lay ahead."

At this point in his story, Collin paused, in order to momentarily figure which way to carry his presentation from here. It was not only a crucial time in his story, but he was recalling a very complex part of his life, the experiences and consequences of which were extremely difficult to narrate. As he paused, the group members sat in silence looking to him for more. There were no questions or remarks. As difficult as it was for him, the sustained quietness compelled Collin to continue on with his story.

"To continue," responded Collin to the silence, "I was beginning to have these new insights into my own self understanding. A crack was opening in the hitherto formidable wall to give me a new view of a more outgoing personality and character. Touches of confidence and glimpses of being accepted as a part of the team were creeping in. I was beginning to realize that my work was looked upon by my superiors as being very good indeed. I was no longer struggling to be received into something, but was already in there and wanted as an integral part of the operation. Now, I thought to myself in my improving but still limited self-understanding, if only I could loosen up with people I could truly do well with this progressive corporation.

"While reading one of the city's main newspapers one evening as my custom was, I came upon a human interest article on the subject of psychiatry. The story told how psychiatry was now beginning to be more widely available, and more frequently used by people generally in a preventative manner and not only for those who were seriously mentally ill. Again, I remind you that this was nearly fifty years ago. At that time in many areas of this and other lands, the words psychiatry and psychology were to the average citizen, words in the dictionary that described some vague and far from fully explored phenomenon. It was commonly believed that these people of extraordinary insight into the human mind were on the threshold of being able to do wonders for those afflicted with any mental malady.

"Here in this article was portrayed a new image of psychiatry that helped, not just people who were insane, or who had complete nervous breakdowns. Now, the article said, it was becoming popular to consult a psychiatrist for any personal difficulty that may or may not eventually lead to a serious health problem, but which, at least was causing difficulty in life. The article was supported with case histories, one of which could not help but catch my attention. It was about a young man, very shy, sensitively blushing in response to the least attention in public, and so miserably afflicted with this embarrassing malady that he had been living only on the fringes of life until he had been helped by modern psychiatry.

"You may readily see why this article caught my attention.

'That's for me,' I thought immediately, little realizing that the article was referring to something new even to most psychiatrists. It was stating what was, at the time and place, more of an ideal than a general practice

"In my naivety and trusting nature, and over the objections of my closest friends and acquaintances and family doctor, I made an appointment with a psychiatrist. It wasn't a common or popular thing to do at that time, but spurred on by the newspaper article, I was determined to do so. Here was my grand opportunity to overcome, so I thought. In my limited knowledge I believed that with my full cooperation in talking freely and openly to him, he would be able to delve into the innermost recesses of my mind, explaining to me what was there that was making me as I was. This in turn, I believed, would help me to overcome my shyness, blushing and feelings of inferiority. That, at any rate was what the newspaper article had inferred.

"The day of the appointment arrived. Walking into the psychiatrist's offices situated in one of the more prestigious medical buildings of the city, I introduced myself to his secretary, whom I must confess gave me the impression of being weird both in appearance and mannerism. 'Ah,' I thought, 'probably a former patient whom the psychiatrist has rescued from the depths of a mental abyss of some sort, reconstructed her, and has now employed her in his office.' Maybe I was right on that. I don't know. Nevertheless I almost immediately regarded her presence as one of the wonders of modern psychiatry. Such was my idealistic overestimation of the profession.

"In due course I was told by the secretary, that the doctor was ready to see me. 'Just open the door and go right in,' she bade me. This I did, entering the inner room closing the door behind me, and standing there expecting an invitation to be seated.

"The psychiatrist, in my estimation about twenty years my senior, sat there behind his desk, leaning on his forearms placed parallel to the edge of the desk just in front of him. He was a very prim and proper man in appearance. Every strand of his thick hair was flawlessly in place and well slicked down with hair cream of some sort which was a custom of many at that time. A medium size mustache was trimmed to perfection. White shirt and tie, the usual professional attire of the time were in top condition. His suit coat, equally spotless and unwrinkled was of an unusual, to say the least, greenish-grey color which only a person of either unusual, or poor taste would choose. The psychiatrist stared at me but said nothing as I stood there.

"'My name is Collin Seldon,' I said, breaking his silent stare, 'I have an appointment with you.'

"'You just tell me how you feel,' he growled at me, pulling his head back into his neck, and his neck into his shoulders like an angry dog facing a stranger whom he did not like to have around and of whom he was afraid.

"'I feel as if I will never get anywhere,' I answered, still none the wiser.

"'I want you to go into hospital,' he growled again.

"I was surprised and stunned by that request. Nevertheless, on thinking it through on the spur of the moment, my very uninformed reasoning and inferiority feelings told me, 'Well, he's a psychiatrist. He should know. No doubt he is sizing me up right now and wants me in hospital for closer and more concentrated consultation and psychotherapy.'

"'Okay,' I said, 'If that's what you want. When will it be?'

"'I will make arrangement for you, and let you know,' he said, a little more civilly, and now straightening up in his chair noticeably, pulling his head up and squaring his shoulders. 'My secretary will phone you when arrangements are completed.'

"'Thank you,' I said, and waited to see what else he would have to say. He simply stared at me some more.

"'Is that all for today,' I asked.

"'That is all,' he replied.

"Saying good-day I opened the door and departed, paying the secretary for my interview on the way out."

Owen, shaking his head in near disbelief, interrupted with a remark, "You really were a green kid from a remote area, weren't you Collin?"

"Yes," replied Collin, smiling a painful smile, "green, gullible, and oh so trusting when it came to a situation like this."

"You weren't able to detect the obnoxious ones then, as you can now," remarked Owen again.

"Not in such circles as that," responded Collin.

Leo's curiosity was aroused. "Was that psychiatrist really afraid of you, Collin?" he asked, "I mean, the way you described his reaction to you when you entered the room. And did he not even ask you to sit down?"

"To answer your last question first, Leo," replied Collin, "No, he did not ask me to sit down. The meeting was as I described it, brief and cold. In answer to your first question, 'Was he afraid of me?' Well, yes, at first anyway. And before that answer sets you puzzling, may I say that this may be a good place in our discussions to begin at least to define what we mean by the term 'obnoxious' people, a term which from the beginning of our discussions, we meant to use temporarily. Owen just used it again with reference to my inability at that time to detect such people. It will follow then, that in the course of defining that term we will be necessarily leading ourselves more fully into the whys and wherefores as we have been calling them. The definition itself will lead us into that."

"I'm all ears," responded Leo, leaning forward in his chair.

"Yes," said Owen, "I too think that this might be the time to clarify and interpret some of the things we have been illustrating by our experiences."

Collin reemphasized, "Yes Owen, this may be a good place to begin defining our terms and giving our interpretations. But there will also be more of that to come later when I tell you the story of my colleague in the land of Terraprima. Only then can our explanations be more complete and illustrated. I hope this doesn't keep you in unnecessary suspense."

The other group members showed agreement and enthusiasm, as if, at long last, they would have some light, perhaps help, shed upon their problems. Collin looked to Dr. Eldren.

"As you wish, Collin," said the doctor, agreeably.

Collin took a deep breath, and thought to himself, *I have never before discussed my thoughts on these matters in their entirety with anyone but my wife. I do not know how it will be accepted, but I have nothing to lose, and I am free to drop out of the group if I wish. On the positive side, it would be liberating indeed to share, and to know there are others who understand that these things are realities that affect life, and they should be recognized and dealt with.*

"We are all aware," Collin began, "that the term 'obnoxious' could cover a whole variety of disagreeable people. In the sense I was using the term, however, I had in mind a segment of people who by their type, can be placed basically into a single category. This type of people will have their differences from one another, naturally, since no two people are alike. but they have certain characteristics in common which enable them, from my observations, to be placed, generally, in a particular category.

"The most outstanding characteristic of such obnoxious people is an erroneous mixture of pride, smugness, and envy. In our time, the word pride is, more often than not, taken to mean a healthy self-esteem. The context in which I would like to use the word 'pride' this evening and throughout the course of my discussions with this group, is the less complimentary of its two general meanings. That is, I will refer to 'proud' persons as persons having excessive self-esteem to varying degrees. Given such a person built up on pride in that sense, and, add to his/her character an element of smugness, and you are getting close to the type of person to which I will be referring, but still only close. I say again, these people are proud. They rate themselves highly with an outward sense of superiority. Secondly, they are smug in the sense that they are satisfied with their inner selves as they are. In their own thinking they have already arrived, so to speak. At some point in their lives they reached prematurely, a stage in their inner being where it is as if they said to themselves, 'I am a mature person now.' Then they shut their minds off to further personal growth. They feel superior and satisfied, and are proud of themselves as they are.

"One of the main short-comings of such people is that being thus satisfied with their over-rated opinion of themselves, they have closed their minds, leaving no 'open end' to their inner thoughts on themselves through which they may continue in personal growth towards a greater maturity.

"This is not to say that these people make no advancement in life. On the contrary, with minds so made up and so cleared of inner thoughts, such people usually learn well the professions, trades and other occupations in life. They are often, to some degree masters at studying and learning to improve their position. But all this studying, even in such subjects as literature and psychology, make no dent or difference in their personal inward growth to further maturity. They memorize, retain, recite, and quote with ease, getting sometimes the highest grades in their studies, but still it moves them not an iota towards an open and changing mind that would bring them further along the path of individual growth.

"Such people often attain good positions in life, since they know their work well. If it is written anywhere in a book at all they will probably be able to quote it or find it. If, by chance, they cannot, they may get to work and study some more. They may be masters at improving themselves in that regard. But it all makes not a bit of difference to their proper inward development as human beings. That is to say, there is no further change or development of personal character. It only makes them all the more proud. In some cases it is academic pride. Add now to this pride the element of envy, and you have a person of which people like *us* have to beware.

"The trouble with this mind-set in which these people place themselves is that it is only secure until someone appears on their scene who, most likely very unintentionally, pricks a hole in the balloon of pride. Then the someone who punctures, or even unintentionally threatens to puncture the balloon, is in trouble."

Leo grinned broadly. "Is that where people like us come into the picture, Collin?" he asked, "are we the balloon puncturers?"

"Yes," replied Collin, "that is what we are, or rather, that is how they perceive us."

"In addition to the pride, there is the element of envy I mentioned, and it is much more dangerous than the element of pride by itself. The proud and envious person hitherto thinking very highly of himself, then sees a person like 'us'. Either he wants us down beneath him, or, out of his sight, so that we cannot puncture his balloon, or shake that false, outward sense of security in which he has enveloped himself. The envious element takes action when this person sees in one of us something he would like to be. Rather than take an example from us and learn, which his pride will not let him do, he may try to drive us away, or, will set about to convince himself in his own mind, and others around him, that we are not as good as he, or as good as we might appear to others. In order to do this he has to discredit us in whatever ways he can come up with to do so. He may even become vicious enough to ruin us, for example academically or financially. More than anything else they would like to destroy a fine personality that they feel may threaten their pride in themselves.

"These things happen more frequently than most people realize, doing devastating damage that, except for a passing thought or two has never been openly recognized. These proud and envious ones have to somehow in their own minds stay on top, remain in their lofty echelons where they can look down on other people, and from where they pursue their demeaning defenses unchecked. Their rationale on the matter goes this way: 'As long as that other person is on top,' at least that's where they see us, 'then I cannot be on top. I can only be on top if I bring that other person down beneath me.' So their foul deed is pursued, often with the use of even fouler means, as we shall explore in this group.

"There are two ways a person can be on top in this world or in any given environment in it. One is by earning your way to the top if you are endowed with the potential to do so. The other is to stay where you are and to push those around you down beneath you. As we have already discovered in the telling of our experiences, there are various opportunities for people to do the latter, and that is where our adversaries come into the picture.

"When their high estimation of themselves and the false sense of pride and security that protect it is challenged unintentionally by one of *us*, then their defense mechanisms go into action. These mechanisms manifest themselves in many ways, but all the manifestations stem from two basic weapons of warfare they use at will. These are *rivalry* and personal *belittling*, and of the two, the latter is the most commonly used, the most damaging and deadly, and by far the most difficult for a victim to cope with.

"In one sense the word *belittling* may sound like a trifling little word, but in the sense we will be using it from here on, it is a vicious weapon. They use *rivalry* only when it is safe for them to do so; that is, when they are sure they can win and get away with it. But such a weapon requires skill and some facet of knowledge superior to that of the opponent. When they do not possess such a superior element themselves they sometimes create one by blocking or fouling up or by shooting down in a forceful manner the work of their victim, and then promoting some often cock-eyed idea of their own to replace it. This is a form of belittling that attacks the person through his work.

"This method works especially well for the obnoxious ones in an environment where belittlers have the upper hand and will openly give their support to such tactics. Note again that although I have stated rivalry to be another weapon, it really is another form of belittling. They will use rivalry only when they feel sure the odds are in their favor. Personal belittling is a weapon they can, mostly unnoticed, use on anyone under most any circumstances as we have already seen and which we will demonstrate further. They are masters in the use of this weapon. So, my friends, in future, let us refer to them, not as obnoxious persons, though they are that, but let us categorize them as only one type of obnoxious persons, the only type in which we are interested in this support group. Let us call them, from now on, *belittlers*."

"Well, I'll be!" remarked Leo, gleefully.

"Super!" came a joyous note from Gilda, "fits them to perfection."

The group members looked from one to another as they broke into spontaneous smiles. Collin felt assured by their response. He pondered momentarily to himself, *that part of my theory passed their test. So far they are with me. But the greatest test of all is now to come so I'd better get right on with it.*

"So, you understand, group members, what I mean by belittlers?" asked Collin, and then answered his question himself, reemphasizing what he had said before. "They are people who belittle anyone whom they deem to be a threat to their security, which is not well-founded, and which they themselves have over-rated and on which they have closed their minds. They have left no open-end to their minds through which they may continue in personal growth towards a greater maturity of character. Such people keep themselves on top, at least in their own warped thinking, by pushing those whom they envy and/or whom they perceive to be threat to them, down beneath them. They do this mainly with their weapon of belittling. So I would suggest we leave our definition at that for now. Then after I have told my story and the story of a friend in Terraprima, we will be able to add further adjectives and indeed rather shocking descriptions to belittlers and their devastating and unchecked belittling in crucial places in society."

Collin continued on without allowing time for discussion at this point in time.

"There are many of these belittlers in society. In fact I would estimate that they make up about one third of the population. Not all of them are openly active in belittling people. Many do not have the ability to do so, and they merely support sometimes quietly, sometimes openly through chuckles, laughter or sneers and jeers, those who practice belittling openly and actively. But beware of the potential danger of the more capable belittlers who guard their pride, their overly rated self-esteem, with all the hatred and viciousness at their command, and often it is much. Rather than have those made up and closed minds cracked open by people like us so as to let new personal growth in, they will put down, discredit, even destroy if they can, the person who threatens their false sense of security and superiority."

Collin glanced around at the group members as he spoke, and as he did he felt he had struck a good note with them. This was positive, but it could stir many questions which he sensed were already arising in their minds. However, Collin decided to himself quickly that to get bogged down in discussion on definitions at this time would do just that, bog down the activity of the support group. Besides, there was a psychiatrist present who although well trained and very efficient in his profession would find no precedent in his training or practice where definitions being presented by Collin existed. *I will finish my definitions without allowing room for discussion during my presentation of them,* Collin thought quickly. *Then if these definitions are accepted I will prove them out through illustrations from my life's story and the stories of the others. If they are not accepted, by either the group members or the psychiatrist present then I may have to leave the group, but here goes.*

"Since people like us are the ones who threaten that phony sense of security and superiority, then it follows that it is people like us who bear the brunt of their belittling. As I said earlier the word belittling may sound simplistic. But I am sure you will be satisfied with it as it is illustrated through my story and yours, which will show its devastating effects. But first we need a definition of people like *us*."

Collin went on without hesitation. "The belittlers see in us, favorable, sometimes exceptional qualities. If we are not put down, driven away, discredited or destroyed, we may shake their false security in which they have encased themselves. What is it about people like us that so riles up the belittlers that they will go sometimes even so far as to destroy us as persons? The answer to that," continued Collin resolutely, "reveals something more of the hollowness and incompleteness of the belittlers.

"You may have surmised already that these belittlers are a vain people as well. Pride and vanity are closely related. There are many characteristics that the proud, smug belittlers get envious of. But there are three which stand in the forefront almost always, and of those three the one they are usually most concerned about, believe it or not, is our appearance as compared to theirs. When this aspect of their lives is challenged by us, their pride is ruffled, their envy is stirred, and their hatred put into action. The kind of appearance that infuriates them the most is a fine, clean cut looking appearance that reflects from the inside a character of similar qualities; a strong graceful character based on integrity."

"Vanity indeed, to be so concerned about someone's looks." quipped Leo.

Collin smiled and kept talking in an effort to finish his definitions without entertaining discussion on them. "The second thing that stirs the belittlers to envy and hatred and belittling is your financial means as they perceive it. They themselves are often preoccupied to a large measure, with the acquisition of money for themselves. Yet they envy and hate anyone of us if they think we have or may gain more than they, or if they perceive we have had a financial advantage over them that has put us where we are and given us what we have."

"My father, that fits my father in many ways!" exclaimed Owen barely aloud, as Collin sought to go on.

"And thirdly," said Collin, "the belittlers are stirred into action by the peculiar intelligence of people like us."

"We can all think of some of those," interjected Gilda with emphasis.

"Yes," replied Collin, "we can, but I remind you, were it not for your appearance — appearance subject to certain favorable character qualities, it is much less likely that the belittlers would envy you for your financial standing or your intelligence."

"How vain can they get!" quipped Leo once more.

Collin spoke again. "To use yourself as an example Leo: when you were telling your story you implied that you were discriminated against, or belittled as we can say now, because your father was a judge, a well-to-do man in a respected position. But when I asked you if your brother and sister were picked on as you were, you were hesitant and just vaguely replied that they had been picked on some, but not as much as you."

"That is correct," said Leo.

"I would ask you to take note then that you were picked on excessively because of your appearance plus other character qualities that all together made you into a nice person who stood out among others. Oh, no doubt you had it slapped up to you that your old man was a big shot and his money put you where you are, all that trite, but the real reason you were put down was because of, among other qualities, your excellent appearance and your likable character."

"How can you tell, being so far removed from the scene?" asked Leo.

"Easy Leo," replied Collin, "experience and observation! Be objective, honest and factual for a moment now Leo," continued Collin, "we won't accuse you of vanity or conceit, but, is not your appearance more outstanding than that of your brother and sister?"

"Yes it is," replied Leo, embarrassed for talking about himself so.

"Then it stands to reason, Leo," Collin summed up, "that since you have a finer appearance than your brother and sister, and since they were not picked on except perhaps to the usual degree anyone is, therefore you were excessively discriminated against and belittled for your fine appearance, and for the fine person you are. And since belittlers, and especially male belittlers, will never admit to so vain an act as being envious of another persons looks, their defense mechanisms come up with an alibi. They reconcile in their own minds, and imply to others that they are down on you because 'your old man is a big shot' with lots of financial means to put you where you are, which is, in the back of their minds, ahead of them. They also try hard to establish that you think too much of yourself. This to them justifies their putting your down. We will establish that mind-game more fully later on. Much of the world supports those who are against the rich, the well-to-do, and the conceited. So their phony defense of their pride and envy stands supported."

"Men envious of other men's looks?" queried Leo in partial disbelief, "I suppose it is so, it must be, yes, it has to be, given the evidence."

"I believe it," added Gilda assuredly.

"I know it," supported Owen. "As with Collin, I too know it from experience and observation."

"I'm with you on it, Collin," remarked Donna.

Albin found the confidence to speak on the matter. "It certainly makes sense to me and explains another reason why my mother's attitude towards me was different than towards my brothers, one of whom was older and the other younger than myself. I knew it wasn't with me as with Owen and his brothers — the younger Owen getting ahead of the two older ones. In fact," Albin added, "I think now the real reason both Owen and I were belittled beneath our brothers was because of our finer appearance and character, and possibly variations of those other characteristics Collin has mentioned."

"Right on, Albin," joined Brett, "and Collin you should know already how I stand on this issue with you. My experience and observations have convinced me over and over again that you are right. I am with you all the way."

Dr. Eldren sat in silence, though his actions spoke well. Partly smiling, partly amazed, partly puzzled, and with eyebrows raised he nodded his head gently.

"Thank you Brett, thank you everyone," said Collin, and continued the discussion. "Now that we have some idea, as incomplete as it presently is, of what I mean by people like *us*, we need a better name by which to refer to ourselves in our group. We are envied by the belittlers for what they see in us as exceptional qualities. Actually these qualities, due to the excessive problems we encounter because of them, are to us liabilities rather than assets when we come into confrontation with belittlers. Nevertheless we have these qualities. For us to say so would likely be labeled vanity by our opponents, and perhaps by many others. But again I call us to look at the matter in an objective and factual way. Time and again I have heard people refer to so and so as a 'gem', meaning a genuinely fine all around person. I can say of every member of this group, not from our own estimation of ourselves, but from other peoples estimations of us, and there is a vast difference between the two, that we are looked upon as somehow specially endowed with a combination of favorable qualities which make us stand out beyond the ordinary. We are respected for this in some circles. In other circles we are hated for it, hence the exceptional amount of problems we encounter in life as people who are exceptional in many ways, and with few defects of character by which belittlers can discredit us to any great extent. So, my friends, without any trace of conceit, and relying not only on self-assessment, but the assessment of us by others, I will, in future group discussions, refer, without apology, to people like *us* as *fine* persons; exceptional persons in some ways; some refer to us affectionately as gems or even rare gems. But for our convenience let us utilize mainly the term *fine* persons, and for ease of conversation among ourselves, the tag of people like *us*.

"I used the description 'exceptional in some ways.' It is important to take note of that description. The worst kind of pride of all is academic pride. An overly proud scholar often takes the attitude that academically is the only way one can be exceptional. When people like us are described as exceptional it often brings scoffing and laughing from the belittlers who have done well, perhaps exceptionally well academically, but are of doubtful character in some, perhaps in many ways. As persons of fine character, we are often so harassed by belittlers that we seldom have the clarity of mind to excel academically. So when I refer to fine people as being exceptional, I do not necessarily mean academically, but rather of exceptional quality of character.

"And by the way," Collin cautioned the group, "you may already be aware from experience that an overly proud academically exceptional belittler requires people like us to keep up a most careful guard. On the other hand, what I would call a person truly educated to maturity, whether exceptionally so or not academically, is a delight to study under.

"Of course Dr. Eldren," said Collin further, and immediately, "all of these definitions of mine will require qualification. I have already indicated that not all persons of good appearance, nor all financially endowed people, nor all intelligent people are put down by the belittlers, but, as I have stated, appearance is a key factor. However, not all people of good appearance stir the envy and hatred of the belittlers. There are other factors involved. For example, a person of good appearance, who has a shabby personality, or is poorly behaved, will not be put down by the belittlers. They may or may not envy his appearance, but in their eyes he is already to where they can look down on him. Some of them will simply shrug him off as in inferior character. Some of them may even befriend even admire such a person, utilizing the attitude that although that person looks like a big wheel, he isn't really. They may label him a little mischievous, or a hard ticket, or something like that; anything to, in their minds, keep him beneath the belittlers themselves. For a person to be set upon in a major way by belittlers he has to be an all around fine person. Fine appearance is the major revealing factor, but it is when the belittlers cannot find some other reason to discredit the person of fine appearance, that their envy and hatred stirs them to various concocted modes of belittling.

"My definitions will be further qualified by illustrations as I tell my story and refer to the stories already told by the other group members."

Dr. Eldren smiled a friendly smile. "I think that is the better way," he said, "and since we drew you into this, we are obligated to hear you through." Then the doctor gracefully added, "have no fear of my professionalism, Collin. You are being very logical throughout your presentation, and you have something very worthwhile for us. Continue as you wish."

With that assurance Collin experienced an inner sense of relief as he had never felt before. "Thank you doctor," he responded. "Thank you."

Collin paused, looked at his watch, then said, "At this point in the discussions, I should pick up where I left off in the story of my first encounter with a psychiatrist. But I would like a five minute recess before I continue. It will give me time to gather and process my thoughts."

Dr. Eldren suggested a break for five, even ten minutes if needed. Everyone agreed.

It seems Dr. Eldren had by now surmised Collin Seldon's wariness of psychiatrists. In future sessions his conjecture would be confirmed. In the meantime his words of assurance to Collin 'have no fear of my professionalism', were very helpful. Dr. Eldren was a person who possessed human understanding. Surprisingly not all, not nearly all psychiatrists, nor psychologists, are endowed with this quality. True and accurate insight into the behavior of people in interaction with one another in what is generally considered a normal society is a gift possessed by relatively few within or outside the field of psychiatry/psychology.

Of course, any successful student in the profession learns the symptoms of the various abnormal modes of behavior, and their beginnings in early childhood, as far as it is understood by the science at the present time. But when a client or patient who is not abnormal is plagued by the realities and malpractices of the present *normal* world around him there is limited hope of his obtaining practical and useful help from the professionals. In addition to having no training in the sphere of every day human coping with life in its reality, the professionals seldom have had much personal experience in that normal world themselves. Most of them possess very little understanding of present adult life circumstances which would enable them to be of help to people like *us*. For that matter they couldn't be of much help to any people who are having trouble in the normal adult world presently around them. They are professionals of the abnormal, and mostly of the past.

So therein lies the danger for a fine person going to a psychiatrist for help with some very real problem concerning present life struggles. Generally the psychiatrist with little or no experience in that life, and trained professionally to detect abnormalities, seeks in his first inclination to find what is wrong with the patient. Every human being has weaknesses of one sort or another. If a psychiatrist seeks, he will surely find. Then the patient is in real danger of being placed in one or the other of the abnormal behavior slots and treated for such. This had been the experience of Collin Seldon. Now he was going to discuss it before a very distinguished professional man whose total adult life had been lived within the confines of his profession where the raw realities of the world seldom touched him first hand. Dr. Eldren, however, was one of those rarities who made allowance in his own mind for that which for him was yet unlearned and yet to be experienced. Collin would trust him and be at ease with him.

Collin was pleased to have this opportunity to share with others of like predicament to his own, the lessons of life he had learned through similar experiences as theirs. Having been through life's school for many more years than they, he was hoping, and felt he could, help them to earlier understanding and better methods of coping, where possible, so that they could progress in life more nearly as they would be able to were they not fine, exceptionally charactered people.

On the other hand it would be therapeutic for Collin to go over his past once again, to bring the sore spots to consciousness, air them and analyze them. He hadn't done so for many years, and age brings new insight. Contrary to what psychology generally believes, traumatic experiences not only of childhood, but of adult years too in the busyness of life, become imbedded in the sub or semi-conscious, and worst of all in the conscious itself, and there lurk to affect the present reactions of the person afflicted with them. Even when a person has attained the awareness that comes with old age, an emotional trauma can leave the person in a state of nervousness that then lurks, not in the subconscious, but on the surface of his life where the person may be fully conscious of it, yet not able to bring it under control. Emotional shocks can happen and do their damage at any age.

Collin now found himself facing a support group that was waiting to know the remainder of the story to which they had been introduced by him as the most dramatic, the most traumatic, and certainly one of the more devastating and life altering experiences in his existence.

"I will pick up my story where I left off in order to formulate our definitions," said Collin as he continued the session after a five minute recess.

"On that ill-fated day when I had kept my first ever appointment with a psychiatrist, I left the coldness of his office still hopeful, and still wanting something done for me about my shyness. In the days that followed though, the effects of the visit began to play on my mind, first a little, then gradually more so, until I became a very heavily burdened person. As the colder aspects of this city in general had done to me over the period I had lived there, so now this psychiatrist had clobbered me with a severe blow in the same direction.

"As weeks went by, I did not hear from either the psychiatrist or his secretary or a hospital. I was left wondering, guessing, surmising what he saw in me that day that was so terribly wrong with me. During that time my thoughts wandered back over my past life and that of my family as I remembered and understood it at the time. There came to my mind every bit of trouble, every deed of mischief, every wrong doing I had ever fallen into, and they were few, very few in comparison to many people's, and especially to many of the present day environment. I became burdened with the thoughts of being a terrible person.

"Everything that had ever gone awry in my family's interaction with one another and within our social setting and they were few in comparison to what I have witnessed since, foundered in on my young and struggling mind so that any reasonable opinion of myself and my family foundered. All the idiosyncrasies of the environment in which I grew up, with its mixture of the crude and the highly cultivated, fell in on me to make me feel it was all so inferior to the society in which I was now living.

"Every important decision concerning both my personal and business life I had made in recent years, and which in retrospect I now consider to include some of the best major decisions of my life, foundered in on my now devastated mind as wrong decisions that may ruin my life. I thought I was a derelict badly in need of help in social adjustment.

"My thoughts were that surely these are the things this psychiatrist in so elegant an office in a highly prestigious building, was seeing in me. I would confide in him, I thought. Yes, I would tell him everything about my past. He would understand it and straighten our my life for me. Day after day my mind wandered and became absorbed in thoughts of how I would approach all this when confronted by the psychiatrist in hospital.

"One day at work, after about three weeks of this mind muddling, I received a phone call at my desk from the corporation doctor. He asked me to come down stairs to his clinic. I had met him before through routine corporation procedure. He was a nice man whom I respected.

"On entering the doctors office, he asked me to sit down. 'Collin,' he said, 'coming to the point, your supervisors and some of your working colleagues are concerned about you. They say something has come over you these past weeks. You are a changed person, and now you are making mistakes in your work. You know the nature of your work is such that each error made causes untold trouble all down the line if not caught and corrected. It goes on to the customer who then becomes a dissatisfied customer. Tell me, can you, what's wrong and what can we do to help?'

"I was dismayed at the news that there were errors in my work. It sent my spirits so much lower.

"'I'm sorry,' I said, 'that I am making mistakes, I didn't know.'

"'Previous to this you were coming along well with your work,' said the doctor. 'Your superiors tell me they were very pleased at your progress. Something has gone radically wrong just recently. Can you tell me what it is.'

"'Yes,' I replied, 'I can. I have been to see a psychiatrist about my shyness and he wants me to go in hospital. I will see him again soon to try to speed up the process so that I will get it over with and come back with a clear mind and able to do my work properly. I will ask you to sign for a leave of absence for me to do so, if you will please.'

"The doctor sat up and gasped, 'going in hospital for shyness?' he asked.

"'Yes,' I said, 'that's what the psychiatrist wants, so it must be necessary.'

"He shook his head, 'No, no. You were doing fine. Give yourself more time. I'll call this psychiatrist and talk with him.'

"'I'd rather you didn't interfere, doctor,' I responded courteously, 'I feel I need help badly.'

"'The doctor talked to me some more about how highly satisfactory my work had been, and how I should just give myself more time. He was right, I know now, but at that time I was down more than ever. I insisted that I must go.

"That evening, at home, as Vita and I were eating dinner, she looked greatly troubled.

"'Your corporation doctor phoned me today at work,' she eventually said, apprehensive as to how I would take it. 'You asked him not to interfere, he told me, but he said he is so concerned that he felt he should talk to me regardless.'"

"'He is a very nice person,' I said, 'and it was good of him to be so concerned. What did he say?'"

"'He disagrees with you going into hospital,' said Vita, 'and he wants me to try to persuade you to drop the idea.'"

"'What did you tell him?' I asked.

"'I told him I had tried, but would try again,' Vita continued. 'Then I got off work an hour early and went to talk with our family doctor. He disagrees with you too. He did at the beginning when, at your insistence, he reluctantly made the appointment with the psychiatrist for you, and he still does. He wants you to go over and talk to him about the matter.'

"'No dear,' I said, 'it's a psychiatrist I need. Please bear with me, I have to do as the psychiatrist says. In a few weeks it will be all over and I will be back at work better than ever, and most of all, happy.'

"'You know I'll bear with you, no matter what,' she assured me.

"'Yes, I know,' I replied, 'and I appreciate it.'

"The next day, I took time from work to visit the psychiatrist's office. Upon inquiry with his receptionist I found that no arrangements had been made for me to go into hospital. I wonder now if the psychiatrist had changed his mind in the interim period, perhaps realizing how he had treated me on my first visit. Nevertheless, in the time that had lapsed, I had well prepared myself mind-wise that I was going in hospital to be made whole. I waited in the office that day until arrangements were made. After consultation with the hospital, the psychiatrist's receptionist told me I was to be admitted that coming Sunday afternoon — just four days time. At my place of work I made arrangements for sick leave and the dubious deed was about to get underway.

"In the few days that remained before I was to enter hospital, my wife talked to me several times about the whole issue. Psychiatry at that time was as vague to her as it was to me and to most people. Yet she felt inclined to heed the advice of the corporation doctor, the family doctor, and her own intuitions.

"'Collin,' she said to me one evening as we sat and talked, 'this city has gotten you down and you shouldn't let it do that to you. There are many nice people in the city. Since coming here you have had little opportunity to experience this. For some time now I have been working with a major corporation were there is a good cross section of middle and upper middle class people. The majority of them are nice well-meaning people. There are also many unfriendly, obnoxious belittlers among them, but since they are not in control of things I have only to be careful of their tactics and align myself with the better people.

"'You, Collin, have not had enough opportunity to experience the nicer people of this city yet. In your job searching, you experienced mainly the obnoxious belittlers who wanted to keep you beneath them. Don't let them do it to you.' Vita continued, 'you and I grew up with better by far than the middle and a good part of the upper middle class that I am now working with in one of the foremost corporations in this city. I don't mean necessarily in material possessions, although that too in many instances; but in things like culture, decorum, sociability, general knowledge and practicality in life, you and I are out in the front lines, by far, in the majority of cases. You have no reason to feel inferior to any of them.'

"And she was right," said Collin to the group.

"'Give yourself time in your new environment,' my wife pleaded.

"'Well,' I said to her, almost convinced, 'there is a lot to what you say. However, arrangements have now been made for me to go into hospital. No harm can come of it. I will talk to them for a few days, and if nothing satisfactory comes of it, then I'll come home again. I can't lose.'

"'All right,' she agreed reluctantly.

"On Sunday evening," Collin told the support group, "I quite voluntarily entered the psychiatric ward of the large general hospital where the dubious psychiatrist and his receptionist had made arrangements for my admission. On signing myself in, I trustingly signed whatever papers I was asked, without question. Then I was shown my private room. Vita accompanied me and stayed until visiting hours were over. After her departure I lay in bed, alone with my thoughts, and with some mixed feelings, but generally trusting, and still hopeful that at last I would get the help I had read about, and which I sincerely believed was available for me. After some time had passed, the stillness of the room and my thoughts were interrupted by a nurse who entered to take my blood pressure and check my pulse.

"'Would you like something to help you sleep?' she asked, as she was about to leave.

"'No thanks,' I declined, 'I have no trouble sleeping.'

"'No?' she responded in a questioning manner.

"'No,' I replied. Then giving in a little for the sake of courtesy, 'very seldom anyway.'

"'Okay.' she said, skeptically, as she left the room, 'have a good night.'

"Left alone, I fell asleep with ease, to be awakened only by the early morning hustle and bustle of hospital routine. In due time I saw breakfast trays going past my door, and wondered why one didn't come my way. Soon, another nurse entered. 'You are to take this pill,' she said.

"I took it without question. The nurse left. In a matter of minutes I felt myself drifting uncontrollably into a deep sleep. I knew nothing more until later in the day I slowly awoke in my bed, drowsy, and with a terrific headache the like of which I had never known before. As I lay there, the drowsiness in time wore off some. The headache lingered but improved. I felt hungry. Ringing the bell for nursing attention, brought a nurse to my room.

"'I guess I've been sleeping and missed breakfast,' I said to her. 'May I have something to eat now?'

"'Why didn't you eat your lunch?' she responded snappily.

"'Lunch!' I exclaimed. 'What time is it?'

"'It's 2:30,' she snapped again, then added, 'mid-afternoon.'

"I looked for my watch on my arm. It wasn't there.

"'My watch,' I said, 'its gone from my arm!'

"'You'll find it there in the drawer of your bed table,' she said, without offering to find it for me.

"As I lifted myself to enable me to reach the drawer for my watch my head felt as if it was about to split in two. Never before in my life had I experienced such a feeling. I retrieved my watch, looked at it, and sure enough it showed 2:30 o'clock.

"'There will be a snack wagon in the hallway at 3:00p.m. You may get something to eat from it to do you 'till supper is served at five,' said the nurse curtly again, adding, 'but you will have to get out of bed and get it yourself.'

"'That's no problem,' I said, 'I have no desire to stay in bed.'

"'Oh,' she responded skeptically, and left the room.

"On getting out of bed, I went to the clothes closet with the intention of getting dressed. My clothes were not there, only my bathrobe and slippers. Putting these on, I walked around a little to work off the remaining drowsiness. My headache improved only slowly, until the snack wagon arrived and I was able to have cookies and hot chocolate. Shortly after that I felt much better, and much more alert. With the return of alertness I began to wonder what was happening to me, but really didn't know enough about the business of a psychiatric hospital to guess, or to ask intelligent questions about it.

"At five o'clock supper was served. By now I was really hungry. To my dismay I learned that in this hospital, the main meal of the day was served always at noon. I wasn't yet sure how, but I had missed the noon meal. Supper was light. I was hungry that night, having had for the day only a few cookies and one light meal.

"Evening visiting hours began at seven, and Vita came to spend the time with me.

"'Are you all right?' she asked anxiously as she came through the door with an expression of great concern on her face.

"'I suppose so,' I replied. 'Although much of the day is a blank to me. They gave me a pill first thing in the morning. After that all I know is that I woke up at 2:30 in the afternoon feeling as I have never felt before in my life, with an awful headache, and a drowsy, cloudy mind. Guess I slept most of the day.'

"'I know you did,' responded Vita. 'I spent my lunch hour here with you. I tried to wake you so you could eat your dinner that was there waiting for you. I wasn't sure which would be better for you at the time, the sleep or the food. Since you were so sound asleep, I eventually figured it was better to let you sleep on. Did you get something to eat later?'

"I explained to her the events of the day and what I had to eat. 'I'm okay for the present,' I said, 'had supper just two hours ago. But now I'm wondering what's going on, and what they are doing to me.'

"'Have you seen a doctor,' Vita asked.

"'No,' I replied, 'have you?'

"'Not me either,' she replied. 'When I was here lunch time and saw the state you were in I asked to see a doctor concerning you, but was told she wasn't available today. Apparently you do not have the same doctor here as you had the appointments with in the medical office building, who, if I am correct was a man. Now you have woman doctor. Obviously you have been handed over to someone else.'

"I was surprised. 'Let's both go down to the desk and see what we can find out,' I suggested to Vita.

"She agreed.

"We walked to the nursing station. I addressed my conversation to the nurse who appeared to be the senior of those present, probably the head nurse of the floor.

"'Can you give me some information please?' I asked courteously, as was my usual manner.'

"'I'll try,' the nurse responded. 'What is it you wish to know.?'

"'Can you tell me,' I asked, 'what is being done to me here in the hospital, and by what doctor?'

"'I'll have to look up your chart first,' she replied, 'since you are a new patient, and this is my first meeting with you. Just a minute.'

"The nurse walked over to the pigeon slots, took out a chart, read it for a minute or two and returned to the counter. In cold and efficient tones she said, 'you are scheduled for a series of electro-shock therapy treatments over the next three weeks. You had the first one this morning.'

"Then she told me the name of the doctor whose patient I was to be in those three weeks. It was a name I had never heard before.

"'Can we see the doctor now?' I asked, urgently. 'I didn't ask for shock treatments.'

"The nurse looked at me curiously. Then went back to the chart, leafed through the pages, read briefly, and then returned to the counter. 'You signed a paper granting authorization for these treatments when you entered hospital,' she said in the same tones as before.

"'That's news to me,' I said, 'may I talk to the doctor and find out what this is all about.?'

"'The doctor isn't available this evening. You will have to ask for her tomorrow,' came the reply.

"I stood there a little stunned. This was certainly different than I had been expecting, receiving treatment when I hadn't even talked to a doctor yet.

"'That's all I can do for you,' came the final words from the nurse as she sat down to checking records.

"Vita and I, disheartened, walked to my room to talk things over. I too was beginning to be skeptical about this venture, as she had been all along, but I tried to keep a positive attitude towards it. It was my nature to be trusting. And besides, there was nothing we could do at the time. As Vita left that evening she was very concerned about me, and rightly so. It was a heavy burden for a young woman alone in this part of the world to carry.

"The next morning, early, the nurse came in with another pill for me to take.

"'Is that another sleeping pill?' I asked.

"'Same as yesterday,' she quipped impatiently.

"'Then I am to have another treatment this morning?' I asked again.

"'Yep,' she said, 'every morning this week. Then next week every other morning. The third week we'll see how many are necessary.'

"'I began to protest. 'But this is not what I came in here for.'

"'Mr. Seldon,' she snapped back, 'If you refuse these treatments now, we cannot be responsible for what happens to you.'

"In my naivety, and lack of knowledge of psychiatry I was intimidated and took the pill as ordered.

"The next thing I was aware of was Vita sitting at my bedside trying to awaken me to eat my dinner while it was still available.

"'Wake up and eat,' she pleaded gently. 'You can't get by on one meal a day.'

"'I can't eat yet,' I replied. 'I'm too sleepy, and my head is bursting. It will make me sick.'

"Vita sat smoothing my brow. A nurse appeared in the doorway.

"'What's happening in here today,' she asked in a cold efficient, and very impersonal manner that was obviously the usual atmosphere of the place.

"'I've been trying to get my husband to eat his dinner,' Vita informed the nurse, 'but he is too sleepy at present. Can he have his dinner brought back later?'

"'He could eat it now if he wanted to. It's not his sleepiness at all. It's just his contrariness,' snapped the nurse, and walked away, obviously a malcontent with her work.

"Vita spent the noon hour with me, and then returned to her place of work which was not far away. In the evening she visited me again. By now, as a result of the treatments my memory was getting hazy. I had only a vague recollection of Vita's noon visit or the attitude of the nurse that day, or of our conversation with the nurse the evening before. Strangely though, although I could not remember the exact words of the nurse who had given me the pill in the morning, I was convinced that I must now go through with these treatments or something drastic might happen to me. In reluctance and with a painful heart Vita stood by my decision to see it through. So for the remainder of that week, each day I went through the same routine; a pill, to sleep, an electro-shock treatment, of which I knew nothing except to wake in the early afternoon feeling as miserable as could be, drowsy and with a terrible headache, and my dinner tray taken away untouched. Then at three o'clock cookies and hot chocolate, at five a light supper, augmented later, when we caught on to the system, by fruit and snacks brought in by Vita in the evening. Needless to say, my weight fell drastically during that week. My young wife was greatly distressed. However, her several efforts to see a doctor that week were refused. We would both be interviewed by the doctor the following week, we were told.

"The following week, my second week in hospital, the electro-shock treatments were every second day. On the alternate days I had interviews with the doctor to whom I had been assigned in hospital. I can only barely recall glimpses of these interviews. The heavy and frequent treatments had all but obliterated my memory. If there was any counseling involved in them it would have been of no use to me anyway. I just could not remember much that was said in the interviews.

"It is common knowledge now, of course, that shock treatment impairs memory, and of course doctors claim that the memory comes back after a period of time. Many people, both doctors and patients, have doubts about how completely the memory does restore itself. What I did not realize then, but learned through later experiences, both of myself and of others, is that both electro shock and drug treatments affect individuals differently. It affects some of us to the extreme. This I didn't know at the time, and no allowance was made for it by the hospital staff. In retrospect I know now that my sleeping until past the noon meal time, and my extremely bad memory lapse were the side effects of the sleeping pill and shock treatments respectively. The reactions were extreme in my case partly because of my natural reaction to certain drugs, which condition by the way still exist to this day, and secondly, because of the degree of heaviness of the shock treatments I had received.

"In my first interview with the doctor on Monday morning, I remember only vaguely telling her why I had gone to a psychiatrist in the first place. To my recollection she was silent on the matter. She did insist on probing into my childhood, my family background and my life since getting out into the world on my own. I could later recall just glimpses of it.

"As I told you earlier in my story, during the month of waiting to go into hospital, every family flaw and problem, every deed of mischief or time of trouble I had ever experienced became compounded tenfold in my mind, or misinterpreted by my topsy turvy mind altogether. These things I now poured out to the psychiatrist."

"Also, as I look back now, this psychiatrist, and also the one with whom I had the original brief interviews, seemed to me to be both people who had never experienced the realities of life as the average person does. They impressed me as having been brought up in, and were now still living in their protected environments. Now they were trying to work in a world which they had never experienced, and of which they knew very little in true reality.

"This woman psychiatrist made little or no attempt to understand that I had grown up in a society quite different from the one in which I now was. My opinion is that also she did not know enough about life in her own society to understand that there are a lot of cut-throats out there as colloquialism would put it, including a lot of obnoxious people like we are talking about in this group. These are ready and trying to take advantage of, bring down to their level and below, to break altogether, or just plain hate with envy and jealousy, anyone they considered to be a cut above them. To her there was a rosy world out there with all nice people waiting to befriend me. All my troubles she attributed to my childhood. She established that I, who had so trustingly placed my life in her and her colleague's hand, was too suspicious of other people.

"As I indicated earlier about psychiatrists and psychologists generally, she also was schooled in the psychology of the formative years as much as was then known. She knew little or nothing about the adult work-a-day world, more especially as it existed for me and people like me.

"Being schooled about the formative years, she therefore questioned me pressingly about my family. At that time I was very vulnerable on that issue. As I said earlier, every family flaw loomed oversize before me. She established that my main problem was that I had had a harsh father. She was able to establish this because I had told her, as I have already told you people in this group, that my father defended himself from belittlers by being firm to the point of shouting at them or telling them off as we would say. The psychiatrist interpreted this as my father being a harsh man. As with Gilda Emerson of this group, so it was with my father, he became known in certain circles as a terror, but he had no other choice but to defend himself or be plowed under.

"Although I do not remember telling it, there was another incident that was on my mind throughout that traumatic period. I may have related it to the psychiatrist. It was one of two only incidents in which I saw my father lose control of himself in a type of rage. I did not understand it or the cause of it myself at the time it happened, or at the time of my telling it to the psychiatrist. I have since looked into it carefully and found that due to the extreme circumstances of the time it was both understandable and excusable.

"I will give you an example of such behavior on the part of others. You no doubt have seen the classic movie, 'Its a Wonderful Life,' (originally by RKO Radio Pictures, starring James Stewart as George Bailey). At one point in the story, everything that George Bailey had struggled for was foundering in on him. He, his reputation, his family and his business, his very livelihood, all were approaching ruin. Under such great pressure, George Bailey snapped, and in his irrational state was harsh to his family.

"When I was very young, a similar incident happened to my father. Due to what would now be considered an irrational practice by insurance companies at that time, my father's good fortune ran out. He had just begun to make his way well in business in spite of the great depression and many other obstacles to success, including belittlers. Our house and store were all in one building he had purchased some time earlier. When at last he could afford it he began to have the whole building renovated. At that time, I am told, when a building was being renovated the insurance company temporarily cancelled the insurance policy, and then re-established it at a different value when the renovations were complete.

"My father had put what money he had into these renovations. They were nearly complete. Then it happened. The building next door caught fire. The fire spread to our building. Both store and home were totally lost to us, my father's money was spent, and there was no insurance. Soon thereafter, as we were housed in a small cumbersome home with a bleak future ahead, my father one day snapped, 'psychologically,' and during that hour or so of being more or less out of control of his wits he treated his family with extreme impatience, not harmfully, but somewhat harshly. However, with a good night's sleep and rest he gained control and became his rational vibrant self again. Starting again from nothing, he went on to build a new place of business; also a separate house for his family, one of, if not the best in the town, and did far above the average of the time for his family.

"I do not remember telling the psychiatrist this incident of my father 'snapping', but I think I must have, because she established firmly in her report, which in later years was passed on to another psychiatrist, that my father was a harsh man, terrorizing his family and other people. It is a distortion of the facts. My father was basically a fine, highly respected person; respected by the right people. He was looked down on by the belittlers, but they couldn't bring him down. He fended them off with superior intelligence, and with a firm voice of authority demanding that he be treated fairly and competently, and putting them in their place in a manner that was often interpreted as bad temper. Sometimes he was in error, as anyone might be when fighting such a continuous battle in life.

Generally though, his action was justified. It was his defense from ruination. Many people respected him. Some held him in awe. Those of the obnoxious mind-set and others not wise to them, looked upon him as a terror. I consider him to have been one of the best friends of my life."

Collin paused with the story. Then to the group "In the years of my ministry since my brush with that psychiatrist, I have known several people to 'snap' temporarily like that, some for a much longer time before getting a hold on themselves. In later years, when tranquilizers are more commonly available, some people temporarily resort to these to regain control."

"I have known that to happen to people," said Owen, "and I've heard my minister father talk of such incidents."

"I suppose you could say that's me," responded Gilda. "I'm a woman and I may not sound as loud and terrible as a man, but still it is my defense for survival and for getting ahead in a life in which the odds are against me."

"Thanks for the support," replied Collin, and continued. "The psychiatrist paid no attention to my present environment except to say I was paranoid and was taking it all wrong. She blamed all my troubles on my childhood, with my family at fault; the usual course for most psychiatrists. I maintain that at age eighteen or so, I had overcome the deficiencies caused by my childhood. The regression I experienced while establishing my bridgehead in life at the mid twenties would never have happened if the world which I went out to face was as rosy as the psychiatrists believed it to be. On the other hand, if I had had an ideal childhood, the extremeness of the pressures brought to bear on me by obnoxious belittlers as I tried to establish myself in the outside world would have played havoc with me, if not in just the same way, then in some other way or ways. Healthy adults too, can be damaged and or broken.

"In addition to being very negative on my father, this psychiatrist also labeled me a dubious and doubtful type of character because of a few youthful antics and errors which I now consider mild compared to the average for the time, and much better than average for the present time. My low self-esteem brought to the extreme by the attitude of the first psychiatrist, helped bring this on. Every error of my youth bore down on me at the time, and I had come to think temporarily that I was the world's worst. From what the psychiatrist said to my wife, and from the little I can remember, all this became a part of my recorded history.

"Of my mother, whom, with my limited analytical ability at that age, I described as a person not very understanding of a person like me, and whom I would today simply define as a belittler, she said very little. Actually my mother was a firm believer in a cultural idiosyncrasy of her time and place, and which still exists on a large scale in some areas. The belief is that it is wrong, even disgraceful, for a younger member of a family to get ahead, in any way, of the older members of the family. This was beyond the psychiatrists knowledge. Her diagnosis was that I had come from a terrible family. In her older years, and after I had made a good place for myself in life, my mother changed her attitude completely on this concept, and made amends to me in various ways.

"I vaguely remember a discussion of my in-laws. In this regard only my mother-in-law was upsetting to me during this down period I was now in. Again in my limited ability at that time to describe the mind of another person, I tried to explain to the psychiatrist that my mother-in-law wanted to be possessive of my wife and I. At the same time she wished to keep us beneath some other siblings, to whom she was partial because they were like her side of the family. Actually it is a common wayward notion found in many families. According to what the psychiatrist said to my wife afterwards, my explanation was like a strange foreign language to her. However, with the knowledge and experiences gained over the years, I can now say with self-certainty that my mother-in-law at that time, in addition to not knowing the proper way to treat a son-in-law and a married daughter, was indeed a belittler. In future years she changed drastically, but I was right at the time, even though I realize I may not have been able to explain it as I can now. As I said the psychiatrist insisted that my mother-in-law was only trying to help me.

"In her older, more mature years, my mother-in-law apologized for her behavior towards us at that time, which according to her own admission, included rivalry and attempted belittling she had practiced in some areas of life that were very important for us, and indeed would be in anyone's life. From there on we got along very well. At times it was a struggle for her not to regress to her old ways, as it is for any older person who has made a major change in mind-set and lifestyle. On the whole, however, she held the line quite well and we generally had good rapport.

"Sometime during the week of interviews came discussion concerning my present life in the society around me. Here too I was experiencing belittlers, as I always had, and know I always will. I just wish that at that time I had use of the word 'belittlers,' and could have defined what I meant by it, even if imperfectly. But I did not. In fact, not only did I just have an average pass in high school English, but it had been several years since I did much formal composition, except to write business letters. Just as one not very experienced in English composition might make frequent errors in composition, so I made a critical error in expression that day. I had come from a land where words were often thrown around loosely, and the hearer of them deciphered them to a practical meaning. Now I was in a culture where practically every word was weighed before it was spoken, because it would be taken at its face value.

"So in the conversation with the psychiatrist, I vaguely remember, and the psychiatrist told Vita about it, that I said simply, and carelessly, as one might without harm in Lower Secundaterra, 'Aw, everyone is against me' What I really meant was, 'a lot of people are against me.' I suppose, even if I had said it that way it would have brought repercussions from a psychiatrist who was green to the ways of the world as it was for a person like me.

"And why did I think a lot of people were against me? Because I had experienced the belittling of passivity, trivializing and slighting during my growing up years. I had experienced the belittling of envious hostility during my young manhood years. And I had, during my year of job hunting in this city, and was presently experiencing, the belittling of both passivity and hostility according as I used restraint or tried to launch out into the breadth of life. Either way, I was put down by a strong and sizeable element of society.

"For people like us, out in the world things like that are always going on. I think you, the members of this group, understand clearly what I was up against in life. The psychiatrist thought I was overly suspicious. One would get the impression from her that all the people of the city were of good and friendly character.

"Referring again to my period of dejection during the weeks prior to my going in hospital, during that time I had become remorseful about giving up what I had in Lower Secundaterra and coming to Secundaterra to live. In fact, as I said before, practically everything I ever did fell in on me as being wrongly done. Things I now in my health reflect back upon as smart moves loomed before me then as grave mistakes. So even though overall, I had done well in the brief business career of my young manhood, the psychiatrist now chalked it up as a dismal failure. She may have had some help from me on this latter item, due to my own attitudes during that down month. However, no allowance was made that my judgment might be affected at such an upsetting time.

"I remember these interviews only vaguely, and at that only bits and pieces of them. Any accurate memory of them was blotted out by the heavy electro-shock treatments I was receiving. Vita's interviews with the psychiatrist helped us piece together my interviews afterwards. I do remember vividly though one brief incident. At the end of an interview, the psychiatrist reached forward to a tape recorder sitting on a table to the side of her desk, and shut it off. The conversation had been taped without my knowing it. I thought nothing of the incident at the time, nor for many years after. But one day it would come back to haunt me for a period.

"Years later it caused me immeasurable stress when during a very difficult period for which I sought help, these tapes, or the content of them, made during such an extreme down period were now handed on to another therapist. They were being used supposedly to help me but in reality were having the effect of continuing to label and treat me for the unsavory character I was not. It also branded my family as very questionable in ways it really was not. In many ways it was very good and upright, and in comparison far above average.

"In reality, my family was well regarded throughout the area where we lived, and beyond. Every family, including some of those known worldwide, has its private idiosyncrasies, some of them notoriously so. A part of my family had one wayward peculiarity that did me harm as a child. They inherited it from a segment of the surrounding culture. It is a psychological quirk found in many cultures in various countries, and pursued also in adult life against people like us whom belittlers deem to be too smart to have around.

"As I reflect back now, decades later, I grew up, on the one hand by being trivialized, and treated as insignificant by many, and despised by some, all of which caused me extremely low self-esteem; and on the other hand being looked up to as a nice, fine person by many others. The first of these was the most emphatically expressed attitude; the latter, sometimes expressed, but often was silent support only. Therefore the first scenario played most on my young mind, especially during difficult times.

"Those first psychiatrists in my life were right in that my problems started at home in childhood even though they overlooked my acquired ability thus far to cope and to overcome. But they were wrong in saying I was too suspicious or paranoid and that the problems I was faced with in society in my youth and adult life were not actually there and being the chief cause of my current problems. In reality the same idiosyncrasies that caused my childhood problem has with increased intensity been worked on me all my adult life either by or with the approval of, I would guesstimate, about a third of the people with whom I come in contact. This intensity and the quantity would vary in different locations in which I lived, it being more predominant in some areas than in others.

"Getting back to the hospital scenario: the week of interviews and treatment drew to a close. At the beginning of the following week my wife, Vita, was called in for an interview with the psychiatrist. She had tried hard and waited long for this opportunity, but had been denied it until now. Little did she know though what was coming.

"The psychiatrist questioned Vita about such routine matters as my family life during childhood, our married life at present, our sex life, and the kind of person I was to live with. More particularly she questioned, with emphasis, on my rapport with my mother and my mother-in-law, and my thoughts of and my relationships with acquaintances at work and in life in general. Obviously she was aiming at what she regarded as my over-suspiciousness. When Vita gave an appraisal of my mother-in-law which was almost similar to my own, the psychiatrist suspended the conversation for a moment. Then after changing her stance so as to look very official, and calling Vita by name in very authoritative tones, she made a statement that would devastate anyone with lesser mental stamina than my young wife. 'Your husband,' she said, 'is an extremely sick person. He is a paranoid schizophrenic, and needs a prolonged period in hospital with very concentrated treatment. He is very ill indeed.'

"At this, Vita's ability to stand up for herself, and for me too for that matter, was agitated into action. 'How on earth woman do you come up with a diagnosis like that?'

"The psychiatrist came on with a loaded question to my wife: 'Do you think that both your husband's mother, and your mother, and also several persons among his social and business acquaintances at times are down on your husband and would seek to bring him down?'

"'Yes, I certainly do,' replied Vita briskly. 'I not only think it, I know it. I do not give them all as much credit as my husband does for having the ability to do him harm.

My husband is an over-anxious person in some ways, I'll admit that. But he has them figured right. Down they would bring him if they had the opportunity. Furthermore, at least some of the avenues my husband is concerned about that may be open to some of them to do so are realistic. They are possible. It is only for his adversaries to think of them.'

"The psychiatrist's professional pride was disturbed. Her defense mechanisms came into play. 'You are paranoid too,' she told my wife. 'In fact, I think you are in worse condition than your husband in that regard.'

"For Vita this was one of those moments when she didn't know whether to laugh or get angry. But out of her consideration for me, in that she did not want to make things bad for me in the hospital, she quietly but firmly stated, 'No, I do not think I am paranoid. I think you are wrong.' That ended my wife's interview.

"Later that day, I was interviewed again. This time the psychiatrist emphasized to me how sick a person I was, and how I needed extended treatment. I protested that I was not that sick, that the problem I came to get help with had been overlooked, and that I had not, since entering the hospital seen nor heard from the doctor who had sent me there. A gulf was now beginning to widen between me and them.

"The next day I was scheduled for an electro-shock treatment. I was given a pill as usual. I do not know whether the pill was of a lesser strength than usual, but during the course of the treatment I could hear as I had never heard before nor since what seemed at the time like an amplified voice talking to me. It was the voice of the psychiatrist who had sent me to hospital in the first place. To my knowledge this is the only time he was present in the hospital while I was there.

"The following day I did not have a treatment. I was approached by a staff member and asked if I would sign myself into hospital and authorize treatment for an extended period. I not only refused but became perturbed over the fact that I had never been granted an interview with the psychiatrist who had talked me into going into the hospital in the first place. I emphasized again that the actual purpose for which I had gone to a psychiatrist had never been to my remembrance discussed in any depth if at all.

"A report of my refusal must have circulated among the staff. They had never shown any warmth towards me. They were not the type to do so. But now I could sense an outright coldness and rejection. The next day without notice I was exempted from treatment again, and spent much of the time out of my room, walking around the ward and reading in the common room. Upon returning to my room at supper time, I noticed my street clothes had been returned to my clothes closet without my being informed. Curiously, and cautiously optimistic, I inquired as to what this meant. 'You may go home tomorrow, Friday afternoon for the week-end,' the head nurse informed me, and come back Sunday evening.'

"'What if I decide not to come back,' I asked, 'what would happen then?'

"The nurse looked at me hostilely. 'Mr. Seldon,' she scoffed, 'if you don't appreciate what we are trying to do for you here, then my opinion is there is no point in you being here. But you cannot leave permanently, without being signed out.' Being taken aback by the tone of her statement, I did not have the presence of mind at the time to ask just what being signed out entailed, but I decided definitely there and then that for my own good I had to get out of this mad house.

"Vita visited me as usual that evening. On being informed of my weekend leave she said she would pick me up and take me home after work the next day. She went home happy that night.

"Although enthused about going home, even for a week-end, the next day seemed very long to me because I was now being shunned throughout much of the ward. As I observed the attitudes of many staff members, I came to the conclusion that they didn't want me there anymore. They were actually trying to push me out. Yet, I must be careful, I realized, and do this right or they may get me or my wife into trouble of some sort.

"On the week-end at home, Vita and I talked the matter over in detail. I wanted to get out and have nothing more to do with them, I informed Vita. She agreed I should be out of it, and would gladly help to bring it about. We decided we would definitely ask for my release when we went back Sunday.

"We returned to the hospital mid-Sunday afternoon. As we

entered the ward through the swinging door at the end of the hallway, the woman psychiatrist was coming hurriedly out of a room through a door just ahead and to our right, and headed down the hallway away from us. But as she took the turn after coming out the door, she caught sight of us, turned toward us for a second, and said sarcastically, 'Oh you're coming back are you?' Then she strutted quickly away.

"'I think we had better go right to the desk and see what has to be done to get me out of here,' I said to Vita. She agreed.

"We approached the nursing station, and I noticed the same head nurse was there who had told me I could not leave the hospital permanently without being signed out.

"'I wish to leave the hospital permanently,' I informed her. 'You told me Thursday, I had to be signed out. Could you tell me now the necessary steps to be taken in order to be signed out?' I asked.

"'Someone who is willing to take responsibility for you will have to sign papers to that effect,' she snapped, glaring at my wife.

"'I'll do that,' said Vita.

"'You will be taking on a very grave responsibility, Mrs. Seldon,' retorted the nurse in her continuing hostile tones. 'Your husband is very sick and needs extended treatment. If you take him out you carry full responsibility for what happens.'

"Vita answered, 'If I do not take him out now, he may never come out, so I will take full responsibility for taking him out as soon as possible.'

"The nurse turned, picked up from the desk behind her some papers that obviously had been prepared before hand. She returned to the counter for Vita's signature on them, then strutted angrily down the hall to the psychiatrists office where I assume she got another signature. Upon returning she snapped again, 'You may pick up your things and leave now, but remember, Mrs. Seldon,' she added, shaking her finger at her, 'he is your total responsibility if anything happens.'

"It was a burdensome farewell for a young woman to bear. But Vita knew she had to do it or lose her husband to destruction. We left the hospital glad and relieved in a sense. But life would never be the same for us again, as you shall see.

"The day after leaving hospital I went to see the original psychiatrist at his office. I wanted to be sure he was aware of what had transpired concerning me at the hospital. I was also curious to fathom his mind as to what he had thought of me and what he had had in store for me as his patient.

"Going without appointment, I entered the secretary's room of his suite, and asked his secretary if I could see the doctor for a few minutes even though I had not made an appointment.

"'You may be in luck,' she unwittingly informed me, 'a patient is late for an appointment, and there is nobody in his office right now. Just wait a minute please and I'll ask the doctor.'

"The secretary went into the psychiatrists office, leaving the door partly open. I walked over closely to it, suspecting I may not be willingly permitted to see him. On hearing his protests to the secretary, I pushed the door open a little more, and stepping inside, said, 'I just want to see you for a minute or two, doctor, it won't take long.'

"As he had done when I first visited him, so also now, he pulled his head into his shoulders and growled at me, 'I'm having nothing else to do with you.'

"'Well,' I replied, 'you didn't have much to do with me before. Just passed me over to a novice.'

"'I gave you treatments,' he retorted with a snarl in his manner and voice.'

"'I know of one treatment you gave me,' I said, 'I heard your voice, but you have never told me why you had me started on those treatments in the first place, and you have never discussed with me the problem that brought me to you originally.'

"'I'm having nothing else to do with you,' he retorted again, 'you have been uncooperative in hospital, and have left the hospital against our wishes. I am through with you and suggest you leave my office now.'

"'Okay,' I said lightly, endeavoring to avoid unpleasantness on my part, 'I know now how it is. Goodbye.'

"I left, not only with nothing more in the way of help than when I originally came, but actually with a whole lot less. I was badly crushed in a lot of ways. I also now had a psychiatric hospital record to contend with throughout my lifetime. It would re-occur every time I made out an application for a job, or anything else important along that line. For example I would never be able to buy life insurance again. There are those who say there is no stigma anymore about such a record. That is so among nice people, but again, not all people are nice. Also, most employers are very cautious about it to say the least. Belittlers and other mind-game players play havoc with it all the time."

Collin continued, "The world was strange to me when I re-entered it to try to put my almost devastated life together again. Heaven knows I had little enough confidence in myself before consulting a psychiatrist at all. Having now had myself, my wife, my family, my experiences and accomplishments in life all blasted to bits psychologically, and, having one of my cherished desires, that of getting help with my shyness, completely demolished, I was, to say the least, a bewildered person.

"Added to that was the devastation of my mind in a physical way. This was due, perhaps somewhat to my bewilderment and its accompanying emotional stress and trauma. But to a much greater extent it was due to the memory erasing effects of the electro-shock treatments and I think, severe brain trauma of some sort, caused not only by the treatments but by the manner and environment in which they were given. A very large portion of my memory had been obliterated. I do not mean to exaggerate the extent of this memory damage. I know that most patients complain that shock treatment impairs their memory. I know also that doctors claim the memory returns in a short time. It is not my desire to argue the validity of each side of that argument, but only to tell you how it affected me. You may remember the pill given me each morning I had shock treatment, had a heavy effect on me so that I slept through the lunch hour until mid afternoon. In years to come I was to find that certain types of medication had either an adverse or over effect on me quite often. Likewise the electro-shock treatment had a powerful over-effect on me also. I think this was caused to a great extent, by the heaviness of the treatments I was given at that time. However, let it be sufficient to say now that my memory, at that time, was devastated to the point where, when I sat in our car which I had been driving for years, I had with the help of Vita, to make a special learning effort several times in order to figure out how to drive it again. It was to take many weeks, and much 'back seat' driving from my wife, before I was to gain a substantial portion of confidence in one of the few things in which I did previously have a high degree of confidence, namely my driving.

"You may surmise, from the difficulty I had with getting back to driving my car again, what a problem lay in front of me with regard to my highly technical job which required indeed a keen memory and knowledge of the product to be produced. I went back to work, as the old saying goes, 'like a fool'. I hesitated and stammered over the names of working acquaintances I had known for more than a year. Names and telephone numbers of business and branch office contacts across the country that had been quite familiar to me were either a blur or a blank. As for the essence and technicalities of my job I couldn't even remember how to go about it. You will readily guess that this lowered my already troubled confidence all the more, and worsened my shyness acutely. Had I stayed on there, I know many people there would have been nice to me. However, my chances of being confident, more outgoing, happy and accepted there as a whole person had been shattered beyond repair. Realizing, correctly I now believe as I look back, that I had been turned into a clumsy, incompetent zombie like creature of some sort, the best I could hope for was to be regarded as a struggling invalid. I quit the job I had wanted to become my life's work, after only a few days back to the office.

"My old problems had been added to. I was now out of a job and felt less competent than ever to have one. Then there was my concern that if anything did go wrong with me, my wife would be blamed. She was to take enough blame as it was, in the weeks and months to follow, as time would tell. Relatives and friends who didn't know the full story behind it all, kept on with such accusations as, 'why did you let him go to a psychiatrist in the first place,' or, 'why did you take him out of hospital before his treatments were finished?' Furthermore, to be in the same city as the doctors whom we knew would blame my wife for any crisis that might arise, and whose reports and diagnosis would be handed on was a burden we need not carry. We had some relatives in a distant city. We moved there and they helped us to get settled."

At this point in his story Collin paused, and looked around at the group members.

"There you have one episode of my life's story," he said, "an episode which increased my problems in life, rather than diminish them as I had hoped."

Gilda came on with questions immediately. "Do you consider now that both these psychiatrists you dealt with were belittlers, Collin?"

Collin replied, "First let me say Gilda, that the incident took place when psychiatry was overconfident in itself and thought it had or was in close pursuit of all the answers to life. Keeping that in mind, then I would also say the first psychiatrist, the one who sent me to hospital was definitely a belittler. In retrospect, this is now evident to me in view of how he was disturbed and taken aback the very first time I entered his office. I had had absolutely no contact with him either visually or verbally before that meeting. You may remember I described him as being immaculately groomed. When I entered the room he was visibly disturbed. It had to be my appearance that did this to him."

Gilda smiled, "He thought he was just it until you appeared."

"That's my interpretation of it," replied Collin, "and similar interpretations with other people have been born out over the years."

"I feel sure you are right, Collin," Gilda said assuringly. Then asked, "Why do you think he recommended hospital for you without even talking to you?"

"Well Gilda, my observation is that on judging me instantly by my appearance alone, he unconsciously felt that I was too much for him. I was punching a hole in his balloon. He sought to overcome this by exalting his professionalism where he had all the answers for me without even having to think about it. I have met many similar people since. They have perhaps a high degree of specialization in their field, whatever it may be. They are proud and smug about this. Then when this pride and smugness, in their minds, is threatened, and note it is only in their minds, then they lay on the pride, arrogance and superiority, which to them is a buttress against the imagined threat. Yes, Gilda, this doctor belittled me by placing himself above me, so far above me, in fact, that he could not condescend to talk with me, or, for that matter treat me, until he did so just to be able to say he had a hand in my treatments and thereby get himself off the hook.

"As for the second psychiatrist, apart from her naivety about the outside world, I believe it was more her professional pride rather than her personal pride or personal superiority, which caused her to treat me as she did. As I already mentioned, this was at a time when psychiatry was believing it had all the answers. This doctor, who was really just learning the psychiatry profession as a resident in hospital, was probably, in her enthusiasm for her chosen field, under the impression herself that psychiatry really did have the answers. So it was her professional pride that was hurt when I balked at their methods of handling my case. In addition to that it is a trait of the character of many people, especially insecure or proud people, never to admit a mistake but to rationalize and make themselves out to be right.

"Most of the staff in the psychiatric ward had an arrogant air about them as you may have already noticed from incidents in my story. I believe this was due to the smugness of the belief of these people in psychiatry at the time, that it was a superior field with far more capabilities than it was in later years realized to have.

"Just what did they expect to accomplish by giving you all those electro-shock treatments Collin," inquired Gilda further.

"It appears to me to be amazingly stupid,' replied Collin, 'as I have come to observe over the years, how some psychiatrists use shock treatment as if it had a strange power to change a persons lifetime established way of thinking. I know, of course, that shock treatment can, for example, lift a person out of a depression. Even at that, I suspect the depression is taken away only because the cause of it has been temporarily blotted out by memory loss. When, in time, the memory restores itself sufficiently, the untreated cause of the depression sets to work again eventually causing further depression, and if shock treatment is given again a continuous cycle is perpetuated requiring it to be given again and again. I would ask you now to keep this observation in mind for future reference in my story. Now that I had had shock treatments once, I would be asked to sign in for it again in the future when I needed help because of my unresolved problems. However, I was able to devise my own way of getting off the treadmill, avoiding the continuous cycle, and begin living a normal life again without ending up in hospital time and again.

"The manner in which the treatment was used on me as far as I can piece it together, amounted to this: the psychiatrist would talk to me mainly to convince me that I had this fault or that shortcoming, that my family background was this or that, good or not good, usually not good, that my marriage had this wrong with it, or that not quite right about it, that my approach to my work life and social life had such and such flaws in it — all negative attributes, extremely negative. Then these would be followed by shock treatments, as if these treatments had some magic way of making all that was said to me become a correction to my permanent mindset. But shock treatments have no such powers. Furthermore all of these negative attributes were according to the interpretations of the psychiatrist. But she did not have a first-hand knowledge of the everyday world that you and I have to live in, much less an open mind to the fact that I grew up in a different culture. She was way off base, and offering me an idealistic pie in the sky. Moreover, all that she was telling me was becoming a blur after the shock treatments anyway, so it was all futile.

"I could not accept what they were trying to brain-wash me into, and that's what it was, an attempt at brainwashing. So the more I resisted accepting it, the more they thought I needed further treatments. But alas, there is no way that approximately twenty five years of thinking can be obliterated and replaced by inexperienced interpretations. No rational person can accept such from someone who has probably never experienced the world of everyday that you and I have experienced each in our own way, and in our own environments.

"When approached properly we can be helped to better understand and have a clearer perspective of our past and present environments.

To try to obliterate ones complete mind set and replace it with another is not only impossible, but is cruel and immoral tampering with the ground of one's being. Added to that, as I pointed out earlier, it was basically negative thoughts on myself, and my whole life that they were attempting to implant in me.

"I remember, Gilda, you telling of your brief experience in hospital, how your psychiatrist's attitude towards you was one of negative self blame for all your problems. He was tearing down what bit of self assurance you had, but not helping you to appreciate what good qualities you did have. Some of the psychiatrists I have dealt with, and there are some exceptions, are geared to finding something wrong with you. On that only do they concentrate. You were lucky, Gilda, you got out from them before they tore you apart. I got out before I was completely ruined, although much damage was done to me as I shall continue to tell you later. But had I followed their wishes I would have ended up, I am sure, a degenerate, too mind shattered to ever take my place properly in the world again.

When Collin paused at this point, Leo's legalistic mind came into play. "Collin," he said, "it seems to me that your first psychiatrist, as I will call him, when he saw that the second psychiatrist's treatment and handling of you was failing and coming apart, came to the hospital and gave you that one treatment just to cover himself before they pushed you out to get rid of you. Do you think that is so?"

"Yes Leo," replied Collin, "I think there is ample room to surmise that that is so."

"And your clothes back in your closet at such an opportune time, and the papers prepared and already on the desk?," said Leo excitedly. "Isn't it obvious they were pushing you out, and setting your wife up to take the blame and the responsibility?"

"Yes," said Collin again, "I think one could safely suspect that, without being suspected of paranoia," he added with a grin.

"It's the paranoia part I cannot fathom at all," chimed in Gilda. "You were so trusting of them, yet they labeled you as being paranoid."

Collin shrugged his shoulders in silence. He was tired.

Owen spoke supportively, "Collin, by leaving the hospital when you did, I would say you showed your preference to stay in your own world of reality, rather than be transported into a fabricated world that would never exist for you."

"Yes, that is what it amounts to, Owen," agreed Collin.

Owen spoke again, "I am sure you have had enough for this evening, have you not, Collin?"

"Yes, I have," replied Collin with a tired looking smile. "Shall we gather in our coffee shop at the corner, for refreshments and fellowship in a lighter vein?" he asked.

All agreed it would be a good way to finish the evening.

Brett spoke supportive thoughts. "The past is usually best left in the past. But when it becomes necessary to recall it, it is at times as if one is reliving it, and it becomes very mind-draining. Diversion is the best antidote at a time like this.

Collin added, "with my thoughts of the past so stirred up, I cannot promise you my mind will be present with you totally, but I know now you will all understand. Therefore your presence will be a great help to me in unwinding for the evening. After all I have just related to you the most tragic part of my life. In the meantime, Dr. Eldren, shall I plan to resume my story next week?"

"By all means," replied Dr. Eldren congenially, then taking leave from the room as he said good-night to all.

The group dispersed and proceeded to the coffee shop down the street, joining with Vita Seldon at the library entrance on the way.

# Chapter Eleven

After so smashing a blow as he had received from his hospitalization, with the subsequent turmoil of mind and memory, and the lack of ability to perform efficiently at work, Collin Seldon saw a necessity to resign from a job he had intended as a lifetime career. This together with the logically felt need to move to another city and begin again, all under the burden of being told and pressured to believe that he was a paranoid schizophrenic, and that his young wife Vita would be held responsible for anything that may happen to him, was no easy pill for a young man to swallow. In spite of it Collin was undaunted in his quest for a place in life for himself, his wife, and later family.

One would think if he really was a schizophrenic, Collin would not even have the motivation to begin life over again elsewhere. Disappointment hits hard to any young person who is smashed on the bridgehead of life. A paranoid schizophrenic to the depth that Collin was said to have been would hardly take on the comeback that he attempted, taking up new opportunities, not only this time, but at other times throughout his later years. Yes, time and again, Collin would have to re-establish himself in life. Why? Because he was a schizophrenic? Not at all; rather, because he was what was now being called in the support group, a fine exceptional type of person — a rare gem, as people sometimes referred to him and others like him; smashed time and again as he attempted time and again to establish himself and make a place for his wife and family.

Such thoughts and recollections as this ran through Collin's mind as he approached Quilibet University for another group session. His wife, Vita, his constant companion and help in times of necessity, did the driving this evening, allowing him time to be immersed in thought on the matter. Now as they approached the library entrance once more, he lifted himself out of his lostness in thought, bade her pleasant reading and proceeded to Room 405.

There after the usual exchange of greetings and notes on happenings of the week the group went into session again.

"I wish to tell you this evening," began Collin, of my attempt to reestablish myself in another city. As I related to you during last session, we felt there was a need, and rightly so I still believe, for us to move to another city. Relatives helped us find housing, and also with the basics of getting established. However, these relatives, it seemed, neither grasped our full story nor much understood what little of it we tried to tell them. Therefore Vita and I were essentially on our own in making our way in life. This is the way we felt was best for us, as it would be for any young couple, although we have always appreciated some help if it is offered under the correct motivation and context.

"We were in a different culture again now. Generally people were more outgoing and friendly, even to strangers in this city at that time. That was as we had been accustomed to in our growing up years. Both my wife and I found jobs before much time had passed. I was surprised that I had so little trouble to obtain a job here in this location. In the beginning, to a very large extent, I was treated as a human being here. There were exceptions of course. This area too had its allotment of belittlers. In time I would find out they were even more harsh than the belittlers of the previous city. Just as the nice people were more outgoing toward us in friendship, likewise we found that the belittlers were more outgoing towards us with their hostility. But as I said the more friendly people were very openly friendly. This helped me considerably. However, even though I indeed had my shortcomings before hospitalization, I wasn't the person now that I was then. The blow had hit me hard.

"I obtained a job in the office of a medium size corporation. There was opportunity for advancement, even if more limited than in my previous job. It took some doing, but in time I took hold and used my initiative, as I had done before regardless of my shyness. However my shyness was no better, I had less confidence in myself than ever, and my terrible memory was a disadvantage to say the least.

"Vita and I realized fully my state of mind, and together we made efforts to restore it and to set it on the road to new growth. For example I could remember very little of the details of the years of my childhood, youth and young adulthood in Lower Secundaterra. Except for my more immediate family, I could not remember the names of relatives more distant in relationship, and acquaintanceship. Only slowly, with much help from Vita did this come back. We often spent long periods talking about it and the circumstances of my younger years, with which, I am happy to say, my wife was familiar.

"Also, in order to help restore my mind, to improve it, and to at the same time qualify myself for a better job, I registered in some evening courses at a university. Here I was fortunate to have an added advantage of participating in a self-awareness peer group, having by coincidence learned of it from fellow students. In addition, my wife and I attended church regularly now. We both since childhood had been religiously inclined. Now we made a concerted effort to renew this part of our lives after a lapse of some time, which is characteristic of many young people. In addition to the religious nurture and inspiration there was the benefit of the exposure to the social life and contacts the church offered. Such was my program of restoration and effort to make a comeback.

"Some aspects of this worked out well, others didn't. With such a broad program as this, one would think I was well on my way in life again. But alas, the belittlers were in this city too, and I, already deeply scarred, was young and not able for them, in fact, less able than before. And the help I needed was not available. After some attempts at the peer group meetings I soon refrained from discussing my concept of belittlers, as I call them now, because it was an unexplored theme to the psychiatrist in charge of the group. Added to that, I was now terrified of being accused of paranoia — a fear that was to remain with me for many years and haunt me every time I had cause to defend myself. I did learn much about self-awareness techniques and this gave me a beginning, only a start, on learning to cope with belittlers on my own.

"First I will tell you of the belittlers at the university of my evening studies. Having registered in three courses, it was a heavy load for a person who had been away from studies for several years, and whose mind was in such a state as mine. But it did not help at all to have out of three professors, two belittlers. Out of these two, one treated me mainly with passivity, but occasionally with a cold, even a little hostile attitude whenever I approached him either privately or in class concerning course work. Especially once when in an essay, I came up with some knowledge of a land and people among whom I had lived and travelled for a period, and which I could relate and authenticate with reliable quotations from notable people, he turned noticeably cold towards me.

"The second belittling professor ignored me completely in the beginning. However, when an essay was required for his course, I did not have the time to complete the required reading for it. I had taken too heavy a course load for the time I had to spend on it. So with only a little reading done to give me a basic knowledge of the subject, I set about to write the essay using my own originality. In my high school years I had received some favorable comments on my ability to do this, as I have many times since in my studies of later years. It doesn't usually give top marks for obvious reasons, but it usually gives a fairly good one. Top marks come from a satisfactory combination of knowledge of the scholars on the subject plus ones own originality. In this paper I was somewhat short on the scholars, but very good on the originality. With the return of this essay, however, came a failure mark and the comment 'This essay is nothing but a repetition of the reading material.' That remark surprised me since I had read very little indeed of the prescribed material. On reading it afterwards though, I found there were very few similarities between the reading material and my essay."

Gilda Emerson interrupted, "I must comment, Collin, before you go further. It seems your essay was in stark contrast to the reading material, yet he condemned it giving the opposite reason. That says something to me, knowing this type of people the way I do."

"Tell us Gilda, what it says to you," replied Collin, "and I will tell you if I agree."

"Well," said Gilda, "if the originality of your essay was rubbish or unworthy material, he could have easily said so and marked you accordingly. But when he said it is a repetition of the reading material, I think he knew your essay was good thinking, in fact too good, for him that is. So as well as failing you, in order to defend his own pride and ego he said also, in effect, that you are incapable of writing an original essay. He had to defend himself that way because he knew he himself was incapable of original thought on the subject. He would like to have that capability, but he does not. So being envious of you because you have it, he had to put you down beneath himself so you wouldn't puncture his balloon."

"Yes Gilda," agreed Collin, "I believe you have it pictured as it is. Envy, more than any other character weakness, has a strange effect upon peoples' minds; so strange that logic is lacking entirely from their actions when they are perturbed enough. I will elaborate on that more fully at some future group meeting. Meanwhile, you Gilda, have pinpointed one of their major offence tactics. They put you down on the things you are good at when it is safe for them to do so without getting exposed for what they are doing. More especially do they go after you when their envy is aroused by something at which you are good and they are not. I was good at original thought. He wasn't. So he hit me hard and put me down. It was safe for him to do so. Who was I to put up an argument in philosophy, or to lodge a complaint against a seasoned professor? I was just a first year evening student, with hardly an acquaintance in the place."

Leo Aidan spoke up in sympathetic and disturbed tones, "The cowardly brute! He knew you had no defense against him." Then in more controlled tones Leo asked, "They put us down on points in which they figure we may be ahead of them, do they Collin?"

"Yes," replied Collin. "But often on other points as well. Their envy is usually stirred not only by your outstanding appearance, but by something you do exceptionally well, and which they would like very much to be able to do but cannot, at least as creatively original as we can. As I said, if it is safe for them to do so they will go all out to destroy what they either consciously or unconsciously, according to their degree of self awareness, consider to be your better attributes. And often they consider these better attributes to be the ones they lack and long for. However, Leo, once their envy is aroused by one of these valuable attributes sufficiently to make them hate you, then they will if at all possible put you down on any points they can find or in some cases invent."

"Invent?" questioned Leo.

"Yes, Leo, 'invent'" replied Collin. "Let me explain briefly now what I mean by that and I will in later discussion draw your attention to examples of it.

The belittlers, when possessed by enough envy and the hatred that ensues, will attempt to bring you down by any means possible. They twist and warp the truth as their defense mechanisms go into action to defend their own pride and ego. When it comes to confrontation with them, they are never wrong. You are always wrong. They will support their position by any means at their disposal which they can safely use, not the least of which is the superiority of their position and authority over yours. This, for them, is a position of power to promote themselves. I will touch on that later also.

"By using this and other means safely, I mean their using tactics that will not expose them as being in the wrong or as being envious. They are always very careful to cover themselves from being accused of envy. To have it said by someone else that they are envious of you whom they have pushed down to where they can regard you as inferior and make others think so too, would deflate their pride in what to them would be a devastating manner. So they play it safe. They keep themselves well covered and have a high score of success in avoiding open accusation.

"Another among the foremost of those means of belittling is the mechanism of their immature minds wherein the truth about you becomes distorted against you, and, the truth about them becomes distorted in their favor.

"Psychology only touches on this with its concepts of

'projection' and 'transference.' For a very immature belittler with a low degree of self awareness, these concepts may well cover many of his envious actions. However, for the well seasoned belittlers who know full well what they are up to, these psychological concepts fall far short of explaining the actions of their warped and twisted, envious minds. They are overly proud with hollow, empty pride, and can when they feel threatened become prejudiced and discriminating far beyond any accurate objective thinking, and far beyond what projection and/or transference covers. They become slanderers.

"They are very adept at twisting the truth to their favor. They can take your highest ideals and your most cherished positive abilities and invent ways to demean them. If you do something well they will look for the one imperfection that may be in it and put the whole thing down. Or, if it is safe for them to do so, they will invent an imperfection to pounce on. If you do something near perfect, as occasionally we all do, they will, for example, attach a wrong motive to your accomplishment, and intimate that you are a glory seeker, which is really what they are. Later in my presentations I will tell you with illustrations, where all of this in another land, is a highly developed and deadly way of life for belittlers." After a brief pause Collin added with a grin, "that's about the only area in life where they are inventive and creative."

"Thanks for the explanation of tactics, Collin," responded Leo.

"It explains an awful lot of incidents in my life as I flash back over them now. Thanks."

"I guess I knew this all along, sort of in the back of my mind somewhere, Collin," remarked Donna Coyne, "a semi-awareness, I guess you would call it. But this is the first time I've heard it put into words. In future I will be able to deal with such matters more consciously and openly."

Gilda remarked in turn, "I have been dealing with them consciously and as openly as I dare, ever since my recovery from my setback and hospitalization. But my problem has always been that I lacked the words with which to discuss it with other people, even my parents, as close as I am to them. Now as a dilemma occurs, I think I will be able to put into words and give a clear explanation of what a belittler is doing to me, instead of just saying he or she is a funny person, or a contrary person or whatever."

"This may turn out to be our basis for a more complete definition of a belittler, Collin," said Owen Winslow. "Perhaps we can enlarge on it through more illustrations as time goes by."

"Yes, I think so," replied Collin, "also we will no doubt bring out other characteristics of the belittlers to help with our awareness which in turn helps us to deal with them."

"When my self awareness was developed only to a small degree," added Brett Culver, "I had the blessing of direction from my father, and my father's business friend to guide me. Otherwise I could not have made my way through. Self awareness of how the 'belittlers' operate is crucial I would say in dealing with them."

"Right," responded Collin. "It took me years to learn it through trial and error." Then looking at Albin Anders, "are you getting a picture of what you must learn, Albin, in order to prevent the belittlers from keeping you down?"

"Yea, yea," replied Albin, now startled from the awe and wonder of it all. "Yea, I see what you mean, Collin, and I hope I can master it."

"Give yourself time, Albin," said Collin, "and it will grow on you and eventually become a part of your nature."

Dr. Eldren it seems, although present, had in the minds of group members slipped into the background. Now the members were engrossed in each other and in the new light that was beginning to shed upon their lives. They all could relate to what was being said. Dr. Eldren offered no comment. Collin was aware that although Dr. Eldren may or may not have had some personal experience with belittlers, today's revelation was beyond the scope of his professional training as a psychiatrist. To Collin's mind and experience psychiatrists are not trained in matters concerning the world of reality. Rather their training concentrates on the unrealities of the sphere of mental illness. So Collin decided to continue with his story.

"I did have one professor at that college who wasn't a

belittler," said Collin, "and my brief acquaintanceship with him was to have reflections in my life for years to come. It was not altogether for what or how he taught me, although I appreciated his friendliness and fairness, but for one simple, casual suggestion he made to me one evening. He had apparently noticed that I was lacking in confidence. He was treating me well, and I was doing well in his subject. Perhaps, since I was doing so well in his class, he thought I should have more confidence in myself. Or, perhaps, as some people do, he surmised that since I was what we are now referring to as a fine person, I was having a difficult time in life with what we are now calling belittlers. A minority of people are aware of this predicament in life. Regardless of why, he made it obvious in various ways that he thought I should think more highly of myself. One day in a brief discussion about some reading material, he suggested the names of some books I could use for reference. Then he smiled pleasantly and said, 'May I suggest to you for personal reading a book that is becoming popular on the market nowadays. It is titled *The Power of Positive Thinking* by Norman Vincent Peale. You may find it helpful. I would like for you to try it.' I thanked him and said I would look into it. I purchased that book and read it, but it didn't take hold of me. This may have been due mainly to my unsettled life at the time; also with work, study, and family there seemed little time to really delve into something of a self help nature. It is ever so true that one should always have time to grow. Such time is all the more necessary and in larger amounts when a person has specific needs as I had. However, there was presently no spare time in my life.

"By the end of our first year in that city, I could tell things weren't going to go really well for me there. The belittlers were at work on me at college, and more so at my place of employment. My shyness was my chief stumbling block as usual.

"My state of mind did improve an enormous amount over the smashing it had received in the previous city, and this in spite of the pressures and set backs brought on by the belittlers who were coming down on me as I tried to establish myself in life. Well into the second year, a planned departmental reorganization at my place of employment brought on the horizon a supervisory job, and it was intimated by the manager and his assistant that I was earmarked for it. I was pleased, and gained more confidence.

"A little later though it became general knowledge throughout the office that I was to be the supervisor of a new section to be created. The belittlers throughout the staff went to work on me — shunning, sneering, tossing work papers at me in disgust, instead of handing them to me. There was an occasional snide remark, not to me directly, but within my hearing distance, about the ambitious man going to college at night, which I should add, was a rarity for many at that time. This kind of treatment became common for me at the office. It started with just two or three. Soon they gained supporters. About a third of the staff I would say. After so many set-backs in life by this type of people whom I was only now becoming to understand, this latest onslaught was discouraging me deeply. Furthermore it was aggravated now by the fact that I was terrified of talking to anyone about it except my wife, for fear of being accused of paranoia and schizophrenia. Vita and I shared this unique and heavy burden alone. There was no help, and as far as we could see there was nothing we could do ourselves to bring us to victory.

"We struggled on as best we could. Some weeks before the new supervisory position was about to be established, I noticed that the manager was fraternizing more than usual with my opponents. Then one day came a cowardly blow. Out of the blue, the manager called me into his office and informed me that I was to be let go from my job, that I was no longer needed by the corporation. Upon trying to pin him down to the reason why, I could only get vague remarks about my studying at night, and maybe some day I would move on to some other career anyway."

Gilda quickly shot in a question, "Did he know, Collin, when he first intimated that you would become a supervisor, that you were studying?"

"Yes he did, Gilda," replied Collin. "It had been general knowledge around the office for some time and I had mentioned it casually in conversation with him one day and he thought it a good thing."

Collin continued, "His flimsy attitude was the giveaway, Gilda. People always come up with excuses and/or reasons for what they do, but their attitude reveals the motive. It was clear to me at the time and even more so now as I reflect back, that he was appeasing the belittlers, in order to remain popular among them. His excuse was flimsy and was flimsily communicated to me. It was quite clearly an excuse only. He had shown no signs of being a belittler himself, but he was joining them now to win the situation — at least that was his way of winning."

"And again, I may say, attitudes are difficult to describe and to prove. I talked about the matter freely to Vita but to no one else, as fear of the paranoia label was now deeply rooted within me.

"During the days that followed the loss of my job, Vita and I spent many hours discussing and exploring our situation. In many ways we liked this city — it's free and open manner, where people usually could be approached with ease. Through an acquaintance I was offered the opportunity of another job in the offices of a medium size manufacturer. But in summing up our situation we came to the conclusion that this city, also, as well as the last city we lived in, was a city where the belittlers got their way. This city as well as the other was a part of Secundaterra. The belittlers were at work on me at the university, and for sure they would be at work on me in any new place of employment as in the old.

"I had to be in business for myself, we reasoned. That was the only way we could see for me to live as near normal as a person like me could, to have my own business. We reasoned further that I had neither the money, the connections nor the experience in the more sophisticated business atmosphere of Secundaterra. In the lesser developed Lower Secundaterra, however, with our previous business experience and record in that region, we could, we felt sure, with a minimum of financial help, establish one or more of a choice of several small businesses. Of course, the belittlers would be at work in Lower Secundaterra with as much vehemence as in Secundaterra. But that we would have to contend with, and there were ways to do so when in business for oneself. Also our growing understanding of how the belittlers operated would help us in dealing with them better as time went by. We became convinced it was our best way to survive. We not only wanted to survive though, but to live a happy and fulfilling life. Yes, we would go back to the land of our birth and growing up years, we definitely decided, although with much trepidation."

"Wouldn't that be going back to the land where you experienced belittlement by passivity during your growing years, Collin?" asked Owen curiously.

"Yes Owen, it would," replied Collin, "but we weighed the odds. In Secundaterra I had by now tried in two cities to establish myself to the point where I could live and work as most other people do. It was clear to us now that this was going to work only fairly well for Vita, and not at all for me. All we could see in sight for me was getting pushed down, squeezed out, going from job to job and merely existing in a world in which it was impossible for me to really live. The best alternative we could come up with was to return to our native Lower Secundaterra where we could see the possibility of establishing ourselves in our own business where I would try as much as possible to live a low profile life so as to keep at least some of the belittlers off my back. We felt we could not only survive that way, but also live comfortable, perhaps in time happy lives in the reserved quietude of close immediate family relationships which we had already affectionately developed, for we had children by now."

"I see now that your plan was well thought out," responded Owen, "I'll be anxious to know how it worked out."

"You are in for more surprises," smiled Collin painfully. "I have yet to tell you of the second most traumatic experience in my life; an experience that when compounded with the first, was to gravely and adversely affect my life for many, many years to come."

Owen shook his head in silent astonishment.

Gilda asked, "Collin, couldn't you have kept searching for the right place and job for you in Secundaterra and eventually find a niche for yourself?"

"Possible, Gilda," replied Collin, "but at the time it didn't look probable to us. The chances were slim. Vita would have been able to do that. She is something like you, pushed her way through with sheer determination. But a woman can do that and get away with it. When a man tries that, he gets in trouble all the more, gets himself accused of being nasty to others, of upsetting others, even of bullying other people. A male fine person cannot assert himself as firmly as a woman can, Gilda."

"I agree," supported Brett, "a man has to tread lightly or he gets accused of all sorts of things. When in business for yourself there are ways to tread lightly through such strategies as choosing for yourself who you do business with, maneuvering around people, avoiding certain circumstances and latching on to some other, as you cannot always do when employed by someone else."

"Yes, Gilda," added Collin, "and perhaps as our group discussions proceed it will be demonstrated how in many instances a male 'fine' person cannot assert himself as forcefully as a female fine person sometimes can."

"Your points are well taken, Collin and Brett," Gilda now agreed. "I can understand there would be instances where people would not accept firm talk from a man, when they would from a woman."

"Good," remarked Collin, "and now folks, before I get to telling you of our return home, I first must relate to you more of the background of the culture and circumstances of the land where Vita and I had grown up and the atmosphere to which we would be re-entering.

"Previously I had briefly described the culture of Lower Secundaterra in contrast to that of the city which we first experienced in Secundaterra. I had told you that Lower Secundaterra during my younger years had had a well cultured, middle and upper middle class people as the basis of its society. Within these middle classes, culture was very well developed, and from it the lower classes took their example for life, and by so doing, often bettered themselves immensely. Many of these middle and upper middle class people owned their own businesses of various sorts and sizes, ranging from a modest general store to a large and complex fish exporting business. They were generally a good class of people, but their reputation was badly besmirched by the usual exploiters among the business people. Although in my opinion the exploiters were a minority of the business class, they earned a negative reputation for the group as a whole by the champions of the poor. An honest business man had to strive very hard, and be very, very careful not to have his reputation included with that of the exploiters. It was in such an atmosphere as this that my father, an honest business man and also a fine distinctive person, had lived out most of his life."

"Oh boy!" interjected Brett, "I can just imagine your father's story, Collin, he being an honest business man and a fine person, in an atmosphere like that!"

"It wasn't easy for him, Brett. Yet he did make the grade, although with a very great toll on his being. I will give you now a brief outline of his circumstances and life, since my living there was to be affected at times by other people's reflections of his life and their real and imagined public image of him. I have mentioned some things about his life earlier, but it is worth repeating and adding to at this time.

"My father was born and lived his early years in Lower Secundaterra. When still a young man he was seriously wounded in World War I, survived, and later lived with his wife and growing family in Terraprima for a few years where, due to complications from his war wounds he was advised by doctors to return to the climate and supposedly slower paced life of Lower Secundaterra. That was the best that medical science could do for him at that time.

"So my father, with his family, returned to his native land, set up a business for himself, a general store, in the hard times of the twenties, and with great difficulty made a living for us. The thirties were even more difficult, as you can imagine. The whole family had to pitch in in order to make the business pay its way and to keep us reasonably well off. The belittlers were at work aplenty. My father's experience and knowledge gained from living in

Terraprima made them all the more envious. As careful as he was, they tried to lump him in with the exploiters. As tightly as we, the whole family, had to pinch the pennies, they labeled him a wealthy man and therefore a person to be despised by many. Of course in the circle of the belittlers this was popular propaganda for them.

"Due to my parent's extremely prudent management, my father did own a modest car, having brought his first one from Terraprima, and was able to buy later models as time went by. Also through prudence and hard physical work he acquired a piece of land beside the sea, on which was an old fishing gear storage shed, which he rebuilt into a modest summer cottage. He spent very little time there himself, but liked for his family to enjoy it. So enterprises like these, which he developed through a minimum of money and a maximum of hard work, earned for him from the belittlers the name of 'rich man.' My father was never rich, but did get the best out of a dollar. He was not stingy either. Many, many times, he created a days work for some man who would come along broke and looking for food for his family. He was always willing to help the down and out by as much as he could afford, which wasn't a lot, but which often saved the day for someone.

"But alas, because he didn't splash money around in large sums, because he didn't hire lots of help for the business, but rather out of necessity utilized his family, the belittlers branded my father as stingy, greedy, miserly and so on. And, of course, belittlers usually don't want to do anything for a man they have branded so. Therefore, as I mentioned in a previous session, my father developed a defense against them similar in nature to the one developed by Gilda of this group. He made people afraid of him. When he spoke in a commanding voice which at times became a roar, people in the ordinary walks of life hopped to it so to speak. In addition, to meet the threat of belittlers in higher places, he had a keen sense of the law to keep them in check.

"Such was the circumstances of the major portion of my father's life. He was honest, prudent, hard working, and generous. Yet he was branded by the envious belittlers as a crooked, stingy, heartless exploiter and above all, rich! There was nothing concrete to substantiate such a branding. Whether my father ever made any major errors in judgment that would cast a shadow of doubt upon him I do not know. I do know for sure, however, not only from my own estimation of him, but from the opinions I was to gain later of good people throughout various parts of Lower Secundaterra, that he was a good man."

Collin paused, then added. "Group members, my father may be entering my story again from time to time, but I have given you the tone of his life. I wish to add to your information that Vita's family was also a well known business family in our area of Lower Secundaterra, having had a large general store handed down through the family. To the knowledge of my wife and I, the main problem this caused the family from the belittlers was the occasional inference in a contemptuous manner, that they were 'rich'. Of course they were not. They were about as well off as my family. However, the extra problem my father had in addition to theirs was that my father, a fine person, had been courageously involved in many areas of public and political life at a time in the history of Lower Secundaterra when it was not popular to do so."

"One question," interspersed Owen, "Collin, did other people in the area have a car or a summer cottage?"

"Yes, several," replied Collin, "and they were people of various stations in life including average workers. Many people who had the initiative and know-how could manage it. But my father, being an outstanding person, was, in the minds of the belittlers, disgustingly rich because of it. In future years cars and summer cottages became quite common for average people, which signifies that it didn't take wealth to have such things, either now or previously. It's just that my father and a few others were ahead of their time."

"Thanks," said Owen, "that tells me a great deal."

Donna shook her head gently and with a quivering, compassionate voice remarked, "Collin, I shudder at the thought of you and your wife going back to make a life for yourselves in the shadow of such a tormenting past as that. Yet I know there was not much else you could do except go from job to job in Secundaterra with a slim chance of finding a niche for yourself. Even with the prospect of having the freedom of your own business, it wasn't an entirely joyous prospect for your future."

"That is true," replied Collin, "it wasn't a top-notch prospect by any means Donna, but it was the best we had in sight. My father had made the grade there, although with much difficulty. We felt we could also. And that is something we couldn't see our way to do in Secundaterra. And when we did return to Lower Secundaterra we found that feelings about my father, who had been deceased several years now, had subsided and fallen into the background, at least to a tolerable degree. People generally were more prosperous there too now, and so the whole situation of rich and poor was coming into a changing focus. This we were to have confirmed in our minds when we did return. In time we were quite pleased about this, and things could have worked out well for us, but they did not. A whole new twist to our lives, would bring on the second most traumatic event in my whole life. And now I would like to take that five minute break we have been having. It will allow me to change gears and go into a whole new phase of my life."

During the recess, Owen and Gilda, Leo and Donna, stood in a cluster together making plans to go as a foursome to a musical concert that was playing in the city. As Collin, Albin and Brett stood aside together, Brett showed his curiosity and remarked, "Collin, you have me wondering. At this point in your story and life you are forming at least some insight into the behavior of the belittlers and ways to cope with them. You are heading towards owning your own business in a business environment in which you have familiarity and experience. And the envy over your father who obviously was a target for stigma, much unfounded, has faded into the background, at least to a more comfortable degree. The indications are you should have succeeded in this next round. But you say instead that you are headed for the second most traumatic event in your whole life. You knew the business world there. Even if terrible things had happened in business life, you would have been expecting it. So as hard as it would be on you it should not have been traumatic. Something quite unexpected happened didn't it?" Brett asked.

"Yes, you are right, Brett," answered Collin heavily. "But it

wouldn't be fair to talk about it apart from the remainder of the group."

"I know," responded Brett favorably, but its got me guessing since in my estimation you could have done well with your own business."

Albin, feeling more relaxed with the smaller group, spoke confidently, "I'm wondering how and when through all this you became a minister, Collin. Did you eventually find a sort of peaceful sanctuary in being a minister of the church?"

Collin smiled a broad smile and laughed aloud in contradiction.

"A peaceful sanctuary in the church, Albin?" he kindly and laughingly questioned, shaking his head. Then answering himself, "No way."

"Ah," said Brett, "now perhaps I see where you're headed. The church comes into your story soon, does it not Collin?"

"Yes, that is so," said Collin, "Albin has led you to the clue, and I am glad. Now it won't be such a shock, at least for you two."

"The shock has already been somewhat buffered by Owen's revelations," said Albin, 'And I sometimes reflect on the matter with regard to my own and my family's connection with the church."

"I'm glad you have a pleasant church relationship, Albin," said Collin affectionately. "One thing I dislike doing is damaging peoples respect and reverence for the church. I have always tried and will continue to do my best to prevent that happening, short of distorting the truth of course. It is time the church openly faced its present day shortcomings rather than hush them up, which originally was its way of protecting itself from the chronic and sometimes unfair criticism it received for simply being made up of imperfect human beings."

"It is going to be interesting and helpful, I am sure," said Brett approvingly, "but let us change the subject and get you off the spot for now, Collin."

So the conversation swung to the current news and issuing small talk until the group was ready to go into session again.

Brett spoke first as the support group members all came together to continue hearing Collin's story. "Whether of much significance or not, members of the group, it is only fair to tell you that Albin and I have had a preview into the origin of the next great traumatic shock in Collin's life. We know nothing of the details. Our conversation stopped short of that a few moments ago." Then addressing Collin, "I don't know whether you want all of the members to know now what we know, Collin. Whichever, I will leave it to you to tell them. But if, as the story goes on, Albin and I indicate some knowledge of it, as little as it is, everyone here will know how we got it."

"Thank you, Brett," responded Collin, then to the group as a whole, "Since the matter has been raised I will give you a brief sketch of the equally short conversation that took place on the matter during our recess. It came about by Brett expressing wonderment he obviously could not contain at the time, about why I would have a traumatic experience coming up in my story when I already pretty well knew what I could expect in business for myself in my familiar homeland. Brett expected I would do well there in business for myself, and he was right. I did do well there, and no traumatic shock came from my being in business. The shock was to come from the church."

"The church!" exclaimed Leo in astonishment.

"Doesn't surprise me," said Owen, coolly.

"Me neither now, nothing surprises me, in any line of life anymore," added Albin to everyone's delightful surprise as they once again noticed his progress in gaining insight and confidence.

Donna spoke as if on behalf of both women present, "we women of the group are learning to take all surprises and shocks in our stride, are we not, Gilda?"

"Yes indeed," replied Gilda. "We are ready for your story Collin," she remarked expectantly.

Enthusiasm among the group members had grown tremendously over the weeks. They were now well at ease with one another, even in the presence of a psychiatrist. There was also on Dr. Eldren's part a corresponding tendency to drop into the background. It was as if the matters at hand were out of his professional orbit, even though he was interestingly absorbed in the proceedings of the group. His low-keyed participation was overshadowed by the groups exuberance.

Collin began the next episode of his story. "My wife Vita and I and our small family returned to live in Lower Secundaterra. For a few weeks we stayed with an uncle of mine who lived in a village several miles distance from the area of Lower Secundaterra in which we planned to make our home. The people of the village, although they wouldn't know me well, would know who I was from former family connections in the village and also from my own boyhood years when I spent much summer vacation time there.

"One event from our brief stay in the village stands out in my mind. I went to the general store to buy groceries. The elderly wife of the store owner was there, and also two female employees. There were no other customers present. As one employee helped me with my needs, the owner's wife and the other employee, a woman nearing middle age, stood at a distance sizing me up and down. I remembered from childhood who these women were, but due to my shyness, plus the fact I wasn't sure they would know me, I didn't go to speak with them, but with the help of the third employee, went about my shopping.

"But then, as if intending me to hear, the owner's wife spoke to the woman standing beside her, 'I know who that is, I remember him from his youth.' The other woman remarked, 'Yes, I remember him too. He was always a nice boy.'

"The older woman remarked as she continued to look me up and down, 'too good for his own good, I would say.'

"The other woman remarked, 'That's the way he's always been, if I remember correctly.'

"'Well,' said the owner's wife, 'if he stays around here, they'll whittle him down and ruin his life for sure.' Their conversation made me feel conspicuous to say the least. Soon my purchases were ready and I made my exit.

"In the days that followed, I pondered that conversation many times. On the one hand it wasn't at all comforting to be informed that if I stayed around, I might be brought low and ruined. On the other hand, it was very comforting indeed to know that there were at least two people, and if two, then no doubt many more, who were familiar with the world of reality as it existed for people like me, and that at least some people wouldn't label me a paranoid if I tried to defend myself."

Gilda interjected quickly, "that store owner's wife knew more about life than the psychiatrists you had in Secundaterra."

"Yes she did, Gilda," replied Collin, "and she will never know what she did for me. I am grateful to her for the assurance she gave me that day, that I wasn't a paranoid, I wasn't imagining persecution. She gave me just a glimmer of renewed confidence, which at the time was only tiny, but which grew as the months and years went by. In the long run, her remark lifted the level of my awareness that there are people out there in the world who will ruin good peoples' lives, simply out of envy and hatred. And, of course, as one's self-awareness of a problem like this increases, so does one's ability to cope increase with it if one has the courage and stamina to do so.

"I should add here," said Collin, "that since that time, that little village has evolved into a more sophisticated place, with people of higher caliber living there. At the time of my story, Vita and I, returning from life in the broader world would have been far too much for many people there. We would not have been accepted, nor would we have fitted in. The women in the store were right.

"One further note, although we didn't stay in that village very long, one person did turn mean towards us and sought vigorously to belittle us. It was an indication of what would have been at the time had we stayed there, but we had no intention of doing so. Eventually we took up residence in Vita's home town, which, although not a far distance from the town in which I grew up, would be a more kindly town towards me. It had been so to my wife always and that would be a help to us. For some time we stayed with relatives for relaxation and reorientation, during which time we explored business possibilities and became enthused at the prospects, although we would have to start from small beginnings.

"However, it was not without a measure of apprehension that I was establishing myself and family anywhere in Lower Secundaterra. In one sense I was happy to be returning to the familiarities of home. On the other hand I had a very pronounced feeling of going back home in defeat. At that time, very few people ever returned to Lower Secundaterra from Secundaterra. Since that time that trend has very definitely reversed. But here I was returning with this frame of mind that put myself in the category of one who had been smashed badly by the more complex life of the outer world and was returning home a failure in the eyes of all who knew me.

"Vita was the only one I could share these feelings with. Together we came to the conclusion that it was mostly my own inner feelings that were making me feel that way, and that no one except us knew what had happened to me in Secundaterra, and we would keep it quiet between us.

"There were a couple of major problems though. One, I was as shy as ever. There was a bright note in this area though, and that is, I was now becoming aware, on my own, of the things that were contributing to my shyness. This was a major step forward. Understanding is the forerunner of better coping. The other problem was that as I moved around that area of Lower Secundaterra I was meeting people whom I at one time knew, some of them very well, but could no longer remember their names, or in what connection I had once known them. Often times I would speak to them not knowing for sure if I should. At other times I would refrain from speaking because I, perhaps, couldn't remember their names, or where I had met them before, or indeed whether I really knew them at all. I blame this on the severe electro-shock treatments I had had in Secundaterra by now more than two years previously, but my memory had not yet fully restored itself. I covered very little territory socially without Vita by my side to whisper to me as we approached someone, 'that is so and so, you knew him or her at such and such a place." There were embarrassing times when my wife didn't have time to coach me beforehand. However, with her endless patience and our tackling the problem together, I did in time become very well reoriented.

"I have time and again since explored the possibility that the memory loss may have been from a psychological effect, but can find no tangible evidence of it for so young a person. After all these years, I am still of the opinion that my memory was severely damaged by the heavy electro-shock treatments. It was a genuine physical impairment of the mind that had to be overcome by a relearning process. I had no notion of looking for pity or the like. Vita and I kept it and all that had happened private, and handled my readjustment quietly, and, we think, well.

"During these months of readjustment and reorientation I also endeavored to brighten up my life by reactivating myself in a recreation at which I had been quite adept when I was a youth of age twelve to eighteen. At that period in my younger years it was quite popular among the boys to sport around the hundreds of square miles of forests, lakes and rivers that were sitting there for anyone who wished to use them. In these youthful years a small group of us, two or three, or occasionally a half dozen would put a pack of food and bedroll on our backs and trek five, ten, fifteen miles and return, into virgin or scarcely worked forest, following rivers, fishing in streams, sleeping on the ground, or in a trappers cabin or old logging camp. It had been the sport of our teens, requiring exceptional physical and mental stamina to trek from two to five days, taking of course, plenty of time to fish, cook, eat, swim, pick wild berries and nuts, and enjoy the freedom of nature. By the time I was age fourteen, I was a master of this recreation. I might emphasize the mental stamina required, in that sleeping on the ground at night became scary at times, as there were bears and lynx around. We did not carry guns, but trusted in our ability to keep cool when we heard strange and disruptive noises at night. We had plans formulated to protect one another, and to scare animals away with fires that could be quickly lit from materials always gathered beforehand and prepared for instant use.

Occasionally, we did falter and fear, and ask ourselves why we did this sort of thing for recreation. But that was part of the growing process. Before each trip was over, we were planning the next, often deciding on our homeward trek, where the next outing would take us.

"So now in this year of my return to Lower Secundaterra, I fitted myself out with a new kit bag, hunting knife, axe, and a few utensils; the minimum equipment required. Sometimes with others, sometimes by myself, I began to make occasional trips into the forest again. The longing for it had never really left me. Somehow rugged nature has a way of keeping hold of a person once he has experienced it. Now at this age and stage of my life I became more adept at it than ever. On one such trip, in two days I built a small size log cabin with only an axe. My body was more powerful than even back in my youth. On the next trip, I utilized that powerful body to carry on my back and shoulders, along with my usual food and equipment, a small roll of roofing and a small steel drum for a stove. With the installation of these, the only items from civilization, my cabin was ready for use.

"Now, as never before, I preferred to go on these trips alone, because this gave me an opportunity, in an environment which I loved and which lifted my spirits tremendously, to be quietly and gainfully introspective. This was something I needed at the time, and gave me opportunity to put my mind in order after the defeats I had experienced. In talking, at a later date, to a friend who had a professional understanding of my state of mind at the time, he expressed the opinion that I made great strides forward during that period of my return to nature.

"When not on these trips, however, Vita and I together participated in social activities, going out often together to public and social events. As I said earlier, I was again gaining, this time quite immeasurably, personal insight into my shyness. Self awareness was really awakening in my hitherto troubled mind. Vita and I were both pleased with my progress.

"There soon came a time when the material aspects of life had to be taken into account. When we had decided for sure what small businesses we each would go into, it was time to put excessive recreation aside.

"Vita, with my help in looking after the family, took a six month concentrated course in beauty culture in a little more than two months, and attained advanced certification. Such was her ability and drive when necessity called, as it often did. Meanwhile, while she was away from home studying beauty culture, I was at home studying photography, and dark room techniques and procedures, and devising and preparing and constructing my own equipment for same day film processing. For a few hundred dollars I was able to put into action a system that, with a little extra labor on my part in the processing would do the work of a system that if purchased ready manufactured would cost several thousand dollars, which we could not afford. Incidentally, I am speaking in economic terms of several years ago. Today the prices of such equipment would be much higher.

"My system and I were ready at approximately the same time as Vita was ready to operate her own beauty shop. Relatives, knowing that we were desperately in need of a way to make a living, helped us with a building in which to house our business, and also ourselves in old, but adequate, furnished quarters. Doing carpentry, plumbing and decoration ourselves, we arranged two high quality shops in this building.

"We had been previously aware that among the relatives who helped us with the site for our business were some belittlers. So it was no shock to us that when they saw how good a system we were setting up and that the prospects looked good for us, they turned sour on us, and there was no further help forthcoming. However, we had the building clinched for the present, and our good credit rating at the local bank was still recorded from previous years. This helped us to obtain a loan to buy beauty shop equipment. Because of the necessity of the loan, we would be on a tight budget for two years, but we could see our way through especially after we opened for business and everything went better than expected from the start.

"As we had surmised and planned on, Vita's business brought

in the major portion of our income to start. We calculated from our own knowledge and information from other contacts in the field, that my business would have to be built up slowly and steadily over a longer period, and would then eventually become the greater source of our family income. Our setting was in a small town. We would never get rich here, we were well aware, and we had no ambition to do so. We did want to earn a living and bring up our family.

"Whether this would be our life's work we were not sure. Sometimes we thought it might be, more often we regarded it as a starter or a stopgap that would soon be eaten up by small town competition. However, there were other more promising businesses, one of which we could start later when we were able to raise larger amounts of money. In the meantime, this was it for now. We worked long and hard, each of us with many hours on our feet every working day. And between the two of us we cared for our pre-school family.

"We were pleased to be earning a living again and to have a measure of family security. Vita being the strong charactered type she was, as ever was able to make herself content in any circumstances that were truly livable. She pursued her business with enthusiasm.

"I too was happy, but not all of the time. For me there was a difficult personal struggle of the mind to continually contend with, especially now that I spent many hours each day in a darkroom alone. The peace and tranquility of nature had helped me to overcome, and had allowed me to grow. But now alone so much in the darkroom, there were sometimes the wounds of the past and the resulting sense of defeat trying to crowd in on my degree of contentment.

"The blows struck to me in Secundaterra, and especially the resulting loss of the good job in the first city, out of which I had intended to make a career, were playing on my mind. At times I felt I was now working at something far less challenging; also, as I said, my work required that I spend a great deal of time in the photography darkroom alone, processing rolls of film and producing the snapshots there from. My mind would occasionally go from periods of enriching introspection to periods of disappointment and discontent, and a resulting frustration at what the world had done to me.

"It soon became apparent that in my off work hours we, and me particularly, would need enriching diversion. There was no time now for my trips into the forest, and neither did I desire to continue such recreation. Rather, on the one week day we set aside as our day off, we as a family would go to some outdoor location, of which there were numerous available, and enjoy nature as a family together. This we all enjoyed immensely.

"On Sundays, in accordance with our Christian convictions, our businesses were closed. We started attending the local congregation of the denomination with which we had maintained association since infant baptism.

"As I began to attend church I was well aware, even at that time, of the problems some people like Brett and the others of us here tonight may at any time have in some congregations, but not in others. From what Brett told us earlier, he can go to church in some places but not in others. It depends mainly on two factors; whether the minister is a belittler, or even just uncomfortable or afraid of people he sees as 'big shots' in his congregation, and whether the congregation is dominated by belittlers and/or people who don't feel comfortable with 'big shots' around. The congregations that prosper are those whose people feel at ease with each other regardless of their occupation and standing in life — Christianity can overcome all barriers. I made up my mind that I would have no such problem as just described. I would intentionally play low profile before the minister and the mainstays of the church, participating and helping but letting them run the show, so to speak. It wouldn't be easy to do this and still gain the necessary growth experiences I would like, but I would do it, I was determined. I wanted to belong to the church, and I wanted no trouble with it. I would be so cooperative with them and so good to them, I thought, that they would have no reason to dislike me or reject me.

"All went well to start, and this gave us a tremendous boost in spirit as, among other things, we felt we now were a part of the community in which we were living. That, of course is one of the functions of the church — to incorporate people into a fellowship where we are one under God.

"But attending church now became more than that for me. I mentioned earlier that I had entered a period of reawakening and self awareness. Now within the fellowship of this church I began to grow again in mind and spirit, rethinking my relationships to people in the close atmosphere of congregational activities; and much much more, rethinking my relationship to God in an adult frame of mind. The main extent of my religious training had hitherto been on a youthful Sunday school level, although I had attended church considerably as an adult. I began to realize now that my Christian convictions, which had been a definite part of me always, needed nurture to bring them to a more developed measure of maturity. Vita was very happy too to be back into the fold of the church. In her pre married years she had developed a very consistent relationship to the church and had always lived in close partnership with God.

"I was becoming aware of the cause of my shyness, but the overcoming of it was very, very gradual indeed. Joining the men's club of the church was a major step forward for me. I attended their meetings and enjoyed them immensely, but as yet had little or nothing to say. However, on various work projects the men were to carry out in the work of the church, they included me in their activities. Apparently some of them, at least, took a liking to me and enjoyed having me working with them on their projects. It may not have been visible to others, but in my own mind I was loosening up and growing and improving immensely in mind and spirit. I was beginning to feel really glad and happy to be back in Lower Secundaterra. There were some belittling scoffers, though not many. They were ever ready to remark about my quietness. This served to tighten me up some again, occasionally. However, scoffers are going to scoff no matter what. I practiced not letting it bother me. I began to teach in Church Sunday School. This was a valuable growth experience for me in that it gave me opportunity to practice expressing myself. This experience was before children only, but nevertheless an invaluable one in helping to overcome shyness. Despite my shortcomings, and the problems encountered from the few belittlers, I was getting well on my way in life again, being gradually restored, and not only that, becoming better than ever at socializing; more than I had ever been, actually developing a well rounded life.

"Not only was I growing into the fellowship of the church, but also into the study of the Bible and the Christian Way itself. As well as serving my growth experience of the time, this also gave me more pleasant things to have on my mind during my long hours alone in the dark room, for there my hours for introspection were too long and too many. With such long periods as that, healthy introspection was prone, as the hours passed, to deteriorate into damaging self dissatisfaction. As an antidote, I began to dwell more on the Scriptures and the Christian life.

"One day, there came into my mind out of the blue, a recollection of the book the professor of one of my college evening courses had recommended for my reading and use, and which I had not found to be of any help to me at the time. The book, you may remember was *The Power Of Positive Thinking* by Norman Vincent Peale. I no longer had this book but decided I would get it again. Perhaps during this period of growth I would see it in a different perspective and get some help from it.

"There was no problem in acquiring the book. It had become more popular than ever, not only for the practical help it offered troubled people, but also for the controversy that had arisen over it in the mainline churches, of which to that date I was only vaguely aware.

"Upon reading this book again, I realized that it was not of help per sé with social or psychological problems. But it very definitely could help me with the aggravating symptoms that were at times plaguing me daily in my darkroom, and sometimes elsewhere, making it more difficult for me to overcome. In addition to being indeed a very practical self-help book to better thinking of oneself, others and God, it was inspirational, and I needed that in no small measure.

"One suggestion of the book especially attracted me. That was the idea that when you are down and feeling blue, have several inspirational scripture passages available to repeat over and over in your mind. This, I thought would be the very thing for me in the darkroom. When the periods of introspection would begin to deteriorate because of their length, I would repeat these inspirational scripture sentences. This worked out well for me. As time went by, I found that I not only wanted to repeat these scripture passages, but to dwell upon them and their significance. This led me to a more extensive reading of the Bible and a corresponding study of Bible commentaries. I was now being lifted from a long standing Sunday school level of religious thinking, to a more mature level of Christian growth. As with many young people, there had been a gap in my Christian nurture. Now that gap was being filled. Weekly Sunday worship and its accompanying sermon I also looked forward to each week as a means of grace and growth. My spirit was lifted immensely, and my introspection was no longer a problem.

"We had opened for business in the spring of the year, and everything went well throughout the summer and winter that followed. Of course, as I said, there were the usual belittlers at work. Vita had always been able to deal better than I with these. Now, with my new awareness of how and why these people behaved as they did I too began to successfully handle experiences with them, at least in my mind."

"I knew you wouldn't escape these," quipped Brett. "However, being in business for yourself allows you more scope with which to deal with them, but even then they will do you harm if you're not aware and wise to them."

"Yes," replied Collin, "there was one in particular, in the business of supplying products for beauty salons. Vita had purchased a small amount of what she considered superior products from a supplier outside Lower Secundaterra. Consequently she didn't pay the Lower Secundaterra sales tax on these purchases, but rather, had paid tax on them to the government of the land from where she had purchased them. A Lower Secundaterra supplier had visited her on several occasions to sell his goods. Neither his goods or his prices or his belittling attitude appealed to her, but she did buy a token amount from him.

"It became obvious to us that he wasn't satisfied with that when a Sales Tax Inspector arrived at our door one day, informing us that he wished to inspect our books.

"I pressed him for a reason as to why he wished to do so. Reluctantly he revealed that he knew we were purchasing products from outside Lower Secundaterra and that we hadn't paid the Lower Secundaterra tax on these purchases.

"We replied that we didn't know we were supposed to pay the tax. The supplier we had purchased them from was in another land and was for obvious reasons not a collector of such tax for Lower Secundaterra, but rather for his own government.

"The tax inspector then informed us that there was a provision in the law of Lower Secundaterra stating that people are on their honor to submit tax to Lower Secundaterra on goods they purchase outside its jurisdiction.

"'Does anyone submit such taxes,' I pressed him.

"'Well, that's not the point,' he said evasively, 'I am here to inspect your books, and if such taxes are owing, you have to pay them.'

"Calling the obnoxious business man by name, I said to the tax inspector, 'he set you on to us, eh?'

"The tax collectors face flushed, 'Oh,' he said, 'I can't say, but now I have to see your books.'

"He inspected our books and extracted from us at that time the total sum of twenty four dollars and some cents. As he was leaving I remarked to him emphatically, 'we will still purchase our supplies from the people we like, rather than from the man who is putting the pressure on us.' The inspector blushed and replied, 'that's up to you,'

"I don't think the inspector was a bad sort, but he had been put on the spot by this business man. I should mention here folks," interjected Collin, "that any competitive business person of tricky practices could have pulled such a pressure tactic on us. But in addition to being a high pressure man, this one was also a belittler, as we well knew from his attitude towards us. Also I wish to say here that I tell of this incident now to point out that Vita and I were coping with such incidents quite successfully, realizing that they are part of reality. At the time though I would never discuss them with anyone other than my wife, always for fear of being branded paranoid. Such a fear and secrecy was part and parcel of my character now.

"Summer was approaching again. As we glanced back, Vita and I were able to take satisfaction in the fact that we had been able to pay our bills for equipment and supplies on time and earn a fairly good living. What enthused us most was that we were getting well established socially in the town and in the area again. The progress of my reestablishment in life, was continuous. To many, I suppose, I was just another quiet person trying to be sociable and they were willing to help. None knew the circumstances of my predicament, and therefore had no idea of my need for reestablishment in life and of the struggle going on in my mind.

"Our modest businesses were going well. Church and social life were going just great. Furthermore, Vita and I had befriended the minister and his wife, had invited them to our house occasionally and also visited them at their home. Our families seemed to synchronize well and a good friendship seemed to be developing. We were very pleased about this.

"One fine day as summer was approaching and it was our day off, we invited the minister and his family to accompany us at one of our favorite outdoor recreation areas, a quiet, almost secluded beach with a backing of beautiful trees; a place we had discovered the previous year and kept secret as a private picnic and resting place for our weekly one day free in our taxing work week. The water was yet too cool for swimming, but the sun was warm that day. We were quite comfortably able to walk, play and rest on the beach, and picnic in comfort. The minister's wife and children enjoyed it immensely. I had no reason to think the minister wasn't enjoying it either. On the way home, however, as I drove along the highway nearing home, the minister's wife complimented us and expressed appreciation for the lovely day we had given them. As she did, the minister shuffled in a perturbed manner in the front seat beside me. His face flushed red. I gained the impression that he was actually dissatisfied with the day. Apologetically I remarked, 'Well, perhaps our hideaway beach is too secluded for you. Some people would rather be where there are lots of other people.' His face flushed all the more, and he shifted around in the seat again. I didn't search for further reasons for this, but passed it off thinking the reason I had already stated was the reason he didn't enjoy the day. I had no idea at the time that he was a jealous or envious person.

"In the days ahead, without further thought of the minister's dissatisfaction with our outing, Vita and I were happy about this and other new friendships and activities that were developing for us.

"With our lives now centered around our Christian faith, and much of our extracurricular activities taking place within the fellowship of the church we both had a renewed interest in the deeper aspects of our religion. It was our nature that anything in which we became involved, we immersed ourselves into it deeply. As for me, the inspirational Bible verses that I repeated to myself so often in the loneliness of the dark room, continued to stir my desire to read them and the background in which they were found in the Bible. I began the habit of reading the Bible each night before going to sleep.

"One day as I was working away in my darkroom, I was repeating to myself, yes more than repeating, I was dwelling upon the inspirational Bible verse from the Book of Revelation, Chapter 2, verse 7, of the King James Bible, "To him that overcometh will I give to eat of the tree of life." I knew little of the context from which this verse came, and I understood less that mystical book of the Bible in which it was written. But I did know and I am sure God knew, that I wanted desperately to overcome, and to have life in its fullness. So now as I pondered and repeated thoughtfully this verse that had become so meaningful to me, I felt as never before or since, a deep religious experience to the depths of my being. Though I heard nothing audible to the ear, I felt deeply as if God had answered my plea for the means of grace to overcome and have life.

"That night as Vita and I lay in bed with the light still on, I picked up the Bible, opened it to Revelation, Chapter 2 verse 7, read it to Vita, then told her of my experience in the darkroom that day, and how I felt so different now toward my whole outlook on life. She understood. We both had tears of joy in our eyes as we set out to read together the whole chapter that contained that verse. The chapter made little sense to us as it was a part of the most mystical and most difficult part of the Bible.

"After reading the whole chapter, I returned to read verse seven again. Again, there lying in the bed with Vita beside me I once again experienced God deeply in my life, not exactly the same as the experience of earlier in the day, but still very emphatic, and now giving me a sense of reassurance that I hadn't been imagining things in the darkroom that day. A new sense of well being and a glimmer of direction for the future was stirred in my being that day and night. It filled my heart and mind with faith and joy. I even remarked to Vita that I would like probably to be a minister.

"As time went by this idea grew on me more strongly. I wasn't perceptive enough at the time however to know that although my Lord, whom I was experiencing anew, had long ago borne the ultimate cross, there were crosses out there waiting for his followers of today. In fact there are plenty of crosses, especially for fine people of integrity and distinctive quality who seek to follow Him in churches that unwittingly have members, ministers, officers and administrators, some of them in high places, who are belittlers, sometimes of the most deadly kind.

"The Bible was now a fascination for me. I had read it quite regularly as a child and a youth, at which time I always found it an inspirational and effective influence in my life. Then came several years in my early manhood when it slipped into the background. Now it was a more fully alive element of my life than ever before; an element which Vita had never lost sight of in her life. The Book of Revelation appeared before us as a puzzle we wished to know more about. It would be to us just superb now to talk to an authority on this mystery.

"The day after my profound Christian experiences, Vita had occasion to drop in to the minister's home to talk to his wife about a church organizational matter. As they were ending their conversation over tea, the minister came upon the scene. Vita spoke to him of our desire to know more of the Book of Revelation.

"'The Book has helped my husband a great deal,' said Vita to the minister, in her relative naïveté of the time on such matters. 'He has also been reading "The Power of Positive Thinking" by Norman Vincent Peale. This is the book that led him to this part of the Bible. I would never believe, unless I was there yesterday to see what happened to him as he read the Bible,' she added, then emphasizing mainly the change in my frame of mind that had culminated at that point in time. 'He may even be interested in becoming a minister,' she told him.

"'Is that right?' replied the minister, in a non-committal attitude.

"'Perhaps,' asked my wife, 'you would talk with him sometime on these matters, and help him with some clarification, particularly on the Book of Revelation, with which he is both fascinated and puzzled?'

"'Sure,' replied the minister vaguely, as he gave a casual excuse to leave the scene and leave the matter up in the air.

"The following Sunday Vita and I with our family, were in church for worship, spirited with our new found zeal for Christian living. It turned out to be a negative, unforgettable though not overpowering experience. The minister, as he conducted the service appeared edgy and so perturbed that his face was flushed. We had no idea what the problem was until the delivery of the sermon. Here, in tones bordering on anger, and with gestures and animation even more uncontrolled than his usual emphatic manner in that regard, he told that he too had had a deep experience of God in his life. With flustered face, he pranced back and forth the pulpit telling how when as a younger man lying sick on his back for a prolonged period with a serious physical illness, he too heard a voice speaking to him. The voice said to him that he would come through all right, and that he should be a minister. He left the impression on me at the time that he had actually heard an audible voice speaking to him in his experience.

"I was astounded, to say the least, at this minister's behavior. It seemed he had misinterpreted Vita's remarks about my religious experience, and this led him to believe I had heard a voice speaking to me. Now, in his enraged envy he was going to outdo me by rivalry as belittlers do when the time is opportune and they feel they can win the contest. It was clear to me now that this minister was envious of me. I knew now what had been wrong on the day we had taken he and his family on the outing. It was not that he was bored, it was that he was envious of me. It was not that it wasn't good enough. Rather, it was that it was too good and his nose was out of joint about it.

"It made me wonder at the time why a well established minister of the church would be envious of me considering the life's circumstances I was in. I hadn't realized yet that I belonged to a particular type of people that I now call fine people, and that some well meaning people even refer to as 'gems' or 'rare gems', of whom belittlers become very envious regardless of our real circumstances. They measure us by the whims of their own immature minds. Then regarding us as a threat to them, they seek when they consider it safe to win, to exalt themselves above us. When they fear of losing such a battle, they seek rather than rising above their folly, to remain as they are, and by belittling bring us down beneath them. For the present, this minister was striving to exalt himself above me. In later years, I would be able to observe this minister's interaction with another person and see that he was also envious of certain people in business for themselves. Experience has born out that he was envious of me on many counts.

"Vita and I returned from church that morning discouraged, but not totally dismayed. This was an experience with one minister only. The church at large is not like that we told ourselves. In the immediate weeks that followed I talked to Vita more and more about my becoming a minister of the church and eventually decided that this was definitely what I wanted to do with my life. I wouldn't let this one erroneous minister discourage me from doing so.

"Before much time had passed we visited and talked with another minister in the area, who was more senior in years and position in the church. He was of a different type, without envy, and lacking any obnoxious characteristics that would cause him to be prejudiced against a fine person, although he showed some signs of nervousness in my presence. He advised me of the procedures to follow in order to process an application and fulfill requirements for acceptance into the ministry. The part of this procedure that was to be done through the local church, he advised me to do in the church I was already attending, and to do it in spite of the 'contrariness' he called it, of the minister. He indicated that he had had problems with that minister himself. He suggested I work on this immediately in order to be ready for processing by the governing body of the wider church at its late spring meetings, which incidentally were to be held this year in our own local church.

"You will be asked by the elders of your church to prepare and participate in a worship service," he advised me. Then he proceeded to give me a few books which would provide resources for sermon and prayer material.

"'I don't suppose you have gathered any such books or material yet,' he said helpfully. 'Take this. You will find it very helpful, and God's blessing on you both!'

"I took the books without paying much attention to their contents until I had reached home. Then, lo and behold, I found one of them was writings on the Book of Revelation. It was a pleasant surprise and coincidence, as I had not mentioned to this second minister anything about my personal experience and its connection to the Scriptures of that Book of the Bible.

"After submitting an application to the elders of the local church to be received as a candidate for the ministry, I was indeed asked to conduct a worship service. I prepared my first sermon using a theme from the material given me on the Book of Revelation. It had not been long since I had written many essays while studying at evening college, so I felt that my sermon was adequate. And although I had never spoken publicly before, and as you know had always been a very shy person, I somehow had no fear now of participating in this service.

"As I participated with the minister in a regular Sunday morning worship service, the Scripture readings and the prayers I seemed to be able to do matter of factly without either fear or strenuous effort. Meanwhile, in the back of my mind I just didn't know how the sermon would come out of me. I had practiced at home before Vita, but here I was now before a congregation, the elders of which were not only here to worship, but to scrutinize me. I was too busily involved in the service as a whole to get nerved up about this, but still I was aware of it in the recesses of my mind.

"Then came the time for the sermon. Standing at the pulpit I first said, 'Let us pray.' And I prayed the prayer from Psalm 19:14 (RSV), 'May the words of my mouth and the meditation of my heart be acceptable in Thy sight, O Lord, my rock and my Redeemer. Amen.' The thought flashed through my mind, 'If this sermon is acceptable to God then it will be adequate for the purpose for which it is intended. So I will do my best for God and it will be o.k. for His people. With that my whole being loosened up as I stood there. To me it was another religious experience I will never forget. It was a vivid religious experience of being free from shyness. That experience, over a period of time, would enable me to attain a very high degree of freedom from shyness in all aspects of my life. I preached well — 'like an experienced preacher,' I was told later by one elder. After the service there was a meeting of elders, minister and myself. Heads nodded in approval. There were warm handshakes, coupled with such remarks as 'well done, fine sermon, quite good especially for your first time.' The minister's only remark was a disgruntled 'He had to look at his notes a lot.' The elders voted unanimously to receive me as a candidate for the ministry. I had passed successfully the first hurdle. However, the envious minister wasn't giving up his side of the game yet, as I was to find out.

"It was some weeks before the area governing body of the church at large was to meet, by coincidence, at our local church for a two and a half day session. During those weeks our minister was cold and unfriendly towards us, his total attitude now openly negative. This took the edge off the wonderful and joyful Christian experiences that had literally lifted my life to a new plateau. A damper was being put on my exuberance for, and my growth in, my newly refurbished faith. It took a conscious effort on my part to avoid regressing in some ways again.

"However, one thing was certain. My shyness had received a smashing blow. I would seldom again feel too shy to tackle any public situation, nor have any hesitancy about speaking in public when circumstance called for it. After that experience in the pulpit for my first time, although I never developed a desire to be an ad lib debater, I had not the slightest hesitancy about preaching, or, for example, presenting a prepared report and then defending it or answering questions on it. My gain in that regard was certain. But another dread was taking its place. The more I tried to establish myself in society, the more confrontation I had with belittlers. And the more confrontation I had with belittlers, the more I feared being labeled paranoid, or worse still a paranoid schizophrenic.

"As we have previously established envious belittlers are often very subtle in their belittling. It is usually very difficult to bring them out into the open for what they really are. So though my shyness was gone, I now had a still increasing dread of being labeled paranoid, and often feared to bring the actions of my assailants out into the open and defend myself against them. This would plague me for several years, till it too, after causing much adversity would in time subside to a large degree.

"The time arrived for the governing body of the church to meet, when my application to become a minister would be submitted to its jurisdiction. As I earlier indicated, the meeting took place in our home church. I was to meet with the appropriate committee on the evening of the first day's sessions. It was somewhat awesome for me as I had never before in my life had contact with or participation in the larger church. My connection had been limited to a local congregation only.

"The committees were to meet at seven o'clock that evening, with a plenary session scheduled for 8:30 p.m. As I walked into the sanctuary of the church to await being called by the committee, many delegates, clergy and lay representatives stood around in clusters talking. Our local minister was there standing in one of these gatherings. On seeing me enter and stand there looking around, wondering where to go or what to do, the minister looked from me to his colleagues and back two or three times with a contemptuous look on his face that portrayed the unspoken, yet discernable message, 'what's a guy like that doing applying for the ministry?' Obviously, he was, in this instance putting me up to his colleagues for scrutiny on the basis of my appearance alone. That is an important and meaningful factor to keep in mind. After implying emphatically this rejection of me, he, instead of greeting me and offering help and direction, turned in the opposite direction, giving me a scornful over the shoulder glare as he disappeared through the door of a meeting room.

"I approached the cluster to whom he had been talking, and saying good evening I told them what I was there for and asked them if it would be in order to just remain in the sanctuary until called by the committee. They looked at one another, then at me and nodded, then to one another again and dispersed leaving me standing there alone with a deep sense of rejection settling in upon me. The envious, belittling minister had already done his work on them.

"As I stood there my mind did several flips. *Am I really being rejected by the church?* I asked myself, *or, is it only the way I am interpreting it. Am I taking it all the wrong way? Maybe I am paranoid. That's what the doctors would say anyway.*

"Struggling, I kept my frenzy under control. *No time to think this through now. No time to get lost in thought. Remain alert as best you can*, I told myself. But in spite of my best efforts I was astounded by the silent blows that had been dealt me. Beads of perspiration broke out on my forehead."

Brett interrupted Collin's story telling at this point."Collin," he said, "you were no doubt able to get to know your minister fairly well at the time. Now with all your years of experience in discerning people, you must be able to reflect back with confidence and perceive with a degree of accuracy what contemptuous and erroneous thoughts were probably on that minister's mind concerning you in the church sanctuary that night. To my mind of the present time, and discerning from my own past experience, I think I can state with a good degree of accuracy what was on that minister's mind. May I state what I think it was?"

Collin smiled. "We are getting drawn into the deeper aspects of things step by step, and I am glad of that," he said happily. "We are truly going to get to the bottom of things in this group." Nodding to Brett, Collin added, "I would be pleased to have you state your discernment, and I will comment on it as much as is expedient to do so for our present purposes."

"Thanks, Collin," responded Brett. Then gathering his thoughts together in a second or two Brett explained his insight on the incident. "Well, I'd say it was his conception of a minister as that of a humble per son, and humble to him meant lowly in station. In his eyes, you, fine looking person you were, were from the upper crust, so to speak, and because of that, and especially since you were in business for yourself, he perhaps perceived you as rich. You just weren't of the class of people he associated with ministry. Furthermore, my guess is, that even though this minister perceived himself to be lowly in station, he probably was filled to the brim with hollow pride, and pretentiousness aplenty, which would make him anything but a humble man."

Collin was pleased and replied confidently, "I think you are quite accurate in your assumptions, Brett. Pride was there aplenty, but also some other characteristics, such as envy, related to pride. We can also discern how this proud minister set the whole tone of the evening with regard to my place in it. Most of the other people present, not being wise to him, picked up that tone automatically, and, as though I really was the wayward one, inadvertently treated me likewise. We may see from this how important it is that people be wise to belittlers. I will elaborate on this at future group meetings when I am at a point where I can illustrate it more effectively. Then we will also be able to discern how widespread this malady is. It was very appropriate to bring it into discussion at this time though."

Brett nodded in approval of Collin's response. "I should let you go on with your story now, Collin," he said.

"Here we go," responded Collin. "I stood around the aisles of the church sanctuary, cautious now about approaching anyone else for fear of being rejected again. I did make an attempt to approach one friendly looking man, but just as I spoke to him he was called away to a committee meeting by another man who had just come into the building rushing, as he was late arriving. For another ten minutes or so I fingered through a hymn book in an attempt to keep from getting nervous. This helped, but only to a point. No doubt about it I had been hurt. Presently a door at the side of the chancel opened. A minister whom I did not know came out and asked for Mr. Seldon."

"I am here," I responded, "Collin Seldon," I added.

"'Would you come in now please and meet with the committee?' he asked matter of factly.

"At his request I entered the committee room. Five people sat around the little area in a semi-circle, with one of them sitting in a more imposing place facing them all, and whom it turned out was the chairman of the meeting. He looked me up and down with piercing concentration. Appearance was a factor to him also. The man who had called me in, after a moment of hesitation, jumpily pushed a chair from the wall to one end of the semi-circle and invited me to sit down. I was now sitting very close to the chairman who in a stern manner stared me in the face and asked bluntly, with no introductions whatever, 'Why do you want to go into the ministry?'

This cold approach in the committee room added to the misery heaped on me in the church sanctuary a little earlier. I became a little more astounded. Had I been even reasonably accepted in a pleasant atmosphere in the church that evening, I am sure that with the gains I had made over my shyness, I could have expressed myself fairly well. But it wasn't shyness that blocked me that evening. It was the grossly negative attitude towards me that astounded and dumbfounded me no end. Needless to say, I didn't do well with the interview. The chairman became impatient with me to the point of raising his voice at me, which astounded me all the more and made it even more difficult for me to express myself. The shock of their attitude confounded me throughout the whole process; an attitude set in motion by one envious minister to whom at least most of the others were not wise. Out of his pride and envy, he had set up, from the very beginning of the process, a negative attitude towards me. Most of the others, not being aware of the tactics of belittlers, had been led astray by him to my detriment.

"There was one official looking man sitting with the committee, whom, it turns out, was a church official with authority. He asked me relevant questions in a purposeful manner. His attitude was more positive. By now, however, I was so disconcerted with the whole happening of the evening, that I did not respond well to his questions. He, being unaware of all that had transpired, became impatient with me.

"In spite of all the negativism and coldness of attitude, I did the best I could under the circumstances to be amicable and cooperative. Feeling I had to be honest with them, I told them that I had had psychiatric treatment in Secundaterra, but that I was well now. The well-meaning man asked me to meet with them again when they had further meetings in a city considerable distance away, and at the same time they would make arrangements for me to have a psychiatric examination. I agreed to this and my meeting with them that evening came to an end.

"The church meetings were to continue at our church all the next day. Then the next night there was to be an honored visit from the person in the highest office of our denomination for the whole nation. It was to be a once in a lifetime event for our town and our local church, and it was to take the form of a grand finale worship service with only a wrap up of business the next morning. The public was invited to this grand finale which was to be covered by the media and broadcast on the local radio stations.

"Vita and I could not attend church that night. It was on a week night that our businesses were advertised as open. We had to take advantage of every bit of business we could get in order to make our payments on loans and meet our living expenses. We would listen to the service on the radio. So at the time of the service, Vita worked in her shop, and I worked in my workroom in another part of the house in an endeavor to get ahead on the next day's work which was going to be heavy, each of us listening to a different radio.

"Regardless of my setback with the committee, the service inspired me as it progressed. *All of the church is not like the part of it I have experienced*, I had told myself. *The greater church is a good institution*, I had convinced myself, *and I will get fair treatment from it on the whole*.

"Then came time for the sermon from the nationally known, outstanding preacher, with a string of degrees, both earned and honorary after his name, and now holding the highest office of our church. As he began to speak I at once detected he was displaying the pulpit manner and attitude of that time. It was a time when thoughts of the 'gentle Jesus meek and mild' had fallen into oblivion. Now the thrust was on two fisted preaching, with emphasis on the theology that portrayed a revolutionary Jesus who opposed the establishment of His time, and who upset the tables of the money changers in the temple. Before he was long into his sermon he was blasting the rich and upholding the poor in very emphatic terms.

"I thought to myself, *well you don't have much reason to upset my money tables, there is so little on them that doesn't go right out to pay the bills.*

"Then the blow of blows came — the second most traumatic experience in my life."

"Oh, Oh, brace yourselves, here it come," interrupted Leo in his usual satiric manner. "What's the church up to now?"

"It won't shock me," responded Owen.

"Me neither," declared Brett.

The others present bounced between smiles and expressions of wonder.

"Let's hear it," added Brett again.

"The honored guest was preaching forcefully and angrily, blasting the rich once more. Then he gave his over simplified remedy for the world's ills.

"'What the world needs,' he said in deep and angry tones, 'is the Gospel of Jesus Christ — not someone to lead us into positive thinking with their drug store literature.' And he was roaring on about being led astray by false prophets with their drug store concepts such as 'positive thinking', when I lost track of him, no longer able to follow, my mind being so upset. Jumping at the radio I turned it quickly off and ran to Vita's shop in the other part of the big old house. Vita was just finishing up with a customer. I paused just outside her shop to await the customer's exit, hardly able to restrain myself. When the customer had gone I rushed in frantically.

"'Vita,' I asked, 'did you hear what I heard on the radio?'

"She rushed to me and embraced me. 'Yes Collin, I did, and we are in deep trouble aren't we?'

"'Oh, yes' I said, 'We are!'

"Then Vita turned towards her radio to hear what else he might say. He raved on about the church's obligation to the poor and how the rich had too much, and how 'positive thinking' is only another ruse.

"'Turn it off,' I shouted, 'I don't want to hear any more of it. Please turn it off.

"Vita turned her radio off promptly and we sat down in her beauty shop chairs in despair, looking at one another speechless for a moment or two that seemed like hours.

"Then Vita broke the silence. 'We have to keep going Collin. Time will tell what damage has been done to us in this town, but in the meantime we have to keep going. I'm expecting another customer any minute. Will you be all right 'till I'm through?' she asked, looking at my paled face.

"'Yes,' I replied. 'But I need your company badly. Please put your customer through as quickly as possible,' I asked.

"'I will' she replied.

"When Vita had finished work in her shop for the evening, she and I sat in our living room to talk and review our situation. The church, which we had grown to love, and in which we had placed our hope for renewed life and fulfillment, had not only rejected us, but had openly and publicly denounced us in our home town through its highest office."

Then Collin changing the direction of his story somewhat, said, "I should pause in my story here to explain why this incident was so devastating to us right from the start. You see, the people of Lower Secundaterra generally feel beneath the people of Secundaterra. So when they get support on an issue from someone of account from Secundaterra, then it becomes the gospel truth for them. Before that happens, there is some room for doubt, and some place for debate on an issue, or a person, over which there may be controversy. But when they receive support from Secundaterra, that resolves the issue for them. For any person or persons, such as I and my family, if we are up against it in Lower Secundaterra, any significant support from Secundaterra would protect us immensely. In our case the support had gone to our adversary. So now in the eyes of most all who knew Vita and I we would be outcasts. And, of course, that would for us, be a large segment of the people of the town in which we lived, for it would surely spread around a small town and in addition to many people of the surrounding area; to those who took an interest in such things that is. Not only would our church life and social interaction with the people be affected, which was detrimental to our living a full life, but, also we knew in our minds that our businesses would be affected drastically and our livelihood threatened."

Leo spoke up. "This experience you tell us of, that is, you being denounced by the leader of your church, would that not amount to a public excommunication, at least to the ears of the people who heard?"

"Yes, that is what it amounted to in effect, Leo," replied Collin heavily, "and it was without forewarning or opportunity for defense or rebuttal of whatever story the local minister had fed into them. And you may depend he fed it to them with his own defense mechanisms in high gear, defending his pride.

"You see folks," continued Collin, "usually when a belittler wants to put you down, he does not tell a story as it is, but rather as he twists it in his mind to suit his own purposes. And his purposes are, first, to keep his pride high and intact; secondly, to put the persons he deems his adversary, beneath him. To accomplish this, he will in his prejudice take the true facts and slant them untruthfully. This is the way such an immature mind works. In the meantime he will convince himself, and if possible, everyone around him, that he is telling the gospel truth. If someone were to accuse him of lying or distorting the truth, he would never agree to it, since he has convinced himself so thoroughly that he is right. In his own eyes he has to see himself as the knight in shining armor, the true dove of peace, the epitome of righteousness. His imagined adversary is to him the devil in disguise, a terrible person who by his very being upsets the unadmitted pride of such 'good' people as he has himself believing he is.

"I will never know what was said behind the scenes concerning me. But from what was said by the leader of our church, from the attitude of the ministers standing in the cluster, from the negative atmosphere of the committee right from the start, and from the way we were to be in future treated by the local minister and many people of the town, we can only believe we were put down very hard indeed.

"However, some people did stand by us. From what they were able to tell us, we were able to piece together that my innocent utilization of the book, *The Power Of Positive Thinking*, was turned into some kind of a great heresy. Also being in business for myself had put me in the category of, what was to them, the despicably rich. Last but by no means least, my appearance had, in the warped thinking of belittlers, placed me in the echelons of those in higher stations in life and therefore among the proud, and so unsuitable for ministry."

Leo chuckled, and remarked, "that minister himself was the proud one, as lowly in station as he might have been. Anyone can tell, and no doubt could have then, that you are not a proud person."

"Almost anyone can tell, Leo," answered Collin. "But a belittler couldn't if he didn't want to. A belittler will find any excuse or distort any truth, to make his gain, and in the doing of it he makes himself come out as the righteous one. The belittler will take anything good about you and find some way to make it bad. He will take anything bad, any minor fault or flaw or weakness, and turn it into the worst. It is all accomplished by his distorting of his own mind. By those who can see through it, it is simply brushed off as immaturity, or ignorance and with little realization of its potential for destruction.

"But now to get on with the story," said Collin as he changed direction again. "Vita and I sat and talked for an hour or two that night. We surmised life would never be the same for us again here in our home environment. However Vita kept a strong and positive attitude.

"'The church has rejected us,' she agreed, 'but God has not, and never will. There will be a way out of this for us Collin,' she sought to assure me throughout our conversation. Then she suggested, 'Collin, we are both very tired now, after a hard days work and with this blow on top of it. Let's go to bed and rest. In the morning our perspective may be clearer.'"

"It was hardly a fair match, was it?' Owen remarked sympathetically. "I mean, the highest officer of the denomination, with all the weight that carries, together with a number of degrees, many of which were no doubt degrees in theology, all that pitted against a guy with nothing more than what he had received in

Sunday School in his childhood!"

"Hardly fair," remarked the others almost in unison.

"Right, but that's how it was," responded Collin, and continued with his story.

"We went to bed, saying our prayers before hand and asking God to sustain us in our dilemma. It was only after I lay in bed in silence for an hour or so that the extent of the possible damage done to us began to really sink into my mind.

"*We have a right to live here in peace*, I thought to myself. *Vita and I were born and brought up in this area, and belong here. We may not have had much similar right of belonging, in Secundaterra, but here in this section of Lower Secundaterra we have rights, birthrights if you will. And now these two churchmen, both from outside the area, come in, and in their hatred which they perceive as righteousness, destroy us. They may have destroyed the only way we can see at the time of our making a material living for ourselves, let alone enjoy fulfillment in life. What will we do now. I have my family to support, and no way to make a living for them if our business falls through.* The pressure on me was greater than I had ever felt before or since. Lying there in bed I grew weary and the pressure grew heavier. Then my whole body went into a severe palpitation. As I trembled immensely Vita turned to me quickly, "'What's wrong?' she asked.

"'I feel as if life is slipping away from me,' I told her frantically.

"She moved close to me and held me, to try to contain my shivering. It helped a little but my body continued to tremble all over.

"'More bed clothes' I suggested. 'Perhaps more heat will help to stop my shivering.'

"Vita jumped out of bed and rounded up more bed clothes, piling it on me. 'Get in bed with me again,' I suggested, 'it helped when you held me.'

"'Shall I call the family doctor,' she asked.

"'Not at this hour of the night,'" I suggested. It was about 1:00 a.m. now. 'I'll go to see him in the morning.'

"It took nearly an hour for this attack of palpitation to pass, but it left me feeling terribly weak. Throughout the remainder of the night, I dozed and slept lightly until the early hours of the morning. It was then I had my first experience with 'early morning waking' that psychiatrists so often look for in a patient. However, this first early morning waking was extraordinary. I awoke to find my body slipping into severe palpitations once again. This time it was extremely pronounced in my stomach. I felt surely now that life would slip away from me. I explored my mind briefly and as best I could under the circumstances.

*"Is this just psychological,* I asked myself, *a trick of my mind?* Then answering myself, I thought, *no it isn't. This is physical, brought on by the extreme pressure and my exhaustion from it, and I'd better do something about it quickly, for life really is slipping away from me.*

"'Vita,' I called, 'get the doctor quickly, or I will die. I cannot hold out any longer.' Daylight had just broken. The doctors response was fast. He came into the bedroom, observed quickly, my paled face and severe trembling. His first action was to feel my pulse, or should I say feel for it. He went from one arm to the other and back again. Then said to Vita, 'his pulse is so weak I can hardly find it.' Checking my chest with a stethoscope, he remarked to my wife again, 'he is in a bad way.'

"The doctor was unaware of what had befallen us the previous evening, and we saw no gain in telling him. Most people didn't understand such things, so we made no effort to tell him, as it would all be extremely involved. Then again we were concerned that as nice a person as he was to us, if the church had condemned me, he might think the church right and me in the wrong.

"'I'm not sure what to do,' said the doctor honestly to Vita. 'I suppose it has something to do with the psychiatric treatment he had some time ago, and of which he told me for my medical record of him when you people first arrived in town.'

"Then turning to me he said, 'Do you have something in mind I can do for you Collin?'

"'Yes,' I replied quickly, 'I need sleep badly. I'm exhausted and rest and sleep will help me get over this.'

"'All right,' the doctor agreed. 'I'll give you something heavy to make you sleep. If that doesn't put you on your feet, then we will have to get further help for you.'

"He gave me two powerful pills, and I soon felt myself drifting into sleep, with the doctor standing there feeling my pulse. I slept all day, not even waking when the doctor came in to see me again at noon and to check my pulse.

"At about six in the evening I awakened, but was still groggy from the sleeping pills. Vita fed me a light meal in bed. Just as I had finished eating the doctor arrived again. Feeling my pulse, he informed Vita and I that it had improved.

"'Can you make it on your own now, of do you feel you need more sleep?' he asked.

"I replied that having slept all day, I may not sleep tonight and that might exhaust me again. 'Can you give me pills to make me sleep through the night?' I asked.

"He agreed, but added, 'If this doesn't do it for you, we will have to get further help for you, as we cannot continue this kind of treatment for a prolonged period.' I agreed, and was grateful for his kindly concern. I remind you here in the support group, that this incident took place before the common use of the tranquilizers that are so effective in controlling various types of stressful situations today. I felt that this doctor was doing very well for me with what was available to work with at the time.

"He gave me more pills as he instructed Vita to call him as soon as I awakened in the morning, whether it be early or late. As I drifted into a deep sleep the clock showed about seven thirty. I awakened at about eight the following morning feeling well and quite able to cope with my thoughts.

"When the doctor arrived, I was up and dressed and eating breakfast. After checking me over, he felt I would be all right, at least for the present.

"In the days that followed, it became evident to Vita and I that our business had been severely damaged. We had not over-reacted on the night of our sick and cowardly public rejection by the head of our church whom we felt had been wrongly influenced by the envious minister. We knew then what we were in for, and now it was happening the way we surmised. Appointments for Vita's shop slowed down considerably the very next day. In fact there were two cancellations. My business was affected to a like degree. Out total business, that should normally have increased during the summer, was cut in half. The only reason we could survive and keep up with our expenses temporarily was because it was summer time and heating and other winter expenses were temporarily non-existent. Previous to this blow, we had been looking forward to this summer as the period when we would get ahead a little financially and solidify our businesses. Now the opposite was true. It would be the beginning of our undoing. We knew we could bring our business through the summer, but the winter would be impossible. What would we do? This was the question we pondered.

"I still was not ready to accept that I may be a total outcast of the church. 'Vita,' I said determinedly one day. 'If we can gather enough money for me to do so, I will go to the next meeting of the governing body of the church. I will submit myself to the psychiatric examination they requested, and I will try to obtain my acceptance to the ministry and we can go back to Secundaterra where I can study for the ministry. We will find a way to somehow get me through. I know there are student pastorates, near the seminary I would choose to attend, and also if necessary you can work to help out. You will, at least, be no worse off than you are now, working here.'

"Vita agreed it was worth a try, but she had reservations about the outcome. Ministers in Lower Secundaterra didn't usually go to Secundaterra to study, and at that time there was resentment towards those who did. On the other hand it would be impossible for me to study successfully among the ministers of Lower Secundaterra because of the attitude now created towards me, and which now was already very negatively established. Nevertheless, we both agreed there was nothing to lose by trying.

"The psychiatric examination was arranged for me. The doctor was a very excellent sort and I did well with him. The report of the psychiatrist was that he could find nothing wrong with me, but that he had no way of telling how I would measure up to a crisis. What he didn't know was that I was already in the crisis of my life and coping with all the meager means at my disposal. I did not tell him this, for fear of being labeled paranoid if I told him so many ministers were negative towards me. I still believe today that it was a logical restraint, because over the years I have found very few, more especially among the young, including those in psychiatry or related fields, who know anything much about the aspect of reality we are dealing with in this support group.

"The psychiatrist who examined me was young. I couldn't take a chance on him. Ironically enough though, many years later I had occasion to talk with the same psychiatrist and dared to discuss with him some aspects of obnoxious ministers. He responded by relating to me that he knew of some such people in his profession as well as in ministry. I surmised from that, that he had learned of such people through life's experiences, but there had been nothing in his training concerning it. He was, however, one of few with whom I was ever able to discuss the matter. Through life's experiences he was not only wise to his obnoxious peers in psychiatry, but also in ministry, I always have retained great respect for him.

"Regardless of the positive results of the psychiatric examination, the general attitude of the committee at the church governing body was negative. Some of them placed emphasis on the fact that the psychiatrist couldn't affirm that I would stand up well under a crisis. I still wonder today, who can affirm that about anyone until the person is in the crisis and going through the test.

"The one church official who had been positive towards me at my home church meeting with them tried again to be positive with me. In later years I would come to know he was a highly regarded man of integrity. He suggested I do some church work among them as a lay pastor. If I did well, then they would recommend me to study for ministry at a seminary in Secundaterra. Consequently in retrospect now, I may have missed out on a loop-hole whereby I could have been given an opportunity. However, at the time, first, I wasn't knowledgeable of the hierarchy of the church and the levels of authority, so was not aware that this offer was from an authoritative top echelon. Secondly, to work among the sea of unfriendliness presently being experienced from most of the others, overshadowed the positive reaction of the one individual. As in my youth, so now again, the good, being lesser in volume, was overridden by the much larger negative volume. In addition, I was practically dumbfounded by it all. In retrospect again, if I had taken that sincerely meant offer, it may not have worked out, simply because I would not have had the general support of other colleagues in ministry. It would, to say the least, be an unhealthy atmosphere to be in for long, especially when I had to be so careful with the paranoia concept. Regardless, I came away from the meeting empty handed, as well as dumbfounded.

"On the overnight trip home by train, as well as sleeping some, I did a great deal of thinking and weighing of circumstances, trying to decide which would be the best way for us to proceed from here. We did not have much in the way of assets. Whatever course we took it had to be the right one as there would be no room financially for a second course, and we would be in dire straights if another plan should fall through. The pressure was enormous.

"As soon as time allowed after my return home, Vita and I, after discussing together the discouraging events of my meeting with the church committee, courageously, if I may say so, faced up to our dilemma and struggled to find the surest way out of it. First and foremost, I would try to find a job in the area where we were living, for here we had a house, fully furnished in which to live rent free indefinitely. The house was old and larger than we needed, but adequate. the relatives who owned it had moved away, and were not yet sure if they wanted to sell or keep it for retirement which was many years in the future. Our only obligation was to care for the property, keep it up, and improve it if we wished.

"Jobs were very scarce here, and if I failed to find one, then we would have to move away. If there was nothing at all for us here in

Lower Secundaterra, then we figured we would, in the larger scope available in Secundaterra have a better chance even though it had been so cruel to us before. If a move became necessary, we decided that the second city in which we had lived in Secundaterra would be out for us now. Although we had well liked the culture of that city, there was now much political and civil unrest in the whole area, with a far reaching problem that did not welcome outsiders. The only other alternative we could see how to manage, was to return to the first city of Secundaterra. A few years had passed since my hospitalization there, so the uneasiness of that experience had subsided. Still it was our second choice, so I searched diligently for a job at home.

"Reactions were mixed as I inquired from place to place, and person to person. Jobs were not plentiful at best, in the area, with openings occurring only very occasionally. Generally, one had to keep an eye out for them usually over a long period of time. Some reactions to my inquiries were typical of areas such as this as they exist in various less populated areas of the continent where jobs have to shared around. I received remarks such as, 'Why would you be looking for a job when you already own a business?'

"Then there was, in some instances, a back-lash from the past, such as a look of surprise and disbelief and such remarks as — 'a rich man, the son of a rich man looking for a job!' Or again, I would hear, 'You have your business and your father had a business — looking for a job eh? Well!'

"Then, of course, there were the proud, would-be belittling type who wouldn't want me around anyway because I was a fine person and therefore too much for them. I was practically told so on two occasions. In one case: 'You've been involved in business all your life, and you have been away, and well, I have my pride too.' I knew what he meant and knew it was no use trying. In another case it was simply, 'What, you work here!' I would have been glad to work there if he had been glad to have me. It was a large company, of which he was branch manager. I had known the company and the man for some time. I also saw the flaws in his character makeup, and could detect his unspoken attitude at the time of my asking. What he really meant was, 'you cannot work here, you would make me feel uncomfortable, perhaps even wreck my pride.' Of course there is something lacking in a person who thinks like that, but there are many who do, and they make life difficult for people they regard as a cut above them. Needless to say, there was no job forthcoming for me after my trying all summer.

"We kept our businesses going for the summer, but with the volume reduced by more than half. This was discouraging enough, but the greater burden was what had been done to us socially. Vita particularly was finding the latter aspect weighing heavily on her more than ever I have known her to be distressed before or since. She had always been a strong spirited woman and has remained so to this day. Many, many people can witness to that fact.

"However, the blow that had been struck this time cut so deeply because she and her husband had been wrongfully, deceitfully and in a cowardly manner discredited in her own home town. She had grown up here with the greatest of respect and not only the liking, but the admiration of the majority of the people of the town. This high spirited, intelligent, friendly, helpful, outgoing, hard working, good living, all around girl, who had grown up with the overall respect of the area, was now with her husband and family near the bottom of the pile.

"Furthermore, she had been put down by the church in which she grew up with a childish and later youthful zeal that would delight the very being of any honest to goodness Christian Pastor; as a little girl, the first in church on Sunday mornings, placing and spacing hymn books around the church; putting the chancel in good order, and whatever tidying and fussing she could find to do. The first in Sunday School, arranging chairs and materials. She was the delight of her Sunday School teachers; lessons well prepared, always well behaved; inquiring and delightfully serious; joyful and helping others to be so. Such was the quality of life that had won for Vita the respect of most of the town in which she had grown up. Now, the church which she had learned to love and grow by and which professed the faith from which she drew her exemplary spirit, had struck her a devastating and destructive blow. As she stood on her feet day by day in her shop, even with her working hours now lessened, she began to develop chest pains that she had never known before. She consulted our family doctor about it.

"'First your husband,' he remarked, 'now you. Listen,' he said authoritatively, 'either your business, or this town, or something is not agreeing with you two. I've heard something about there being trouble in the church concerning you. I don't know much about it, and I doubt if it's your faults. But I would suggest that if it can't be straightened out you just as well sell out and live somewhere where you can live a normal life. I can only surmise that this town hasn't been kind to you. If you stay now after what has happened to you in the church and whatever else, and working as hard as you two work, your health will be at stake, and that would be a crime at so young an age. I would suggest you give up your business real soon.'

"He was speaking words of wisdom, and we knew he was right. We had no choice now but to go. After advertising Vita's equipment, we sold it within a reasonable time. We also sold our very good late model car. We were into autumn now and had to move to something else before winter. Our advertising of Vita's equipment publicized throughout the town the news that we were leaving. One day we received a visit from a woman, the wife of a prominent teacher in the local school. She and her family had been good friends to us for some time and on occasion we had visited with them in their home. She was a woman who could see through to the truth of life's situations.

"'I'm sorry to hear you folks are moving away,' she said. 'We will miss your friendship.' She added, not knowing what we were headed for, 'I know you will be better off up there.' Then, as if wanting to unload her mind of thoughts on our circumstances, she spoke in concerned tones that were disturbed and angry, 'Of course you would have done alright here if it hadn't been for the envy and jealousy of our minister. There are people here you know who feel you would make a good minister, Collin. You are quiet, but it's a nice kind of quiet that most people like when they get to know you. Lots of people here like you, you know, or they did until you were blasted by the head of our church. And some people know what happened there too. It wasn't you. I know lots of people in the ministry in Lower Secundaterra who couldn't hold a candle to you, and they were accepted. It was jealousy and envy that got you turned down. Some of us know that. If I ever get the opportunity, I will tell it to church officials.'

"It helped us to know that someone understood. But we also realized there was nothing she could do for us. The ministry there at that time was closed to us."

"At that time?" Leo asked, quickly and keenly. "Do you infer by that that there is a time coming when you will be associated with them again?"

"Oh yes," replied Collin with a smile. "I'll be telling you about that later. I was indeed to have still more association with the church of Lower Secundaterra. There were and are a lot of good and wonderful people in the church of Lower Secundaterra, as there is throughout the land itself. But like the other lands I'll be talking about, there is insufficient knowledge known there about belittlers, and therefore little or no means of coping with them effectively.

"When the time drew near for our departure, I ceased to operate my business. Dismantling my home made set-up, I discarded what I had put together from practically nothing, and packed the equipment I had purchased. Making arrangements to store the bulk of our goods with an acquaintance and with plane reservations made we awaited our day of departure with sadness.

"The departure was desolate for us. Apart from the periodic well wishes of the teacher's wife who kept contact with us often and up to the day before our leaving, there was only one other good-bye. Ironically enough it was from the minister's wife by phone the morning of our departure. She phoned to say good-bye and to wish us well. I have never known whether she understood the intricacies of what had happened to us or whether it was just an innocent call of a person who meant only well. There had been no word at all from her husband for some time, nor was there now. We had phoned the bus service to arrange transportation to the airport fifty miles away. As the small bus stopped in front of our house, we shut the house door locked behind us, leaving the keys inside for a previously arranged caretaker to pick up with the use of another key he had been given beforehand. We boarded the bus and left behind a fully furnished house in a land we loved in spite of all the inadequacies, to go live in rooms, in the city of Secundaterra that had previously been unkind to us. In this city there was a housing shortage which would cause us to pay high rents for accommodation far inferior to that which we were generally accustomed. For some time also we could only afford a car much inferior to what we had before. It was in many ways a come down for us indeed.

"As we now set out to establish still another bridgehead in adult life, there was yet to be one other traumatic event for me before I fully realized what I was and always would be up against in society. After that I accepted my lot in life and began to devise ways to cope with it. I will tell you more at next week's session.

"That friends is the end of my presentation for this evening, and I am exhausted from the telling of it," said Collin in conclusion.

"Would this be a good night to gather at the coffee shop, Collin?" asked Owen.

"Yes it would, Owen, diversion would be good for me tonight if you folks can join Vita and I there."

It was a night when they all agreed they should and could be there to lend support and provide enlightening fellowship.

# Chapter Twelve

To pack up and leave home for another land because one wants to either for the adventure of it, or to be nearer one's family members if they are affectionate, or because one sees better opportunity for livelihood and life as a whole, can be a wholesome, exhilarating experience. Such was not the case with Collin and Vita Seldon and family as they returned again from Lower Secundaterra to Secundaterra as fugitives from a foul deed. Having to give up so much of what they loved, and the prospect of once again trying to make their way in a city that had previously been unkind to them gave them no delight. Rather than possessing a sense of adventure, which was quite often a characteristic of their nature, they now braced themselves for the realities that existed for them, and for Collin in particular, in this city.

The pain of the experience showed across Collin's face as now years later, at yet another meeting of the support group at Quilibet University, he continued to relate stories from his life's experiences.

"Some things did go well for us in Secundaterra," began Collin, "and luckily so, for what little money was ours had begun to diminish very fast in this city before we had an income to meet our living expenses. Before long Vita found a job with a very good corporation whose employees were mostly female office staff and therefore there was ample opportunity for a woman to do well. Good quality day care was available for children in well run nursery schools. This, as well as being good for our children, left me free to search for a job.

"This Secundaterra city, through an influx of people from elsewhere, had broadened out much since our first period of residence there, but it was still no place for a fine person to flourish unless he was vocationally qualified to command a job high up the ladder, above reproach. Time after time I was turned away from jobs that I could have done easily and well, until, at last, I happened upon a large municipal government office that was taking on temporary help at a busy tax time of year. There were several dozen of us hired to tabulate tax data on large tabulating machines that handled data sheets approximately two feet by one and a half feet in size as near as I can remember. The work was complex to learn at first and required keen concentration. But being exhilarated over finding employment it came easily to me.

"On the second day I fell right into the niche of it, my fingers racing over the keys at top speed and producing completed data sheets much, much faster than was expected. Some of the people nearby took an example from me, pulling themselves up to a faster speed in their work. Others, perhaps more than not, took offense, reacting in such a manner as pushing up their lip or sneering in contempt. Although this bothered me some, I wasn't really affected by it until the supervisor, as he frequently walked around the floor, or as he at other times stood in a prominent spot before me, began giving me hostile glances. At other times as he passed by me he would rap his knuckles on my desk, then go to talk freely and friendly to those who were scorning me, or simply patting them on the back."

"*I'd better slow down*, I told myself. *I'm working too fast to please them.*

"This I did, but to purposely work slower was to affect my performance in other ways. I now caught myself at times groping for the proper keys to punch. This made the job a burdensome drudgery, not unlike an experienced typist reverting to thinking about each key before he punched it. It also caused me to make errors which I then had to locate and correct. Other people were making some errors also. This was noticeable when they scanned their sheets to find where it was out of balance.

"I knew I personally could do better work at the faster pace. On thinking the situation through at home that night, I came to the conclusion that I should have the right to work at the speed that came naturally to me, for it was at that pace I did the better work and felt more comfortable personally. If that bothered others, then they had a problem. The problem was not mine. Further, I resolved that rather than get a bad name from being awkward and error ridden, I would prefer to take whatever came as a result of my working speedily and accurately.

"The next morning I settled in to work at my own fast pace, again producing completed data sheets accurately and in abundance, and again to the consternation and antagonism of many of the employees around me. Regardless, I kept working until alas the supervisor came to my desk with a data sheet in his hand from the day before."

"'You're working pretty fast,' he said coldly.

"'Yes,' I replied, 'I seem to have gotten the hang of it, and that's the way I do my best work — fast.'

"'Hardly,' he growled. 'I have a sheet here from yesterday which shows it didn't balance out until you corrected your errors.'

"My heart sank. 'You are right,' I replied again, 'I did make errors on some sheets when I was operating at a slower pace, and I had to correct them in order to make the sheets balance. But if you will check the sheets I have done at my normal fast pace you will find them to be accurate and balanced without any correction.'

"The macho supervisor growled back at me in subdued but very hostile tones, 'Are you telling me how to run this office?'

"I was speechless and didn't respond. Sitting there in limbo, my head swirled as I desperately tried to hold the line on my reasoning. The domineering thought in my mind, for several seconds however, was, *Good heavens, is there no place in the world for me. First the psychiatrists condemned me, then the church, now the government. Where in the world can I go; what in the world can I do in order to live*?'

"I guess I appeared to be as upset as I really was. Perhaps that's what caused the supervisor to move away without further conversation, and to stand leaning on a high counter some distance away, near the exit, but still peering down on me intensely. I gathered my faculties as best I could, quickly thinking through my situation. *If I work fast*, I thought to myself, *he will bear down on me again. If I work slowly I will make errors, plus now that I am upset my concentration will be affected and I will make errors anyway.'*

"Which ever way I looked at it, I was up against it and could see no way for me to win in that situation. So, standing up, I walked straight towards the exit, pausing only briefly to speak to the supervisor who had been standing there glaring at me.

"'I'm quitting,' I informed him as I paused. 'You can mail my salary to me.'

"'Did anyone say anything to you?' he snapped back at me with eyes piercing as if to frighten me from challenging his hostile actions towards me.

"'No,' I replied promptly, with fear of paranoia racing uncontrollably through my mind. I made my exit without further delay.

"As I went out into the street my body began to palpitate as it had that grim night in Lower Secundaterra when I thought I would die.

"Standing on the sidewalk I suddenly felt a need to sit down somewhere. Looking around I could see no place to do so. Just then a city transit car pulled in to a nearby transit stop. I hopped on board, dropped a ticket in the receptacle and quickly sat down to rest my trembling legs and body. I soon became concerned that this car was taking me farther away from home, rather than towards it as I ought to be going. In time I could see a church a few blocks ahead. Church doors were nearly always unlocked in those days. At the stop nearest the church I left the car, and crossing the street entered the church to sit down, rest, and try to get control of my mind. As I approached the church my mind was upset all the more at the sight of an elderly man in worn and shapeless clothes, and with dirty ragged beard, seeking hand-outs from those who went by.

"*But for my wife*, I shivered to myself, *that might be me*.

"The thought was not comforting, but if it were not for Vita's income, that could well be a reality for me. Dropping some change I could not afford into the poor man's hat, I passed by into the church sanctuary to sit in a pew. There was no one else to be seen. I sat in quietude to think things through.

"First, I reviewed in my thoughts the incident back at the office. The supervisor had obviously aligned himself with the slower workers, and had come down on me with hostility. I wasn't mistaken. His attitude towards me was definitely negative. His open friendliness with the slower workers was very obvious. In later life I would experience time and again that there is no reward from belittlers for exceptional work. In fact it is not wanted; neither are the workers of it.

"I had never in my life before shrunk from any person, whether it be a bully, or a challenger, or for that matter from a sincerely superior person, as many belittlers do. But I had now in this no win situation withdrawn from this bully and belittler for fear of being labeled paranoid. He had asked me bluntly, 'Did anyone say anything to you?' True, he hadn't said much. But of his hostile looks there was no mention, and could not be by me. I knew from my limited previous experiences, and have had it confirmed by numerous later experiences, that such people wrangle their way out of such predicaments by saying they hadn't said a word. He had been working there much longer than I and would have been believed. Such people often lie unabashedly. You may ask, 'how can they do such a thing?' Later in my story, I will tell you how and why and give you illustrations of people you would never dream would do such a thing. As I have said before it is generally referred to simply as immaturity by the few people who can see through this obnoxious characteristic of the belittlers.

"My mind was soothed somewhat by the thought that it is wise at times in life to withdraw. Many wise generals and people in other walks of life incorporate temporary withdrawal or retreat into the normal patterns of their lives and careers in order to make a better advance thereafter. So to that part of it I became reconciled.

"What made this experience so traumatic was that, as I mentioned earlier, it followed being squashed, first by doctors, then in commerce, later, the church, and now a branch of government. It seemed everywhere I turned I was condemned by someone. However, something helpful did come out of this incident. The idea eventually entered my mind, and in time grew on me that this all was a part of my lot in life. I being what I am, would always have trouble with certain kinds of people. It would never be traumatic for me again.

"In the meantime I was in a bad way, and I needed a job. The money we brought with us from Lower Secundaterra had all but run out. Vita was bringing in barely enough to, on a tight budget, pay the rent and keep us eating. Having sold our good car in Lower Secundaterra and bought on credit a much less adequate car in Secundaterra with the opportunity in sight of a job requiring a car — which job by the way turned out to be a dud — we now had payments to keep up. We did want to keep the car, as meager as it was. We had never known life without one.

"*Vita will be so discouraged*, I thought. *She was so happy when I found work. Now its gone. And me! Is there no place in this world at all for me*? I didn't fully realize it at the time, but the seeds of what would be termed an undiagnosed and unnamed mental illness had now been well implanted in me. These seeds had been sown there, not by some childhood experience still lurking in my subconscious and being triggered by a current event. Rather, they had been embedded by a barrage of traumatic experiences hurled at me in my early adulthood as I tried vainly to establish the bridgehead of my life. These experiences were too severe to be withstood by almost any young person who had not yet acquired a secure place in life, and who had had no time to let the realities of his particular life grow upon his being. Had I had time for personal growth after the new awakening I experienced in Lower Secundaterra, I might have somehow withstood these onslaughts. Instead I was almost immediately tossed out into a world that would be to an overwhelming extent hostile towards me. Time for growth was replaced by struggle for survival.

"It would be several years before I would have any chance for real personal growth to the point where I would have stability even in the face of such traumatic experiences as were befalling me and would in future always be a common part of my life which I must withstand. As it was at the time, although I was in my early thirties, I reminded myself of being like an adolescent who had gained a new and sound perspective for life but hadn't had time to really grow into that perspective. Instead he was tossed out into the world to flounder as best he could with little or no material or moral support.

"Leaning forward in the church pew, I placed my head in my hands, staying there in thought and despair I have no idea how long, when I heard a nearby voice saying gently, 'Hello, can I help you?'

"Stirring slowly I looked up into the face of a minister. 'I don't know if you can help me,' I replied, 'but I just wanted to sit here to rest and think.'

"'Your voice is quivering, indeed your body is shaking,' he responded. 'Are you afraid of something?'

"'Not really,' I answered, and then to cover myself, 'I'm just having trouble finding a job.'

"'Are you new to this city?' he asked again.

"'Yes,' I said, 'I came here from Lower Secundaterra.'

"'Oh,' he replied, as if the problem were now solved. 'Then you are not used to the big city life yet. But give it time, and it will come. It's a nice city. People here are very friendly. You just have to get used to the faster pace and then you'll like it and feel comfortable here.'

"I forced a smile on my face. 'Thanks for the encouragement,' I compelled myself to say.

"'Are you connected with a church here in the city yet?' he asked next.

"'Yes I am,' I told him. And upon telling him which church I had become associated with he offered to telephone the minister of my church and make an appointment with him for counseling. 'I think you need it,' he said, 'you are still trembling some.'

"He phoned the minister of my church who offered to see me as soon as I could arrive there. *Maybe he could help me to find a job*, I thought, *or maybe he could help me to get involved in the church again to the point where I could become a minister. Surely I would get treated well in that occupation in Secundaterra.*

"About two weeks previous to this I had gone to talk with a

national official of the church about my desire to become a minister, and gave him just a sketch of how my desire had been handled in Lower Secundaterra. He was an older man who knew the score in life and was fully aware of many of its prejudices and injustices. He was also, and no doubt for good reason, a very cautious man with regard to what he said straightforward. Implication was more his style. He did, however, say that he was very impressed by me. That remark, in such stark contrast to what I had heard from ministers previously, was like music to my ears. He suggested I work in Secundaterra for awhile, become active and known in the church I was now associated with, and 'see if you are the type of person they would recommend to the ministry.' He felt sure that they would, he said assuringly.

"I was pleased with his suggestion, even if he little knew how difficult it would be for me to find work in Secundaterra. Even omitting that difficulty, it would mean getting established in this city where it was hard to get a job unless one intended to stay with an employer for many years or a lifetime. That was often an expected requirement at that time. If my plan worked out, in a year or two I would be uprooting again to go into preparation for ministry. Even with all the obstacles it entailed, I told him I would follow his suggestion. So here I was now, off to an appointment with the minister who hopefully, would help me through to some feasible road in life.

"This minister of the church we were attending was also aware of life's realities. He reflected the maturity of his years and the diversity and intricacies of life, learned in the country from which he had come to Secundaterra. He was a fine, elderly and wise man. His interest in my well being encouraged me. I could not help but notice previously that he had taken a liking to me as he shook hands with parishioners leaving the church on Sunday mornings. Now in the interview we talked at length about where I was from, my goals in life, and how he could help. Without telling him of my experience with ministers in Lower Secundaterra I told him of the suggestion of the national officer of the church, whom he knew, that I seek admission to the ministry through this congregation.

This minister not only agreed to it, but was really pleased.

"Also, I told him, rather sketchily of my experience that day with a 'supervisor who didn't like me,' as I put it. 'We'll help you find a job somewhere else, Collin,' he responded, 'but in the meantime you have had a bad experience with a bully today, and I want to send you to talk with a Christian psychiatrist whom I know. Maybe he will be able to help you further. In future, Collin,' he added, 'remember that a bully is coward.'

"As I have already said, this minister meant well. He was an older, experienced, wise and concerned man, with a knowledge of the realities of life one finds among the more knowledgeable people. So I agreed to follow his suggestion, even though I doubted either he, or very many others realized the full extent of the harshness of the realities of life as they exist for me or for you, fine people as we are or rare gems as some people call us.

"Going immediately from the ministers office to the psychiatrist whose office was in a general hospital in another part of the city, I was interviewed by him for ten or fifteen minutes with me making sure our conversation centered on present circumstances, and saying nothing about my past experience with psychiatrists. He impressed me as being a pleasant and sincere person. He spoke idealistically about the city in which we lived. It was indeed fast becoming an outstanding city, but no city has all nice people in it. This psychiatrist took a similar attitude towards me as had the minister in whose church I had taken refuge earlier in the day. His remarks and attitude towards me could be summed up this way: that I was new here from Lower Secundaterra and finding it rough getting adjusted to big city life and that with a little help in adjusting, I should be all right and perhaps even make a very good minister someday. He was trying to be encouraging. However, during the course of the conversation it became obvious he was not knowledgeable of the circumstances that brought me to him. To him it was a matter of getting adjusted to big city life. To help me with my adjustment he wanted me to attend a day clinic for a week or two. He had a psychiatrist colleague there who would supervise my program. Thinking perhaps this might be a good opportunity for me to have some talks with a Christian psychiatrist, I agreed to go.

"Arriving at the center at nine o'clock the next morning, I was before long introduced to the young psychiatrist in whose care I was to be during my attendance there from nine to four each day for a brief period, perhaps two weeks. In the course of my initial interview with this doctor he asked me what my long range plans were for my life.

"'I would like some day to be a minister of the church,' I answered enthusiastically.

"'Well,' he replied, 'no doubt you will be some day, but I'm not sure I can help you with your plans for that. You see I am Jewish.'

"My hopes were dashed for help in the sphere of spiritual matters, an area I would have liked very much to discuss with someone with knowledge and understanding of very personal aspects of Christian spiritual life.

"Steering the conversation to matters other than spiritual, I brought up the topics of envy, jealousy and rivalry out in the world. Not daring to go into the whole story with a person I did not yet know well, I gave him just a brief sketch of the incident of envy and jealousy I experienced with the minister in Lower Secundaterra. Also, without saying where, I gave him a bare outline of the supervisor at work who was envious of me also. In both cases his reply amounted to the same thing.

"'Why would a minister be envious of you who are not yet even started on your training?' he asked with unrestrained disbelief. And 'why would a supervisor be envious of a clerk? I don't understand that!'

"I could tell he didn't understand, and that I had better steer myself out of this conversation quickly. Whether he would draw on his professional training to label me paranoid I wasn't sure and didn't intend to take the risk of finding out. I formed the opinion that most likely this doctor, who was not a belittler but an inexperienced nice young person who in his naïveté, if I were to talk to him about such things as envy, would turn to me to learn something about the world or reality and I would become his teacher. That I wasn't willing to risk either, not with a psychiatrist.

"So after saying very emphatically that he didn't understand how a minister and a supervisor, both so far ahead of me in life, could be envious of me, he then said, 'now lets put you through some psychological testing to try and determine what is the cause of your problem.'

"Through the tests I went, and the young psychiatrist came back with the summation that I would hear again and again in the future. 'We can't determine from the testing what is wrong with you, but whatever it is, it can't be very much.'

"With only a little effort I managed during the remainder of my stay at the center to steer the conversation to discussing what I was and would be doing at the center over the next week or two. In this area he was adequate.

"At the end of ten days or so, during which time I had participated in group discussions of various sorts, did crafts and associated socially with other clients and staff, all the while taking pills that had been prescribed for me, I had a final interview with the psychiatrist.

"In response to his inquiry as to how I felt now, I told him I was doing well and would have to get searching for work very soon. He agreed that would be best for me. 'If you need help, come back any time,' he suggested.

"That was reassuring even though he could not help me with the root of my problems. As I left the center I expressed appreciation for his sincere and kindly though incomplete concern and care. Other psychiatrists would of necessity come into my life in the future, but there would come between me and them a fixed barrier, they with their eye and ear trained to detect symptoms of mental illness which they would not be able to find in me; me with my first hand knowledge of the world of reality as it existed for me, and, the two very incompatible. I devised a way to deal with it which in the long run was to my detriment, but which saved me from the label of a hopeless paranoid.

"When a few times in the future I became worn down and

exhausted by the antagonisms of belittlers and ended up in need of help, I would automatically blame my troubles on overwork. Often the advice forthcoming was that I had to learn to pace myself. Again there would be routine psychological testing, the result of which was always a message to my wife that there was not much wrong with me, but whatever it was they couldn't quite discern. With colleagues in the church and at work and with other acquaintances I always used the overwork reason to explain my illness. The end result of this necessary tactic was that I escaped being labeled a paranoid, thereby avoiding long term hospitalization and extensive treatment, which would amount to brainwashing for paranoia to make me believe such things weren't happening to me. On the other hand, I became known as a person of low work capacity. Actually I was just the opposite, but for many years I got the mediocre jobs, and at times the same for churches.

"Coming back to the moment of my story: eventually through parishioners of the church which I was now attending, and with whom I was put in contact by the very efficient minister, and, through getting to know neighbors, and also through contacts Vita had made through her work, I was able to get jobs. They were short term for a while, but with a very good permanent job eventually coming through for me.

"Simultaneous to this Vita and I were developing our church activities and the social life stemming from it, with me developing the ground work for my possible future entry into the ministry. At this point I was developing both a secular career and the preliminary preparation for ministry, leaving till later the decision as to which route I would follow according to what doors would open for me.

"It was a large upper middle class congregation in which we were now involved. Vita and I were not in that class financially, by any means, but were extremely well received there. We were able to take our places well, becoming active in a broad range of church spiritual, social and business activities. We got along well with both ministers and were able also to select a broad range of acquaintances and friends. The congregation was large enough to facilitate our avoidance of involvement with belittlers. We could pick and choose the activities in which we wished to be involved, and avoid those in which we did not.

"Concerning my career matters in the church at large, I was gradually making contacts in the church administrative structure from where I obtained some guidance which helped me get started on liberal arts studies, a prerequisite to theological studies. This arts studying I would do part time. The theology would have to be done full time for three years.

"Mostly because of the desire to avoid confrontation with belittling professors in class sessions, I chose to study liberal arts courses by correspondence. Before the days of video and computer this was a time consuming, grueling method. Instead of listening to lectures, a student did all the reading privately and submitted a series of essays, often a dozen or more, on various aspects of a course. Then a final exam was required, which, in my experience, always contained questions on aspects far different than any covered in topics prescribed for essays during the semester.

"After working at brain work all day at my job and then studying in this manner all evening, I did not do well, but managed a pass mark. Had I gone to classes, however, even though the method of study is much easier, I am of the opinion I would not have been able to get through at all. The belittlers, I am sure, would have blocked my way. How I would get through three years of full time theology studies at seminary I did no know yet, but kept an open mind and a prayer line to God open on the matter, hoping and praying that seminary would be a delightfully different experience.

"Incidentally, I would like to tell you at this time that during the course of my visits to our denomination's large and quite comprehensive book and supply outlet, one of the first books I saw sitting there on display in a most conspicuous place, was *The Power of Positive Thinking*, by Norman Vincent Peale. On seeing it, I thought to myself, *a church that on the one hand condemns such a book and me with it, and on the other hand promotes its sale to its members, owes me some explanations in the form of theological instruction.* This now was one more incentive for me to pursue theological studies.

"So here I was in this city with its good, though sometimes naïve side, and definitely with its mean side, making my way in secular life as though I might do so for the remainder of my working life, and therefore going about my employment as if it were to be permanent. At the same time I was pursuing my preparation for life in the ministry of the church as though it might become my life's work, but not knowing yet whether such a career would open up to me. So I was living a dual life, both aspects of which had to be temporary and permanent at the same time. This caused difficulties but we were able to cope with them well. Concerning housing and its furnishing, we avoided getting involved heavily or permanently in these, because if I was successful in becoming a minister, both housing and furnishings would be provided by the church. Consequently we had to live under conditions barely adequate and of far less quality than we had been accustomed to.

Collin continued with his presentation: "As you already know I eventually did get into the ministry of the church. In due time I would learn through experience that most, not all, of the people at or near the top of the church pyramid of influence were people of well cultured Christian character. There was much evidence of the presence of dignity, integrity, and varying degrees of maturity and stature as persons. For people made up of such, I am always grateful.

"However, as much love and respect as I have for the church as a whole, I must later this evening tell you of my adverse experiences in ministry out in the field. Indeed, out of that same love and respect it must be told.

"First, though, I must relate some further experiences I had in secular life before I began full time studying for ministry. Early in the period of my re-establishment in Secundaterra I had for several weeks, a job as an elevator operator in a large high-class hotel. You may think that here working among unskilled, and generally not well educated people in the service industry, I would have a very difficult time with belittlers. Such was not the case. On the contrary, I did not experience one belittler in this place. There are a variety of reasons for this, not the least being that people working in a high class hotel have to accept that there are going to be high class people around and that they must be treated with respect. Anyone not willing to respect such people would not be kept on the staff there. The hotel had excellent management who would see to that. So the most I had to put up with was an occasional comment passed from one employee to another such as, 'what's a person like him working at this for?' But there was no belittling or animosity toward me of any kind, and to me this is very significant in that it proves wrong the usually accepted assumption that such envy and animosity stems from a lower class of people. These people I was working with were not highly educated, yet there wasn't a sign of envy or enmity coming from them. Because such enmity was lacking in this hotel is not to say that envy and belittling does not occur among less educated people. It does aplenty, depending on the environment, and often on the management of any particular organization. On the other hand, such envy and enmity comes in abundance from well educated people also. It is a major and very trouble producing, misery causing character flaw or disorder that is prevalent in people in all walks of life, from the least to the most educated. Call it immaturity if you will, and that more nearly describes its cause, but it cannot be truthfully brushed off as ignorance as it often is. Neither does the term 'personality conflict' accurately describe it. Two persons are required to make a conflict. But here, the problem is initiated by one person only, the belittler who has a character disorder. The victim who is defending himself is doing just that, and not intentionally doing anything wrong to the belittlers as they often suppose or claim. Nor is it a character disorder of the majority of people. I would guesstimate, it includes about one third of the population, causing untold misery to countless people, and most especially to people like you and I; indeed at times destroying some of us.

"Another job I held was with a heavy industry corporation. This work called for the steady inflow of various types of steel and steel products from suppliers near and far. My job consisted, in essence, of keeping inventory records, again before the time of computers for such work. When any of the various steel supplies went below a designated level I would have to order from the appropriate domestic supplier, watching that it was available on time, and at a competitive price. When it was not available under these circumstances, then, under supervision for the present, I would reroute the order to another supplier, sometimes in another country. Such a job, as you may imagine, could become complex at times, but this brief outline of its description is sufficient for our purposes this evening.

"The person who had held this position before me had been promoted to another position in the same large office. Therefore he was present to help train me. He had been at the job for four years and knew it well.

"My observation revealed that it gave him a sense of importance to be teaching me such a complex and responsible job on which depended the continuous operation of the plant. He was not friendly in his dealings with me, but cold and efficient. When, however, it appeared to him that I had all but mastered the job in four days, he became hostile and abrupt in manner, speaking snappily and tossing papers at me rather than handing them to me or placing them on my desk in a mannerly fashion. The nature of the problem with which he was struggling was revealed when he said angrily to me, 'perhaps you will learn this job faster than I did.'

"He was unsuccessful in his personal struggle to overcome his envy and hatred, but did succeed in turning a large number of the office staff negative towards me and into sympathy with himself. People often sympathize with the envious, hateful one, placing the blame for the problem on the one of whom he is envious, when all that person has done has exercised his God given gifts to their fullest extent, which is the way they are meant to be used. God doesn't give us extra gifts in order that we may suppress them so as not to arouse the envy, jealousy and hatred of someone with lesser gifts. He gives us such gifts that we may use them to the fullest for good. If someone else has contempt rather than respect for such gifts, then that person has a serious character problem that needs correcting.

"As I said earlier, about one third of the population, I would guesstimate, are belittlers to varying degrees and in need of such correcting. By the same method, I would say that another one third can be swayed one way or another, not having a real understanding of the issue. The other third are wise to what is going on but remain silent because of the largely unexplored nature of the issue. Consequently we can have as many as two thirds of the people seeing the main belittler as the underdog. They sympathize with him, side with him, support him, and turn against the one at whom the envy, jealousy and hatred are aimed.

"There was little sympathy shown for me in that office. I was treated like dirt under their feet by the majority for several days. Working at such a responsible and exciting job, normally I would have thrived on it. But working at it under inhumane circumstances, I became exhausted, ending up in hospital for what was termed there as a 'nervous breakdown.' This, in turn, resulted in the loss of my job.

"It was obvious to me that although the office manager had at least some inkling of what was happening he was not capable of handling the situation. This, I think is mostly due to the fact that there is little or no human understanding of the dynamics of such a happening. Nothing explicit has ever been written on the matter. There is no resource available that can teach people the workings of the human mind on this matter. It has never been put into words that give a concrete explanation. Therefore, even people who recognize it as wrong, simply shrug and brush it off mostly as ignorance, sometimes as personality conflict.

"The psychiatrist who cared for me in hospital was not of any more help. On my trying to find out what position he would take concerning envious people causing problems for me, he responded, 'you shouldn't let such little things bother you. And now, let's try to find out what's causing your problem.'

"So again they set about trying to find causes through psychological testing. From it I received what was as I said earlier to become a usual response to my wife Vita that they were unable to determine from the tests what was wrong with me, but whatever was wrong, it wasn't very much.

"In response to one of my attempts to explain to the doctor what was happening to me, the doctor asked, 'do you think everyone is against you?'

"I knew what was coming — the paranoia issue, and I had no desire to get involved in that and its consequences ever again. 'No,' I quickly replied, 'it's just a person here and there who causes me a little trouble, which I must get used to and take in my stride.'

"Again I utilized the *overwork* reason for my condition. The doctors became convinced that I was prone to overwork myself. Actually, under favorably working conditions, I had a far above average capacity and stamina. Now I would be labeled as having insufficient capacity and stamina to carry a job requiring responsibility and perseverance. This label would be to my detriment, but it would save me the consequences of being labeled paranoid. Again the only advice I was given for this supposed overworking of myself was that I would have to learn to pace myself within my 'limited capacity.'

"On another occasion I applied for a government office job through the civil service employment agency. Various tests were required and the information was that with so many people applying, only those with a very high score would be given further consideration. This did not pose an obstacle for me since I knew from experience that I always did very well indeed with general knowledge and I.Q. tests. Actually I found the tests to be a breeze — surprisingly simple. I did extremely well in them, which in turn qualified me to take an oral examination on general knowledge of the country and its government. Of this I had no worry at all, since I was very well read in the affairs of all branches of government, and all sections of the country. Keeping up on public and political concerns both domestic and world wide had been a keen interest of mine for years. Not only was I widely read in these matters, but had travelled the country from one end to the other.

"Two men conducted my oral interview. Both were friendly at the beginning. They asked me questions as to what elected representatives held what positions in government. What major civil servants held what positions in government. What major government policies and projects were being carried on in the country and where at the present time. I answered each and every question without hesitancy. As this process went on, I could easily notice that the one interviewer was astoundingly pleased, while the other, who appeared to be the senior officer of the two was getting noticeably colder as I answered and discussed question after question without any problem.

"Then there came questions on the geography of the country. Frequently, I could not only impart knowledge that I had read or seen in pictures, but in many instances I could say, I have been there and have seen it for myself. This displeased the senior officer immensely and he was unable to keep from showing it. I would guess he had not travelled much. I knew then I would not get the job, for the senior officer's nose was out of joint.

"As the interview ended and I was about to leave, the senior officer growled in cold tones, 'If you don't get the job for which you have applied, we have several openings for mail carriers, and you are free to apply for one of these.'

"The other officer's mouth dropped noticeably as the shock of that statement hit him. A week later I received notice that I would not get the position for which I had applied.

"So you see folks," said Collin to the group, "no one can read another persons mind with one hundred percent accuracy, but with years of experience in dealing with all types of people, we get to be able to figure them out reasonably well. In the instance I just related to you, I think it is reasonable and rational and very true to reality to say that the senior officer turned me down, not because I wasn't good enough, but because I was too good—too good for him, that is. He could only bring himself to approve of people on whom he could look down. He found no way in the interview to put me down beneath himself, yet his character disorder would not allow him to look up to me and respect me for my near flawless presentation. The way he devised to belittle me was to offer me an opportunity for the lesser job. This not only made him appear in his own mind at least, to be the condescending patronizer but also covered his prejudice towards me from any verbal protest. That is, if I or someone else were to accuse him of being prejudiced, which he definitely was, he could easily argue, 'but look, I even offered the guy another job.' In his mind there could be no standing argument against him. By the way, I didn't apply for the letter carrier's job. It was a job with very good remuneration, but it just wasn't in my line of interest, and besides, I knew very well that if I did apply for it, the belittler would find some way to stop me there too, or, endeavor to bring me down some more. Most likely he would see to it that I got the worst of the several letter carrier openings that were available. Once you find an organization dominated by that kind of people, it is just as well to bow out. They will continually find ways to put you down, and if they can without revealing themselves as the kind of people they are, will eventually do you in.

"On another occasion I applied for a job with another government office; that is a different level of government within Secundaterra. There was the usual testing, with which I did well. But this time there was a difference in that I had a connection in the right place. Through Vita and I making friends through our developing social life we had come to know well a person who was in a position in government to ensure that I received fair consideration. So after going through all the required procedure, I was placed in a government office position that held promise for a good future. Due to our friend's general oversight of the situation there was no room for either favoritism or prejudice to be shown in my obtaining this position. There was no way I could be unjustly shafted in the process, therefore I had no problem in landing the job. That, incidentally is something we should keep in mind in future as we prepare to help one another, and Albin the younger of us in particular, to take our rightful places in this university and in life outside it; to use our influence to see that people like us get fair treatment.

"The manager of the office in which I was placed was of very high caliber and delighted in having similar people work with him. He looked down on no one, respected high quality work, and yet had adequate patience with those of average ability. To my delight, he was not a belittler, and in time I was to learn that right up through the department there were non-belittlers in charge.

"You may think that now I really had it made, but I didn't. There were belittlers among the employees, one of whom was very open and prevalent, brazen I would say, in his belittling activity. Apparently he had been mildly belittling some others continuously with sarcasm and innuendo as long as he had been there. Since it was only mild, his victims took him with a grain of salt. Others supported him to varying degrees mostly by their supportive chuckles or by their just plain friendship towards him.

"Some of you may now think, 'but he was only one, and you had a good boss.' My answer to that is, yes, I had a good boss, and good management up through the ranks, and some near-by support from some of the employees in the office where I worked. But I was brought low, and I will tell you how and why.

"Unlike some previous incidents it took a while for trouble to brew up for me in this office. The belittlers were there, but were not very troublesome at first, and this gave me time to prove my abilities and capacity in all areas of my work. I won the respect of my superiors and some others in the office and throughout the department. After my probationary period of three months I was informed by usual channels and procedures that my work was satisfactory and that I was now on permanent staff. Sometime after that, perhaps a month or two if I remember correctly, I was given an indication that if my work continued at its present high standard I would over a period of time be promoted upwards to an eventual administrative position. This news became common knowledge among the employees of our office. In fact I heard some sketchy news of it from fellow workers before I heard of it from the supervisor. Regardless of the awkward communication, the news pleased me immensely and gave me an always needed boost of confidence in myself.

"Shortly after that news broke, however, the prevalent and brazen belittler of the office began to show his colors more openly, and also I began to learn who his friends were, and who were mine. Mine were about half, most of them silent. I might have succeeded this time, in grinding my way up the ladder of success, and with such odds against me it would have been a grind, had I not been also studying part time, and by correspondence at that, for my prerequisites for ministry.

"At this point, I considered extensively whether or not I should give up the idea of ministry and put all my energies into this promising government position. *I would if necessary be content to make a career here,* I often thought to myself. Looking at my situation in a practical way, I deemed that a person who because of belittlers, has had such trouble as I in obtaining jobs and being able to stay with them, could not afford to let go of any reasonable opportunity, whether tentative or concrete until a door had definitely opened allowing me to proceed with another career.

"Even more strongly than these considerations though, was the sense of duty to answer my felt call to the ordained ministry of the church as long as there was a possibility the church door might open to me. So I eventually made a firm decision and stuck to it. I would continue to pursue both careers until I was sure which door, if either, would open widely enough to assure me of a genuine possibility for the future.

"To make it more clear to you now just what I was up against in this office, I will explore again the phenomena of belittling. I wish to point out to you at this time that not all, not nearly all belittlers are openly hostile, active and aggressive in putting people down. Only relatively few of them have the cold brazenness to be so. The others, non-active, we'll say, support the active ones in various ways: by merely befriending them with the implication of taking their side, or, by showing sympathy for them as an underdog because of the way, in their minds, a fine person towers over them in appearance, intelligence, integrity, personality and perhaps real or imagined material possessions. They also, at times, by snickering, grinning or smiling in mockery, try to add to the embarrassment of the fine person when they deem the belittler has gained a victory over him. These people, often many in number, are near silent supporters of the active aggressive belittlers. They add immensely to the burden we have to bear."

Owen interrupted. "Collin, I would like to explore again some percentages you mentioned earlier. What percentage of people would you estimate are belittlers, either active or non-active, as you have classified them?"

"First let me emphasize," replied Collin, "that I have no scientifically arrived at figures for this. There are none available, and I have no means to establish any. I would estimate from experience and observation, however, that one third of all people on our continent are belittlers, and one third are non-belittlers who would definitely support people like us even if only silently. This may vary from area to area; within some areas, the belittlers being more numerous, and more outwardly active, are actually predominant over the human environment."

"And the other third?" asked Owen.

"The other third," Collin continued, "are like sheep who follow which ever shepherd captivates their mind or fancy in any given circumstance. This latter third of the people have a limited human understanding, due perhaps to limited exposure to life in the market place or due perhaps to their overriding inclination not to bother themselves with the deeper intricacies of life. They are not 'street wise' people. So if and when their attention is drawn to a contest between a fine person and a belittler, they are not likely to discern the real reasons for the contest. Consequently, some may take the side of the fine person because they see him as a nice person whom they like or as an intelligent person with something good to offer. Others may take the side of the belittler out of pity, seeing him in their mind's eye as coming from less fortunate circumstance or viewing him in the present as the less fortunate of the two because he is not so smart or good looking, or rich or as fine a person."

"This latter third of the people, then, are naive about this area of life," added Gilda.

"That is my opinion," remarked Collin, "very naive. And in far too many instances we find such people in responsible positions."

"So it is possible," surmised Leo, "that in a given situation you may have two-thirds of the people at odds with you."

"Nearly two-thirds sometimes, Leo," replied Collin, "but usually you will have at least a few individuals of the naive one third who are supporters, but like the one third who know what is going on, they most always have to remain silent. It takes keen detection to know that they are supporters. No supporters can be of much tangible help to you that way, but you learn to detect and appreciate their silent support which gives you a boost in morale.

"Continuing with my story," said Collin, "It wasn't altogether the numbers that went against me in this experience, but rather the circumstances of it. My daily work required of me a lot of brain drain, but in itself not too much for me. I was quite capable of it. My studying by correspondence, with all the required reading in lieu of lectures, plus the dozen or so essays for each course, was an added brain drain at night, but still I think not too much. I felt then, and still think today I could have handled it well were it not for the continuous mind disturbing annoyance caused by the daily hounding of the main belittler of the workplace.

"He apparently was much annoyed by my 'gentlemanly' ways as he inferred them to be, and was determined to bring me down to his level or break me. Like a mad man he would busy himself about the office, and as he did so he would talk, not to others, but mumble audibly within my hearing and usually that of some others, what he would in future expect of me in terms of my personal behavior. I was to go out 'on the town' with him at night and 'have some fun,' which I did not get in church life. He would not expect me to drink, because he did not drink himself. How kind of him! But how self centered also. He did however have two girl friends, divorcees, he said, who miss their husbands and who craved his loving because they had no other. These I was to share with him. He was not married. Apparently it made no difference that I was, and very happily so. He demanded to hear a little cussing from me now and then, so that I would be more of a man like he was. As he went about the office he would at times slam his one fisted hand into the other open hand and mumbling threats of giving me a good trimming if I did not succumb to his wishes for me.

"His actions were always and only carried on in my presence and within my hearing for the purpose of intimidating me, yet it was done in such a way that no one would be able to prove it was actually aimed at me. Everyone there, except a few of the naive ones knew right well it was aimed at me, yet when one of my supporters said to him one day, 'that's a sin what you are doing to him,' he replied snappily, 'I'm not doing a thing to him.'

"I did my best to ignore him, knowing that if he dared to fulfill any of his veiled threats I would have him out in the open where I could enforce discipline upon him either through superiors in the department or through the process of law. He did not come into the open, however, but it was the continual hounding, days, weeks, months, of it that eventually began to get on my nerves, especially when I would be a bit spent from days working and nights studying.

"As bright a man as my supervisor was, it seemed he was only vaguely aware of my problem with this most strange belittler. When I spoke to him about the matter he passed it off lightly saying, 'aw now, that guy is not really going to do anything to you.' Some time later however, I learned that the supervisor knew that this belittler's family had a personal connection to someone much higher up in the department. I formed the opinion that the supervisor chose to gloss over the problem lightly because of this.

"The supervisor was right with regard to any physical interference towards me by the belittler, but my nerves were slowly being wrecked and that of course was his game. One day the belittler and his supporters were coming down on me heavily. They may have noticed I was very tired that week, and this was their chance to break me, as the belittler often implied he would if

I didn't follow him into his ways. I had been studying hard and writing essays at home. it was a busy time of the month at the office. The continuous tactics of the belittler were wearing heavily on my nerves. I felt a haze coming over me. As I continued with much effort to do my work a kind of stupor came over me. I sat in the chair at my desk, hearing everything that was going on, but unable to respond to any of it. My mind was so exhausted, it just would not work any more. It had simply shut down. It is my opinion, and deep inner feeling that the exhaustion came not from my work load, for which I believe I was well able. Rather it was from the constant aggravation of belittlers while I was under that heavy work load.

"Vita was notified. I was taken to hospital. After two or three days of rest and sleep with the aid of appropriate medication I recovered. However, my condition was termed some sort of a 'nervous breakdown' again, so I had to go through all the usual testing and treatment for such a condition. There were the usual pills, tests, and the resulting 'we don't know what's wrong with him, but it isn't much.'

"Immediately on my return to work the belittler started on me again, this time with added mumblings that I was 'nuts' and had to go in hospital for that and that he would in time make a man out of me. With this new line added, he continued his previous tactics. It soon began to get on my nerves again.

"Searching for a way to hold on to this job out of which I knew I could make a career, I decided to speak to the minister of my church. I had confidence in his discernments on many matters of life, although I wasn't sure he would be able to handle this for me.

"On telling him of my predicament, he said, 'I can help you Collin. The elected representative who has authority over that government department is an acquaintance of mine. I will speak to him about it as soon as I can get in touch with him.'

"Thinking now that my situation would be secured in my favor for sure, I was alert each day at work for an indication of change in the belittlers attitude. In the first three days there was no change. Then on the fourth day I heard voices in the hallway just outside the door that was a short distance from my desk. The first voice spoke and I could not discern the words. Then as the second voice responded, I could easily tell it was the voice of the belittler. He said, much more loudly than the first voice, 'I'm not doing anything to him.' The first voice spoke again, and again I could not discern the words. The belittler responded a second time, loudly, clearly, and most emphatically, 'it's a lie. I'm not doing anything to him. He's lying.'

"There was further brief conversation in more subdued tones, making the conversation of both people indiscernible to me. Soon the door opened and the belittler entered, shutting the door hard behind him. Standing over some work at his desk, he began muttering to himself again, 'I'll get him for that,' came the words, as he slammed his fist into his open hand again. 'Nobody will do that to me and get away with it. I'll get him,' he repeated, punching his own hand with his fist again, and casting glaring eyes my way.

"The tactics this belittler was using on me were similar to those being used in some areas of Secundaterra by high school students to break teachers they didn't like; teachers you and I would consider the better type of teachers who have something extra in the way of character, sincerity and performance.

"Envy and hatred can do strange things even to a person who has been chastised about it by a senior authority. The belittler kept working on my nerves as though no one had spoken to him about it. I was an obsession with him. In time it began to bother me more and more. To make matters worse, having had the previous breakdowns, I was becoming more prone to them. I was weakening under the continual bombardment. On speaking to the minister of my church again, he said, 'we will find you another job.'

"I appreciated his sincerity and effort, but knew also what he even in his wisdom, did not know, and that is that chances are I would have similar problems wherever I went in Secundaterra. The choice I had was, be worn down to chronic illness, or get out.

"Through all of this I had kept up my part time studies for the ministry, although my performance in them was affected adversely. I had for about a year now been recommended to the ministry by my local church, so I decided to visit the offices of the church at large to try and open some doors for myself to serve as a lay pastor while studying. My previous contact person there had moved away, but I had some other names of departments and people. I was hoping to get a rural church appointment that would allow me more time for study, and hopefully in a more pleasant environment. With such a church, I could be ready in two years for full time theological studies, when it would be possible for me to obtain appointment to a student pastorate near the seminary.

"Upon making my needs known to the appropriate department, and they upon their learning that I had grown up in Lower Secundaterra, offered me a church in the northland of Secundaterra thinking it was like my former home, but it was not. There was very little comparison between the two very different parts of the country, but they in their lack of accurate knowledge thought there was and were determined that I could fill the need there where they hadn't been able to get a minister to stay for very long. However, regardless of its unfamiliarity it did take hold of me as an adventure I would love to tackle.

"Vita and I discussed this possibility for two or three weeks, in the meantime contacting people who knew the area, and also people from the area.

"As we reviewed the situation, Vita and I realized that it was not what we had hoped for, but surely, we reasoned, if we accept this appointment and do well with it, then the church would see to it that we get something better in the future. So with this confidence in the church, and with an opportunity for me to be in a healthier atmosphere, plus our sense of adventure running high, we accepted the appointment. Within a matter of a few weeks we set sail on a ship for the Secundaterra northland. As rugged as life would be for us there, it would not be near so hard on us as the later realization that our confidence in the part of the church we were dealing with now at any rate, was misplaced.

After pausing briefly Collin interjected, "I think it is of much significance I state now that as I was leaving my government office job for the northland, the very brazen belittler admitted to me verbally that he indeed had tried very hard to break me. 'You're a tough nut to crack,' he said, 'and I apologize for what I tried to do to you. I wish you well up there. You've got more guts than I have. I'm sorry for the way I treated you.'

"It's not often a belittler makes such an admission," added Collin, then continued with his story.

"Life in the northland, we were soon to find out, was rugged indeed, and made possible for us newcomers only by the help of a very practical people with an inborn friendliness. Arriving there in September, we were soon taught how to order food, have it come from a thousand miles away and store it in for the winter. Before freeze-up time came, I and sometimes my family with me also quickly learned to travel to the various little villages along the coastline that were included in my pastorate, by boat with rugged fishermen at the helm. On the first of such trips I travelled with two men who handled the boat extremely well in a wild wind and rain storm in which we were caught on the way. We arrived at our destination safely but all three of us soaked to the skin by the almost icy northern waters. Waves had washed over the boat time and again, and even through the cabin in one side, out the other through the glassless window spaces. The men thought I would never travel with them again, but I did many times.

"As winter freeze-up and snow came we soon learned to travel by dog team. I did not drive a team myself as it takes considerable time to develop such a team for personal use. Sometimes my family would travel with me for the adventure and pastime, utilizing two teams between us and the two accompanying drivers.

"At that time snowmobiles were coming into common use, and a city church of mainstream Secundaterra supplied me with a snowmobile. After a few weeks of getting to know the area and its supports and dangers for humans, I was able to travel the long distances by snowmobile, first in the company of other men, but soon, on my own, and then I was able to serve my parishioners more adequately.

"There were very real dangers always present to the traveler in the northland. I was however quite able to take these dangers in my stride. To me they were not near so damaging to my being as the hardships I had faced daily with the belittlers in the south. There would in time prove to be belittlers here in the northland, as there are everywhere, but here I had ample support to make life pleasant regardless of the rugged physical elements of terrain and weather.

"On one occasion, my family and I in the early part of winter were travelling by snowmobile to another community about ten miles away, using two snowmobiles and a second driver besides myself. We had been travelling on ice, and were now about to leave it and go onto the land. Both land and ice were heavily snow covered near the shore. A few hundred feet from land our snowmobiles became bogged down in wet snow. Everyone got off to help push the snowmobiles, with engines working hard, toward land. My machine was the last. I walked out to it after helping to push the other to land, revved the motor and began pushing by myself as the others had lagged behind. The snowmobile started to move slowly. I noticed the others didn't come out to help and thought it was because I had it moving already. I noticed them waving and shouting, and thought it was just to encourage me on. As I pushed, I saw water coming up through the snow. *This would bog my machine down all the more*, I thought quickly. Revving the motor up to full throttle and meanwhile steering and pushing with the full force of my then muscular body, I was able to bring the snowmobile to land. When I did, my companions pointed to where the snowmobile and I had been out on the ice. Now the ice and snow had sunk below the water for some distance around.

"'We tried to warn you,' my companions said, 'but the sound of the motor prevented you hearing us. We wanted you to leave the machine and run. As you progressed towards the shore the ice was caving in behind you. It was a hair raiser, but once you got the machine moving we could see you were going to make it.'

"'Is the water deep out there?' I asked.

"'About forty feet,' the man replied.

"I thanked God for a powerful engine and a strong body. To put us in a lighter vein again, I quipped, 'but travelling is much better than being bogged down in ice water. Let's get on our way!'

"On another occasion in mid-winter when ice was thick from intense frost, and snow generally was packed hard by frequent strong winds that a few times registered more than one hundred miles an hour, I was travelling alone by snowmobile on a Monday morning. Having had Sunday morning and evening worship services at a village down the coast I was now returning to the village where we lived. It was always the custom to phone ahead and let someone know you were travelling and what time you expected to arrive. There were only a few phones, placed in some homes and other buildings where they were needed most. We had no phone at our house, so on this occasion I phoned ahead to the doctor of the village, telling him when I was leaving for home. He would keep a check on me as the custom was.

"A part of this journey was over wooded land of rolling hills. Among the trees and in the valleys, sheltered from the strong winds, the snow didn't pack down hard as it did in the more prevalent open country. The resulting loose snow in the valleys between the sometimes steep hills would, on occasion, cause difficulty for snowmobiles which at that time were heavier machines than they are now. Just where a fast run was needed for a hill, the loose snow would slow you down. On occasion, people got stuck in the valleys and got out only with help, or with great difficulty.

"The last part of this trip was over a causeway of solid ice nearly a mile wide and three miles long. In winter the water here would freeze because it was sheltered from the open sea. On either side of this ice passage way, however, lay open icy waters. To cross this ice pan with its thin covering of snow, we would follow the tracks of others who knew their way well from years of travel over it. In time a person also got to know land marks towards which we would travel.

"So soon after I left for home this day it began to snow, not too badly at first. The hills and valleys among the trees had been in poor condition, but passable all week. This new snow made them a little worse, but I got through the valleys with only some difficulty.

Then there was a stretch of relatively easy going for a few miles. By the time I got to the open ice span, however, a full blown storm had developed with strong winds and literally blinding snow. I was caught in a dilemma with little time to choose. To turn back was to surely get stuck in the new snow in the valleys; to continue towards home was to depend on my following the tracks made in the snow by previous travelers. The tracks were visible now for a distance of only twenty feet or sometimes less. Only very occasionally could I catch a glimpse of one of the few tiny islands dotting the causeway, and there was no sight at all of the far shore three miles distant toward which I was heading. I did not know the scattered islands well enough to use them as a guide in a snow storm, but at least I could get a glimmer of them occasionally. 'If it becomes necessary, I can somehow make a shelter on one of these,' I thought. There were a few small scraggy trees on them, and I could make a hole in the snow and a roof of tree boughs. This would be a last resort of course, but in the meantime there was a chance I could follow those tracks across the ice span, so I set out on my way.

"About halfway across the three mile span, the storm became even more blinding —the worst snow storm I had ever known. I would estimate the winds were about seventy miles per hour. In order to be able to follow the tracks I had to slow down considerably. Snow was drifting madly, but also catching in many places on the ice, the surface of which had previously been roughened by mild snow freezing into it. Before long I was able to see a track only occasionally. It was becoming more difficult by the minute to follow the worn travelway. Eventually I lost trace of it altogether. Criss-crossing, I endeavored to pick it up again. Occasionally I did in tiny spots, but could ascertain no definite direction for it, since such tracks, even though they are all going in a general direction they criss-cross each other in an amazing tangle. From the occasional glimpse of this criss-cross of tracks I established some sort of direction as best I could. But eventually the tracks disappeared altogether and in the course of trying to find them I lost all sense of direction. Then right out there in the middle of it, the snowmobile motor quit. There I was stranded on an open ice field, with winds at about seventy miles per hour, temperature about thirty below zero, and visibility zero in a blinding snow storm. I tinkered with the machine as best I could under the circumstances, but could only take my heavy mitts off for a minute or so at a time. It was too risky to start walking as I had no idea at all of the direction I should go. I decided to stay where I was and wait for rescue, hoping the doctor would not forget me. I felt he wouldn't as he was a man very adequate and precise in his dealings with the northland, with which he had reckoned for many years.

"Meanwhile, back home, after sufficient time had lapsed that I should have arrived, the doctor, trying to appear casual, dropped in on my wife. 'Is your husband home?' he asked.

"'No,' replied Vita, 'I was expecting him, but I assume by now he didn't set out in this storm. Is there something I can do?'

"'No,' he replied, 'just wanted to talk to him.' Then he left.

"Vita knew a doctor didn't come visiting during a snowstorm such as this, just to talk about something unimportant. She feared for and prayed for my safety.

"The doctor alerted several men of the village and they began a search. One of them decided to travel to one of the islands amid the ice span and use it as a lookout. He would know every island, and every aspect of the surrounding landscape and seascape. Taking up position on the most imposing little island, he just sat there peering through the storm. As happens in all snow storms, now and then the wind lets up and you can catch a glimpse of better visibility. On one such let up in the wind, this man saw a speck out on the ice that he knew shouldn't normally be there. On his snowmobile he headed straight for it and it turned out to be me. He gave me a ride home. The next day after the storm had abated, he, with a helper, went to get my snowmobile. The engine started without difficulty and he brought the machine home to me, informing me that if I had continued in the direction I had been going I would have driven into open water.

"'God has been good to me,' I said, as I thanked the man and

God. I was thankful also that church officials in the general office had taken out heavy life insurance on me for my family's sake. They were efficient in that regard.

"The people of this remote area had been in the past, neglected by the governments. But recently there had been an awakening, by the people who wanted better, and by the new government which was just becoming aware that this area too must progress with the remainder of the country which was going through major growth and change. It was with this outlook in mind that there arose the need for a church operating year round instead of just in the summer months as in the past.

"I saw that the first need of our church community there in establishing a permanent year round service to our people, was to build a new residence for the minister. The old one had not been used by the church for many years, but had been rented for a long time and finally condemned by the local people as unsuitable for the cold winters of the north. My family and I would have a very difficult winter in this house, but we realized that some minister had to pioneer, organizing the people to build a new one. I cheerfully decided to take on the task.

"At the same time, education in the area had been neglected in the past by governments. Only by the efforts of the local people was a viable program kept going. Now at this time there was an awakening need for drastic upgrading in the local schools. A school inspector sent by the government to assess the areas educational needs stayed with us during his visit. The present educational circumstances of the whole area he assessed as way below the usual standards of the remainder of the country. It would take a few years to raise it to acceptable levels. He informed us that our children would have to repeat their grades when they left here and attended a regular standard school again. Consequently, for our children's sake, he advised us not to stay any longer than one year.

"Incidentally, to get ahead of my story a little, that is just what did happen when we moved back to the city after one year. The school authorities insisted that our children repeat their grades. We only averted their action by explaining to them that we had sent for school books from the city and Vita taught our children herself to keep them abreast of the accepted curriculum of the school system. At the insistence of Vita and I and particularly of the children themselves, they decided to give them a trial period in the next grade. It worked out well in the children's favor.

"But back to the northland for another while. With the help of the local church board, members of the congregation with building experience, and the doctor who knew how to utilize local conditions for modern conveniences, we set about planning a new house. I had hoped to see the job done before I left, so that the local people would be able to have a full time minister in future.

"Choosing a house plan that was popular everywhere at the time, and for various reasons suitable to the area and building site, I drew plans from it, adapting it for use as a church house with office and modern conveniences as much as were possible there at the time. All materials for the building would have to be ordered by mail and come by ship. It was a tedious job making out such an order, or several orders I should say, for the required goods at the right time to keep them coming in proper sequence as needed.

"Also there was no construction machinery available except a small motorized cement mixer and the use of a jeep. Building would be slower and more labor intensive than elsewhere. It was a pleasure to work with local church officials on this project. They knew what they wanted, when, how and where. There was no problem with them. But there were problems aplenty with the church hierarchy back in the city, under whose authority I was doing this project. They just didn't understand how such a project had to be done in such an area, so I had to oppose them many times. It wasn't easy and it would later take its toll on me personally because of their hurt pride.

"My choice was, one: to listen to the local people and my own observations of the project and build a good house inexpensively at the risk of crossing up the hierarchy; the other choice was to listen to the hierarchy and be a laughing stock of the people in the village, send them hopelessly in debt and put the church there in dire straits for years to come. Naturally I chose to side with the local people.

"The essence of the differences of opinion between me and the hierarchy was this: they were used to letting out contracts and writing checks. In this case the contractors would have to come in from elsewhere. This would cost a small fortune. The government had built a house that way at a cost of fifty five thousand dollars, a lot of money at that time. Even with promised help from the wider church, there was no way the village people could pay their share of such a sum. But village men who usually went out in summer and worked for these contractors agreed to stay home for a summer and build the house at the going wage. The total cost of the house would be fourteen thousand dollars, one third of which the local church people would raise themselves.

"Soon I could detect in the correspondence from the hierarchy, and would later have affirmed in personal meetings with them that they were miffed at my approach to the matter, taking the attitude that I thought myself superior to them. This to me was a silly reaction on their part. It wasn't that they were stupid in mind. It was that their stupid pride was in the way of the opening of their minds to a situation that was new to them. I was determined to see the project through for the sake of the local people and in a way satisfactory to them.

"A shipping strike prevented the building being completed before we left the area. But with the basement in and the walls and interior partitions up, and everything else planned in detail, including electrical, plumbing, and financing, nothing much could go wrong with the project. I left feeling my year there had been worthwhile. Time proved this out. The building was soon completed and to this time our church there has flourished for years with seldom a problem in getting, as I had recommended, a minister without children, to live there, and even ministers with children in later years when education had improved.

"At the end of the church year my family and I returned to the same city in Secundaterra we had left a year earlier, to face we knew not what in the realm of employment for me and education for our family.

"Soon after our return to the city, I visited the general offices of the church with the hope that they would come up with an appointment more suitable to my present needs. There were three men heading up the department that had oversight of my northern ministry and that concerned me now. The chief of them, an older man firmly set in his ways, snubbed me outright by silently passing me by as he insultingly furrowed his brow at me and refused to speak even when I spoke to him. Pride does strange things to some people when it is hurt pride. The second, a middle aged man listened to my request for a new appointment and offered me something worse than before, especially with regard to education for my family. I wasn't sure then, nor have I decided since whether he made that inferior offer just to spite me and put me off, or whether he just didn't know enough to grasp any concept of my circumstances. He was a difficult person to read. However, I politely declined 'for the present.' His offer wasn't at all a suitable one for my needs and that of my family. I turned it down, realizing I would not get any better unless and until I was further educated for ministry, and maybe not even then.

"The third was a younger man, about my own age, with whom I did much preparation work before leaving for the northland. He seemed to be listening to what I was saying concerning what I had tried to accomplish in the northland, and my reason for not staying, but he was noticeably non-committal in his opinion about it all. He was playing it safe in that regard, but remained friendly towards me.

"My family and I continued to attend our church, but at a different congregation now. I didn't want to go back to our previous congregation because people would ask questions about what had happened to my ministry. In response to their curiosity I would of course have to tell them the truth about the inadequacy of the church at large to handle such a mission as that which I was sent upon, and of their treatment of me afterwards. This would for some have a devastating effect on their respect for their church. I had no desire to disrupt anyone's faith or their respect for the church. Some others on hearing my story may simply keep their distance from me. Without thinking it through they would simply interpret it as trouble and want nothing to do with it or me. So we attended another congregation of our denomination and it worked out well.

"Meanwhile Vita had no problem in getting her previous job back. Before our going to the northland she had been well established in a supervisory position with a good corporation run by people chosen for character as well as working skills. The management were non-belittlers who appreciated top-notch employees. There were some belittlers working there, and they tried to do their usual damage, but in this corporation they were so outnumbered by quality people, that they dared not go very far with their trouble making. Another thing that made this place the good environment that it was for a woman was the fact that the employees were nearly all female, and female belittlers of Secundaterra at that time were not so outwardly vicious as male belittlers. So the point is Vita was soon settled in a pleasant good paying job. My family was, after the difficulty described earlier, well settled in school.

"As for me I put ministry out of my mind, but continued my part time studies in arts, and went looking for a job. Throughout the ensuing academic year I landed two jobs, but for me the environment was the same. One way or another I was put down. I knew it would eventually destroy me to try to continue living like that. However, I worked as did Vita and we were able to put aside a little money, with the idea of me entering on a new career come next September. This came about through my correspondence during the winter with an official of a university other than the one from which I was taking courses.

"Through several rounds of correspondence with him I had made arrangements to enter his university to prepare to become a teacher, and I would be able to utilize the courses I had already taken by correspondence. We would have to make another long distance move to do this, but it was necessary for I could not survive where I was. This was an attractive and feasible opportunity. We could see our way through this venture financially also.

"One evening as the time was drawing near for us to pursue this plan, I received a phone call from a minister I had met only briefly once before. 'I notice your name has been on our records for some time now as a candidate for the ministry, and I am wondering if you intend to pursue it,' he inquired.

"'I have tried to pursue it,' I said, 'but it hasn't worked out well.'

"'Would you come to my office in my church tomorrow morning and let's talk about it?' he invited.

"'All right,' I said, without much enthusiasm or intention to get involved again. 'I will come and hear what you have to say.'

"The next morning in his office, I sized him up as one of the better ministers I had come in contact with to date. On telling him the story sketchily of my association with the church in the northland experience he replied, 'Okay, but now that you have sufficient credits to attend full time theology studies you can qualify for a student pastorate near a seminary. That means a small but sufficient income and a house to live in, within commuting distance of seminary. I will give you the name of the person to see. Phone him for an appointment. He is a very nice man. You will like him.'

"This persuasion was convincing enough to make me say 'yes, I will go and see him and then decide what I shall do.'

"Very soon after making an appointment I took a day to drive to and visit the seminary many miles away where I met the Dean and some other members of the staff. The Dean was a gentleman indeed. He came across to me as a man of quality, dignity and reasonable decorum. I knew almost immediately I could study successfully under him. It was also obvious to me that day, on meeting other faculty members that this man had chosen for his staff, people compatible to his own ways and characteristics. I would be able to study under them too, I felt for sure. To make the prospect even more enticing, the Dean showed a liking for me and indicated that my qualifications were acceptable and that I would be eligible for a student pastorate.

"For some days after the visit I weighed matters carefully. I had been accepted at the other university to study to become a teacher, and I knew the man who had processed my acceptance would be all right for me to get along with. But I had no knowledge at all of the various other professors under whom I would have to study. Some would be good I knew from the reputation of the university. But as is always the case, especially in undergraduate studies, there would be a mixture, with some belittlers to put me down. This would be detrimental to me now because through the actions of such people I was gradually becoming more prone to 'breakdowns,' though they were brief and minor. Short periods of exhaustion—complete burn-outs, they actually were. "At the theological school I would have no trouble with the staff. Having met most of them I assumed, and rightly so it proved to be in time, that they and I were compatible. It did seem there was a door wide open, and a welcome mat in place at last for me to enter the ministry. To enter that door would be to answer a felt calling. So I decided to try to answer the call once more rather than take the route to teaching. Although this latter opportunity had held out much hope for me in a time of dire need, still now it held up to me a partly unknown road to follow, on which there would likely be at least some belittlers creating pitfalls for me.

"So for the next three years I studied full time at theological seminary, meanwhile also ministering to three churches. The main one of these was of fair size as smaller churches go. The other two were country cross-roads churches. It was a good three years for me and my family; some of the best of our lives. It was also a good three years for the churches. Overall I did well during that time.

"There were absolutely no belittlers among the staff of the seminary. I do suspect, however, that there were a few, only a few, among the students. I say I suspect because I cannot be sure. In such a good environment with such an excellent staff, if there were any there, they wouldn't dare show their colors.

"One of the events that still makes me think there may have been some belittlers among the students was a particular public speaking class. Together with some other students, it was my turn to make a speech before the class, and as the custom was, there would be class discussion and constructive criticism following each speech. I had made an extremely good speech on a previous occasion, with good emphasis, and as my natural style was, with a distinctive voice and expression that was uniquely mine, so I would in time come to realize. On this day however, I was very weary, having taken care of a late night emergency on my pastorate the night before. As tired as I was I tried now in my speech to do my best, but my style faltered. I did as I have heard many speakers do when they are overtired, I spoke in a drone. My efforts to emphasize in the appropriate places became merely a raising and lowering of the pitch of the drone. I have learned since that time to compensate and do well in such a circumstance. However, at the time I was unaware of such a pitfall until receiving the criticism of the class. Two or three of the students seemed delighted to comment that I had not done well that day. It seemed to give them satisfaction that I had flopped. Other students either during or after the class remarked understandingly about how tired I was. Most students by far showed friendliness toward me, and sought, as they usually did, to support and increase my self-esteem.

"Meanwhile, things were going very well for me on my student pastorate. One of the most influential families of the town in which I now lived and had my larger church, were members of my congregation. They had a wonderful respect for me as a person and as their minister. This family were well regarded people and their influence in the town and in the church was very high. They were in many ways the role leaders of the area. Their liking for me helped a great deal I am sure in bringing about the warm acceptance I received in that town and area. Within a short time of our arrival there, they and most other people had received myself and my family very well indeed. I had a good pastorate there for the three years I was permitted to stay as a student minister. The pastorate prospered under my care, and in years to come went on to higher plateaus of ministry.

"I did make an error that student ministers too frequently make.

I allowed myself to slip gradually into full time ministry while doing full time studies. It cannot be successfully done. Some students who fall into this, lose ground on their studies, getting lower grades. Others, realizing their situation, ease off on the pastorate work, although this is not easy to do once you have things rolling. I tried to keep up both ends, until I became totally exhausted. After a much needed period of rest, and after ironing out some misunderstandings about it, I bounced back again. Then with my priorities and schedules adjusted, I was able to do well enough with both my studies at seminary and my duties of student ministry.

"As indicated previously, I had exemplary reception and treatment from people of quality character at seminary and on my pastorate. This enabled the best three years of our lives up to that time. In later years I had to learn to slow down and rest more whenever I was prone to allow myself to be drawn into too much church work. Church work has a way of doing that to people if they are unaware; you can easily slip into doing too much. But more especially, in the future, when under belittler induced stress, I would need to get plenty of sleep. That would be for me a key factor in surviving the belittlers; getting enough sleep to keep me sufficiently rested so as to retain a clear perspective that would enable me to cope well. This factor will later come again into my discussions.

"In due time I was ordained a minister of the church. In the years ahead I would be out in the field rubbing shoulders with the general ordained ministry, and the laity, many of whom are also of quality character, but many of whom are not, at least when it comes to dealing with people like you and I. And to me that is a test, one among many perhaps, but at least one key test of truly quality character. It is a test as to whether or not envy and hatred will set in on a colleague, or on anyone for that matter, when he feels overshadowed by someone he deems as being a cut above himself. The church at large has its share of belittlers, both in ordained ministry and among the laity. In a church founded on love for all people, the envy and hatred of belittlers sets in and takes its toll. I will tell you more about that tonight and at future group meetings. For now, since I expect this to be a longer session than usual, I would appreciate that five minute break we have been taking."

A recess was agreed to by all present.

One wouldn't expect to find, on any large scale, envy, jealousy, and belittling at work in an organization such as the church, which places so much of its emphasis on fellowship, brotherly and sisterly love, and the commitment to love all peoples—all peoples that is— in all walks of life.

In the Bible incident of Pilate bringing about the decision to release Barabbas or Jesus we read in Matthew 27:18 (R.S.V.) "For he (Pilate) knew that it was out of envy that they had delivered him (Jesus) up. Apparently Matthew could observe that Pilate had detected their envy. Matthew also must have agreed that their cause for delivering Jesus up to crucifixion was envy, or he would never have written it so in his gospel.

Mark also, in his gospel (15:10, R.S.V.) writes much the same thing, "For he (Pilate) perceived that it was out of envy that the chief priests had delivered him (Jesus) up. Regardless of the close relationship of the material used in the writing of the two gospels, it is obvious that Matthew and Mark agreed with Pilate that envy was the cause of Jesus' crucifixion.

Of course some modern pseudo theologians will give other reasons, radical political or even economic reasons, why Jesus was crucified. But it still stands that Jesus was sent to death because envy incited it. Whichever way one may interpret the other issues of the time, it was envy that caused the cruel deed of killing. Take note also, it was not rich business people who instigated the deed, but the proud and envious religious hierarchy and their like-minded followers.

Envy is alive and active indeed in the twentieth century as it was in the first. Christianity has scarcely recognized it, let alone eradicated it even from its own ranks. Many years of hardship were to be endured by Collin Seldon and his family before he was able to make the segment of the church in which he lived and worked, see through the mask to the hatred and hostility that ensued from envy. It was continually robbing him of the life in its fullness that the Christian gospel is able to give. Even when Collin's church, the church at large that is, saw through it and tried to put a check on it, they were unable to grasp fully its devastating significance. So added to the destructive and oppressive treatment Collin and his family had to take from the secular world, would be more of the same from within the church.

Collin hoped that this support group at Quilabet University might be some small beginning towards rooting the problem out into the open. With a prominent psychiatrist, Dr. Eldren, overseeing the group, who knows where the results of this small gathering may go from here! It was such thoughts as this that Collin Seldon had as the group session resumed.

"I wish to relate to you this evening some experiences with envious belittlers following my graduation and ordination," said Collin to the support group which had settled down in session again.

"Before long after my ordination, I had a fairly large congregation, large for the area at any rate; preaching to just under three hundred people each Sunday. It was an active congregation, and it became much more active under my ministry. I was very busy, and I thrived on it, for a while, that is. I need not go into detail about it, except to say that the majority of the congregation cooperated with me. In fact there were no visible dissenters until long after two envious and belittling ministers began their work on me. One was a retired minister attending my church. The other was a neighboring minister with whom circumstances caused me to be working with him on certain projects. I may add, there was another retired minister in my congregation, with whom I got along very well. There was also another neighboring minister with whom I became good friends.

"You in this group now have an adequate idea of how belittlers work. These two belittlers not only came down on me themselves, but in time drove a wedge between me and a segment of the congregation. To add to this problem, the city on the edge of which

I lived was not one of the more friendly cities of the area. Belittlers were predominant there. Within fifty miles there was another city to which I loved to go. With its mostly friendly and fair minded people it would have been a nice place to be living. But here I was living in this generally belittling area. I kept up my heavy activity load through all the trouble but eventually it wore me down to where I could work no longer. I was exhausted in a similar manner as I had been when worn down on my secular job.

"I went to see a renowned psychiatrist in the pleasant city which I just mentioned. He helped me with my predicament for which I was grateful. His diagnosis of my problem, however, gave me a boost for life. He diagnosed my problem as 'emotional fatigue', adding that I had no symptoms of mental illness, and that there was no evidence of such illness in my past or in my family history. Here at last I had something with which to protect myself from the paranoid schizophrenia label. I have been grateful to that doctor ever since. In future some other psychiatrists would come up with the same verdict of me.

"On going back to my congregation, I simply told them what was the easier for me to explain and for them to understand; that I had overworked myself. I could have stayed there, and many of them would have lightened the load for me. However, the real problem was still there. Most of all, I wanted to leave for reasons of a different educational system for my family. So we moved back to our native and beloved Lower Secundaterra where upon making my desires known, I had been offered a church."

Collin now turned his thoughts towards his experiences in the church of Lower Secundaterra and began to relate them to the group.

"On our arrival at our church in Lower Secundaterra, we were delighted at the friendliness shown us by most of the townspeople. Even more so were we enthused by the friendship offered us by the nearby ministers. My congregation was much smaller than the one I had just left behind, but that made no difference to us. We were happy with it. The school for our family turned out to be just what we had hoped for; teachers mostly of what I call the classic teacher type, people of quality culture and integrity; also a good core of friendly, well behaved students with whom our family could make friends. Before long, Vita and I were making friends throughout the area, with business, professional, political, and average people galore. Our friendship with the nearby ministers was a special delight to us. Before a year had expired, however, there were signs that some of these latter friendships were not sound.

"At Christmas time, the local area newspaper, according to its usual custom, asked the area clergy to write a Christmas article for publication. My article was different from the usual extolling of the birth of Jesus, God's Son sent to redeem God's people. My approach was creatively different. The hitherto friendly colleagues were visibly miffed.

"I did my best to continue to foster the friendship. Then on one visit and in discussion with them, I came up with an idea which would be good for some churches other than the ones we were serving; it would save the church at large considerable expense, and I would do the work involved, at no extra financial benefit to me. Both me and the idea were shunned. Twenty years later the idea, now derived from another source, was in use and working well.

"Another piece of work I did put me still further on the wrong side of the belittlers. The minister's residence in which I was living was basically a good house but badly in need of some improvements. I asked the local church for a small amount of money to buy materials and I would do the work myself. The man who held the sway in the congregation more than anyone else had previous to this been zealously protecting his position of prime influence in the local church, and at times showed he felt threatened by my ministry. Being a belittler of sorts, though not very adept at it, he turned thumbs down on my request for money, and no one counteracted him.

"There were some things that needed doing badly, so I bought the materials with my own money. That wasn't easy on us after my only recently coming through three years of seminary on a shoe string of money. However I was able to afford a medium quality product and did the several days work myself. Much to my delight, before long, the women's group of the local church, on hearing of my project, not only raised money to reimburse me for the cost of the materials I had used, but also came up with money for other improvements. Before long we were very comfortable. The only reaction from my colleagues in ministry was criticism for my using a medium instead of top grade product in the first job.

"A minister well up in the ranks of the church of Lower Secundaterra visited the area. I invited him to come for a brief visit with us as his time allowed, which he did. I didn't bring up any of the local problems with him. I felt I should know him better before I did that. In the course of our conversation, we talked about ecumenical affairs, in which I had a keen interest at the time. I showed him a copy of the "Common Bible," a Bible only recently approved by both the catholic and protestant church world wide. Just before returning to Lower Secundaterra I had bought a copy of it very new off the press. The visiting minister looked at it casually, 'O we've got that in our book store back in the city,' he said curtly.

"From the tone in which he said it, I doubted the accuracy of his statement. A little later, when I visited the city, just out of curiosity I went to the book store. On not finding the Common Bible on the shelves, I asked the manager if they had it. He told me they did not have it, and it would be some time before they would get it, the demand being more than production could keep up with. I knew now that there was at least one high ranking minister I wouldn't be able to turn to for help.

"My general ministry was working out well and Vita and I were still making friends with people in all walks of life throughout the area. They liked us and liked my style of ministry. The envious ones were getting colder all the time. As the friendship of my colleagues grew less and less and eventually disappeared, and as other belittlers did their work on me, and with nowhere to turn for understanding and help, I was again getting fatigued, in time nearing the point of exhaustion.

"I couldn't keep up my normal daily pace of ministry with the weight of all the hostility on my mind. Suffering from debilitating fatigue I went to the local doctor who had only recently come to the area from another country and another culture. His background was oriental and he was of a religious faith other than Christian, so he revealed to me in friendly conversation. Out of a combination of my love for the Christian church, and my shame at its behavior, I refrained from bringing before him the shabby behavior there was to be experienced within the church. It may not have done any good to do so anyway, for there was nothing he could do about it.

"'You seem to be under great stress,' he said to me in his broken English, and maybe it is making you depressed, yes?'

"I do not feel depressed," I replied.

"'You can be depressed without feeling depressed,' he said, 'displaying a professional knowledge of the matter.'

"Do you have psychiatric training," I asked him inquiringly.

"'Yes,' he said, 'sufficient for a general practitioner.'

"Okay," I said, "what do you suggest I do?"

"'I will give you some pills,' he said, 'and I suggest you slow down considerably, and try to avoid your stress areas for a while. But sooner or later, as you take up your full duties again, you will have to find some way to take care of your stress areas so that this does not happen again.' Then he remarked, 'You do not give me the impression of being a person with any serious psychological disorder. Maybe the people of your church get difficult sometimes, eh?'

"I responded vaguely that it does get difficult at times. But I could not bring myself to reveal to him the extent that envy and hatred exist even among clergy in a church founded on love.

"Changing the emphasis somewhat, I said, 'I have some vacation time available. How would it be if I took two weeks vacation, and went away to rest for that period?'

"'That would be even better,' he replied enthusiastically. 'If you can do that, then good.'

"Some months previously, a friend had offered me the use of his summer cottage beside a quiet lake, whenever I would like to use it. So off we went to the cottage. After a little more than a week I was feeling myself again. We stayed a few extra days, meanwhile visiting some friends in the area. These friends had seen me when I was exhausted, and were simply amazed at the difference they saw in me now that I was rested and well. The contrast in before and after was so vivid, they could hardly fathom there could be such a difference in a person. Upon returning to my pastorate I was relieved to find that most parishioners welcomed me in a concerned and friendly manner, all except two or three. Another relief, from the overall experience was that I was gradually getting better understanding from doctors. The renowned psychiatrist I last went to in Secundaterra diagnosed my problem as emotional fatigue. Now this latest doctor's diagnosis was that my problem was stemming from excessive stress. This was all progress to me.

"I went back to my ministry in the parish amid the same problems. If anything they were worsened, because now some of the belittlers were saying I shouldn't be in ministry because I couldn't carry the work load.

"To make matters worse a new problem soon arose. I went to the local bank to obtain a small short term loan, for about three months to make a particularly good purchase that came my way. I had a modest savings account in another bank in a city a considerable distance away. But we believed in meeting our present circumstances with our present earnings. We had been banking at this local bank since moving to the area, and already had a car loan from them. I approached the branch manager for a loan of a few hundred dollars for a period of three months. His reaction was, for such a small loan for so short a period, I could simply overdraw my account. He would okay it, and there would be an interest charge. Amid my skepticism about doing that, he assured me it would be okay. I overdrew my account for the amount needed, and it seemed to go okay, for a while that is. On telling this to an experienced bank person later on, I was told it was a wrong practice, and that the person who led me into it probably just didn't want to bother doing up the papers for a small short term loan.

"A month or so later I received a stern letter from the bank area head office. A bank inspector on his routine rounds had noted my overdrawn account and demanded it be corrected immediately or it would be handed over to a collection agency. I went to the bank to discuss the matter and was told the manager was away on vacation for three weeks. The inspector was still there. I tried to explain but he very abruptly told me it was wrong and neither he nor the bank would have any part of it. He treated me as though I had done something very wrong and dishonest.

"I left there and went to my bank in the city, a bank with which I had an excellent credit rating for years. Upon explaining to them what had happened they gave me a bank draft to pay off all my debt including our car loan in full, and I would repay the loan to them. From then on I did my banking at the bank in the city, and never did business at the other or any of its branches again.

"However, it is the repercussions of this experience I wish to point out. As often happens in a small town atmosphere, news of something like that often leaks out, as it did in this case. Here I was with belittlers around me looking for reason to put me down. Now they had something to use. Rumors went around that this minister was in debt and the bank had to come down on him. He wasn't capable of handling his finances well. I tried to explain it to a high officer of the wider church, whom I knew had heard the rumor. He snorted at me and would not listen.

"In time I became worn down and fatigued again. Another high officer of the wider church came to visit Vita and I. He was genuinely concerned, and beginning to have some understanding of what I was up against, but only some. He suggested I make arrangements to see a psychiatrist in the city. I did so through the local doctor I had seen before. The psychiatrist to whom he referred me asked that I come into the hospital in which he worked, for a few days of observation. This I did. During these few days I had plenty of medicinally induced sleep and rest, plus I had some interviews and was under observation at all times.

"Then I was called in to the psychiatrist's office for another interview with him. He was one of the keener psychiatrists I have ever met with. He had come to Lower Secundaterra from one of the most developed countries in the world. He knew western culture well. Moreover, and to my delight he was not only a 'street wise' person, but a fine person as well. He knew, not just psychology, but he knew adult people and their ways out there in the world of reality.

"'As far as I can ascertain,' he told me, 'you have no disorder requiring hospitalization. I do get the impression, however, that you are working under extreme stress,' he continued, 'and this is not the place for you to come and get out from under that stress. It is neither necessary nor good for you to be here.'

"Then he questioned, 'you have had a few days rest here. Tell me how well you are now, using a scale of one to one hundred?'

"After a moment of thought I replied, 'eighty five percent.'

"'If I send you home to rest more with the help of medication,' he said again, 'do you think you can gain the other fifteen percent.'

"Yes,' I replied, 'I feel sure I can with something to help me sleep well for a week or two.'

"'Okay,' he replied, 'I will give you a prescription and send you home to rest. But in addition, I want you to come back to see me as soon as you are rested, and once in awhile thereafter, to tell me about your work and conditions surrounding it. I can only surmise there must be difficult people in ministry and/or congregations of your church, as I have found there to be in the field of medicine. When you are having difficulty with such people, come back and talk to me about it. Maybe we will be able to help you fare better.' His statement surprised me pleasantly. At last I was on my way. So it seemed at the time anyway!"

"O, Oh," quipped Leo, "not yet, eh Collin?"

"No, not yet," replied Collin. "I'll tell you about it as we go along, but you seem to know by now how it goes with me anyway. To continue, I went home, rested up and was back to work within two weeks. After the next two or three weeks of observing and experiencing the belittlers attitudes towards me again, I went back to see the psychiatrist as he had instructed me to do hoping this was my chance of a lifetime. I entered his office with Vita by my side, and told his secretary-receptionist what I was there for.

"'Oh my,' she said, 'you won't be able to see him. You see this is his last day here. Tomorrow he is leaving this city to take a position in another city.' She told us the name of the city. It was three thousand miles away. 'The remainder of his day is taken up with meetings and he won't be taking any appointments.'

"The disappointment was great. But to see him just that day wouldn't have been of much use anyway. I would need follow up for a while. So the whole hopeful idea fell through then and there.

"To make a long story short, I went back to the pastorate, and before long moved to another church hoping to find a better environment. The move was a calamity. Vita and I were total misfits in this community. With a few exceptions we were just too much for people in the community. Our family, by the way, were away to university. In time this new environment caused me to go down hill again. Eventually, I ended up going to the same hospital again for help, hoping to find another wise psychiatrist. This time however, the psychiatrist in whose care I was placed was from the far east, an entirely different culture and religion altogether. He wanted to give me a series of shock treatments, something I hadn't had for a long time. Vita refused him permission to give them to me. Then she went to the church area office and talked to the same officer who had first suggested I go to this hospital away back in time. He was getting to know me by now and to understand my problems somewhat. Being a minister with many connections he was able to communicate with the superintendent of the hospital.

"The next morning a hospital orderly came to my room. 'You are requested to come to the office of the hospital superintendent,' he said.

"'What for?' I asked with much apprehension.

"'Don't know,' replied the orderly, 'but you must rate highly to get such a request. Come with me, I'll show you the way.'

"The superintendent, a kindly, and I think astute man, after conversing with me briefly about where I grew up, where I lived now and how I fitted into the environment there, and all the while sizing me up and figuring me out, said to the orderly, 'I think you can go back to your ward now. If I need you I will call.'

"As the orderly left, the superintendent suggested I sit down. Referring to a file on his desk, he said, 'I have examined the record of your previous brief stay in this hospital and I think there is a lot of merit in the approach taken by your psychiatrist at that time. It's too bad for you he moved away.'

"Yes sir,' I replied, 'I had intended to see him at intervals.'

"'That sounds good to me,' he remarked. 'I will discharge you from the hospital, and your wife can come for you this afternoon, but I want you to give me your word that you will keep contact with a psychiatrist in private practice for several months in case you run into problems again.'

"'I will do so,' I told him.

"'In the meantime,' he said, 'I will see that you get a prescription for medication to help you get rested further. Can you find your way back to your ward yourself?' he then asked, trustingly.

"Yes,' I replied, 'I can.'

"'Then stay on your ward until your discharge this afternoon, and good luck to you.'

"I thanked him two or three times outwardly, but a thousand times in my heart. Now I was getting to where I didn't have to fear being labeled paranoid and schizophrenic, not even depressed. There were some people now who had at least a partial idea of what my problem was. This was a great relief to me. It relieved much of my stress.

"When I returned to my pastorate and began taking the prescribed medication, something clicked in my thoughts. The majority of doctors over the years had prescribed the same type of medication for me. They usually prescribed the average dosage for that medication, about two hundred milligrams per day. This dosage made me sleep more than well. It kept me sleepy most of the daytime as well. Now I began to experiment with the dosage. I knew that if I could get regular sleep, I would never get fatigued. I was getting quite able to cope with the belittlers and all the regular duties of life if I was well rested. In my experimenting, I gradually brought the dosage down to twenty five milligrams per day, taken only at bedtime. This amount enabled me to sleep regularly for approximately eight hours each night and not leave me sleepy the following day. Very occasionally when I couldn't get to sleep at night, I would cut a twenty five milligram pill in two and take an extra half pill. That became my maximum dosage. I would sleep well at night for approximately eight hours, and be able to work next day at my usual above average capacity without either drowsiness or tiredness.

"In future I would have a problem convincing doctors from whom I sought a prescription for this small dosage, that such a small amount would do me any good. Some of them would prescribe only a regular dosage of the average size of two hundred milligrams or more per day. At times I had to go along with that and pare down the dosage on my own. However, I kept taking my own dosage that I knew was right for me, and regardless of all the continuous tactics of belittlers, I never again became fully fatigued or had a 'breakdown' as it was usually referred to.

"The small dosage of medication did the trick for me. But I must emphasize, knowing that some people were beginning to recognize and understand my problem correctly, relieved me of a great deal of the stress under which I had been continually since my first traumatic experience with a psychiatrist.

"One of these people who was beginning to understand me and my predicament was the church officer with whom I had rapport about going to a psychiatrist in the city in the first place. He eventually made arrangements for me to become minister of a developing suburban area just outside the city. Actually over a period of time this area had grown from a rural village to a suburban town. The church there needed to be upgraded to meet the changing life and circumstances of the town. It was a challenge I and Vita with me gladly took on.

"In this town we would be among people who wouldn't feel uncomfortable with us because of our wider experience in the outside world. These people were experienced in city life and felt confident to take their place with anyone. They welcomed and accepted us, and we all worked hard and in harmony to fulfill our task of upgrading the church to meet the needs of an already changed and still changing and growing community.

"The very small number of belittlers that were there, soon dropped out when the remainder of the congregation very emphatically and overwhelmingly accepted us and supported our leadership.

"My ministry flourished in this community. In time our activities, for example among youth and children far exceeded in numbers those of the larger nearby city churches. All phases of church activity prospered. Vita, as a well as working a full time highly responsible job in the city, was organist and choir director for two choirs; oversaw, without holding office, all the women's activities, giving guidance but leaving it to women of the congregation to benefit from the experience of holding office; served on various committees, including a very busy property committee; and in the wider church was very active with the women in a variety of activities that often took her out of town evenings or Saturdays. She worked very hard. So I did myself; preaching, teaching, overseeing building programs, pastoral care work in several hospitals and nursing homes. We both had a very busy life and worked hard and long hours. Everything was going so well for us I decided to leave off taking my small dosage of medication. I did very well without it for some time, until I ran into belittlers again.

"When activities were well established and running smoothly at the local church, I turned my attention to becoming involved in the denominational and ecumenical activities of the wider church of the city, as all ministers were expected to do. It was there I ran into belittlers of various sorts. This didn't stress me as much now as it used to because I knew there were doctors and other people who knew my circumstances and to whom I could talk in case I needed help. This was a great stress reliever. Furthermore I had occasional visits with a psychiatrist in private practice in the city, as I had promised the hospital superintendent I would. This psychiatrist had assured me there was nothing radically wrong with me; just that I had to develop better ways of dealing with obnoxious people as it would be a part of my life always. He often experienced the same in the medical profession, he revealed. I could not help but notice, he too was a fine person, highly respected in his practice and by people generally. He too experienced belittlers.

"I would like at this time to tell you group members of my experiences with belittlers as I endeavored to participate in the wider church; as I tried to establish a bridgehead in the city. I will tell you of incidents rather than a continuous story. These incidents will illustrate further the concept we of this group are trying to establish.

"Eventually I became involved as a committee member of some of the organizations planning and carrying out the work of the wider church. At one such committee meeting with eight or ten members present I began to participate in the discussion, making a suggestion as many others of the group had already done without any problem arising. When my suggestion was made, one of the more senior members of the committee became pouty and perturbed. His perturbance was not because of the content of my idea; it turned out in time to be a sound suggestion. His perturbance was solely because of my effective participation. He was envious of me. My participation deflated him; he could not stand for me to take my rightful place on the committee. He went into a near frenzy. But I continued to participate anyway. It near devastated him, so much so that after the committee meeting I passed through a hallway where he was in a frenzied state of mind and a more mature lay member of the committee was comforting him and trying to help him see the light as he whimpered."

Brett interrupted, "it's easy to see what that guy's problem was. He didn't know how to accept or react to someone he saw in his own mind as being a cut above himself. It wasn't your problem, it was his, and he was badly in need of therapy for it."

"Yes," agreed Collin, "that was *his* problem. He was well up in the church as a leader, doing good work, well respected, and coming up with a lot of ideas of his own, yet he was bothered that another person, a fine person, might come along and perhaps outdo him on it. I had no intention of trying to do so. I just knew I had a right to participate. It is a common characteristic of belittlers that they do not know how to accept or react to people they deem to be in some way a cut above themselves. You have hit the nail on the head, Brett.

"At another committee meeting with a different group of people, there was a minister who had tried to show some arrogant dominance over me at times before. During an intermission in this all day meeting he asked if I would like to go for a walk with him. I thought to myself, this may be a chance to befriend him and bring about a proper relationship. I agreed to go for the walk. He was taller and bigger than I and much younger. As we walked, I had to exert myself a little more than he to keep up with him. He noticed this, and grinning at me said, 'having a job to keep up, eh?'

"'Not bad,' I replied, 'you're a little taller than I but its okay.'

"With that he speeded up more, now silent, and grinning at me still. I just smiled back, and kept pace with him. Before the walk was ended back at the committee meeting place he had tired and was lagging behind me noticeably. I pretended I didn't notice. He was cold toward me for the remainder of the day, visibly showing perturbance at my participation in the meeting.

"This incident shows another characteristic of belittlers. They are, in their minds, always in rivalry with those who inadvertently upset their proud sense of superiority they wish to maintain.

"Meanwhile my ministry in the local church was going exceedingly well, including my pastoral care work in the city's hospitals and nursing homes where I continually had people to visit and give spiritual care. I became well known by various staff members of these hospitals.

"One day the supervising chaplain of hospitals for the whole city, a minister of another denomination, approached me. First he told me something I already knew, that the hospital chaplain of our denomination was to retire at the end of the church year. Then he surprised me out of the blue.

"He said, 'The hospital staff people with whom we chaplains

come in contact would all like for you to apply for the position of chaplain of the city's hospitals for your denomination, and work with us as a team throughout the city's system of pastoral care. They all feel they can work well with you and they like you.'

"I was surprised indeed, very pleasantly so. I had always enjoyed that part of my ministry and was delighted at the invitation. I told him I would look into it and consider it.

"The minister who had previously been so snooty over the 'Common Bible' incident was the chairperson of the committee to oversee chaplaincy work. Soon after the invitation, I approached him on the matter. He was cold and flippant in his response, as though I were trying to interfere in his work. He said something to the effect that he had been looking after that aspect of the church's work for some time now, and he would continue to do so. With a contemptuous scoff he turned away from me. I dropped the matter, knowing full well that I would have no chance with it. In time another minister was given the position, and he did the work very well.

"I might add here for information sake that this was not the only time I was eyed for a good position. For example, on behalf of the church at large I once conducted a meeting at a church much larger than the one I presently had. Several at the meeting asked me to be their next minister. I knew there was a lot of support for my style of ministry, and for myself as a person. This helped to sustain me as the belittlers kept trying to put me down.

"There was another incident where at a large gathering we were, during the course of the event, divided into groups of about fifteen people for seminar type discussions on a church matter. As I tried to participate in my group, the leader of it, a minister who was doing well in a large church, took objection to my participation. As I started to speak, and before I fully expressed a thought on the matter, he whimpered angrily like a spoiled child, in objection to my participation. It was as though he thought I had no business to participate and spoil his day on him.

"A month or so later, there was a similar conference, at which again we broke up into the same committees. I was feeling tired and edgy on this day, and decided not to participate for concern that I might tell the seminar leader off for his maltreatment of me. I knew nobody would understand, and I would have to take all the blame for causing a fuss, so instead, I went for a walk. This caused a very real problem for me. A church official saw me out walking around. The fall out from the incident was that I was lazy, too lazy to attend the meeting. As I said, I was tired that day. Yes I was beginning to fatigue again and starting to show it. Soon I went back on my one pill per night and saved the situation.

"Some time later, I attended a different committee meeting, at which would preside the church officer who thought I was lazy. It was to end around one p.m. However, far past that time the work still wasn't covered so it was suggested we all go out for lunch together and then come back to finish. I asked to be excused. The church officer jumped on me quickly, before I had time to explain why.

"'Why don't you want to participate further in this committee?' he asked abruptly.

"I explained to him that since this meeting was planned to end at one o'clock, I had an afternoon event planned with a class of twenty three youth for 3 o'clock as they came out of school. No way would I let these children down. There was no more objection. Twenty three youth was far more than some of the big city churches were mustering. Still the inference of laziness stuck for some time.

"Eventually, a minister who could see and appreciate my abilities, asked me to be the secretary-treasurer of an organization within our denomination that carried out needed projects at large throughout the city. I accepted. As secretary-treasurer I worked very closely with the chairman of the organization, himself a minister. He was a good sort, with no hang-ups, and we got along very well. I helped him keep completely informed of our finances and the many aspects of our work. With both of us working so well together the organization had a bumper year. In his closing summation at the end of the year, and before a new slate of officers were to take over, he first spoke of our attainments. Then he paid me a tribute, one of few I have ever had in my life. He said he could not have done the job so effectively if it were not for my work and support. Most of my belittlers were present to hear that tribute, but it changed them not an iota. Their long faces were blank.

"At that time, however, as I looked at their expressionless profiles, a most emphatic thought came to the forefront of my mind. It was as if it was from my mind's recesses where I knew it only vaguely but now it would become a part of my full consciousness. The thought was something like this, 'Collin, you will never know a time in your life when belittlers are not looking down on you or trying to put you down and keep you down. You have to accept that as an integral part of the life of a person like you. However, it is not a normal way to live. Abnormal characters are inflicting wounds upon you continually. The only way you will be able to stand up to it is to get your sleep, and the only way you will get your sleep is to take your pill at bedtime for the rest of your life. Accept your predicament as a part of your life and decide to live with it.' It was like a new religious experience in my life.

"From there on," said Collin to the support group, "I very consciously accepted my lot in life, learned to live and cope with it better as time went on, and did the best I could under the circumstances. That was several years ago, and to this time I have not been fatigued, or broken down since."

"Hurrah!" exclaimed Leo, as he clapped his hands lightly.

"You found a way, didn't you?" remarked Owen.

"Yes, I found a way," answered Collin, "and on top of that, at least some people began to understand, at least partially what I had to contend with in life. I will tell you another incident or two that will illustrate belittling in high places, and how some people were trying to come to my rescue.

"There was to be a very special ecumenical church service in a city cathedral, with the highest dignitaries from every denomination, and some from across the land. It was a national occasion. On the spur of the moment I, being present, was asked to participate in the service in place of a church officer who was suddenly unavoidably absent. I was thrilled to do so. Being designated to lead in a litany, I found a robe and sat in the chancel with many other clergy. When the time came for me to read, the awesomeness of the occasion set the adrenaline flowing through my system. I knew that the natural response of my voice would be that it would boom out in a notably distinctive style as it always did on very special occasions. For a split second, thoughts flashed through my mind, *Should I repress my voice in order to avoid future retribution, but also go down as mediocre in my performance, or, should I give it all I've got and take the consequences.* I quickly chose the latter. As I read the first lines a hushed awesomeness came over the huge congregation. Then in reverent and emphatic tones the responses came back. It turned out to be a highlight of the service.

"A few days later, while standing among a crowd of people waiting for the door of a public place to open, I approached a minister of the denomination in one of whose churches the special ecumenical service had been held. It was a minister who had always been friendly to me. Standing with him was the church dignitary who had been in charge of the ceremony that day. He held a very high office with jurisdiction over a large portion of the nation. As the friendly minister attempted to introduce me to him, he turned his nose in the air and away from me. The minister friend was distraught. 'But,' he protested feebly to his church official, 'this is a good guy, he's all right.' I walked casually away to save my friend further embarrassment.

"Shortly after that, this same church dignitary was speaking at a major function in a church of my denomination. I sat several pews down the aisle with members of a procession. And now before a congregation of several hundred people, he focused his gaze on me and apologized that he had hurt someone. Many could tell who he was focusing on. It was very embarrassing to me, but I sat motionless and without visible reaction.

"This story illustrates the instinctive attitude against excellence and success that is prevalent among many people, even among people who themselves have been successful. I would note here also that someone had gotten through to that dignitary, no doubt the minister who had been with him at the doorway. There were indications also that officials of my church had been talked to about it also. I mention this to show you that at last some people were beginning to understand what was being done to me, and trying to ease or correct the situation.

"It is ironic that at that same function where one belittler apologized to me, another snubbed me openly. As we gathered in the church hall, robed for the procession, the minister of the 'Common Bible event' chose to practice his belittling again. He still hadn't learned anything new about his behavior. As I stood among the crowd talking to a very good minister friend, this belittling minister would come by, say a few words to my friend, then glare at me, put his nose in the air and walk away without speaking to me even to say hello. He did this no less than three times. My friend recognizing the snubbing that was going on remarked, 'Collin, its rough all right.'

"To me it was a part of the course by now, a fact of my life.

"Again it is even more ironic that some of the worst belittlers of Lower Secundaterra used as an excuse to belittle me that they didn't need smart alecs back from Secundaterra showing them what to do. Later they went to live in Secundaterra themselves.

"Another occasion of snubbing comes to my mind. At an area church committee meeting with several people present, a debate took place on the floor concerning a financial matter. Since I was the secretary-treasurer of the committee, I felt I had every right to speak on the matter. I had already formed my own opinion on it, but as my custom was, I waited to see if someone else would come up with the same view. I could play low profile and let them decide for themselves. Two different plans on the matter were expressed. One of these was almost identical to mine, so as the plans were being summed up, I agreed with the one nearest my own thoughts, making only one suggestion for a minor amendment. The amended plan was accepted by the body as a whole. Strangely enough though, after the meeting, and during the refreshment and fellowship period that followed, the two who had proposed opposing plans socialized with each other quite amicably. After they parted, I went to socialize with the person whose plan was not accepted, and he very clearly snubbed me and walked away.

"Again I would bring to the attention of the support group," said Collin, "that this is still another characteristic of the more extreme belittlers. They don't want people like us to do anything or be anything. They will put us down no matter what."

Owen asked, "what do they expect you to do with your life?"

Collin replied, "most of them don't think that far ahead. They are just bent on putting us down, not thinking beyond the moment. Or at least that is so for Secundaterra and Lower Secundaterra."

"What about in Terraprima?" Owen jumped in anxiously.

"In Terraprima it's a different game altogether. In many cases they know full well what they are doing, and they do it mercilessly. Starting as soon as time allows I will tell you of the experiences of a minister friend of mine who went to Terraprima, what happened to him, and what could have happened to him had he not been able to salvage himself."

"Sounds drastic to me," commented Gilda.

"Drastic but not hopeless," responded Collin. "I will tell you about it later. But for tonight I wish to finish my story to where it puts me where I am now in life."

"Carry on," agreed Gilda.

"To continue with another incident with people in high places, I will tell you of a Terraprima professor of high standing, from a renowned school of theology, who was invited to Lower Secundaterra to present a continuing education course on preaching.

"Advanced instructions had been given to all who registered for the course, me among them. We were to have certain readings done and a sermon prepared on one of a choice of topics. I went to the course well prepared, but would soon find my preparation was of no avail. The professor, I would soon discern, was a belittler to the Nth degree. From the beginning he showed no friendship towards me as he did the others.

"During the week of the course, the previously prepared sermons were presented at intervals, interspersed with discussion and other teachings on the art of preaching. The professor chose to begin with the student who sat on the side of the oblong table opposite to me, and then work his way around in a direction towards where I was sitting. On the morning that it had become the turn of the person sitting beside me on my right, I fully expected to be called upon after him. The person on my right made his presentation and there followed the usual evaluation of it. It was not yet mid morning, and time for two more presentations. Now the professor quite openly and brazenly went back to the starting point at the side of the table opposite to me, and asked the person to the right of the starting person at the beginning to make his presentation. From there the presentations continued around the table in the opposite direction, working towards the person on my left. I knew I was being snubbed of course, and reconciled my mind to being last. As the week ended, however, I was to learn that I would not even be last. The professor worked his way around the table until the person on my left presented his paper, and the follow-up discussion was through. Then he blatantly announced that was the end of the course, that we were through more than an hour early, and we could go.

"My path crossed with that belittling professor only once more. He was invited to preach at a large combined Lenten gathering of a number of our churches. Because of the way that event went for me, I acquired the impression that some church officials may have either redressed him or consulted with him concerning my peculiar circumstances which some of them were by now getting to know. I knew it was a custom of the Lower Secundaterra clergy to consult on a variety of matters, with visiting dignitaries. The incident I have in mind made the event a memorable occasion for me. At one point in his sermon, he stuck his eyes into me as I sat in a pew towards the rear of the church and he said introspectively and sulkily, 'I guess I am a coward of a sort. Yes I suppose I am, since I don't stand up to those troublesome and obnoxious people in the church, but rather avoid confrontation, in which case they generally get their way.'

"As he spoke, I thought to myself, *my dear man, you are not merely one of the cowards, you are one of the most obnoxious of people. You need a whole lot more introspection yet before you get the matter into proper perspective.*' Outwardly, I just smiled at him and he abruptly changed the subject, turning elsewhere in the congregation.

"Following the service, I purposely stood in line to greet him, wondering how he would behave in close quarters. As I attempted to converse with him, his eyes got shifty and he said, 'I haven't met you before. I don't know you.'

"I replied, 'yes, we've met on occasion. God bless you,' and I walked away, thinking, why else would he single me out among four hundred people, all strangers to him to tell me he didn't know me, other than to cover himself for his shabby behavior.

"Here was a belittler from Terraprima, of the most seasoned kind. As I would learn much later, they quite commonly play the belittling game there, in high places and low, in a much more sophisticated and skilled manner than ever the dirty, destructive game had been played in Lower Secundaterra, or in Secundaterra either for that matter. In these latter places, belittling was practiced by individuals and in a haphazard way only. In Terraprima, the game is highly developed into a widespread, conspiracy type, vicious, destructive weapon. Here was this *Christian* professor spreading his discriminatory and poisonous venom into territory where it had never before existed."

"Now you really have me wondering about Terraprima, remarked Owen. You know I have a vested interest in the place. You will have to tell us about it."

"I will indeed," assured Collin, "but first I wish to finish my own story tonight."

"Carry on," Gilda said eagerly. "Here you are with us in Secundaterra. We need to know how you came to be here and your present circumstances."

Collin continued to relate his circumstances and experiences.

"Many in Lower Secundaterra with whom I rubbed shoulders

were beginning to see my problem and were understanding of it. Also, now that I was always getting enough sleep I was wearing the belittlers out rather than they wearing me down. They were easing off. There were also some new church officers on the scene, from whom I was getting fair play, and even more important, at least a partial understanding of my predicament. I was being accepted by more and more clergy in the field. I think I could have well made the grade there for life; gradually being accepted by sufficient clergy and officials. We already had numerous friends among the lay people.

"However, our family, now educated through university had moved away for career reasons. Vita and I had to decide whether to stay in Lower Secundaterra where we had already established and put into action some of our plans for eventual retirement there, or, move to Secundaterra to be nearer family. Our plans and acquired property for retirement would have been lovely. Nevertheless, we decided to give it up in order to be closer to family and see them more often. So we moved to Secundaterra again.

"I started there with a small town church in which I had a mostly pleasant ministry. There were some power and control people there who, as they usually do, prevented my exercising a fully effective ministry, and some belittlers did appear on the scene. Overall though it was a pleasant and effective ministry with an abundance of nice people.

"Belittlers were not overly plentiful among the clergy in the general area of my ministry there, but there were occasional incidents. For example a minister of a large city church attended my church when on summer vacation. He became envious of me, showing it in obvious ways; haughtiness towards me, and snubbing me. At a town public function which he and a colleague friend of his attended, he tried a sneaky maneuver. His friend came to me privately, aside from the two dozen or so people present, and in a round about way began to inquire as to the sources of my sermon materials. I immediately suspected what was happening, even more so I figure, than the person who was inquiring. I asked him politely, 'does your friend,' calling him by name, 'want to know this to help him with his work?' 'Yes,' he replied innocently, 'he suggested I ask you.'

"Well,' I said, 'I have read thirty books over the past year. But that alone won't do it. It takes a good mixture of study and the Grace of God to preach worthwhile sermons, the latter being very important.

"His face expressed a mixture of wonder and bewilderment as he went back to his colleague. I don't think he was wise to his belittler friend and the envy motivation that had set him up to do this sneaky task, nor why the belittler hadn't come to make the inquiry himself.

Collin then remarked to the support group, "I'm not really a bookworm. To be honest I seldom read that many books in one year. But I had done so in that year for a special reason.

"Now to continue, from that time on this belittler did his best to plague me. For example again, a wider church official was scheduled to be present and conduct an important meeting with my congregation after Sunday morning worship. The official didn't show, so I conducted the meeting myself, with no time to look up the rules on such a meeting. I did have a good general knowledge of the matter at hand, and the meeting was proceeding very well. The belittler minister had been present for worship and stayed for the meeting. Part way through he caused a disturbance by stomping out of the meeting, telling several people on the way, that I had made a mistake in procedure and the meeting wasn't valid. I would have been happy to have his correction and help if he had been willing to offer it in a satisfactory manner. His actions showed he was more interested in discrediting me rather than helping me. It was a crucial meeting and we did accomplish our purpose to the satisfaction of both the local and the wider church.

"In addition to that, this belittler, quite often at wider church business meetings, would shun, snub, and try to intimidate me by continually showing off to me what a big wheel he was. Some friendly ministers who had known me for years previous, caught on to what he was up to and I assume, in my absence took him to task for it. In future, he did me no harm; even showed indications of remorse and improvement in his behavior towards me."

Said Collin to the support group, "The latter part of this incident shows how readily this problem of belittling can be met and changed. The awareness of it by other people, and the self awareness of the belittler, can often change the mind-set that causes the whole problem.

"In contrast to this I must tell you of another incident which actually amuses me. A minister and his wife from a large church of another city also attended my church each year while on summer vacation. The minister attended regularly during his vacation period, and his wife only occasionally. In conversation with one of my parishioners, the minister's wife revealed that she liked to have a break from church during the summer, 'but my husband,' she remarked, 'he wouldn't miss a service here for any reason. He gets enough ideas from Collin Seldon's sermons to do him for six months after we return to our home church.'

"I had no problem with that. He was a friendly, good natured, well motivated person.

"I will tell the group of just one more incident," said Collin, "this one is of a belittler in high places again. One day I was seated in about the center row, one among nearly two hundred people in a church that can accommodate about four hundred. At the front of the church, sitting at a table, was a panel of three people, among whom was the editor of a major religious publication. This editor fixed his eye contact on me quite frequently throughout the presentations by the panelists. I could not tell whether he had a friendly or a hostile attraction towards me.

"A question and answer period followed, and thinking perhaps the editor just might be viewing me as a person he would be interested in hearing from, I decided to ask a question concerning an aspect of his publication. I did this amiably, much more so than some others had bothered to do, and who had received pleasant replies. I asked him about his perhaps making an effort to fill the gap between the church hierarchy and the people in the pews, intending to go on then to express what I felt that gap to be. The editor could hardly wait for me to finish my first sentence before he began to growl at me.

"'I'm already working on that gulf,' he snarled, emphasizing the word 'gulf' as if to go me one better over my use of the word gap. 'My emphasis has been for some time now to close that 'gulf, and I am doing it successfully,' he went on hostilely.

"Then as he proceeded to name various articles he had published to accomplish this, it became evident to me that we each had opposite views of what that gap or gulf was. What he thought was narrowing the gulf, I looked upon as widening it. Whichever one of us had the more accurate view is beside the point. The point is that other people asked him questions, some of them sticky and negative questions too, and he responded in a civil manner. When I asked a question his response was hostile and defensive. Here is a classic example of a defensive belittler.

"Another person present took notice of the belittlers problem and spoke out to him, 'it's a good publication; nobody is questioning that, even though it may not be perfect.'

"There was no response to that remark."

"I would add here, the only time I saw that editor again was at another, much larger conference of about five hundred people. There he sat, at a news media table with reporters, and other people of his profession, listening in what appeared to be a very casual manner as though only half tuned in, all the while picking his nose in full view of the whole auditorium of people. His self awareness appeared to be nil. From my first encounter with him it was evident that his natural, even if unconscious bent was to be automatically down on anyone he deemed to be a cut above himself. This incident points out to me very clearly the great need many people have for far more self awareness in many areas of life. In our interests they need particularly an awareness of their erroneous mind-set to be automatically hostile and down on fine dignified people.

"Overall, things went fairly well for me in Secundaterra. Several colleagues in ministry became aware of my predicament with people whom we here in the support group are calling belittlers. These colleagues kept after the wayward ones and eventually I was in a fairly good environment, doing well in the local church and participating well in the church at large.

"In time I began to seek for another, larger more challenging congregation. I asked some ministers with whom I had worked well on committees if I could use their names as references. They agreed, but as far as I was able to discern and find out, the references never came. The reason, one person told me, was that my health record had followed me, and many people did not want to take a chance on me by giving a reference. Whether the laziness label had followed me also, I do not know. I do feel, however, that both Vita and I disproved that one sufficiently to many people. It is notable that even though my predicament with belittlers was now kept in check, my helpers, to my knowledge, never did see the problem as the cause of my past adverse health record. Often public knowledge of this area of life in which we of the group find ourselves is next to nil.

"Eventually I did get a medium size pastorate with a suburban congregation; suburban to one of my favorite cities where belittling is present but not predominant; a city in which I would be pleased to live anytime. I will tell you how I got it. I was asked by a church official to conduct meetings with and oversee this particular pastorate's search for a new minister. During the course of the meetings with the appropriate committee they took a liking to me, my work style, ability and personhood. They asked me to become their minister. It was a progressive congregation, not dominated by belittlers, so I accepted their invitation. I am still there, and having a pleasant, truly Christian ministry. Belittlers tend to drop away when they cannot dominate a church or other situation. That's what happened to make this church so pleasant. The better people took over the leadership with me. But still to this day, in my interaction out in society, whether in places of business or of leisure, whether in something special or in the ordinary course of life, belittlers still peck away at me. My age makes no difference, nor does my occupation. They have no respect for either. It is something I have to accept and endure to my dying day."

Collin Seldon paused, looked around at the group members and smiled happily. "Reviewing a mostly unpleasant past," he said, "is burdensome, but sometimes necessary. Now that it is over I feel enlightened. But I have kept you late. Where do we go from here, Dr. Eldren?"

"You have done well, Collin," said the doctor. "Now concerning the story of your friend in Terraprima, how much time do you need for it?"

"At least several sessions," replied Collin, "I can't say exactly."

"Then I'd suggest it wait until next semester," said Dr. Eldren, "If you wish, members, we can meet next Wednesday and have Collin lead us in some reviewing of what we have done so far. Then let us adjourn until the new year when we can take as much time as needed in the winter semester. How does that sound to you, Owen?"

"I'm delighted," said Owen, "that we can have time like that. Is it all okay with you Collin?"

Collin agreed and added, "In Terraprima the whole tactics system of belittlers and mind-game players takes a different twist. There, it is a highly developed, sophisticated and treacherous art, not only of individuals as here, but at times of many birds of a feather, in their own way, flocking very closely together to make it into a conspiracy of sorts to maim or destroy. There is evidence that the phenomena is finding its way to this land and will eventually be practiced widespread here as well, so I think the matter will be relevant to us. Do you find that to be in order, Dr. Eldren?"

"I certainly do," he replied enthusiastically. "We need to cover the whole problem while we are at it. For now we can adjourn until next week."

It being later than usual the members decided to omit a gathering at the coffee shop until the following week. They went to their cars in the parking lot and drove away into the night.

# CHAPTER THIRTEEN

The support group met again on Wednesday evening, Room 405, as usual. This last session of the semester was to be of a review and analysis nature.

Collin began by suggesting, "I would like now for us to go back and review incidents in the life stories each of you have told during our group meetings. We can use your experiences to illustrate further just how society as a whole, and we and people like us in particular, are affected by belittlers. Perhaps we can learn more from doing so. Would the members of the group agree to that?"

The response was unanimously positive.

Collin began. "We can easily see by Leo's difficulty at first in explaining peoples attitudes, why most people don't bother to explain such things, or even think them through rationally to themselves. It can be a mind-boggling experience. Most people spare themselves by shrugging off such attitudes of belittlers as immature, odd, obnoxious, personality conflict, funny person, contrary person, mean person, ignorant person, and the like. Also, as I have said previously, many people do not have problems with belittlers to the extent fine people do, so they have no pressing need to pay much attention to them or their odd behavior.

"But let us briefly explore Leo's experience with the professor with whom he had difficulty. That this professor was a belittler there is no doubt, but what was it that triggered off his behavior? No one knows exactly and for sure except the professor himself. However, had Leo or any one of us been in close contact with him, like working with him all day every day during the week, we would have heard now and then muttering remarks and cutting inferences that would have indicated his problem with us. From past experiences of working with similar people, I can rather safely surmise one or more of the things about Leo that was bothering the professor.

"First, it may well have been that the professor saw in Leo either the clean cut, fine appearance, or, the creativity of his mind, or, a combination of both that the professor would like for himself. It may seem preposterous at a glance, that a professor be envious of a student, but it is not. I have seen people in far higher positions envious over someone seemingly far beneath him or her, yet perceived in some way by the belittler to be a reason for envy. This has been a frequent observance and experience of mine over the years.

"Another twist that may have triggered off this professor as it does many people like him is that he may have seen in Leo what he would like to see in his own son. Whether he has a son or not we do not know, but this is a possibility.

"Or again, perceiving Leo as such a fine person, the professor may have surmised that Leo was therefore from a wealthy family. Belittlers frequently in their minds make such an association. The professor may have always wanted to be wealthy, perhaps so he could look fine too, so he thinks in his warped emotions. So he turns on the one he thinks has accomplished or inherited what he himself would like but does not have.

"Whatever the particular reason of the moment and experience, the belittler is compelled to put the fine person down to where the belittler can feel above him. In doing so he is thereby protecting his pride and convincing himself, and, he often hopes, others around him that he himself is the better of the two. Such belittlers by their nature, live a life of rivalry, but it only really shows when their envy and hatred are stirred into action.

"It is so easy to assume that Leo, in his childhood and youth was discriminated against because he was the son of a notable man, a judge. But in our discussion of other aspects of Leo's life, we find that Leo has a sister and a brother, children of the same notable judge, yet who are not discriminated against to anywhere near the same degree as was Leo. Actually Leo was discriminated against mostly, perhaps totally, for himself, because he is a fine intelligent person who appears to the belittlers to be rich. A belittler could never admit the real reason however, so he justifies his belittling action by making himself, and hopefully others believe that he is simply putting down a disgustingly rich person, or a snobbish big wheel or the like. That is a popular thing to do in many circles, indeed in some surprisingly, supposedly circles of good repute.

"When Gilda was telling her story," continued Collin, "it was obvious to me that she wasn't aware, not fully at least, why she was being picked on. She too assumed, I think, that it was because of her father's prestige and notability in the area. That may sometimes be a part of it, but only a part. When Gilda was telling us of her grade five experiences, in answer to my probing she revealed that there was a girl in the class from a much more wealthy family than Gilda's. The teacher didn't pick on that girl. This was a very vivid illustration. At the time Gilda wondered if I was suggesting that it was somehow her own fault that the teacher picked on her and not on the more wealthy girl.

"It should be very obvious to you now, Gilda, that the teacher was down on you because of the fine person you were, and using your family's supposed wealth as an excuse for doing so. The other girl, although from a more wealthy family than yours, was not such a fine person, and therefore did not disturb the belittling teacher into envious action."

"I remember that incident in our group discussions, Collin," remarked Gilda. "Over the weeks since, I have come to understand quite well the difference between myself and the other girl, and the teacher's very different attitude toward each of us. Also, I realize now that even then I suppressed thoughts in the recesses of my mind that I was picked on by that teacher in grade five because of the kind of person I was myself, aside from my parents position in life. But I was terrified to bring it out in the open and face it myself let alone talk about it to anyone else. It would be so easy to be accused of all sorts of things, conceit, delusions, paranoia — but now I can talk about it, in this group anyway."

"That's another burden lifted now," Collin responded.

Leo added, "I supported Gilda strongly in that discussion. It was near the beginning of our sessions. I guess we have all come a long way since then. Thanks Collin, your key point is very well taken. You stuck me with a similar question when I was telling my story. I was only partially aware of the correct reason for people picking on me. It had been suppressed into the back of my mind for so many years I was unable to bring it out and state it in words for fear of embarrassment. It is hard to talk about such things oneself. To hear someone else talk about them makes it easier."

Donna Coyne spoke next, "I was aware of what your were probing for in these pointed questions, Collin. I thought perhaps you would ask the all revealing question when I was telling my story. I braced myself for it. Since it has been discussed, I am relieved."

"I noticed you became tense Donna when we discussed that your problems with belittlers were there because you are a fine person. I did not know if Dr. Eldren would have understood at that time. He does now, I feel sure."

"Yes I think so," replied Donna with an obvious sense of relaxation coming over her.

Dr. Eldren simply smiled and nodded.

Collin continued, "Again when Gilda referred to herself as a butterfly easily open to attack because of its openness, I added 'because of its color also,' It seems Gilda, consciously at least, found no meaning in my remark at the time. What I was really saying was that Gilda is a colorful person. She stands out, can be easily spotted among people. Because of her standing out as such an all around fine person she, like the butterfly, easily becomes a target for the hawk, as she called one belittling professor.

"A little later when I asked Gilda what the overall appearance of the other belittling professor was like, Gilda revealed that her appearance was not what it could be. It seems she had not advanced beyond her younger girlhood with regard to her choice of clothes and personal care. Gilda's appearance is always very good indeed. There is, therefore every reason to assume that this professor saw in Gilda something of what she ought to be, and probably could be to some extent, perhaps to a significant extent if she bothered to try. Instead, rather than pull herself up, she chose to put Gilda down."

"Collin, I have a concern," Leo spoke up. "You said of the professor with whom I was having trouble that he may have seen in me what he would like to be himself. But referring to Gilda's problem with the professor she called the hawk, he was a male professor. Is it likely he saw in Gilda what he would like to be?"

"That's a good question, Leo," replied Collin. "It is not likely he wished to be a woman like Gilda, although that too is possible in some cases of confused sexual identity. But within our purposes in this group there is indeed the possibility that the 'hawk' as he has been referred to, saw not in Gilda's femininity but simply in her fineness, a person who stood out, a person of stature and high profile. This is one of the usual desires of a belittler, to stand out in the public eye and be recognized. This is quite likely, Leo. I have seen many such instances.

"On the other hand, though, the problem between this particular professor and Gilda could have been that he wished his wife or his favorite daughter could have the outstanding mixture of qualities possessed by Gilda. He should have been broad minded enough to accept and make the very best of what is, to improve where possible, and to realize that life does bestow gifts on some that it does not bestow on others; that each person, no matter what the gifts, has his or her own uniqueness. Instead of accepting this, the belittler becomes envious and seeks to bring down those he perceives to be ahead of him, or his wife, or his daughter, as the case may be."

Leo half smiled, half grimaced. "You speak of a person's fineness as being a gift," he remarked. "I wonder sometimes if it isn't mostly a curse."

"I understand the point you are making Leo," replied Collin. "Many people, perhaps most people, including belittlers and non-belittlers, seem to think it is a great privilege for people like us to be as we are. Little do they know of the tremendous trials and tribulations it puts us through. It is a gift I would say, but the lack of understanding of so many good people, together with the injustice done to us by the obnoxious belittlers and their supporters certainly does, in far too many instances turn it into a curse for us. This often prevents our gifts from being utilized to their fullest extent not only for our own fulfillment, but for the contribution we could make to society."

Collin continued, "There is a point I would like to make concerning Gilda's coping with her circumstances. When she decided to return to university, she told her father, 'this is something I have to do on my own.' Gilda's parents were behind her all the way, but they didn't understand the problems she had to face in life. Neither did the psychiatrist she had while in hospital for a short time. I think Gilda made a very wise move in eliminating these people from her confidence concerning her problems with belittlers. To include any of them, even if they had tried to understand, would have been just an extra weight to carry. It would be only educating others to her problems; an extra and difficult chore that would be energy draining and often frustrating and of absolutely no help to Gilda herself. Throughout my own life, I have kept my problems within the sphere of a very few friends, simply because it would wear me out to include too many others. Here in this group, where we all understand each other, although it is not always easy emotionally, it is quite viable and without undue stress.

"How critically important it is though that more and more people should become fully aware of belittlers, their pride, envy and hatred, and how they drastically affect the lives of people like us and of various people to varying degrees. Had Gilda's parents been aware of the warped ways of belittlers when Gilda was in grade five, they could have probably done something to save at least a whole year of misery for Gilda, and perhaps more. Maybe they could have saved her from a burden she carried with her unconsciously for years afterwards; the burden of having the feeling she had to do well in order to be worthy of her parents respect.

"How immensely important it is for the numerous people like that grade five teacher of Gilda's, to come to an awareness of the terrible harm they are doing to other peoples' lives! Not only do they hinder proper human growth and development, they often destroy people to the extent that they are no longer of use in society.

"I would guess that far more mental illness is caused by belittlers than by poor parenting of children in their early years. A tremendous amount of thorough research has been done on early childhood and its weakening or strengthening effects, as the case may be, on later life. Yet with all this knowledge, mental illness is on the increase. In my own belief, the reason for this is that even if a person has had good enough parenting in his formative years, the continuous stress producing attitudes of the belittlers can and does cause untold numbers of cases of illnesses; what is commonly referred to as nervous breakdowns. They are illnesses that would never have occurred had it not been for the obnoxious behavior of belittlers.

"It is also my opinion that many such illnesses, although they may have some symptoms of the classical mental illnesses, are really, as they were in my case, merely emotional and physical exhaustion. They were brought on by doing much work, especially work with a heavy brain drain, under extremely stressful conditions caused by belittlers. Under such conditions fatigue sets in and our weakest areas, some of which everybody has, show through. A psychiatrist's diagnosis is based on those areas and the cause attributed to a weakening in our childhood. However, I emphasize were it not for the belittlers we would not have such breakdowns.

"Gilda was fortunate in that she had only a brief illness, thanks to the reawakening of her own determination and stamina. Donna has avoided any such breakdowns, due, I would say to her willingness to forfeit, as most of us have to do at some time or other in our lives. Some of us sometimes, due to evolving circumstances, have to forfeit much and often. Due to the circumstances of Donna's final two years of high school, I can easily understand why she was deterred from taking on university. I would like to emphasize though, Donna, as I have in the cases of Leo and of Gilda, you were discriminated against in these two years mostly because of yourself in that you were and are a fine person. Had you been wild, tough, slovenly, hard boiled, misbehaved, any of these and/or a number of other things, whether your father was wealthy or not, you would never have been singled out and picked on as you were.

"This is evident again, Donna, as you worked in industry, for there also you were put down simply because you were too good for the department supervisor. The quality and quantity of your work was too good, and you were too fine as a person. It may have been, foremost of all, your integrity together with your other fine qualities, that bothered him. Because of the way he used you, it was obvious he didn't have much integrity, and lacking this, he would have few other fine qualities. I would say he could see in you what he knew he ought to be. Rather than face up to it, he turned on you and got rid of you; out sight, out of mind.

"The coarse, tough girl was no threat to him personally. She wasn't a good employee, and didn't get as much work done as she should. She made others cower, and blamed the faulty system of the corporation for her shortcomings. The supervisor wouldn't dare blast her for being late. He was a coward all right, but he was a belittler most of all. The tough girl, although making him cower, didn't cause him to take note of his lack of integrity and other fine qualities, nor shake his inner security, or stir his envy and the ensuing hatred, as you Donna unintentionally did."

At this point Donna interrupted Collin's flow of words. Breaking into a half smile, she said, "Collin, if only you knew, how much it means to me to have someone else say, and believe, as I do myself, and did at the time, that the supervisor hated me because I was too good for him, because I am," she paused, "a fine person like the other members of this group!"

"I think I do know," responded Collin.

As if not hearing this reply, Donna went right on, "At the time I told my story, you remarked then that he hated me. Since that experience with the supervisor it has been a horrid burden to me, knowing that he hated me because of the kind of person I was, but never being able to talk to anyone about it because they wouldn't understand, or wouldn't believe." Then suddenly Donna looked around at the other group members, asking with apprehension, "Do the remainder of you believe it?"

"Of course we do," came the reply from Leo.

"And we all understand it so much better now," added Gilda.

The others assured her also, as Donna's smile now broadened. "The lifting of my burden has now been completed," she sighed in relief and tears of joy.

Collin said further, "While that supervisor was stuck with you Donna, he used you to get an abundance of work done, which, as indicated by the general manager's response to you, was good for him and his standing in the corporation. The one morning you were late, however, he used it as an excuse to blast you down hard. This eventually led you to leave the corporation. It was also the final straw, so to speak, for your first year supervisor. She also left the corporation to work elsewhere."

"As you told this story Donna, Albin asked a question to the effect, 'Don't all supervisors appreciate the qualities of good work, punctuality and decorum?' My answer to that is, some do, some don't, and some appear to. They appear to until some super, genuine person comes along, a person who could be an extremely valuable asset to a corporation. But, alas, if that person is more super than the supervisor himself, who has never learned how to supervise someone more capable than himself, then there is a very real problem. If the supervisor has any latent belittling characteristics, chances are that sooner or later, usually sooner, that super person will have to quit, and will be lost to the corporation. Business and industry would do well to become wise to the effects of belittlers on people who have the potential to become their most outstanding employees, but who are driven away. Not only are they sometimes driven away by belittling supervisors, but very often by belittling fellow employees who cannot stand to have them around. It is time to recognize that because a person is a supervisor or manager or owner, does not mean that anyone smarter, or more capable, or finer, cannot work under his supervision. Some of the best brains and personalities in the world go by the wayside because this lesson hasn't been learned, except by a minor percentage of people. The corporation, or any other organization, that weeds out envious belittlers one way or another, will be far ahead in the caliber of its employees and the performance of its business.

"In Brett's stories we see illustrated once again the impact of belittlers on industry and commerce. There was the self centered bank manager who couldn't allow the promising young Brett Culver to get a foot hold in a business that the manager perceived to be different and most likely better than that of his own son. He had to put Brett down, even though the deal was with a sound and solid oil company. In reference to this bank manager, Brett's father's friend indicated that 'birds of a feather flock together.' In all too many instances the sad part about a belittler in a position of authority in any business or organization is that he brings more of his kind in, and if the opportunity arises, places them in positions of authority. This kind of people are attracted to one another by their similar personalities.

"There was the government officer in control of loans for industry, turning down Brett most likely because his nose was out of joint that such a fine young man would be shooting so high. He himself probably long ago had settled for secure benefits and likely a very good, but limited salary. Not only did he turn Brett down, but in an effort to either outsmart him or purposely ruin him, would have led him to destruction. Whichever motive it was, Brett could best discern by the attitude of the government officer at the time. However such an attitude in government is not uncommon, and it can make one wonder of its total effects, not only on individuals, but from there rippling out to affect the nation as a whole.

"We can see the effects on a community when the attitude of belittlers becomes the prevailing one, as we listen to Brett's and his father's experiences of the extremely difficult two years of Brett's high school in such a community. Brett with much close and constant contact with people, wasn't there very long before he found out the school was dominated by it. That factor would have a ripple effect throughout the whole area over the years. In time Brett's father found the same atmosphere to prevail strongly throughout the business, church and social activities of the area. This is not to say that the majority of people in the area were belittlers. I have never known that to be so anywhere. However, they were a dominating influence there, and outstanding persons such as Brett and his father could never get ahead there. Needless to say, such a community as that never excels in anything. It is generally mediocre and to compensate for that they build themselves up on pride, as again is evidenced in the incident of Brett obtaining a transcript of his school record. The quality of the record was according to what would enhance the pride of the school from which it was coming. Again, such pride, and envy, is evidenced in the reaction of Brett's mathematics teacher. She was threatened, not alone by a fine person such as Brett, but also by the fact he might establish that another school system might be better in some ways than this one of which the math teacher was a part. She couldn't let Brett damage her proud concept of herself and the school system of which she was a part. Not that Brett was purposely trying to do that. It was all in her own mind. However, to prevent it she thought she had to bring Brett down to where in her mind, and she would hope in the minds of the students of the class, she and they could perceive Brett as being inferior. They could never admit to themselves that they were picking on him because he was too good for them. That alone would destroy their pride. They have to find fault somehow and bring him down to where they can feel that the reason they don't accept him is because he is no good.

"One further observation concerning Brett's experiences is the permanent effect of belittling action on people's lives. People who have lesser troubles than people like *us*, often advise you not to let it bother you, and, pay no attention to it. However, when you look at Brett's life, how it was altered drastically and permanently, one cannot brush such happenings lightly aside. I wonder further, what would have happened to Brett had he not had a girl friend to support him financially before and after he got into business; also had he not had his father's friend to steer him until he was experienced enough to set his own course! Had he become reduced to dire straights he could have returned to his parents, which would have given him security, but also another defeat with likely little desire to ever try anything worthwhile again. How many, though, have no parents or anyone else to whom they can return! How many people of wonderful potential become derelicts of society, having been put down and smashed by belittlers!

"Also, when you think of it, it is amazing how belittlers in their minds and actions can pit one part of a country against another, or one area against another, in order to, in their minds, support and justify their actions of belittling; our area and school is better than where you came from and the like. Meanwhile Brett has done well with his life. Whether he is better off in business than he would have been as a doctor is beside the point. The fact is the goal he had originally set for himself in life was stolen away from him by others, by belittlers.

"Early in his story Owen raised the question of whether or not people should expect the church to be better than other areas of life with regard to the sphere of human behavior we are discussing in this group. We are discussing such characteristics as envy, pride, hatred, jealousy, rivalry. All of these were brought most vividly to the attention of the early church by the Apostle Paul. Even the pagan and politically expedient Pilate was able to perceive that it was out of 'envy' they brought Jesus to trial and sought his death.

"Obviously, according to Paul's writings, such matters as envy and the like were a very real problem in the early church. Writings down through the centuries indicate the same chronic disease. It exists in abundance today, the writings on the traditional Seven Deadly Sins being largely ignored. It is a problem the church has rarely tackled. It has seldom brought this malignancy, this envy within its ranks, into the open. It is infrequently mentioned by scholars and preachers, because some areas of the church are riddled through and through with it. It is so much a part of the system and the personalities, they don't even want to recognize it as a problem. 'It is just the way people are', is the accepted attitude. There are simple, yet adequate resources available in Paul's writings to the churches, and indeed in the Gospels themselves, to raise humanity's spiritual and moral progress side by side with its technical and scientific advancement.

"The secular world has never given the deadly disease anything but an occasional glance mostly in fictional writing, or worse, a brush under the carpet, pretending that the malady, now out of sight does not exist.

"The unwritten law that says open criticism of the church is taboo, allows the disease to continue its destruction while people refuse to either recognize its existence, or, bring it out in the open. The closest the field of psychology has been able to come to the very visible malignancy is in recognizing the concept of sibling rivalry. In the sheltered confines of classroom and laboratory, they are so wrapped up in the stages of human development, a comparatively tame and decipherable phenomena, that they have failed to stumble upon this area of everyday human behavior. When there comes a widespread awareness and recognition of the problem, then the good people will be free to put the belittlers in their place, instead of the belittlers all too often having the upper hand and short changing society.

"In Owen's family, not only was there rivalry among the children, but the belittling clergy father was involved, and indeed was the instigator of it all. The father perceived Owen to be a threat to himself and his other two sons whom either consciously or unconsciously he perceived to be of lesser caliber than Owen. In order to keep himself and the two other sons, whom he aligned with himself, on top, he had to put Owen down. He pacified his conscience for doing this with a notion commonly used, that a younger member of the family should not get ahead of the older members because it damages their pride. This rivalry in the family was not just among the children. It was instigated by a man whose character was built that way. He behaved that way, not only within the confines of the family, but in all his dealings and associations with people in every sphere of life, including the church of which he was a minister. Sibling rivalry barely touches the edge of this problem of enormous magnitude.

"Owen's father's interpretation of the Magnificat reflects his own prejudice in favor of the 'common man,' and of the poor, which he perceives himself to be, and, against the mighty and the rich like whom he longs to be. My own interpretation of the Magnificat, even after taking into account the writer Luke's known concern for the poor, would refute Owen's father's view. I would say God certainly is mighty enough to do so, and can and has and will scatter the proud in the imagination of their hearts, and put down the mighty if and when necessary, and when they thwart his purposes. They may play havoc with God's world before God sees His time to do so, but sooner (sometimes) or later (at other times) He may do it.

"They may be proud rich people, they may be proud poor people, they may be proud middle income people; they may be behaving mightily in politics, in financial circles, in industry, in commerce, in the educational realm, in common, everyday life out in the world, in the hierarchy of the church, in any congregation of the church. Whatever their station in life, and/or whatever their income, rich or poor or anywhere in between, sooner or later God's righteousness will triumph over them if they are being haughtily proud and mighty in any or all spheres of life. Similarly, whatever their station in life, high or low and/or whatever their material wealth, whether it be little or much, people can serve God faithfully and humbly if they choose to, and God will bless them according to his own wisdom and choice, and can and will indeed exalt them if and when He chooses. God is indeed powerful enough for that. But God isn't automatically for all the poor and down on all the rich and well to do as is implied by the behavior of many. Other Christian doctrine, as well as common sense and human nature, to my mind, support me in this interpretation.

"Owen's mother, it seems, was a loving, innocent person who believed that righteousness was stronger than evil and would eventually triumph in a person's life if that person endeavored to stay with righteousness. Although she didn't understand Owen's peculiar circumstances, still, her love for him as a person was there, and this is what made it possible for Owen to lay the groundwork in his life that would enable him to mature into a solid person. Everyone needs someone. A mother is almost vital in any case, but only almost. If adequate parenting isn't forthcoming from a mother, there are substantial substitutes that help make up the difference. However, a belittling mother can do more harm to her child than a mother who neglects a child's material well being.

"Owen was well over fifty percent blessed by having his mother's love, even though he didn't have her understanding and consequently lacked her verbal support for his personal predicament. This was hard going for Owen. Nevertheless, her love uplifted him to where he could learn to cope for himself and eventually led him to rely on God's love despite his father's lack of it in its genuineness. Owen was further blessed, believe it or not, by his physical size. Bullies are cowards, no doubt about it. Many belittlers would hesitate to openly pick on him because of his size. As Owen said himself, though, he didn't have their friendship either. Silent, as well as open rejection, can lead to dejection, which can and often does for various reasons lead people, especially vulnerable youth to wayward paths in life. Owen was on the brink at times in this regard, but was pulled back by his better side. We can see though, how envious belittling can send a young person down wayward paths in life."

"There may be a further blessing for Owen in the future. There are some fine people who, due to a series of fortunate circumstances, become above reproach. Owen may turn out to be one of these and be fairly safe from belittlers as his career advances. Since he has done well in another land south of the border, belittlers here in Secundaterra will think twice about trying to discredit him. Being successful in getting more formal education and more experience here or wherever, he may have a better chance to survive, either here or somewhere south of the border, perhaps even in Terraprima.

"So Owen has done well, but alas, not in his chosen field of study, but rather, in the one he could best find his way through as he dodged the belittlers. The professor and head of the literature department, whom Owen described is typical of many. He was very proficient in the knowledge of his subject, and in teaching it. But he did not have wisdom or a creative mind. A knowledgeable mind and a creative mind do not necessarily compliment each other. In fact they only seldom do. Who knows? Maybe this professor could have helped Owen develop into a famous author. That would have been a feather in the professor's cap indeed had he possessed the character and gone about helping in the right manner. But no, because this man was not creative to the point where he could gain recognition for it, then no one else must be so either. So he stood on guard at the gate of his domain, letting enter only those he could keep beneath him. "Owen's other professor, although recognizing that Owen possessed creativity, wanted to press him into a mold of the professor's own making, which again was knowledgeable, though not creative, but rather, a continuous copying of the creativity of the writers of the past. This uncreative professor was saying in effect, you, Owen Winslow are creative, so do as I say and I will develop your creativity the way I see it should be developed. One may ask, if that were possible then why didn't the professor become creative himself and do his own creating. The problems that arise in such circumstances as this are many, among which also, the professor wants to totally possess the creative one, mold him his way, then take credit for it all himself. This professor didn't want just a feather in his cap, he wanted the crown and the glory, with puppet status for Owen. He had to come out on top, and the belittled creative person on the bottom. The whole thing is impossible of course, because a creative person cannot become like an uncreative person and still remain creative. Neither can copying other creative people make the copier creative.

"When Owen began to discuss his career in the church, it was no great surprise to us that belittlers were to be found there also. One of the most notable incidents Owen told that supports our views is that in his pastorate of two congregations, he has illustrated the difference between a church dominated by belittlers, and a church that is not. The free church prospered, and the belittling church didn't, while both were under the same ministry. The belittlers of the unprosperous church blamed the minister for their lack of prosperity. Brett remarked as Owen talked to us about the church, that he could support Owen's views on the hazards of people like us in the church, because of his own experiences. I can guess the nature of these experiences Brett, but I would like for you to tell us about them."

"Sure," responded Brett. "I will begin by saying that from much observation I have come to the conclusion that the local churches which are the more prosperous spiritually, financially, in programmings, and in numbers of membership and attendance, are the churches that have not driven away any segment of its people including its business people. There are still some of these congregations around in the mainline protestant churches, depending on location and the predominance of belittlers. It so happens there isn't one of them of my denomination in my area. Consequently I am not a member, nor do I attend regularly any one church at the present time. I forfeited that some time ago.

"The more prosperous I became in business, the more envy, hatred and resentment built up against me in the congregation which I attended, served, and supported well. It came from a minority of people, but enough to make church life unpleasant for me, and to make the innocent and naive ones think the belittlers were right in their attitude towards me, and I was in the wrong somehow. It got to be supported more and more by the minister and his attitude, and including from the pulpit, as time went by, biased sermons about the injustice between the rich and the poor. I tried another congregation where many business and professional people attended. In that particular church the tendency was toward a high and expensive social life to which I had neither the desire, nor at the time the money, to keep up. So now I attend a worship service here and there irregularly. When I am away on business I have located churches of my denomination where I can attend comfortably. But that is only occasionally. I find ways to contribute to the church and to charity. Nevertheless it is all lacking in that I do not belong. I am a member of a well known fraternity which I enjoy immensely, but it does not take the place of church in my life. For me there is no adequate substitute. I shall continue to nurture my faith as best I can, and continue to seek a church home."

"Thanks Brett," said Collin, "a sad story indeed. Condemned by the church for being a fine person who is successful in an occupation that involves more money than the usual.

"It is no wonder that some mainline Protestant denominations are in decline. There are some other reasons involved too of course. But based on extensive observation, my opinion is that these people we call belittlers are one of the major reasons for it. I have noticed time and again how some ministers shun and shy away from fine, well to do people. Belittlers cover themselves on that by blaming it all on the rift that they themselves have helped create between the rich and the poor. One of the results of it is that many rich people have been driven away from the influence of the church by belittlers who are unable to take their place beside them, and who also have a warped and biased concept about business and money and the proper way to utilize it for the common good.

"My observation over the years has been that the congregations, and consequently the denominations that prosper both numerically and financially, are those which have, among other things, two essential ingredients. The first of these ingredients in that belittlers are kept at bay very emphatically, so that fine and nice and well charactered, well meaning, genuine persons of any and all walks of life are not driven away by them. The second is very akin to the first: that there be sound emphasis on genuine Christian character throughout the congregation and the denomination. Slick wheeling and dealing won't do. Greasy, insincere smiles will eventually be seen through. Surface friendliness does not impress. For the Christian, only properly motivated Christian character based on the teachings of Jesus, guided by the Holy Spirit, and undergirded by the Grace of God will do it. There are other faith issues involved in the well-being of the church, but these two have to do with the concerns of this group.

"Referring now to Albin's story," Collin continued with his commentary, "again may I say it is generally acknowledged, by psychology, and by people of human understanding, that one of the worst things that can befall a child is to be left lacking the genuine love of one's mother. Not only does this do harm in childhood, they say, but painfully hurts somewhat all the way up to and sometimes through adult life. Nevertheless my opinion is that eventually one can learn to deal with it adequately in the mind, and in addition over the years can literally grow out of the harm it can do.

"Therefore, even without the ingredient of a mother's love in childhood and adolescence, a young person of ability and drive like Albin can still make the grade adequately in life. He could even make it exceptionally were it not for the many obnoxious persons, belittlers more especially, he still has to encounter out in the world as he begins to make his way in it. At this bridgehead of life the Albin Anders of this world are confronted by belittlers galore, belittlers no different in essence than Albin's mother. It may appear that he cannot overcome the damage done to him by his mother. In my opinion that is not so. He cannot make his way because of the almost continuous repetitions of his mother's attitude toward him; repetitions made by belittling teachers, as he goes through school, college and university, by belittling co-workers as he enters the world of industry, commerce or the professions, by belittling competitors for popularity as he tries to build a social life for himself. If he seeks help with his problem, it is most certain that any help or therapy at all, will dwell on his experiences with his mother in early childhood, and perhaps in adolescence, but not usually in adulthood. Had Albin consulted a therapist about his problems of adulthood, he may have received the same reaction as did Gilda and myself. Either they would look for the answers in the wrong places and ways, or worse, blame all his troubles on himself thereby belittling him all the more, as though he was too sensitive or working in the wrong place and the like.

"It is most interesting and important to note the contrast of

Albin's plight with that of Owen's with regard to his brothers and his position of age among them. Owen grew up thinking he was kept beneath his two brothers because he was the younger of the three and the younger brother must not get ahead of the two older ones. That of course was the reason Owen's father was making himself believe. Such rationalization would placate the father's conscience. In addition, it was quite natural for Owen during his young years to sense and accept as accurate the reason for the belittling that the father portrayed outwardly.

"Then we come to Albin, the middle of three brothers, being belittled the same as Owen, except in Albin's case he is being belittled beneath a younger brother as well as an older one. Owen's father's reason, or excuse rather, would not hold up in this case. The real reason for the belittling by Owen's father, that Owen was too good for both his father and his brothers was kept hidden, either consciously or unconsciously by the father. Most likely, to some extent at least, the two brothers would sense and take up unconsciously, the same attitude towards Owen as did their father.

"What excuse would Albin's mother find for belittling Albin beneath a younger brother as well as an older one?" asked Collin, and then answered himself. "She would come up with some excuse and convince herself and many others that it was a logical and warranted reason. She established the reason that Albin was presumptuous. The real reason, as always, but which the mother will probably never admit to is that Albin being such a fine person was just too good for her. He was also too good for the two brothers in whom the mother took pride because they were like her side of the family. such rivalry happens frequently in families.

"The two brothers were more like their mother and her side of the family in appearance and character. Albin was more like his father and his side of the family in appearance, in character, and in the ability to get along well with people regardless of their standing in life. This latter is evidenced by both Albin and his father fitting in so well at the high caliber church, where the mother on the other hand had all sorts of problems. Albin's mother had set up rivalry in the family by drawing envious comparisons between those like her family and those like her husbands family. She also set up a rivalry of her own in the church family.

"Albin obviously was also associated by his mother, with the fine people of the church which the family attended. Albin's mother had a mixture of hatred and a desire to be like those fine people. In her efforts to be like them, or, knowing her personality better than that, trying to be above them, she resorted to outward measures of rivalry like buying fine clothes. Such measures never make a fine person. She would sense that she still wasn't measuring up to or above them, so her hatred of them would become all the more intense. Then she resorted to putting them down verbally at home, even though she boosted her pride in other circles by boasting of being a member of that church.

"Concerning her belittling of Albin, the mother pacified her own mind and conscience on the matter by perceiving in her own mind that Albin really wasn't much of a person. She rationalized that his fineness was just an artificial effort of Albin in a bid to be like the 'big wheels' at the church. She turned this into presumptuousness on Albin's part, and this contrived presumptuousness became her excuse for belittling him. One can see that her whole conception of Albin was a projection of herself and her own relationship with the congregation. The real reason for her belittling of Albin, regardless of his age standing in the family, was that he was a fine person. She had either always had a hatred for fine persons, or had developed one because of her relations at the church. Chances are it is the former. This hatred was turned on Albin. As similar in character as she was to Owen's father she needed no age reason as he had. She built an excuse to label Albin presumptious and therefore deserving to be put down. Belittlers always contrive an outward reason that covers the real reason.

"It is no wonder Albin didn't pursue his education beyond high school. With his young mind dominated by belittlers, it was virtually impossible for him to experience the mostly silent love and support there must have been also present. This is evidenced by his grade three popularity that was so overshadowed by his problems stemming from belittlers that he couldn't notice it.

"If Albin had had any need of psychiatric treatment at any time through his school years, he probably would have been labeled paranoid with the whole problem based on his childhood relationship with his mother. Attempts would have been made to reconstruct his mind so he could see even the belittlers as his friends, which would be an illusion that would never fit into life when he was released into the world once more. He might never find the world of reality again. Albin made a right move to get out into the work-a-day world where, even though there are belittlers, they are more crude and open in their ways, less subtle and therefore easier to become aware of, to see through and learn to deal with. On the other hand the non-belittlers, and more especially those in business for themselves are often friendly, outgoing people. That after all is how they do business. They would be open in their praise of Albin and his work. He would soon learn to draw a contrast between the friendly and the unfriendly, thereby enabling his mind to dwell not on the unfriendly belittlers alone, but on the good natured people as well, and even more so. This, I would say was a very significant saving experience for Albin.

"When Albin went to university, however, the tables turned on him mightily. Here he was up against the more educated, more subtle type of belittlers. It must have helped him a great deal to have some understanding of them by now, having gained it in the work world. Against his favor now though was the fact that he was doing much more brain work. This is always a heavy drain on a person besieged by belittlers. To try to concentrate and study with a mind upset and troubled by belittlers is an energy sapping ordeal. Albin had a minor breakdown which was attributed to overwork. Had Albin not been troubled by belittlers there is no doubt in my mind he could have done much more work and not become ill or exhausted. The real cause of his illness was the belittlers. Try to tell a belittler he is the cause of someone's illness and he will look at you goggle eyed and deny the whole thing. In his closed mind he would see it as successfully defending his pride against a smart alec who has no business acting so smart. He would be pleased over it.

"We must also note, because of its importance in understanding belittlers, that there was not just passivity toward Albin after he went to university. Albin, while working, had gained confidence in himself, and was now positively and confidently establishing himself in the academic world— something he had never done before. Passivity now changed to hostility, shunning, blocking. This fine person, this smart guy had to be stopped. He was too strong now to be just brushed aside. He kept pushing his way in. Passivity could no longer stop him. It would take something more. The belittlers would now feel compelled to confront him one way or another. Nevertheless Albin had decided to exercise his right to make something more of his life. Right maneuvering would help; still he would pay dearly for progress gained."

Collin paused as if to end his review. "I think it might be repetitious for me to review my own story, since it was told so recently. Also, it is too soon to analyze our concepts further at the present time. The stories of my friends who went to live in Terraprima will, as they are told next semester, enable us to gain much further insight into the problems of fine people versus belittlers."

Turning to Dr. Eldren, and Owen, "I think my presentation should end for now. Perhaps some others would care to add to it."

The members decided to leave all as is until next semester and Collin's presentations of the Terraprima story.

Dr. Eldren left to take care of other duties. The remainder of the group expressed a desire for a leisurely hour at the Corner Coffee Shop. Collin would have Vita join them on the way.

At the coffee shop, with the consent of the manager, two square tables suitable for four persons each were pushed together. The group, now including Vita Seldon who had joined them from the library on the way, all sat somewhat crowded closely together at what for them was now one table. There were not many people in the restaurant at that hour. There were none close by this table of eight near where the corner windows met. Conversation became free and open.

"Vita," said Gilda Emerson across the table, striking up a conversation with her, "I am very curious to know how you fit into Collin's life as he has related it to us in the group sessions. No doubt you are aware that he has been doing so?"

"Yes," replied Vita, and all at the table listened intently. "I am aware that he planned to tell his story. I am sure you are aware by now that it has been a difficult life, to say the least. To satisfy your curiosity, and your genuine interest as well, I am sure, I can only say I have lived through every moment of it with him and shared the resulting tribulations. In addition to that, as you know very well from the experiences of yourself and Donna, women like us have our problems similar to men like Collin and the others present. So Collin and I each had our own individual struggles to wage, but also each others to share. We could only survive by being very close to one another, always ready to share each others encounters and shore each other up with help in diagnosis, means of coping, and encouragement."

"Has such a life as this become easier or harder to take over the years Vita," asked Gilda.

Vita explained, "It just seems like one long hard struggle, with sometimes brief, other times more extended interludes of peace. You long for more of it and sometimes it does come. But as time goes by, you learn that it is only a temporary interlude. Sooner or later, usually sooner, someone is going to come down on you again, so you almost permanently brace yourself for them. I say 'almost'. Once in a while a more lengthy tranquil period may come, and you dare to drop your guard. You have to, just to give yourself a break. Then just as you are really settling down to that peaceful period, a belittler or belittlers will appear on the scene. There is bound to be one or more around. Then having dropped your guard for a while and enjoyed the interlude, it hits you all the harder when it comes again, and you are shaken for a while, until in time you are able to brace yourself for this new onslaught."

"You know Collin's experiences as well as your own, Vita," Gilda continued with her questions, "would you say the problem we in this group all have in common is more difficult for men or for women, or is it equally difficult for us all?"

"It depends to some extent on where you are living," came Vita's reply. "And it also depends substantially on the severity of the individuals with which you come in contact in each encounter. We have these obnoxious people everywhere, but, we have lived in a variety of areas. My experience has been that in one area of Secundaterra for example, and this was some years ago, the women of the generations I had to deal with were well cultured in comparison to the men. It was easy to see why. The girls as they were growing up had an abundance of cultural programs in which to participate. The boys were more or less brought up to be egotistical he-men. This meant that among the adults there were very few women belittlers. I had the best years of my life there. On the other hand, among the men there were many active belittlers, and an abundance of supporters for them. Macho men were the order of the day at that time and place, and especially among the young and young adult generations. Fine people were put down hard by them. So for Collin, life there was difficult, and that made life unpleasant for me also.

"In another area we lived, in Lower Secundaterra, it wasn't much better for me than it was for Collin. In another area still, much to our surprise, things were worse among the women than among the men. Our overall experience has been then, that for a married couple like us, there is nowhere we can go, and have a reasonably peaceful life. I do not mean by that entirely without problems, which we all know is impossible. But for people like us there has been nowhere thus far where we can live without there being people trying to disrupt or destroy us, except as I said, perhaps for a brief interlude that can more often be counted in days rather than weeks or months."

"Would you mind telling us briefly tonight of some of your more difficult experiences in life," asked Gilda sympathetically. Then smiling, she added, "I may be a fine person, married to a fine person some day and I'd like to be better prepared for the onslaught." As she said this, it was barely noticeable that Owen

Winslow shifted in his chair a little and cracked a slight smile."

Vita began, "well one of the harder things for us when we were young and just married, was that there were belittlers in our families, on both sides; there being mostly passive and trivializing belittling, which is hard enough. Even though that was discouraging at the start we coped with it quite well and in only a short time overcame it. However, it bounced back on us a little later, and more especially on me.

"For example, when Collin was duped into going into hospital for psychiatric treatment, his first ever, I had to bear responsibility for taking him out of it when things went so terribly wrong there. Not only did doctors in authority warn me threateningly of the responsibility I was taking upon myself, but also some family members took a similar position. They really did not know all the circumstances of the event, but nevertheless laid responsibility upon me for taking him out before he was quote, 'cured', as they thought of in their usual limited knowledge of the subject that existed at that time. I was very young and this was a heavy burden to bear. Yet I knew I had to do it. It did help some that other family members not only agreed that I did right in taking Collin out of hospital; but that he should never have gone in there in the first place. But you can see the controversy I was caught in."

"Yes, I certainly can," remarked Gilda. "You were dealing with health and life, and these cannot be taken lightly. Also you were alone with your problems to a great extent without much family support and almost alone in a city new to you. I'm not so sure I could have handled that."

"Not entirely alone, Gilda," interjected Vita. "My experiences of God in the very early years of my life kept reoccurring to me. These experiences were influenced, as far back as I can remember, by two very lovely Sunday School teachers, husband and wife, who had no children of their own. I knew that families with me or not I was not alone, and that the God who had made me so happy as a child, even amid many adverse circumstances, would be with me now. I knew God would see me through and make a place with a purpose for my husband and I and later our family. God doesn't promise it will be easy, but he does promise to stay with us. I never felt alone. I felt His guidance and His courage leading me to make the best I could of the adverse circumstances of the present time. Most often, God's church was not dependable in this, for as you know by now it too is infested with belittlers. But God is dependable, and through Him I kept going then as I do now."

Vita continued, "Also outside our families, and more particularly when Collin became a minister, I often had to support him in dealing with belittlers in the church, both laity and clergy. Collin was generally easy going. There are always people around to take advantage of that type of personality. However, Collin could only be pushed so far. Then he would get his back up, which would more often than not get him in trouble by having to take the blame for the ensuing fuss. Belittlers always turn things around like that. So quite often, to protect Collin's career, I would be the one to step in with a word of stern rebuke and have the brakes put on the matter whatever it might be. I, like you Gilda, became known to some people as a terror. Then, or course, they didn't want me around. There developed, at times, by clergy who should have known better, attempts to manipulate my husband behind my back. Collin was aware of it and handled it as best he could without having a wide open uproar which, as I said, would only be twisted around and blamed on him. But again in many of these instances, I became the terror to be avoided."

"But the belittling in the church wasn't directed at Collin only. There was plenty of it aimed at me," continued Vita.

"Would you give us an example?" asked Donna.

"Okay," replied Vita. "As often happened, I was called upon to put on a program for a group of women gathered from the wider church of an area. The program on this particular evening turned out to be very exceptionally well received by almost all of the large number present. There were suggestions that I could have had an altar call. People were really moved and inspired by it. Almost all, that is. There were two dissenters, both minister's wives. They shunned me then and thereafter."

"Then, of course," continued Vita, "as with you Gilda and

Donna, I had the usual 'put downs' by belittlers at places of employment. Where good employees were respected and appreciated I went ahead, being promoted to supervisory positions. It was a blessing to be in such places. At other businesses where I have been employed, I have experienced stress so heavy from the belittlers and from the supervisors who support them that I at times had to give up any other activities that required brain drain.

"Little do some employers realize how much good brain activity I will call it, is lost due to stress caused by belittlers. I would guesstimate it must cost millions and millions of dollars each year in industry and commerce, as well as the damaging stress to individuals. Often I have passed up an opportunity, perhaps a job posted within the company. Although the job was well within my ability, it would require a great deal of brain drain, which, when you have envious, hostile and pouty people around all the time, would eventually wear you out. I have let some opportunities pass by that way, and also the opportunity to study evenings because of the same problem. The work load in itself wouldn't be too heavy, not by any means. But with belittlers on your back, it would do harm. Collin experienced that as you probably know. I protected myself in order to protect and help him as best I could, as his career was more important than mine, he being the prime breadwinner of our family.

"These are some of the consequences I have experienced for being people like us, Gilda. In addition, like all of you here, I have had my own share of routine put downs by belittlers. One of the things that irks me most is how these belittlers can get away with so much in some places of employment. Even, in many instances, where the supervisor is not in sympathy with the belittlers, he or she is afraid of them. The supervisors sometimes will pounce on people like you and I for the least little error or oversight. But the nastier the belittlers are the more they can get away with because the bosses are afraid of them. Often, they promote the belittlers to pacify them. It's very bad for business, and, when such negative people become dominant in a business organization, then that company goes down hill from there on."

"Gilda," said Vita in summation, "I don't mean to be all negative. I have had some wonderfully good positions out there where I was able to do very well. The thing I would suggest, if you find some day you are a fine person married to a fine person, is for you both to search for that rare and hard to find combination where each of you is in a position where belittlers are not in control. Collin and I were able to accomplish that only very occasionally, but it is possible. Search until you find it, and stay there, unless, of course you outgrow it. Then your search starts all over again, and you take your chances. Remember though, you have a big plus going for you in that you have a major portion of your education already. You won't have to work and study and struggle all at the same time."

"Thank you Vita," responded Gilda appreciatively, "you've helped me more than you know. There is hope for a good and peaceful life for me out there. I will search for that niche, and my faith tells me that if I seek I shall find; and if I outgrow it I will search carefully again."

"Do search carefully," added Vita, "because there is no growing when the circumstances are not right. There is only stifling, cramping oppression that comes from the brow beating of the belittlers. But do keep the faith that there is a place and a purpose for you."

"One more question Vita, if I may," asked Gilda, "I am wondering why you didn't attend our group sessions all semester. You could have added a great deal to our discussions, I'm sure. Why did you stay away?"

"There is a reason," replied Vita, "and it is for security reasons; for the security of Collin and I, and previously our family too. You see, years ago Collin was wrongly diagnosed by a psychiatrist. He has been branded at times ever since, and it has caused him untold trouble. In order to keep myself from being a marked for life person also, for family supportive and legal reasons I make a point of avoiding circumstances where I might also be branded by either a belittling or a naive psychiatrist. There are some of each out there who just have to put a tag on everyone.

"In the past, I have talked to psychiatrists about Collin, but never about myself. For safety sake, one of us had to stay above board so to speak, especially after our very first episode with psychiatrists. Since a psychiatrist was overseeing this group, even though I hear he is a nice person, I chose to follow my protection plan, I'll call it. At the same time, I have every confidence in my own stability and marriage and family relationships. I have professional support for that confidence, arrived at in a round-about way through Collin's interaction with some of the better professional help he has had."

Donna spoke to Vita, "from what you have said here tonight, and what Collin has included about you in his story, I know that you have had many experiences similar to mine out in the world of business."

"No doubt we have much in common in that regard," replied Vita, "but I have been out of the employment market for a few years now. How is it out there these days?; much worse than it used to be according to what I hear."

"Yes Vita, I would say it is worse now than even the relatively short number of years since I began working. I am studying again with the hope that the higher up the ladder I can climb the better it might be, but time will tell."

"At least with more education you will have a wider field in which to search for your place in life," responded Vita hearteningly.

"Thanks for your encouragement," said Donna with affection.

There was an interlude in the conversation. Collin drew their attention to the fact that it was getting late. In an enlivened tone he then told them, "The worst is yet to come folks. Next semester I will tell you the story of a fine minister friend who together with his wife went to Terraprima to live. Their trials, tribulations — and their survival, will astound you. In the meantime, Christmas is coming. Forget your troubles for now and have a merry one. And let's look forward to being together in the New Year for the Terraprima story.

In a happy frame of mind they soon all left the coffee shop for the university parking lot beside it. None of them were alone with their problems now. However much they had to wage their battles alone in the past, now each one felt support from others of the group. Collin wondered aloud as he and Vita drove away, "Will there ever be a day when people such as they and you and I will be able to live in an environment pleasant enough to allow each of us to reach anywhere near our full potential?"

**END OF VOLUME 1**

# NOTES

# NOTES

# NOTES

www.ingramcontent.com/pod-product-compliance
Lightning Source LLC
Chambersburg PA
CBHW020600270326
41927CB00005B/110
* 9 7 8 0 9 8 0 9 9 9 5 6 3 *